The
Schooled
Society

*An Introduction to
the Sociology of Education*

Scott Davies | Neil Guppy

OXFORD
UNIVERSITY PRESS

OXFORD
UNIVERSITY PRESS

Oxford University Press is a department of the University of Oxford.
It furthers the University's objective of excellence in research, scholarship,
and education by publishing worldwide. Oxford is a registered trade mark of
Oxford University Press in the UK and in certain other countries.

Published in Canada by
Oxford University Press
8 Sampson Mews, Suite 204,
Don Mills, Ontario M3C 0H5 Canada

www.oupcanada.com

Library and Archives Canada Cataloguing in Publication
Davies, Scott, 1962–, author
The schooled society : an introduction to the sociology
of education / Scott Davies and Neil Guppy.

Includes bibliographical references and index.
Issued in print and electronic formats.
ISBN 978–0–19–902488–9 (softcover).—ISBN 978–0–19–902489–6
(PDF)

1. Educational sociology—Canada—Textbooks. 2. Textbooks.
I. Guppy, Neil, 1949–, author II. Title.

LC191.8.C2D37 2018   306.430971   C2017-906234-4
                                                 C2017-906235-2

Cover image: © vasilkovs/123RF
Cover and interior design: Sherill Chapman

Oxford University Press is committed to our environment.
Wherever possible, our books are printed on paper
which comes from responsible sources.

Printed and bound in Canada

2 3 4 — 21 20 19

Contents

7   Attainments by Gender, Race, Sexuality, and Other Equity Categories   126

Part III • Social Organization and Legitimation   153

8   The Changing Organization of Schooling   154

Part V • Conclusion   257

Preface to the Fourth Edition

This edition builds on previous editions of *The Schooled Society* with a bolstered discussion of educational inequalities and an expanded coverage of a range of topics and theories. First and foremost, we have added a series of case studies that showcase qualitative studies, which we use to animate key concepts in the book. One particular emphasis among these case studies is to examine several different issues involved with Indigenous education. This edition has also updated many references, data sources, and policy controversies. Our book remains one of the most current sources of information on education in Canada.

The Approach of this Book

Over 40 years ago, Ivan Illich composed his famous treatise, *Deschooling Society* (1971). It was a literary phenomenon, selling hundreds of thousands of copies and capturing the attention of a variety of educational stakeholders. A harsh critic of modern education, his tone was decidedly *anti-school*. Illich faulted schooling for being a wasteful and self-serving institution that disempowered its students and stifled more authentic forms of learning.

How times have changed. Who, today, calls for deschooling? Over the ensuing decades education has become one of our society's "motherhood" icons. While virtually all aspects of schooling are criticized today, almost no one questions the general need for formal education. School reformers abound, but schooling is now starting at ever-earlier ages, and may never end, as emerging ideologies of "lifelong learning" and "universal" post-secondary participation take hold. Most people have much lengthier school careers than their forebears. Every family pins the hopes for their children on educational success. The salvation for social problems such as drugs, violence, and immorality is often seen to lie in the classroom. More and more people clamour for school credentials. Illich's worst nightmare has come true.

This book expresses our fascination in the grand institutional extension of formal education. Nations spend billions of dollars on schooling, and individuals spend thousands of days in schools. Politicians tout education to make us globally competitive and prepared for knowledge-based economies. But "school" is also seeping into other realms of life. School forms are continuously expanding, from academic preschools to larger post-secondary institutions. From infants to seniors, more people are becoming "students" in a variety of forms of schooling. There are schools for corporate executives, prisoners, felons, and athletes, to name but a few.

We strive to survey the entire field, but this is a thematic book. We are captivated by the spreading reach of school, defined broadly, in the ongoing history of modernity. Though it focuses on contemporary Canada, our title *The Schooled Society* is meant to convey a historical and comparative sensibility, evoking a not-too-distant past in which schooling was less prized than it is today and not so entrenched within society as a central institution. The book details a mutual process whereby schooling intrudes into more realms of social life while being simultaneously affected by an array of societal trends beyond the classroom. We link schooling to massive economic shifts, from agricultural to industrial to post-industrial, including globalization and the "knowledge-based economy," and to such demographic shifts as immigration and societal aging, traditional political cleavages of left and right, and the evolution of mass culture. Unlike many other texts, we cover all three tiers of schooling—elementary, secondary, and post-secondary.

The book's sociological framework integrates theory with major research traditions in the sociology of education. Theoretically, ours is an eclectic approach, mixing classical and contemporary traditions, and micro, macro, and middle-range concepts, particularly those regularly used in empirical research. We use a diverse range of theoretical tools from across the social sciences (including sociology, education, women's studies, and economics). Further, many of these theoretical perspectives are evaluated using the latest research evidence. Students will be exposed to a set of conceptual tools designed to enrich curiosity and provoke debate.

This book is suitable for sociology of education courses in sociology departments, as well as for social foundations courses in education faculties. It can be used in both one- and two-semester courses, and can be supplemented by edited collections of readings or custom course-packs. Both of us teach sociology of education courses at our respective universities, and colleagues at several other Canadian universities generously offered their feedback on earlier versions of the book. The book includes numerous figures, tables, boxes, suggestions for additional reading, and questions for critical discussion within each chapter, as well as chapter learning objectives, a glossary, and an extensive bibliography.

Organization of the Book

To organize the sprawling literature in the sociology of education, the book is split into three central sections, each representing a core role of modern schooling: selection, social organization, and socialization. Our intent is to provide a lucid framework accessible to undergraduates.

The section on selection covers the bread and butter of the sociology of education: research on inequalities among students by class, gender, race, sexuality, and other student categories. As schooling expands, it becomes a more integral component of stratification systems. To understand how individuals navigate through those systems, we describe the major contours of school systems and how families activate various forms of "capital." The book compares forms of educational inequalities that are entrenched and that are changing.

The section on social organization is unique for a Canadian education book. Here we draw on the sociology of organizations, and in particular, new institutional theory. We ask readers to think of the historic bureaucratization of education, as well as emerging pressures to subject schools to market forces. Governments are insisting that schools should be more entrepreneurial while simultaneously more firmly regulated, often in the name of accountability schemes that are borrowed from business. In this context, we discuss organizational alternatives to regular public schooling, such as alternative schools, free schools, home-schooling, pre-schools, new private schools, and online learning providers.

This section also includes chapters on the curriculum and the teaching profession, discussing concepts like the "hidden curriculum" and drawing on histories of curriculum, theories of pedagogy, and new challenges from feminism and multiculturalism. The section on socialization examines how schools shape and mould their students, beyond their socio-economic role. Our emphasis is on how socialization is changing, both as a result of internal shifts in teaching styles and classroom conduct over the past few decades, and as a result of broader societal forces. We note controversies around the politicization of the school curriculum and the emergence of new educational ideologies in which many (especially upper-middle-class) families see themselves as sophisticated consumers of schooling, and who are cultivating tastes for tailored forms of education. Following on this theme, we devote a chapter to the competing influences on youth and we inspect those social forces beyond the classroom that affect the workings of education today. Examining student peer groups and youth culture, we describe how selection systems continue to sometimes generate oppositional student cultures. We conclude the book with an eye to the future of Canadian schooling. While certainly mindful of the perils of prediction in the social sciences, it is a fitting finale to urge students to think about emerging trends and to ponder the likely impact of a variety of societal forces. Students can decide for themselves whether they indeed share Illich's strident misgivings.

Acknowledgements

There are many people who deserve our thanks. Lorne Tepperman, the late Jim Curtis, and Susan McDaniel were each warmly supportive of the early beginnings of this project. Both Jim Conley (Trent) and David Mandzuk (Manitoba) provided us with detailed and helpful comments that improved the book. We both further acknowledge the assistance of many folks at Oxford University Press and anonymous reviewers who assisted with each edition. In addition, Neil Guppy thanks Samuel Ko, David Winfield, Chris Thureau, and Sarah Brayne for their research assistance; Tom Kemple, Ron Manzer, and Renisa Mawani for their helpful comments; and the many students who have contributed in his sociology of education teaching. Neil is also grateful to his daughter Emma. Scott Davies thanks all of the patient students who have endured his sociology of education courses at both McMaster and OISE, and also salutes his co-authors, including Janice Aurini, Zahide Alaca, Darren Cyr, Eric Duku, Magdalena Janus, Dan Hamlin, Floyd Hammack, Steph Howells, Johanne Jean Pierre, Vicky Maldonado, Mark McKerrow, Jal Mehta, Emily Milne, Bill O'Grady, Roger Pizarro Milian, Linda Quirke, Jessica Rizk, Julian Tanner, David Tindall, David Walters, and David Zarifa. Most of all, he thanks Janice for her love and support during the writing of this edition, along with Elise and Rowan, who are now experiencing much of what this book is about, and Tatyana, who might appreciate its ideas about higher education. We salute both of our families, who have, through their success and dedication, shown us how education systems can be simultaneously effective, infuriating, and puzzling.

Part I

Introduction

1   The Context for the Schooled Society

Learning Objectives

- To understand what is meant by a "schooled society"
- To identify three broad links between schooling and society
- To recognize key elements of the context for modern schooling

Introduction: What Is a "Schooled Society?"

Schooling matters. Education shapes our lives. The central premise of this book is that education plays a more prominent role in our lives now than ever before. Canada is now a "**schooled society.**" By this we mean that formal education has moved to the centre stage of social life over the past century.

Start with the basic organization of our biographies. Schooling is increasingly central to our life histories. School attendance is one of the rare things mandatory in life. Few Canadians *do not* spend most of their teenage years in schools. Most of us attend a post-secondary institution. Just five decades ago most youth did not finish high school. Now lifelong learning is prolonging the hold of education. Schooling grips our lives more tightly now and that grip is more multi-faceted.

Why? The growing demand for formal education partly stems from its rising power to shape lives. More jobs and career paths require educational certification. Not surprisingly, families are increasingly pinning hopes for their children's success on education. With this, schooling has become the major route for **social mobility**. Groups formerly under-represented in positions of power, such as working-class people, women, and some racial minorities, are now encouraged to use schooling as a lever of upward mobility and social change. For them, schooling has been both touted and doubted for its capacity to be a "great equalizer" that can boost opportunities. But in any event, Canadian schools are now *the* institution that is expected to deliver on core values of equity, progress, and technical sophistication that are intrinsic to modern society.

Education not only shapes our future biographies, it also shapes society. Countries spend billions of dollars on education so it can play a pivotal role in modern nation-building and citizenship. Governments and corporations increasingly turn to universities to generate innovative research to fuel wealth creation.

Schools, especially post-secondary institutions, have become more tightly connected to labour markets. More than ever, schooling classifies and regulates who works where, both creating and rationing access to specialized roles, such as "economist," "welder," or "computer programmer."

Working in the other direction, commerce increasingly intrudes on the school. Business schools have been *the* growth field of study in universities and colleges over the past several decades. Large corporations have established their own on-the-job training and certificate programs; some have created their own universities, including McDonald's "Hamburger University," General Motors University, and Dunkin' Donuts University. The institutional boundaries between schools and corporations have blurred recently, a trend some hail and others lament.

Beyond the economy, more and more social problems are seen to have educational solutions. Schools are called on to tackle an incredible variety of social ills, ranging from drug use to racism to violence prevention to health promotion. Whatever the social issue—sexism, climate change, welfare dependence—an educational solution has been devised. Even in the criminal justice system, schooling is increasingly used as an alternative to incarceration. "John schools," for instance, allow people found hiring sex workers to have their charges dropped in exchange for learning about legal, health, and equity issues surrounding the sex trade.

Formal and structured learning is ubiquitous. Schools are designated as the places to learn new knowledge and upgrade skills needed to engage fully with all that life has to offer, whether in the workplace, at leisure, or in your home. As a result, more and more realms of life are being "schooled." Early childhood is increasingly shaped by preschools. Similarly, jobs that in previous eras had little connection to formal schooling now require official certificates. Think of local community college programs that did not exist just 35 years ago, such as security, bartending, and even bra-fitting. Likewise, preventive health care is increasingly organized through school forms such as prenatal classes. As these examples attest, schools now take many different forms—from home-schooling to schools for cooking to the International Space University. There is a school for almost everything.

How Schools Relate to Society: Three Roles

Sociological thinking generates many questions about schooling. Who succeeds at school, and why? Why are schools organized as they are? What impact do schools have on students? These kinds of questions animate the sociology of education.

A useful place to start our analysis is to pose a most fundamental sociological question: what do schools do? Sociologists answer this question from different angles, but commonly look to relate schools to the wider society, examining roles that schools play in society. To answer that broad question, our book is organized into three main sections: "socialization," "selection," and "organization."

First, schools *socialize*. As obvious as this may seem, schools help prepare the next generation, not only passing along know-how, but also deciding what knowledge and values to transmit, and how to teach that material. Because this socialization role is schooling's central mandate, it can be extremely contentious.

Consider how changes in schools reflect changes in society at large. One hundred years ago, Canada was a far more Christian, rural, and working-class society, and so schools focused more heavily on older-style values and virtues, often casting civic responsibilities and moral codes in religious terms. But recent decades have brought a shift. Today, many policy-makers want schools to emphasize the teaching of technical knowledge and skills. Others contest this focus on several fronts. Many worry that our culture already is overly individualistic, and urge schools to revitalize their community orientation. Advocates of the traditional arts also criticize the current emphasis on technical education, noting that any greater exposure of students to the intricacies of polynomial equations and subatomic particles will make for less time for music, languages, and art. A common result is that the humanizing aspect of education is taking a back seat, as evidenced by cutbacks to music and arts programs. Others see schools as not socializing everyone fairly or equally, perhaps celebrating some cultural traditions at the expense of others, and more or less deliberately nurturing some students for positions of advantage and others for a lifetime of subordination.

The work of Émile Durkheim, a classical theorist discussed in Chapter 2, can be used to examine schools' socializing role. Concerned with the waning force of religion and the smaller sizes of families, Durkheim saw public schooling as a tool to combat the rising culture of **individualism** in modern society. His work can be used to frame a series of questions. Just what culture do schools socialize students into? What values and norms are they learning, and are they doing so by questioning and critiquing or by respecting and obeying? It also implies causal questions such as "what impact are schools having on students, just how successful are schools at socializing students, and do they have as great an impact as they intend?" Finally, it also raises questions about social processes: "just *how do* students learn cultures and moral codes?" Sociologists influenced by Durkheim also examine how other institutions compete for the attention of students. You have surely heard the old lament that children watch too much television, or the newer lament that they spend too much time online. Do mass media and popular culture limit the impact of schools on student's lives?

In a second role, schools *select.* They award "badges of ability" by sorting, differentially rewarding, and certifying graduates of elementary, secondary, and post-secondary schools. Think of the endless appraising, assessing, evaluating, examining, grading, judging, marking, quizzing, and testing in schools. Again, this activity may seem self-evident. But a sociological approach looks to the big picture: at a higher level, schooling shapes and is shaped by larger patterns of social inequality and **stratification**. Indeed, obtaining credentials is now more consequential for people's income, occupational success, and other life chances than ever before. To get prized credentials you need good grades, and those with the best marks become the selected winners. As schools have professed to have become increasingly inclusive in some ways, they have become more selective in others. And schooled individuals are entering an occupational structure that in recent decades has created growing disparities in wealth and income in society.

Sociological approaches to inequality prompt a series of questions. While education is obviously advantageous for individuals, are those advantages distributed equally among all participants by class, gender, or race? *Who* gets selected for *what*, and *why?* Why is family background related to school success? What social processes translate family disadvantage into educational disadvantage? Do all school systems have similar ways of selecting students, or are there variations?

These kinds of questions can be traced back to foundational ideas in the writings of Karl Marx, another classical sociological theorist to be discussed in Chapter 2. His legacy is to have brought to the forefront of modern sociological analysis those issues pertaining to how economic structures create patterns of inequality. While Marx wrote little on schooling per se, his twentieth-century followers examined how schooling reinforces economic forces and patterns of inequality. Indeed, the sociology of education has for several decades addressed a profound and enduring debate: is equality of educational opportunity a myth or a reality? Pressures to tighten schooling links with the economy can clash with democratic aspirations to make schooling accessible to all. With more policy-makers expecting schools to help further Canada's position in the global economy, schools are being pressured to be more competitive, but this competition can constrain schools' ability to guarantee equal opportunity, or to be a local cornerstone of democracy.

In a third role, schools *organize and legitimate*. Schools affect how we learn, whether formally or informally, by rote and routine, or by curiosity and inquiry. Education helps create professions and professionals by institutionalizing an elaborate classification system. It shapes how people become, for example, certified welders or economists, by codifying the knowledge requirements for certain occupations, while also assessing and certifying the standards one must meet to enter an occupation. Schooling also legitimates knowledge claims and only teaches what is considered official knowledge (a disputed term as revealed by debates between evolutionists versus creationism, or the appropriateness of sex curricula for children). Another classical theorist, Max Weber, was interested in how modern institutions *rationalize* the world. Schooling, he wrote, organizes the teaching of knowledge in ways that are bureaucratic, proliferating credentials that create formal pathways between schools and labour markets.

Weber's followers over the past few decades have seen **rationalization** as a core social mechanism that creates change in education. They have used his ideas to raise new questions. Why do employers seek employees with school credentials? Is it simply a matter of hiring those with the most skills, or are there other reasons? Some of Weber's contemporary followers see only loose connections between school content and what is demanded in most jobs, and interpret schooling as mainly a legitimating tool used to ration access to good jobs. They challenge the conventional wisdom that schools simply teach skills and employers hire the most skilled. In contrast, they offer different reasons for the widespread use of school credentials. These sociologists question why we trust school credentials and whether that trust can be maintained as more and more people graduate from higher education.

The Schooled Society and Indigenous Peoples

In a schooled society, schooling is frequently touted as the salve for all ills. For example, in seeking to better the lives of women in Canada, the Royal Commission on the Status of Women argued that "education opens the door to almost every life goal. Wherever women are denied equal access to education, they cannot be said to have equality (1970: 161)." Likewise, the Truth and Reconciliation Commission of Canada implores all levels of government to use schooling as a means to improve drastically the lives of Indigenous peoples. The lenses of socialization, selection, and legitimation/organization shed powerful light on how challenging this task is, yet how centrally important it is.

Take socialization. Historically schooling was used by Western nations to forge a new national identity. In Canada that involved transitioning from a rural resource economy to a modern nation-state. But for First Nations peoples that transition became something much more coercive: schooling was used to solve "the Indian problem" and acculturate First Nations children into Western ways. Residential schools played a central role in this attempted assimilation, removing many First Nations children from their communities, often forcing them to speak only English or French, wear European clothing, and adopt Christian beliefs. Simultaneously, other Canadian schoolchildren learned mixed images of First Nations from their textbooks. Sometimes they saw respectful depictions of noble warriors allying with British troops against American incursions, or inventive peoples surviving in unforgiving landscapes and climates. But sometimes they also saw images of cultural backwardness, savagery, ungodliness, and indolence (see McDiarmid and Pratt, 1971). Ridding those legacies is easy in words but far more difficult in practice.

This coercive socialization then shaped many processes of selection. Poverty made it difficult for Indigenous children to succeed in schooling for all the reasons that are discussed in Chapters 6 and 7. Competitions that prize individual success ahead of communal well-being were alien in many First Nations. Generations of First Nations peoples were traumatized by residential schools, causing them to disengage from public education, seeing it as irrelevant at best and as oppressive at worst. Public schools lacked supports, curriculum, and pedagogy that were tailored to Indigenous students. Too many teachers and peers saw those students as different and backwards. As a result of all of these factors, First Nations peoples have long struggled to succeed in mainstream educational institutions, and continue to do so.

Finally, what about the organization and legitimation of schooling? Because Canadian governments saw First Nations largely as impediments to their project of creating a modern, globalizing society, Indigenous perspectives, knowledge, and ways of life have had little legitimacy in mainstream public education, at least until very recently. How, then, can schools be organized to "re-legitimate" Indigenous cultures while simultaneously preparing young people for the challenges of contemporary life? How can schools right many historical wrongs while creating new opportunities for First Nations children? We dig into many of these crucial issues throughout this book.

Setting the Context

To set the context for the study of schooling, we next highlight major social transformations that have altered the social world over the modern era. We begin with dramatic changes in the economy.

Economic Transformations

In *The Coming of Post-Industrial Society*, Daniel Bell (1973) linked major societal changes to massive shifts or "revolutions" in people's work. Momentous changes in farming created the Agricultural Revolution, and then massive changes in manufacturing sparked the Industrial Revolution. By the late twentieth century, Bell foresaw the beginnings of a third great revolution—the advent of post-industrial society or the Service Revolution. This revolution was built on human and professional *services*, such as communications, finance, and sales. In the late 1800s only about one-third of Canadians worked in the service sector. By 2015 this proportion had grown to nearly nine out of every 10 jobs. Now only about 1 per cent of Canadians work in agriculture, with less than 15 per cent in manufacturing. Table 1.1 demonstrates this transformation. Whether measured by the production of goods and services or by jobs, in just over a century and a quarter, economic activity has shifted dramatically from agriculture to services.

Importantly, Bell predicted that this transition would impact not only the location of people's work, but also the quality of their work. He reasoned that theoretical knowledge would be more central to jobs. Just as the plough and the steam engine were central to change in earlier eras, he anticipated that the computer would emerge as the driving force in the contemporary period. Indeed, since the 1970s information and communication technology (ICT) has rapidly transformed our way of life, from the Internet to cell phones through to smart cars and bioinformatics.

Inspired by Bell's image of a "post-industrial society," others have since coined terms like "information society" and "knowledge society." Research and development, frequently done within universities, plays a decisive role in modern

Table 1.1 Percentage Distribution of Canadian Economic Activity by Sector and Period

Economic Sector	Production		Employment	
	Late 1800s	Circa 2020	Late 1800s	Circa 2020
Agricultural	44	2	49	1
Industrial	19	29	15	12
Service	38	69	36	87

Sources: Estimated from K.A.H. Buckley and M.C. Urquhart, 1965, *Historical Statistics of Canada* (Toronto: Macmillan); Statistics Canada, *The Labour Force*, Cat. no. 15–001–XIE; Statistics Canada, CANSIM, table 282–0008.

economies. The examples are legion and include insulin (University of Toronto), BlackBerry (University of Waterloo), and WebCT (University of British Columbia). More fundamentally, modern innovations depend increasingly on the pure research of university scholars. Especially with increasing global competition, policy-makers have been quick to point to education—as a producer and disseminator of knowledge—as critical to national success.

Has Bell's prediction about jobs been borne out? Yes, at least in some ways. The number of knowledge-driven jobs has risen rapidly in the last century. Many new professional and scientific jobs require greater levels of education (Clement and Myles, 1994: 72). More and more jobs require autonomy, cognitive complexity, and mental dexterity. Indeed, subsequent to the financial crisis of 2008, "high-knowledge" jobs provided the main source of job creation, a growth trend that most see continuing (Dept. of Finance, 2014). Increasingly, workers must be able to recognize when, where, and how to apply relevant knowledge. And, as a key consequence, a person's level of education increasingly shapes their economic rewards: more educated individuals increasingly earn greater incomes (Baer, 2004).

The maturing of industrialism and the advent of post-industrialism was accompanied by other institutional shifts in nations like Canada during the period 1950–1980. An array of government-provided services grew markedly, including welfare, unemployment insurance, health care, and of course, education. Public sector and private sector unions grew and raised wages for millions of workers. These co-expanding institutions were supported by progressive taxation in a thriving economy that generated not only an unprecedented amount of wealth, but also distributed that wealth more equally than in previous generations.

But over the past 40 years, two key shifts have occurred in Western economies that were not anticipated by Bell. The first is the movement of jobs and money out of traditional sectors that produce industrial goods and social services and into financial organizations like banks, investment firms, and insurance companies. These enterprises generate their profits not by making tangible products, but by channelling money through financial institutions that have become increasingly complex and labyrinth-like. Recent decades have seen the rise of increasingly arcane and opaque financial ventures like hedge funds, stock options, insurance schemes, and derivatives, many of which operate in hidden ways. This process of "financialization" began in the 1970s and intensified when some financial institutions were deregulated in the 1990s and 2000s (Tomaskovic-Devey and Lin, 2011). This financialization is a prime cause of the deep recession that originated on Wall Street in 2008 and then spread around the globe, its long tail continuing to slow economic progress.

The second shift is rising income inequality. Since 1980, the incomes of Canadians in the bottom and middle ranges have largely stagnated, while those of the top 20 per cent, and especially the top 1 per cent, rose substantially

(Fortin et al., 2012). This trend has several causes. One is a reduction in the proportion of Canadians in unions, and some reductions in government-provided social programs. At the same time, politicians have repeatedly called for lower taxes, particularly for those in upper income categories. A barometer of these twin shifts was the "Occupy movement," that in 2011 imported the "Occupy Wall Street" protests to several Canadian cities. Polls showed that Canadians were generally sympathetic to the protests because they drew attention to these trends. This broad economic shift since 1980—the financialization and deregulation of financial firms, rising income inequality, calls to further reduce taxes, and the weakening of unions and many social programs—has been dubbed the neo-liberal era (e.g., Hall and Lamont, 2012). Neo-liberalism has in many respects reshaped our economic and political institutions, and in turn altered the context for contemporary schooling.

Cultural and Demographic Shifts

These economic changes have been accompanied by great cultural and demographic shifts. One such shift has been the continual decline of religious authority in Western societies. The earliest European missionaries—the Recollects and the Jesuits—were quick to establish schools to educate everyone, including of course First Nations peoples, in the godly ways of the world. As well, many of the earliest university charters were awarded to institutions with strong religious ties (i.e., Dalhousie, McMaster, and Queen's). The Church was instrumental in the formation of public schools in all provinces, and was especially authoritative in Quebec and Newfoundland.

However, the erosion of religious authority has continued to this day in most developed industrial countries, including Canada. Not only are fewer people active in organized religion, but even among those who participate, the influence of religion is now more delimited, more privately spiritual, and less world-orienting (Bibby, 2011). Whereas Sunday schools once provided many Canadian children with their moral compass, religion now plays a far lesser role in socializing most young Canadians.

This decline in religion has altered the cultural underpinnings of modern life. Culture is about people's taken-for-granted social conventions—the principles of action, the habits of speech and gesture, and the recipes or scenarios about how to act. Sociologists think of culture as social "tool kit" or set of implicit guidelines and rules that range from turn-taking in conversations, queuing, or dressing, to deeper social mores.

Picking up on Durkheim and Weber, some suggest that the continual erosion of religion has given rise to a new set of values, one marked by rising individualism and less deferential attitudes. Ronald Inglehart (1995) argues that as newer generations are exposed to economic prosperity and higher levels of education, they undergo a "value shift" that puts greater emphasis on self-development and personal identity. For liberals, this individualism is a good thing, strengthening values of liberty and equality. Notions of individual rights underpin much progress over the past century, including the near-abolishment of slavery and the success of the women's movement. Ideas of human rights and entitlements (e.g., to vote or to own property) are being extended to children, who are increasingly seen to be entitled to their own happiness and freedoms. But among many thinkers, these same things are often deemed to have gone too far. Some conservatives see them as eroding traditional values of authority, respect, and honesty, and condemn schools for not shoring up those values. Many leftists see individualism as promoting too much consumerism and competitiveness, and blame schools for being insufficiently progressive.

Regardless of one's view of the merits of individualism, sociologists cannot help but be struck by how this cultural shift has affected lifestyles. Individualism has spawned self-help, self-actualization, and self-realization movements. Professional counselling and therapy, individual lifestyle choices, and personal coaches (e.g., fitness trainers, financial planners, and education tutors) further underscore this rise of individualism.

This cultural shift has particularly transformed parenting. Children have gradually come to be seen as family members requiring special expertise and nurturing (see Albanese, 2016). Intensive parenting is the new normal (Wall, 2010). As hard as it is for modern sensibilities to comprehend, until the nineteenth century both the abandonment of children and hard child labour were common. Children were, most importantly, economic appendages of families, effectively miniature adults. As a more educated workforce became essential for economic growth, childhood gradually emerged as a recognizable period of life. The prolongation of childhood has meant that the socializing of young children is increasingly supplemented, and sometimes primarily done, outside the family, principally through the education system, but also through the health-care system (pediatricians, child psychologists), social workers (youth workers), and daycare centres. Further, these changes have spawned a litany of experts to provide parents with scientific advice about how best to raise their children (from Emmett Holt's *Care and Feeding of Children* [1894] to Benjamin Spock's multi-edition *Baby and Child Care* [1946] through to Glenn and Janet Doman's *How to Multiply Your Baby's Intelligence* [2005]). Although pleas to leave childhood to children are often made, the cultural pressure grows to intervene and produce "super-babies." The implication for education is that expectations for children and their success continue to rise.

Similar changes in the last few decades involve adolescents, as seen in the rise of a consumer culture devoted to this market segment. The global marketing of clothing fashions from various brand-name jeans and running shoes, each signify the institutionalization of a culture targeted at youth (and adults who seek to remain young!). This accelerating popular culture exerts a far greater influence on the lives of young people than it did in the past, and by doing so, it has an impact on schooling. Increasingly, school material must compete with popular entertainment, advertising, and clothing. Today's schools must somehow "fit into" young people's identities and lifestyles.

Families, another traditional pillar of socialization, have also changed continuously over the past half-century. In 1959 more babies (479,275) were born in Canada than in any year before or after. By comparison, in 2015 the number of births was 388,700 (a decline of 19 per cent). This shift from baby boom to baby bust was consequential for schooling: it first required a massive increase and then a sizeable decrease in the number of schools and teachers. Beyond the sheer number of children, family *forms* have also shifted. The traditional nuclear family—mom, dad, and the kids—continues its relative decline in Canada. While in 1961 married couples with children at home accounted for 62.3 per cent of all families, by 2011 this had declined to below 39 per cent. The proportion of families headed by a lone parent had risen to over 15 per cent and the proportion of childless couples (either married or common law) had increased to over 40 per cent by 2011. As well, children in more recent years have fewer siblings, if any.

The family has also changed in other ways. Common-law unions now represent about 15 per cent of all couples, and just under half of these couples have children living at home. Couples that do marry now tend to do so later, and they often delay having children. More and more children have 40- and 50-year-old parents. As well, the vast majority of school-aged children live in families where both partners have paid jobs. This leads to more frequent parental absences for significant portions of childhood and adolescence (see Hersch, 1998). Divorce is also now more prevalent. Now, every third marriage is likely to end in a divorce; among divorcing couples, over 50 per cent involve children. The result has been a significant rise both in lone-parent families and in children living in stepfamilies.

Regardless of how these changes are interpreted, they have stark implications for schooling. With more parents in paid employment, leading busy lives with multiple demands, their engagement with their child's school varies greatly. Some children have only one parental advocate, while others have multiple parents and guardians supporting them (although not always in unison).

Other population changes have also buffeted schools. Birth rates and immigration fuel population growth. Immigration has always been large scale in Canada and so schools have long been accustomed to teaching the children of recent immigrants. What has changed most recently is the composition of the immigrant groups. Fewer new Canadians have European roots, and more have ancestral homes in Asia. Refugee uptake has also increased.

These changes all bear on schools' relations with children. Grand religious traditions are being replaced by new, rapidly shifting ideals, forcing schools to compete for the hearts and minds of young people. Leaders now proclaim social diversity, multiculturalism, and tolerance as core values to be promoted by schools. Modern teenagers can actively choose among a far greater diversity of lifestyles offered by industries that, in seeking their market share, make school a less central priority for many youth. The smaller modern family can place intense pressures on children to succeed because fewer siblings are available to shoulder the dreams of parents.

Plan for the Remainder of the Book

A few words are necessary to highlight what this book is *not*. We do not attempt to review all types of educational settings (due to lack of space) and thus restrict our focus to organized schooling designed mostly for younger people, as practised in the primary, secondary, and post-secondary systems. Also, we aim merely to understand schooling, not to offer proposals for reform. If you peruse the education section of any good bookstore you will find a wealth of books devoted either to decrying crises in schooling or to offering solutions. Far fewer books are devoted to understanding how schooling operates, with all its entanglements.

We hope to contribute a thorough understanding of schooling using a theoretically informed, evidenced-based approach. This entails not merely accepting what people *say* they are trying to accomplish, but probing what they *actually* accomplish. When studying schooling, this exercise can be contentious. Faith in schooling is strong. Expectations are both lofty *and* diverse. Not everyone agrees on what the priorities or core goals should be. Experiences range widely. Schooling can be a place where they work or study, where they did or didn't get "a leg up on others," or where they have fond memories or horrid experiences. Yet everyone has a lot at stake.

The next two chapters review prominent theories from classical and contemporary sociology in order to highlight questions, issues, and tools that help us to comprehend schools and schooling. Chapter 2 reviews core sociological principles that motivated the key sociological theorists, Durkheim, Weber, and Marx. Chapter 3 turns to contemporary theory and illustrates new tools that have been developed in response to changing societal conditions over the past several decades. Each theoretical approach highlights different sociological insights about schooling, and connects schools to trends in economics, science, religion, politics, the family, and popular culture. We approach these theories as useful starting points for raising issues, posing questions, and conducting research. In later chapters we emphasize middle-range ideas and subsequent research findings, and then reflect back on theory.

Part II focuses on selection and highlights the changing ways that schools both offer opportunities and generate inequalities. Chapter 4 examines the great expansion of schooling over the past century. Chapter 5 examines how the very structure of schooling has changed and become itself more stratified. Chapters 6 and 7 turn to a more individual level to consider educational inequalities by class, gender, race, Indigeneity, sexuality, and mental health.

Part III turns to the organization of schooling and legitimizing of knowledge. Chapter 8 examines schools as organizations, placing them in the context of other types of bureaucratic enterprises and looking at their variety of organized forms. Chapter 9 examines the curriculum, investigating the content of schooling. Chapter 10 highlights the work of teachers and discusses teaching as a profession.

The final section focuses on socialization. Chapter 11 summarizes a broad body of research concerning the impact of school on students, focusing on changing forms of morality, and research on various kinds of school effects. Chapter 12 looks at the limits of this socialization by highlighting competing influences on students. In the concluding chapter we draw together several of the book's themes to outline a prognosis for the future of schooling.

Conclusion

Canada has become a "schooled society." Formal education has moved to the centre of social life. Canadian education has evolved remarkably since its humble origins as a loosely coordinated collection of local schoolhouses. Today's educational systems are huge bureaucracies that are governed by a variety of professional, legal, and political bodies. More and more politicians are earmarking education systems as generators of wealth and skill. As schooling enters a wider variety of institutional realms (e.g., corporate universities), its relation to society grows more complex than ever. It gains an unprecedented institutional centrality. This is what we mean by a schooled society. We next turn to sociological theorizing about schooling's roles in societal selection, socialization, and organization/**legitimation**.

Questions for Critical Thought

1. There are diversion programs in the criminal justice system such as "john schools," remedial driver education, and anti-drug education. How do these programs, or others like them, exemplify our schooled society?

2. Are there any ways that contemporary Canada is *not* yet a schooled society? Explain.

3. Using the themes selection, socialization, and organization/legitimation, compare your schooling experience so far with that of one of your grandparents. Discuss whether today's schools might have a greater or smaller causal impact on students.

Suggested Readings

Baker, David. 2014. *The Schooled Society: The Educational Transformation of Global Culture*. Stanford, CA: Stanford University Press. This book broadly examines how mass education has dramatically altered the face of society and human life. Great title, too!

Mehta, Jal, and Scott Davies, eds. 2017. *Education in a New Society: Renewing the Sociology of Education*. Chicago: University of Chicago Press. A series of authors examine how new sociological concepts can be used to comprehend change in education.

Walters, Pamela Barnhouse, Annette Lareau, and Sheri H. Ranis. 2009. *Education Research on Trial: Policy Reform and the Call for Scientific Rigor*. New York: Routledge. This volume debates the strengths and pitfalls of current educational research, and the value of approaches that are more or less scientific.

Web Links

Council of Ministers of Education, Canada
www.cmec.ca
This website is maintained by the provincial ministers responsible for education and contains good resource material.

Canadian Teachers' Federation
www.ctf-fce.ca
This website is a national alliance representing nearly 200,000 elementary and secondary school teachers across Canada.

Canadian Education Association
www.cea-ace.ca/about-us
The Canadian Education Association website is a useful place to find discussion and research related to current issues in Canadian education.

2 Classical Sociological Approaches to Education

Learning Objectives

- To use classical sociological theories to understand schooling
- To see how Durkheim's thoughts provide foundational concepts for understanding micro-level social situations and reveal broad shifts in the role of schooling in societal socialization
- To discover how Marx illuminates the role of education in selection and inequality
- To understand how Weber's concept of rationalization reveals fundamental changes in the form and content of modern schooling

Introduction: Using Theory to Study Schools

Theories are conceptual tools that provide perspective or illumination. They help formulate intriguing questions and guide our search for interesting answers. Sociology does not possess a unified, grand theory that everyone shares, but instead offers competing perspectives, each having different emphases and starting points. Like lenses of different magnification, sociological theories can focus at different levels of abstraction.

"Macro" theories are pitched at the largest scale, attempting to understand vast horizons of social activity across entire societies and over long stretches of time, sometimes spanning entire continents and centuries. Macro sociologists approach schooling by linking it to broad modernizing forces that have transformed the world, such as the rise of science over the past three centuries.

Next are "middle-range" theories. These theories are more circumscribed, offering propositions that are geared to specific times and places, such as a particular nation in a particular time period. A middle-range theory might attempt to explain why the Canadian higher education system greatly expanded in the immediate post–Second World War era. Rather than examining grand forces of modernity, this middle-range approach might examine more proximate causes such as the growth of the welfare state, post-war economic prosperity, and the baby boom.

Finally, the most specific are "micro-level" theories. These theories are concerned with face-to-face interactions among people, with only a partial eye to broader social forces. A micro-level theorist might observe a teacher's classroom management tactics and other attempts to wield authority and maintain control. These three different levels of explanation—macro, middle range, and micro— allow sociologists to examine various facets of the social world.

Different sociological theories of education are also rooted in different topics. Some focus on socialization, others on school bureaucracies, others on links to the labour market, others in why some schools work better than others, and yet others on gauging the extent of educational opportunity in society today. Explaining these very different things requires different conceptual tools. No single explanatory framework could develop insights into, or answers for, these diverse questions.

Consider school bullying. Competing explanations can take different starting points. Micro-level researchers might focus on the social psychological mental states of individual bullies, or on how they interact with their victims and bystanders. Middle-range researchers, in contrast, might examine the organization of peer groups, trying to understand how such groups are formed and who is excluded from them, who is isolated and why. Finally, at the most macro level, a sociologist might engage in cross-national comparisons, or in long-term historical research, and examine how different cultures define bullying. Some cultures, for instance, may consider rough physical play to be normal, in contrast to our contemporary society that has evolved more expansive definitions of bullying, extending beyond physical intimidation to include social ostracism and demeaning words. A macro sociologist might compare how such cultural definitions vary across vast sweeps of space and time, and how they evolve.

In this book we begin with macro theories to set the societal context for education. In later chapters we work down to middle-range theories to explain particular aspects of schooling, and near the end we examine micro theories to explore the experiences of students and teachers. As we argued in Chapter 1, school activities form a trilogy: socialization, selection, and organization/legitimation. Focusing on these three issues, this chapter presents the major theoretical concepts that assist our understanding of schooling.

We begin with the work of founding theorists. Sociology was born out of revolutions—first, the Industrial Revolution (1760–1830s) and then two political democratic revolutions in America (1765–1783) and France (1789–1799). Understanding the transformations these revolutions unleashed called for new ideas and new models. Three scholars in particular had powerful insights that hold enduring significance for sociological research. Émile Durkheim (1858–1917), Karl Marx (1818–83), and Max Weber (1864–1920) each contributed to the establishment of sociology. In the following pages we highlight some of their central ideas. Following this, in Chapter 3 we present a series of more recent theoretical perspectives that are especially illuminating for the sociology of education. In subsequent chapters we put all of these theories to work to understand modern schooling.

Durkheim and Socialization: The Micro Foundations of Social Interaction and the Cultural Shift to Individualism

In earlier societies, people's deference to tradition tended to make social life regular and predictable in a world that was otherwise turbulent, unforgiving, and unpredictable. Religion prescribed what you did; custom and habit ruled. The revolutions in industry and politics were transformative precisely because they ushered in new social orders that broke radically with traditional societies. Rising *individualism* was central to this radical break. By "individualism" we refer to the gradual ascendance of an individual's personal goals and thoughts over their sense of obligation to other persons. The rise of capitalist markets and democratic procedures tended to promote individualism and undermine traditional, pre-modern notions of collective responsibility.

These changes motivated Émile Durkheim to pose both micro-level and macro-level questions. At the micro-level, the rising tide of individualism made him think about the very building-blocks of social interaction: what social encounters make people feel part of a group, and how do social situations vary in their intensity? These were questions about social solidarity, processes that bind people to an interconnected group, and questions of individuation, those that distinguish them from collectives. While Durkheim has been long criticized for under-emphasizing group conflict at the macro-level, his concepts are useful for understanding micro-level processes in smaller scale settings, such as classrooms and schools.

Durkheim got his ideas from studying religious groups. He observed that social experiences can intensify when people are gathered together and each focuses their attention on the same people or objects. Rituals are especially good at this: they gather people in near physical proximity, encourage them to speak, sing, sway, or dance in unison, and to revere a common object—a cross, statue, totem, flag, or text. Successful rituals boost group solidarity by renewing people's feeling of being part of a collectivity. Durkheim noticed that religious rituals could energize people and give them a common emotional state, what he called "collective effervescence." This effervescence peaked when everyone assembled became deeply attached to a common object, making it "sacred" to them. In fact, Durkheim argued, objects gain a sacred quality precisely because they symbolize the group. But he also noted that rituals have to be repeated to retain their power, and that sacred objects can sometimes lose their power to motivate individuals and bind groups together.

Rituals and symbols can be seen in schools. Some symbols represent the nation, such as a flag in the schoolyard, a portrait of a political leader on the classroom wall, or the singing of a national anthem in assemblies. Others represent a religious community, such as a Christian cross, a painting of a Pope, or the reciting of a prayer. But in an attempt to forge their own community spirit, schools have also created their own group symbols, such as school mascots, uniforms, songs, nicknames, and emblems. These symbols can become charged with emotion when used in collective gatherings, such as sports events or assemblies. That is one of the latent roles of school sports teams. Student athletes wearing the same uniform, adorned with school colours and recognizable school emblems, serve to symbolize the school community.

The gathering of large crowds of students and teachers, repeatedly chanting and cheering, can create an electrifying, ritual-like experience. The entire spectacle can serve to recharge collective feelings of belonging to the school, just like plugging into a wall outlet can recharge a battery. School rallies and assemblies perform similar roles for large gatherings. School clubs, such as Gay-Straight Alliances (GSAs), also play comparable roles for smaller groups, binding their members together in a common cause, albeit in a calmer, toned-down, less kinetic manner. For a modern-day Durkheimian, each sport event, rally, assembly, or club meeting is a micro-level vehicle by which schools generate moral feelings and group solidarity among their members. But not all rituals and symbols equally bind all individuals together with equal force. Some successfully generate group cohesion; others fail outright, leaving many feeling apathetic, unattached, or excluded. Some generate a great deal of solidarity, but at the same time can also stratify people into leaders and followers, insiders and outsiders. In Chapter 3 we will examine more recent micro-level theories that emphasize *variations* in the capacity of schools to generate solidarity.

At the macro-level, Durkheim asked: with the transition from traditional to modern societies, what provides for the social regularity of modern life? For him, industrialization and democratic reforms had sparked greater individualism by making societies increasingly complex, and by giving more people a greater range of social experiences. Cites were growing. More people were geographically mobile, moving across countrysides, regions, even national borders. Fewer people worked in subsistence agriculture, and were instead moving to work in new jobs in an ever-elaborate division of labour. The expansion of mass immigration mixed more and more people of different nationalities and ancestries. This expanding range of social experience, in Durkheim's eyes, provided the experiential bedrock of modern individualism. These societal changes allowed new and central ideas to ascend, like the dignity and worth of human individuals. Both the French and American revolutions stressed the ideal that people should develop their individual talents and capacities to their fullest extent. In its day, this was revolutionary thinking.

As individualism flourished Durkheim wondered what was replacing the authoritative voice of religion which had traditionally supplied the norms that prescribed social behaviour and bolstered social cohesion. What kept individuals from acting only in their own selfish interest, from being uncooperative and self-centred? He offered a powerful sociological response. First, he argued against those who postulated that individual rationality and an implicit social contract were the building blocks of society. That rationality and contract, he reasoned, could only thrive if people trusted one another. Think about two people doing business with one another. For any two parties to agree to a contract, he reasoned, trust had to come first. Trust was fundamental, "pre-contractual." Only when you trust someone to not cheat you, will you ever agree to abide by a contract.

Second, Durkheim emphasized how our very individuality is itself a social product, something forged through social interaction. Our personal identity and sense of self is moulded, shaped, and reshaped through the ongoing reactions of others. We internalize the judgments of family and friends, and eventually those of relative strangers (e.g., new schoolmates), in forming a self-concept, defining ourselves—funny, confident, anxious, good-looking—as we interpret how others respond to us. And in turn, we each contribute significantly to how others view themselves.

Durkheim recognized that historically, religion had dictated the individual's place within the collective. Separate personalities were virtually absent. By the late 1800s, however, people were beginning to form stronger personal identities. The power of people to develop their own individuality, nurtured by the reactions of significant others, was growing. Circles of interaction and chains of interdependence broadened this feedback network.

Third, as Durkheim argued, each of us speaks a language we did not invent. This has profound consequences on which we seldom reflect. Most plainly, we think with words created by others. Mutual understanding is possible only by using a common language, but we did not create that language. Language is, by analogy, a microcosm of society, one example of the social rules and resources that constitute society. Durkheim (1964: 13) argued that all of these rules and resources "exercised on the individual an external constraint." These rules and resources promoted social cohesion.

To summarize, Durkheim argued that social norms provided a moral framework—the basis of enduring trust—that underlay our participation in mutual agreements. Acts of mutual reciprocity (including contracts), presuppose and reinforce trust. The surrounding community provides a moral basis for social cohesion, enabling us to follow guidelines (ethics, etiquette), but also restricting the range of approved action (e.g., no cheating on sociology exams).

Durkheim's university appointment at the Sorbonne was in both pedagogy and sociology. He often lectured prospective schoolteachers on moral education, which he understood as "the means by which society perpetually recreates the conditions of its very existence" (Durkheim, 1956: 123). Fundamentally, he saw schooling to be about the "systematic socialization of the young generation" (ibid., 124). Durkheim (1964: 6) argued that "all education is a continuous effort to impose on the child ways of seeing, feeling and acting at which [he or she] would not have arrived spontaneously."

At the core of Durkheim's lectures on moral education were three things. First, morals had an imperative quality, stipulating how one should act: "a system of rules of action that predetermine conduct" (Durkheim, 1961: 24). Second, acting morally entailed some appreciation for the well-being of others: "to act in the light of a collective interest" (ibid., 46). Third, acting morally meant taking personal responsibility, to "have as clear and complete an awareness as possible of the reasons for our conduct" (ibid., 120).

Taking each point in turn, Durkheim's moral education involved several nuances. It entailed that students learn a "system of rules" that should benefit society (the "collective interest"). But students must not follow rules blindly. They must understand why rules exist; they must accept responsibility for their actions. Socialization is thus a complex activity involving an important reciprocity between the individual and society. For Durkheim, education was *the* institution that could fulfill this broad public mandate, this service to society. Schools were to teach students to be socially responsible, to internalize their obligation to the larger community.

Durkheim also urged that the curriculum needed to include training in scientific reasoning and knowledge; "it is science that elaborates the cardinal notions that govern our thought: notions of cause, of laws, of space, of number. . . . Before the sciences were constituted, religion filled the same office" (Durkheim, 1956: 76–7). This comparison between science and religion signals an important turning point in education. The Church stressed literary study and worked doggedly to restrict the teaching of scientific ideas. Durkheim was pushing new directions by stressing the centrality of science in education.

Before we consider problems with Durkheim's ideas, it is important to note those enduring issues that he correctly identified. First, he recognized the salience of socialization in formal education. He emphasized both virtues and values (for him, morality), and he stressed knowledge and competencies (through the importance of teaching science, both its findings and its methods). Second, he proposed an important view regarding the relations between individual and society, and despite its shortcomings (see below), this remains a powerful statement of education's role in the communal anchoring of social norms (morality).

Third, on balance, Durkheim stressed that education is more likely to reproduce society than to change it: "[education] is only the image and reflection of society . . . it does not create it" (Durkheim, 1951: 372). Education plays a fundamental role in promoting social order, in giving stability to society. Social reproduction, not social change, is the focus of both socialization and legitimation.

Durkheim's thinking stresses a conservative tendency within schools and schooling. Preparing children to take on adult roles implies preparing them for positions and responsibilities in an adult world similar to the existing society. Preparing children for some utopian or desired society would be irresponsible since this would be preparing them for a future that may never materialize. Nevertheless, Durkheim reminded future teachers to "guard against transmitting the moral gospel of our elders as a sort of closed book" (Durkheim, 1977: 13). He encouraged "responsible" social change, but he cautioned against assuming that education could or should be a powerful change agent in society.

Finally, Durkheim was concerned about education providing an equal opportunity for everyone. He was critical of education for being too "aristocratic," stressing that for the majority of people education should be a route to improving "their material condition" (ibid., 205–6). He clearly supported the ideals of the French Revolution, seeing education as a vehicle to foster the development of individual talents and capacities.

Critics of Durkheim, and there are many, typically point to two related issues. His view of society is too consensual. Society appears as one big happy family where everyone agrees. Conversely, conflict is relatively invisible. He implies that everyone in society provides equal weight with respect to social norms, but critics are quick to note that the morality of powerful groups is often the official morality. Power plays a more fundamental role in the social order than Durkheim allows.

A second criticism is equally important. Durkheim tended to point to the moral order, or society, as all-powerful. Society was an "external constraint," it "commanded us," it "penetrated us," and it "formed part of us" (Durkheim, 1961: 98). Socialization took on the aura of pouring the contents of societies' moral rules into the child. A sophisticated treatment of the interplay between "individual" and "society" needs to be more dynamic, recognizing that people actively interpret social rules. Socialization is not like turning on a faucet and filling a vessel (i.e., pouring norms into a child). Children interpret and make sense of social rules in the light of other rules, and do so in their own everyday context, while interacting with others—who themselves are reacting to the same rules.

Finally, for Durkheim the "health" of society could be seen as the ultimate goal. His defining question was one of social cohesion or integration in the face of rising individualism. His lectures on moral education understood the school first and foremost as a socializing agent devoted to instilling in children society's core values and virtues. In contrast, many of the early education theorists in North America took the concept of individualism in a different direction, arguing that schools should aim to develop people's capacity to make the most of themselves. This understanding of individualism is central to John Dewey, a famous American educator and contemporary of Durkheim. Dewey and his followers placed more emphasis on nurturing individual talents, and emphasized active learning—learning by doing—and discouraged rote, disciplined teaching of societal rules.

Marx: Industrial Capitalism, Class Inequality, and the Spectre of Selection

For Karl Marx, the focus of any social analysis must be on the production and distribution of goods and services that are critical to the survival of society. He traced how the earliest economies were based on hunting and gathering. Over time, innovations in ploughing and planting allowed people to become more settled and live off the soil. This agricultural revolution occurred approximately 12,000 years ago as crop cultivation and animal domestication replaced foraging. In both hunter–gatherer societies and agricultural societies, learning was by custom and tradition—mother to daughter, father to son. Families passed along values and virtues, capabilities and skills; organized schooling was non-existent. Tradition ruled; custom was king.

Gradually, agricultural output increased. The capacity of farmers to support a non-agricultural population presaged the next great economic revolution, the rise of industry. In the mid-to-late 1700s, and located initially in England, the introduction of innovative machinery in factory settings accelerated productivity. With the rise of manufacturing came a population shift from the farm to the city, a growing division of industrial labour, and the beginnings of a more globally integrated world. Formal schooling was introduced as something critical to economic well-being, both for the individual and the nation.

For Marx, an important aspect of industrialization was that it generates vast social differences in wealth. From the homeless and downtrodden to the rich and powerful, enormous gulfs divide us. This social inequality surrounds us—rich and poor, esteemed and pitied, advantaged and disadvantaged. Making sense of these differences, both their nature and extent, is a central focus of sociology. Marx has had a substantial impact on sociological explorations of inequality, remaining to this day one of the most read, cited, and criticized social thinkers in history. His key tenet was that **class struggle** was central to any understanding of society. Modern society, in Marx's view, is capitalist, divided between two main groups, those owning industries and businesses and those working as employees. Those owning factories, offices, and businesses are the most powerful because they control *capital*—productive investments. They dictate how economic production and distribution is organized.

The divide between owners and workers, Marx argues, is fundamentally exploitative. In agricultural societies this exploitation was easy to see—workers (peasants, serfs, slaves) were compelled to work for a lord or aristocratic master. In modern factories or offices exploitation is less obvious. Marx argued that workers receive a wage or salary, but that they have no claim on the profits *their own* work generates. Workers create more monetary value in the goods or services they produce than they are paid in wages. Owners claim this surplus amount as profit (after deducting other expenses, e.g., building costs, marketing costs). By reaping this "surplus value," in Marx's language, employment relationships are *exploitative*: one class generates a profit, while another confiscates that profit.

He and his long-time colleague, Friedrich Engels, argued that social power followed from economic exploitation: "the ruling ideas of each age have ever been the ideas of its ruling class" (Marx and Engels, 1969: 125). The creation and diffusion of the dominant ideas in any society are driven by the ruling class, according to Marx. In capitalism this means that the specific interests of business owners and the captains of industry are the most dominant ideas.

Schools are all about ideas. For modern Marxists, mainstream classrooms, along with other institutions like the media and the legal system, unwittingly transmit the ruling ideas of capitalist society. Schooling is seen to play a particularly critical role in spreading the ruling ideas throughout society. Furthermore, Marxists presume that the sons and daughters of the ruling class will benefit most from mass institutions like schooling, being virtually guaranteed the best badges of ability and top academic honours.

But just how do schools disseminate ruling ideas and the dominant ideology of capitalism? Here, Marx was rather vague. He left for his followers, in very broad strokes, two possibilities. First, is an "education–workplace fit." Marxists claim that schools mainly teach those skills and values that are essential for the smooth functioning of the capitalist workplace. Indeed, Marx (1967: 509) referred to schools as "teaching factories." He and Engels saw education, along with "Modern Industry," as transforming children into "simple articles of commerce and instruments of labour" (Marx and Engels, 1969: 124). Second, they argued that education reinforces ideas that sustain and legitimate inequalities in the surrounding society, and vowed to "rescue education from the influence of the ruling class" (ibid.). Both of these lines of argument have been taken up by scholars inspired by Marx (see Box 2.1).

Certainly controversial and decidedly wrong on specific issues, Marx's thinking nevertheless remains influential. His focus on the role of power and conflict in shaping societies is critical, particularly how its economic organization tends to create unequal social classes. No sociologist can properly understand education

Box 2.1 Paulo Freire: Critical Pedagogy

Paulo Freire (1921–97), a Brazilian educator, was a key proponent of "Critical Pedagogy." Most early forms of schooling emphasized rote teaching and memorization rather than critical thinking (see Chapters 6 and 8). Freire was especially caustic about the "banking" model of education that views students as passive, empty vessels into which teachers fill curriculum content. Echoing John Dewey, Freire considered that banking model of schooling to be dehumanizing. Moreover, Freire refused to reduce schooling to a utilitarian means for training or moulding workers—encouraging students to passively accept oppressive attitudes and practices. His central interest was in using education to empower the poor. As the Director of the Department of Education and Culture in Pernambuco during the Great Depression (1930s), he worked to educate the illiterate poor. Freire saw education as emancipating. Educating illiterate workers was a political act because in Pernambuco only the literate could vote. Literacy, he wrote, could push the poor to develop a fuller "critical" consciousness, one that connected their individual experiences with schooling to their larger social-economic context. Only then would schooling help people gain the power needed to transform reality and challenge their oppression.

His influential book, *Pedagogy of the Oppressed*, was first published in 1968 (1970 in English). Dedicated "to the oppressed, and to those who suffer with them and fight at their side," Freire debunked traditional teaching methods, believing them to promote inequalities between students and teachers. He advocated a reciprocal relationship in which students and teachers each teach, learn, and question one another. Freire's book resonated with North American and European professors and students in the wake of the 1960s, and they eventually formalized **Critical Pedagogy** as it is taught widely today in universities. Freire's work highlights the role of schooling in unequal social relationships, ranging from overt battles between the colonizer and the colonized in parts of the Third World, to tussles between employers and employees in the First World.

without being fully cognizant of the power of economic power, wielded by business associations, and to a much lesser extent, unions. In contrast to Durkheim, Marx's view that the "ruling ideas" benefit some segments of society more than others has inspired many followers.

In common with Durkheim, Marx stressed the importance of education in supporting or reproducing the current social order. Marx argued that employers want schools to socialize students into compliant and productive labourers. Today, some Marxist theorists point to similar pressures, such as when politicians use the rhetoric of the "knowledge society" and national competitiveness to call for tightened links between schools and workplaces. In contrast, Marx envisioned socialist societies as having education systems that would truly nurture the development of the whole person.

As noted above, Durkheim emphasized equality of opportunity, the idea that everyone should benefit from schools and schooling. Marxist thinking refines these ideas, suggesting that societies ought to strive not just for equality of opportunity, but also equality of outcome. Both Durkheimians and Marxists note that those from richer and more prosperous families are surely more able to succeed, not because of their intrinsic abilities or efforts, but because of their many, and early, advantages. Because advantaged children are able to start running before the race even begins, and most often cross the finish line in first place, some question whether education ought to be organized as a race at all.

Critics of Marx have questioned whether the economy is always the driver of societal change, and whether class divisions readily reflect only two main groupings, capitalists and workers. These critics contend that economies and classes are not the ultimate determinant in every case of change. It is hard to see the recently won rights of women, which are fundamental to changes in modern society and schooling, as resulting solely from economic class struggles. The economy is critically important to how we live our lives and following the trail of money is often important for understanding how and why things are changing. But other factors influence social arrangements. For schooling especially, change is not necessarily driven only by the economy, even though schools do tend to reflect their local economies in some fundamental ways.

Weber: Organizing and Legitimizing Knowledge

Like Durkheim, Max Weber examined the transition from traditional religious societies to advanced industrial societies. His writing stressed two coincidental processes. First, he underlined the demise of religious enchantment in providing social cohesion. Second, he highlighted the rise of instrumental reason, also known as rationalization, as a principle logic animating modern societies. Let us elaborate.

As noted earlier, traditional societies were characterized by a binding religious narrative—an overarching story that legitimated and explained to all persons their place in the social world. Religion provided the guiding ideals and the authoritative voices. In such traditional societies it was the long arm of history—soaked with religious custom, habit, and tradition—that constrained the present and the future. The Church was the supreme authority in the affairs of economics, education, law, marriage, and politics. But with the gradual erosion of religious authority what fascinated Weber was the influence of this shift on the cognitive frameworks that people used to think and act. Religious prophets and priests used sorcery, sacrifice, and enchantment to claim a transcendental religious or spiritual authority. But in modern societies that form of authority was clearly on the decline and was being replaced by something else.

During the Enlightenment the Church was science's main competitor for the hearts and minds of people. Galileo's condemnation by the Catholic Church typified that struggle between two idea systems. Science became a more pervasive world view only as the power of astrology, witchcraft, and especially religion waned. But science became powerful because of its rising economic utility. Science and engineering featured significantly in industry's rapid growth. Men of science (and they virtually all were men) invented the steam engine, the spinning jenny, and the ships made of iron plate.

Beyond these technical inventions, the rise of science also promoted a new way of thinking. Galileo's observations of the night sky and Newton's laws of motion were remarkable discoveries. Rather than searching for knowledge in the pages of religious texts, people began looking towards science as the authoritative voice demonstrating how the world worked. The sober procedures of science were in ascendance—the formulation of hypotheses, the analysis of evidence, and the public scrutiny and critical reception of new knowledge.

The scientific outlook introduced a new world view, a new way of seeing. Many mysteries of the universe were solved as science came to reveal that the earth was neither flat nor the centre of everything. But of course a new way of thinking needs to be taught. People did not acquire a new attitude to knowledge by osmosis. Organized schooling played a vital part in science becoming widely understood and applied. During the seventeenth and eighteenth centuries, Enlightenment thinkers worked to replace religious dogma with a more reasoned approach to life. For the new Age of Reason to mature, schools were essential.

For Weber, what was fundamental in modern society was that science emerged as a major cultural authority. As Drori et al. (2003: 10) argue, "the modern attribution of competence and responsibility to social actors—rather than, for example, [to] tradition or nature or god—would make no sense" without this scientific cultural authority. A scientific outlook is fundamental to the premise that we, as humans, can act rationally in the world, that we can intervene to change both ourselves and nature. Over the past 200 years, science has increasingly supplied the major cognitive models used by people in Western cultures. As a result, schools slowly became less religious and more scientifically rational. They began to teach, at least at their upper levels, basic science (e.g., chemistry) and scientific reasoning.

Importantly, scientific rationality became one of the prime modern rationales to justify the expansion of mass schooling.

Historically, religion has played a powerful role in society by "explaining" inequality, disaster, and calamity to believers as the will of the Deity. But in the age of scientific reason, purely religious explanations found fewer and fewer adherents. Schoolchildren now learn scientific explanations for plagues, hurricanes, and earthquakes. As the enveloping power of religious ideas eroded, instrumental reason and calculation (rationality) came to dominate. Weber describes this rise of rationality in terms of people's everyday lives. People gradually accepted that a "bus or an elevator, money, a court of law" were "in principle rational." Further, people gained confidence that "these phenomena function rationally" such that "one can reckon with them, calculate their effects, and base one's actions confidently on the expectations they arouse" (ibid.). Think of the clock as a metaphor for rationalization. Mechanical clocks (from the 1300s onwards) helped to usher in a world that was more orderly, precise, and predictable—in a word, rational.

Rationality gradually reduced the spheres of the everyday world in which mystery, uncertainty, and chance dominated. The growing rationality of modern life is all around us—in the economics of profit and loss, in logistical planning, in time management, and in the increasing complexity of legal codes. Predictability is a defining attribute of each example. It is, as George Ritzer (2000) graphically depicts it, the "McDonaldization" of modern society—fast, efficient, predictable processes.

With the diminishing of religious authority and rise of rationalization, Weber saw a new type of authority emerging: **legal-rational authority**. This new authoritative voice claimed legitimacy through careful planning and precise calculation. This was a new mindset where individuals gradually came to assert their power in the world. The world was increasingly demystified; people came more and more to understand that they could intervene to increase food production, reduce morbidity and mortality, manage time, and "see" the most fundamental particles of matter—quarks. Placating the gods and spirits was replaced by rational human intervention. And, of course, schools were prime vehicles for teaching this new world view. However, these very schools had to be rationally organized—or in Weber's language, bureaucratized.

Weber saw this new legal-rational authority as being crystallized in modern bureaucracies. For him, modern bureaucratic administration was both efficient and constraining. Consider the greater efficiency that comes with bureaucracy. As trade routes expanded, as money began to circulate across wider geographic regions, as national populations grew, and as the division of occupational labour accelerated, precise specialization and coordination became imperative. Specialists were needed everywhere, including in transportation, in accounting, in tax collecting, in standardizing time, in town planning, and in schooling. And all of this specialization demanded coordination. Whether in a ballet company, Canada's Institute for National Measurement Standards (INMS, our official timekeeper), or a high school, bureaucracy is the most efficient method we have of coordinating specialized organizational and administrative structures involving large numbers of people.

Such specialization and coordination also drive us crazy. Bureaucracies, according to Weber, are "iron cages" that constrain us from acting spontaneously and nimbly; instead, bureaucracies provide scripted, formulaic solutions for our diverse problems, often generating more "red tape" than inspiration. What is "red tape?" Well, it is the rules and regulations that made bureaucracies so efficient in the first place! Large-scale action requires careful planning and precise calculation, but it simply cannot take every contingency into account, especially as our world evolves. As George Ritzer (2000: 16) phrases it, "rational systems are often unreasonable." Weber recognized this, stressing how the efficiency of bureaucracy allowed it to spread incessantly, while recognizing at the same time that its rationality undermined individual freedom and creativity.

Even more fundamentally, Weber saw two crosscutting tendencies unfolding within society. One tendency was the rise of a world of stable calculations. But with this came, paradoxically, a more disordered world in which different systems of logic competed. Whereas religion had enveloped traditional society, now new and individualistic or competing persuasions of artistic/aesthetic, economic, political, and scientific logical systems began to emerge. These were distinct institutional spheres, each with its own internal, rational logic as, for example, the logical systems of economics and of science. At the same time a powerful logic of rationality was expanding, but coincidentally institutional spheres were differentiating and using the abstract principles of rationality for their own ends.

Only in the last few centuries, and most noticeably in advanced Western societies, could one point to the separate spheres of work and home, of government and religion, of school and health. No single authoritative voice provided overarching moral legitimacy. Each institution sought legitimacy. Whereas Marx saw in the logic of capitalism that the economic sphere was dominating all ideas, Weber saw a much broader set of competing values and interests: the rationality of the marketplace emphasized profit and loss; the world of science valued truth and logic; the world of democracy stressed voting and political parties; the world of art and design valued creativity. Each domain had its own rationality, each had its own logic of efficiency, but each also required its own organizational forms and legitimacy.

In using these conceptual tools to understand education Weber focused mainly on related themes in bureaucracy and inequality. Because bureaucracies required specialists, qualifying examinations were central to ensuring a meritocratic system (i.e., "no hiring of the senior administrator's relatives unless they are the best qualified"). For Weber (1946: 240–1), "special examinations and . . . trained expertness" are "indispensable for modern bureaucracy. . . . The modern development of full bureaucratization brings the system of rational, specialized, and expert examinations irresistibly to the fore."

A characteristic of the modern bureaucracy is that formal, impersonal rules govern staffing and that trained experts earn positions based on merit. As Weber (ibid.) argued, "special examinations mean or appear to mean a 'selection' of those who qualify from all social strata rather than a rule by notables." Bureaucratic authority gains legitimacy in people's eyes because it is staffed by merit, not by family ties or personal loyalties. Importantly, Weber notes that the process "appears to mean" an openness to all. Appearances are critical to legitimacy because, in an oft-repeated sociological truism, "what people define to be real, is real in its consequences" (Thomas and Thomas, 1928: 52). Legitimation may exist only in people's heads, but so long as it exists there, it is a powerful force having real consequences.

Weber's ideas resonate both with Durkheim's emphasis on equality of opportunity and with Marx's caution regarding equality of condition. Examinations may give the appearance of fair selection but, as a sociologist, Weber wants to leave open the question of whether selection systems do actually produce fair and meritocratic selections (see "Talent versus Property" box). Noting that acquiring an advanced education is expensive for students in terms of time and money, credential requirements effectively create "a setback for talent in favor of property" (Weber, 1946: 242). In short, those with income and wealth typically do better in education systems using competitive examinations (although he is vague about the exact social mechanisms that work to reproduce this inequality).

Weber also notes that educational certificates have a certain "social prestige." They purportedly signal the possession of expert knowledge, but can also function as exclusionary devices. Occupational groups that demand higher levels of education prior to entering them may reflect a "desire for restricting the supply for these positions and their monopolization by the owners of educational certificates" (ibid., 241). Effectively, occupational groups (e.g., doctors) can use educational credentials as a way of regulating supply, selecting through examinations optimal numbers and excluding others.

Finally, Weber also comments on the content of schooling, although only in passing. He was himself encyclopedic in his range of expertise and interests, writing about religion, music, accounting, history, and on and on. He worried that the "ever-increasing expert and specialized knowledge" (ibid., 243) was drowning out an education that encouraged "ways of thought suitable to a cultured" person (ibid., 428). He pointed to both Greece and China as historical examples where education had not been narrowed to content that might be "useful" for a specialization (ibid., 243).

Significant lessons flow from Weber's insights. Most importantly, the process of rationalization has deeply affected schooling in many ways. Examinations are all about calculating and predicting. Bureaucracy is fundamental to school administration. Critics worry that school curricula have become dominated by knowledge thought to be "useful" for the economy, though Weber would argue that this perceived utility allows schools to retain their legitimacy in a highly rationalized world. Weber also stressed that in a pure and idealized model of bureaucracy, merit is a core principle for both hiring and promotion. But Weber worried about inequality and gaps between ideals of how bureaucracy ought to work and how it really worked in practice. He was concerned that "property" might distort the actual processes of meritocracy. He was also cynical about what educational certificates actually signalled (e.g., indicators of talent or measures of

Talent versus Property: A Case Study from India

There are now over 20 Indian Institutes of Technology (IITs), often lauded as institutions of world-class excellence that nurture the best and brightest young talent in India. IITs boast of being top-flight universities that are buoyed by the exceptional success of their graduates. The IITs are said to have produced more millionaires per capita than any other university in the world. Some IIT applicants see admission to top universities such as Harvard or Oxford as a safety net, an insurance placement of second choice. But while the IITs are among the world's elite education institutions, whether all talented Indians flourish there is a separate question.

In 2015, about 300,000 aspirants wrote the Joint Entrance Examination (JEE), the sole criterion for admission. About 3,000 (1.0 per cent) gained admission. Successful students usually need to expend extraordinary efforts to prepare for the school's high-stakes admission test, sometimes taking a full year to cram, and sometimes even attending boarding schools that specialize in exam prep. Because admission to IITs is a crucial gatekeeper of upward mobility and class reproduction in India, governments have carefully monitored the demographics of IIT students. But a decade ago, researchers found few women, few from rural settings, few from the lower classes, and few from the lower castes (the so-called scheduled castes and tribes). So in 2007, officials asked the institutes to implement a series of quotas or "reservations" that would greatly boost the representations of students from those groups. Then in 2008, they asked for similar reservations for teachers and faculty. As Gupta (2015: 104) describes it, caste-ridden and hierarchical societies like India need to find ways to provide social justice and economic opportunities to all who are deprived by social and educational disadvantages. But Gupta also reports that IIT directors have voiced their "reservations about reservations," warning of dire consequences such as greatly diluting the quality of the student body and faculty. Some consider these concerns to be products of a deeply entrenched caste-based culture, while others see them as understandable worries over quality. In either event, sociologists can recognize that IIT graduates may be extremely talented, but also illustrate how "property" (using Weber's language for gender, caste, and class) paves the way for talent to show through.

perseverance) and how they were used to monopolize access to jobs, both themes we pursue in later chapters.

It is harder to criticize Weber than either Durkheim or Marx because many of his ideas are very specific to certain contexts, rather than expressed in general concepts. Weber was encyclopedic in his thinking but this very range brought with it a certain level of description. He said little about education as an organized activity, and when he did it was only about certain details. There is little conceptual sociology of education to be found in Weber's own work, although, as we will see, much of the ongoing debate about schooling makes use, often unknowingly, of his insights.

Conclusion: From Classical to Contemporary Theory

The classical theories of Durkheim, Marx, and Weber set the foundations for socio-logical theorizing. They offer a rich heritage that pushes us to think imaginatively and rigorously about schools. However, many key social and intellectual changes have occurred since those classic treatises were penned. The past half-century has brought profound societal shifts, changing intellectual priorities, and a corpus of empirical research, combining to give birth to more refined thinking about schools. The next chapter outlines more recent theories.

Questions for Critical Thought

1. What, if any, relevance do the ideas of these three dead white males have for contemporary schooling? What would you cite as their most informative idea, and why?

2. Can ideas from contemporary feminism make ideas from Durkheim, Marx, and Weber more useful for understanding today's schooled society? Are their ideas useful for understanding women's changing place in that society?

3. Durkheim provides interesting ideas about how schools can promote ritualistic, solidarity-generating experiences. Do one or both of the following: First, think back to your own high school experience and suggest why it might or might not have illustrated what Durkheim articulates. Second, think of a recent movie that might illustrate some of the school ritualism that Durkheim's idea can illuminate. Describe the scenes in the film that illustrate ritualism at work.

Suggested Readings

Collins, Randall, with Michael Makowsky. 2009. *The Discovery of Society*, 8th edn. New York: McGraw-Hill. This well-known American theory text is written with an emphasis on the classics.

Grabb, Edward G. 2007. *Theories of Social Inequality*, 5th edn. Toronto: Thomson Nelson. Grabb's book, now in its fifth edition, is the best-known Canadian textbook on sociological theories.

Prentice, Alison. 1977. *The School Promoters: Education and Social Class in Mid-Nineteenth Century Upper Canada*. Toronto: McClelland & Stewart. In *The School Promoters*, the author presents a popular history of Canadian education.

Web Links

Classical Sociological Theory: A Review of Themes, Concepts, and Perspectives
http://deflem.blogspot.com/1999/09/classical-sociological-theory-1999.html
Maintained by Dr. Mathieu Deflem at the University of South Carolina, this website outlines a thorough review of the major themes and concepts of classical sociological theory.

Module on Karl Marx
www.unc.edu/~nielsen/soci250/m3/soci250m3.pdf
Created by François Nielsen for his sociology course at the University of North Carolina Chapel Hill, this PowerPoint presentation presents a concise summary of the life and works of Karl Marx.

3 Contemporary Sociological Approaches to Schooling

Learning Objectives

- To recognize the limits of classical theories for understanding schooling today in light of important economic, demographic, and cultural changes
- To use contemporary sociological theories to understand educational selection, socialization, and organization
- To compare and contrast a series of theories with different assumptions about core social processes

Introduction

This chapter builds on the classical approaches outlined in Chapter 2 and reviews contemporary theories on the three themes of socialization, selection, and organization. We begin by examining Randall Collins' reworking of Durkheim's micro-level thought. We then shift to the macro-level, comparing structural functionalism's rather positive portrait of schools as passing on values of modern life to that of neo-Marxism, which largely inverted this image, and portrayed schools as inculcating a capitalist culture that benefits only a few. We then shift to the study of inequality, again comparing functionalists and Marxists. Next we examine what is known as "**cultural capital**" and approaches to differing experiences of students, particularly by gender and race. The chapter ends by comparing how sociologists and economists offer different accounts of schools' organizational processes and goals.

Socialization: Interaction Rituals and Hidden Curricula

Socialization is central to schooling. But with the waning of religious influence, contemporary theorists have pondered new, broader relations between schools and morality. Most approaches presume that contemporary socialization in schools is "hidden," that is, tacit or implicit, a concept that we develop below.

Chapter 2 described Durkheim's ideas about the capacity of rituals and symbols to generate social bonds and solidarity. Randall Collins (2004) has recently revised this thinking with his own theory of micro-level interaction. Collins begins by noting that social settings vary in their capacity to coax people to focus their attention on the same thing. Some settings encourage people to synchronize their moods, bodily rhythms, thoughts, and feelings. This process is what Collins calls "**emotional entrainment**": the enhancing of interaction by people attuning their emotional states together. This entrainment occurs easily and spontaneously in small groups of friends and among family members. Lively, flowing, and dynamic social encounters can generate "**collective effervescence**"—a feeling of group membership that can invigorate and energize people (e.g., friends working together to create a rock band). But generating and sustaining such entrainment and effervescence is far more difficult in larger gatherings of near-strangers. Schools face the challenge of recreating similar energy in larger and more anonymous groups. When successful, classrooms can animate students and bind them to the school by provoking interesting discussions, riveting their attention, sparking creativity, and encouraging all to share ideas. But Collins also emphasizes what Durkheim tended to neglect: some social situations trigger little entrainment and effervescence. Their participants can be instead bored by the interaction. It might make them feel sluggish, lethargic, and indifferent. They may exit early. If they are captive without consent, they will cope by day-dreaming, seeking distraction, or engaging only passively in group activities. Such situations can be unpleasant and dulling. Think of a classroom in which few students are captivated, and most wait impatiently for the bell.

Collins's theory can be used to view classrooms through the lens of "**interaction rituals**." His use of the term refers not only to formal ceremonies, but also more generally to any social situation that structures social interaction. He tries to explain why some settings successfully generate emotional entrainment and collective effervescence while others create apathy and avoidance. Further, he seeks to explain why some interaction rituals equalize the energy among all participants while others distribute it more unequally. This latter issue highlights interpersonal stratification in social situations. Collins notes that people at the centre of attention are most energized by rituals; they use that energy to gain further popularity and status. Speakers at a school rally, for instance, can become figuratively drunk by the adoration of the crowd. But rituals can also create fringe members who are cast in the role of low-status followers, and who are only partly invigorated by the interaction. And at their worst, rituals create outcasts who can be the object of negative attention—scorn, ridicule, taunting. Think of cases of gang-bullying, when some children gain energy and status by putting down others.

This interaction ritual framework offers a useful lens for interpreting classroom processes. Good classrooms are those that successfully create interactions with a high degree of collective effervescence and a broad distribution of emotional energy. Bad classrooms stimulate little energy and/or distribute it unevenly. This framework also allows us to illuminate issues of student engagement. Philosophies of teaching over the past 40 years have placed greater priority on effectively engaging students in schoolwork. Modern teachers try to encourage students to become active learners, to connect deeply with classroom activities, and to identify with the school community. The teachers' challenge is to promote lively classrooms in which students do schoolwork in a thoughtful, purposeful manner. Students' attention is focused and engaged, allowing few distractions and little mischievous-ness. This is no simple task! Teachers must compete with student peer groups for pupils' attention. If students channel too much energy and solidarity to their peer cliques rather than to school-sponsored groupings, their interest in school material will wane. (We will return to these issues in later chapters.) Durkheim's early work has also inspired macro-level theories describing sweeping cultural changes that have key implications for today's schooling.

Competing Rituals in a Tough School

Classroom teachers compete with peer groups for students' attention. This is espe-cially challenging for new teachers. Here is how one teacher described his first day in a Bronx, New York high school in the 1990s, as he walked through the halls to a classroom led by a senior teacher (Paulle, 2013: 2–4, slightly adapted):

> The bell rang and the hallway started to empty. The beats, ritualized greet-ings, screams of delight, laughter, and taunts in the corridor finally subsided. The tyranny of the bells, I would later understand, was supported by mobile teams of security guards, "hallway deans," and two uniformed policemen, all connected by walkie-talkies. Kids were discharged from their realm that overflowed with excitement and teenage angst, and entered an adult's private, low energy sphere of influence. I took a seat in front. A few more kids dragged themselves into the classroom.
>
> The class was a disaster. Rather than being impolite or hostile, most kids seemed disengaged. The teacher struggled to get his students even slightly en-gaged in written assignments. They seemed utterly unconcerned with the all-but-irrelevant guy in the front of the room. One boy, slouching almost to the point of lying down on his desk, stared blankly at the blackboard with no pen or paper, proceeding only to take off his black leather glove over and over again. Two kids seemed to be asleep in the back. One girl came in late. She talked to a girlfriend almost perpetually, even as the teacher pleaded with her to be quiet. The non-stop chatting was all the more bizarre because she was sitting in the front row, almost adjacent to the teacher's desk. His proximity had no effect. Finally, he asked her to leave. She stopped talking, but did not move an inch. He asked her to leave a second time. Again an awkward silence ensued. "Whatever," she said at last. Her face expressed a mix of disgust and apathy. As soon as the bell rang to end the period, the hallway sprang to life once more. The pupils returned to the energizing space on the other side of the classroom door.
>
> While this experience seemed extraordinary at first, it later turned out to be entirely mundane. I learned two lessons from it. One, student life in the halls is electric and full of meaning, while most kids seem not to care about teach-ing, the formal curriculum or anything else that takes place inside classrooms. Two, to get along in their classrooms, many teachers let countless "minor" provocations slide and become routine.

Structural Functionalism: Nurturing Modern Values

Structural functionalism was popular in the 1950s and 1960s, and has a direct lineage from the thought of Émile Durkheim. Even though few sociologists today would identify themselves as functionalists, the logic of the theory survives in many forms, often implicitly, and particularly in the theories discussed in subsequent sections, including human capital theory and the new institutionalism.

Functionalists took from Durkheim an interest in how youth are socialized. Functionalists were particularly impressed with the way in which socialization reflected the process of "**modernization**"—the progression of societies from an agricultural to an industrial economic base. But just what kinds of values and culture would schools socialize youth into, and how would they do it?

For the functionalists, schools taught *modern* values. As societies industrialize and urbanize, their cultures become less parochial and more cosmopolitan, and their politics less authoritarian and more democratic. Schools, functionalists reckoned, provide a common culture in societies that were growing increasingly diverse and complex. In their eyes, schools would *function* as transmitters of modern values like universalism, democracy, and meritocracy. Students would implicitly be taught a common culture in which individuals aspired to get ahead, to champion universalism (treating everyone the same), and to uphold meritocracy (where social rewards would go to those with talent who exert effort in open competitions).

Now, to answer the question of *how* students learn this common culture, the functionalists had an interesting idea. Instead of teaching these new values overtly, schools actually taught them through their very form and operation. That is, rather than repeatedly lecturing students on universalism and meritocracy, schools purportedly operated in a universalistic and meritocratic fashion. Schools ritualistically repeated this basic mantra, and still do. Students learned by doing. By treating all students equally using common rules, schools embodied the values of universalism, according to this argument. By rewarding only those students that truly deserved top grades, schools taught the value of meritocracy. And so on. In this view, the *structure* of modern schooling *functioned* by implicitly displaying modern values through its very organization (see Dreeben, 1968). In interesting ways, the very core of this explanation has been reshaped by scholars inspired by Marx.

Neo-Marxism: The Capitalist Hidden Curriculum

A different perspective on socialization in education has been offered by followers of Marx. In 1976, Bowles and Gintis (1976: 132), two American economists, wrote *Schooling in Capitalist America*. They emphasized that different levels of education feed workers into different occupations (see also Anyon, 1980; Bowles and Gintis, 2002). That is, different educational settings prepare students for the disciplines of different workplaces, each requiring distinct types of personal demeanours, modes of self-presentation, self-images, and job identities. The earliest years of schooling were said to *correspond* to the lowest levels of the occupational structure by stressing rule-following and rote activity. In higher grades, schools gradually require students to work with more autonomy and discretion, corresponding to occupations in which work is more independent and less directly supervised. Different tracks or streams in the school system further reinforce this correspondence. Vocational programs stress close supervision and rule-following, while academic streams allow more open-ended curricula. Through an implicit or **hidden curriculum** students were socialized for their allotted labour force positions.

Bowles and Gintis also saw schools as inculcating "**ruling class ideology.**" Ideology is typically understood in two ways. First, it refers to systems of ideas or cognitive frameworks that guide our thinking and acting. Second, ideology includes class bias or class self-interest. Marx understood capitalist ideology as justifying existing patterns of social inequality, serving the interests of the ruling class. For Bowles and Gintis, schools perpetuate this one-sided, biased, distorted thinking. Likewise, Michael Apple, another prominent neo-Marxist, argues that "schools create and recreate forms of consciousness that enable social control to be maintained without the necessity of dominant groups having to revert to overt mechanisms of domination" (Apple, 2004). Schools, from this perspective, help reinforce capitalist inequality through a variety of mechanisms that persuade people to accept it as natural and inevitable. Rarely are students encouraged to question systematically these patterns of inequality and their causes, he claims.

How is this ideology taught? Again the hidden curriculum is posited as the mechanism of socialization. Schools force students to vie for grades and rewards, awarding "badges of ability" to the winners. This practice, the neo-Marxists note, mirrors competition and individualism in the wider capitalist society. Further, capitalist schools prioritize some forms of knowledge, especially scientific forms like chemistry and mathematics, while giving short shrift to non-technical forms such as folk knowledge. This stratification of the curriculum makes it easier to stratify individuals because technical knowledge appears to be more objective. Badges of ability from science courses appear to objectively measure student abilities. Students who fare poorly in school, and are typically from disadvantaged backgrounds, are said to be taught to accept their poorer performance, and hence their subsequent, and often inferior, positions in the labour market (see Chapter 6).

These ideas about schooling's role in capitalism have not gone unopposed. Some critics contend that this portrait of school–workplace correspondence is too simplistic. Perhaps workplaces "need" to have compliant, well-disciplined workers in unskilled jobs, but do schools simply obey and produce these workers? Do schools really create all of this essential compliance? How would you account for non-compliant workers—aren't they products of schooling as well? As in Durkheim's view of socialization, the complex, messy details of contestation, conflict, and compromise are absent from the analysis, both in the functionalist and neo-Marxist guise.

The neo-Marxist assertions about "ruling ideas" may also lack awareness of the complexity of modern education. Rote memorization and rule-following can be key parts of student learning. But schools have also long encouraged critical thinking, although perhaps not enough for everyone's liking. Teachers do far more than simply spout the official rhetoric of the business elite. And, do we really know whether the hidden curriculum is all-powerful? Might students learn many of the traits needed in the workplace or about ruling ideas from other sources? Again, we agree that some ideas are more influential than others and that, more frequently, they are those that support advantaged groups. A more careful theory, however, is needed to understand how different ideas come to be enshrined as "ruling ideas."

Shaping Identities of Gender and Race

Classical approaches depicted school socialization as a largely homogeneous process. They acknowledged differences in the experiences of students from various economic classes, but for the most part, emphasized the common impact of schools on all children. More recent approaches, however, focus on the school experiences of non-class groupings. These scholars take aim squarely at gender and race, and increasingly, ancestry and sexuality.

Gender scholars begin by pointing to the deep inscribing of femininity and masculinity in the history of educational institutions. Until the past half-century, public schools were overtly gendered institutions. While taxes were used from the beginning of public education to finance compulsory schooling for both boys and girls, and while both males and females were seen to benefit from moral education and from basic literacy, the "common" secondary school prepared girls and boys for mostly different social roles. Some girls were steered towards "domestic science" and most boys towards trades, though a few boys were selected for advanced studies. Most young women were trained either for housewifery or a narrow range of "nurturing" occupations like nursing and elementary school teaching. This schooling was based on overt assumptions about gender, assumptions that were not hidden, but were open and assumed to be self-evident.

This began to change in the post–Second World War era. As we document in a later chapter, girls were not only encouraged to go further in school and enter non-traditional fields, but their attainments soon equalled and then surpassed those of boys. This change prompts a key question: might these new patterns of formal educational equality signal the presence of new forms of socialization in schools?

Starting in the 1980s, when those new attainment patterns were emerging, some sociologists of gender answered this question with a flat "no." They asserted that change was only apparent; schools were continuing to reproduce traditional gender roles, albeit in more covert ways (Bennett deMarrais and LeCompte, 1998). Notwithstanding the new patterns in some school outcomes, they argued that the *experience* of schooling was still gendered, due to a "hidden curriculum" that continues to subordinate women. The explicit gender stereotyping of the late 1800s had only been masked, now by stealth, and made invisible. This tacit curriculum was said to alienate females from non-traditional course material, dampen their aspirations for non-traditional fields, and send messages that they are inherently inferior to men.

Likewise, sociologists who examined race also argued that schools did not socialize all students the same way. Sociologists of education have long argued that the schooling of various minority groups is influenced by the wider context of race relations. A stark example is provided by the experiences of First Nations children in Canada. Until the early 1970s, the federal government sent many Indigenous children to residential schools with the express intent of "Canadianizing" them—to socialize them into the dominant culture, requiring them to learn English or French, accept Christianity, and learn industrial job skills (TRC, 2015). The socialization provided by those schools was clearly inflected with power dynamics, aimed to subordinate. Today, through political means, many Indigenous children are taught in schools that aim to be sensitive to their needs, backgrounds, and wants for cultural survival. This cultural pluralism is something that neither the Durkheimian nor functionalist traditions are strong at comprehending.

A similar issue about race and socialization arises when dealing with immigration. In recent decades, large waves of minority immigrant children from a wide variety of cultural traditions have entered Canadian schools, often not speaking English or French as their first language. A huge effort has attempted to determine whether teachers treat minorities differently, and whether they are adequately represented in curricular material, textbooks, and courses. Similarly, sexual minority students have only recently received recognition by some educational officials. While some school boards have developed new inclusive curricula and teacher training, others have been reluctant to follow suit, as the recent struggles to form Gay-Straight Alliance (GSA) organizations in schools have shown. As we discuss in Chapter 7, notions of school equity have expanded to encompass a wider variety of group experiences. Much sociological attention over socialization has shifted towards group differences in experiences and away from similarities between all students.

Box 3.1 Critical Pedagogy: Education for What?

What is now commonly known as "social justice" has long been at the heart of public school ideals. Liberal philosophers have wanted public schools to create equality among citizens, and help everyone reach their fullest human potential through critical thinking. But in recent decades, social inequalities have actually widened, and millions of students fail to thrive in the classroom. "Critical Pedagogy," originally promoted by Paulo Freire and later celebrated by scholars such as Henry Giroux and Peter McLaren, provides one reminder of these gaps between liberal ideals and reality. But what do they mean by "critical?" Their usage is not simply about critical thinking, which involves probing the veracity of statements and assumptions. Critical Pedagogy aspires to be more radical and activist. It sees oppression built into the very heart of Western society. Our major institutions, including schools, are riddled with inequality, they claim. Fundamental change is needed. Critical pedagogues urge us to

continued

resist domination by subverting conventional ways of thinking. This resistance, they hope, will eventually transform institutions, including schools, making them far more inclusive, ethical, and humane (see Breuing, 2013; Kincheloe, 2007).

Does this critical emphasis differ widely from mainstream educational thinking? Not in all respects. Virtually all educators recognize societal inequalities, and support reforms aimed to lessen them. What distinguishes Critical Pedagogy is a bolder claim: that schools actively uphold societal oppression, teaching only the received wisdom and supporting prevailing injustices. Schools are not neutral, objective sites, they warn. Students and teachers must actively strive to thoroughly overhaul the fundamental structure of society.

Those bolder claims do indeed diverge from the mainstream, but as we discuss in Chapters 6 and 7, only some are supported by empirical research. And, Critical Pedagogy shifts the expressed purpose of schooling. Mainstream liberal educators want to help students develop their personal qualities, and help reform society. But critical pedagogues call for a deep-seated transformation of social arrangements. Only radical change can create a better and more just world, they insist. But to realize their ideals, critical pedagogues face a huge challenge: to somehow translate theory into actual, workable tools for students and teachers.

Selection: Inequality and Opportunity

Ideas about school selection have evolved since Marx's time. Marx largely implicated schools in class structures that emerged from nineteenth-century industrialism. In contrast, contemporary theories have had to incorporate profound economic transformations over the past few decades, along with the great expansion of schooling. In so doing, they have developed new approaches to questions linking school selection to inequality.

The Functional Theory of Stratification: Selecting for Merit

Following the Second World War, what did social thinkers take from the societal shifts they saw around them? The structural functionalists believed that those shifts had key implications for educational selection. Their reasoning went like this.

Neurosurgeons make a lot of money—why? In the late 1940s Kingsley Davis and Wilbert Moore (1945) articulated a provocative explanation. Stratification is a "universal necessity," fundamental to the survival of society, they contended, and schools needed to sort and select people to aid that process. Their premise was that different *positions* in society contributed more or less to societal survival. Farmers are critical to ensuring we have enough to eat, but film critics (or maybe even sociologists) are not so intrinsic to societal longevity. "Functionally important" positions were more specialized, playing essential roles in society, with other positions often depending on them.

Equally important, Davis and Moore argued, societies need to ensure that people with skill and talent are induced to take on functionally important jobs, and perform them well. Talent is both natural and trained. Some positions will require rare talents (e.g., the fine hand–eye coordination of neurosurgery). Other positions (e.g., general medicine) require talent that is fairly abundant in society, but that require "burdensome and expensive" training. For the most important jobs, incumbents are scarce because either the training is arduous or the skills are rare. Society thus requires a motivational system to induce people to occupy functionally important positions. Motivators can include not only money and prestige, but also interesting jobs that involve discretion and creativity. In contrast, less functionally important roles have fewer inducements.

In this theory, education plays several critical roles. First, schooling had to become an astute talent-scouting agency, an efficient and rational method to sort and select people for positions that require expertise. Second, in applying our basic knowledge of quarks, quadratics, and quarantines, to name but three examples, schools have an increasingly integral role in contributing to a **knowledge economy**. Schools teach the basic knowledge that allows people to function as employees and consumers. Third, the functionalists developed an explanation for why many students, particularly those from disadvantaged class backgrounds, were still not enjoying school success. To them, lower-class groups were yet to fully embrace modern values, and still do not truly value education, aspire for upward mobility, and embrace the spirit of competition (Hyman, 1953). In addition, these families were seen to disadvantage their children by failing to nurture the basic cognitive skills that support school success. Middle-class families, they reasoned, were more likely to read to their children and engage them in literacy-enhancing exercises.

At first blush this functionalist account is a useful way of thinking about inequality. The idea that rewards follow from effort and ability resonates with a core modern principle. Certainly some jobs pay better than others—judges make more than janitors. Although it rubs against egalitarian ideals, most people would agree being a good court judge requires more advanced training than does cleaning a building. A key problem, though, is that while this may describe society well, it does not explain much.

It is a weak explanation because some abstract entity—"society"—plays a curious role. Society "needs" to survive and stratification "functions" to provide this. It is wise, always, to be suspicious of lazy theorizing that attributes human capabilities to nonhuman entities. Society does not have a will of its own. It may be common shorthand to say "society thinks" or "society needs," but this is an elementary error. Society may be composed of different positions that receive different rewards, but individual people fill those positions, act, wield power, and distribute rewards. To ascribe such action to "society" is to ignore agency or action. Davis and Moore seem to imply that market forces are the underlying mechanism that sets pay rates for different occupations. Judges get paid more than janitors, they reason, because fewer people have the advanced skills required to be a judge, and fewer are willing to complete its required training. So, pressures of supply and demand presumably operate to raise wages for tasks with scarcer suppliers. An alternative explanation (discussed later in this chapter), examines how occupations battle to set their own wage rates, often by establishing licensing and certification that can limit their number of market competitors that might otherwise pull their wages downward.

Other criticisms of the functional theory of stratification follow. Inequality is functional for whom? Does everyone benefit equally? Does this line of reasoning simply make inequality appear legitimate, rather than explain it? Also, how unequal must the rewards be? Most people would rather be judges than janitors, in part because of the money, but in part also because it is a better job. But are movie stars and bank presidents, with their huge incomes, so much more important to society than nurses, janitors, and schoolteachers?

Another criticism is that Davis and Moore focus too much on how inequality motivates individuals to undergo long and arduous schooling. They avoid examining how inequality fails to function for others who are equally motivated but unable to pursue the necessary education. Some families cannot afford to send their children to law school. Some teenagers drop out of school to earn money to support their families. Indigenous children living near Hudson Bay experience far tougher conditions in becoming neurosurgeons than do children raised in affluent families anywhere in Southern Canada. These unequal family conditions prevent everyone from participating equally in the opportunity to pursue education and acquire "functionally important" jobs.

Neo-Marxism: Thwarting Upward Mobility

As discussed in the previous section, neo-Marxists proposed a "**correspondence principle**" to understand links between schools and workplaces, contending that what happens in workplaces is quickly reflected in schools, so that schools generally mirror capitalist workplaces. As examples, they point to common uses of external rewards to motivate behaviour, whether wages or grades in school. They point to similarities between the alienation of factory workers from their work and the alienation of students from the curriculum. They point to similarities in the vertical lines of authority between supervisors versus workers and teachers versus students (Bowles and Gintis, 1976: 131).

But contra Davis and Moore, Bowles and Gintis emphasize that some students need to be selected for the most *subordinate* and thus least attractive positions in the labour market. These students will be the failures, the high school dropouts. They corroborated a finding that was well known in sociology: students from less advantaged backgrounds are far less likely to progress to higher levels of schooling, while those from privileged social origins are likelier to obtain the highest badges of ability. However, using that well-established finding, they offered a bold conclusion: schools in capitalist societies are *designed* to thwart the mobility of working-class youth. Schools make such inequalities inevitable by exposing disadvantaged youth to poorly resourced classrooms, stereotyping them as ill-equipped for schools, and rewarding traits such as docility. By design, Bowles and Gintis argue, schools *reproduce* class inequalities.

This reproduction theory became very popular in sociology, and is often used as a foil to the functionalist image of schools creating a meritorious order. But subsequent approaches needed to correct at least two limitations. First, while the neo-Marxists paid great attention to social classes, they largely neglected other patterns of inequality, such as those structured by gender, race, Indigeneity, and sexual orientation. Second, researchers faulted Bowles and Gintis for not clearly specifying the social mechanisms that reproduce inequalities. The next two sets of theories that we review attempt to address these functionalist and neo-Marxist shortcomings.

Understanding Differential Success: The Forms of Capital

Since the 1970s, educational sociologists have repeatedly sought to understand just *why* some groups are consistently less successful in schools than others. Rejecting the functionalist notion of inadequate socialization, some sociologists have taken a different explanatory path.

Pierre Bourdieu uses the concept of "cultural capital" to explain sorting and selecting. Seeing inequality all around him, Bourdieu asks: how is this inequality reproduced? How is privilege transferred across generations? Like Marx, he focuses on capital as a powerful resource. Following Durkheim, he examines how things become classified as "aristocratic," that is, of high or valued cultural potency. In keeping with Weber, he is concerned with how social groups can monopolize this capital to exclude others.

Bourdieu (Bourdieu and Passeron, 1990) defines cultural capital in education as a widely recognized set of cultural symbols that signify high status. It is comprised of the behaviours, knowledge, values, possessions, and preferences that are hallmarks of a ruling or upper class. Some examples would include being adroit in casual conversation, having an expansive vocabulary, appearing worldly and wise, and being *au courant* with high-brow art, music, and theatre. In short, to possess the sophisticated tastes and styles associated with highly cultured people is to have cultural capital. Why is this beneficial? From eating, to fitness, to holidays, to conversing, to schmoozing, doing these things with elegance, grace, and distinction can impress the right peers. Noting that quarks were named from Joyce's *Finnegan's Wake* would exemplify this upper-class erudition. Students from working-class families can work to acquire these cultural competencies but they will rarely develop the same natural familiarity of those born into middle- and upper-class families because it is akin to learning a second language. Significantly, Bourdieu contends not only that some individuals or families are more likely to possess sophisticated tastes and styles, but that this cultural capital is institutionalized in education.

This latter idea is novel. Not only do individuals from different class backgrounds have unequal access to cultural capital but, more importantly, the same signals of high-status "distinction" are baked into the organization of schooling. Bourdieu develops this from an idea of Basil Bernstein's. Bernstein (1975) focused on language, or what he called **linguistic codes**. His core idea was that ways of speaking varied by social class. Schools rewarded codes that were middle and upper class in style—more abstract, with meanings more explicit (or less context-dependent) than is the language of working-class families. For Bernstein, children from the working class have to learn a new style of speaking to be successful at school, while middle- and upper-class children enjoy a smoother connection between language used at home and school.

In effect, Bourdieu extended Bernstein's observations by arguing that other types of family-learned behaviour, knowledge, values, and preferences also were linked to formal education. School, he argued, is not a neutral institution, but is built on class-specific cultural resources. Those who create the social structure of schooling—the curriculum, the examinations, the daily routines—are from middle- and upper-class backgrounds. While they may not consciously intend to favour one group over another, they take cultural stratification for granted. This is reinforced by other educators who come from similar backgrounds and share the same institutionalized behaviours, knowledge, values, and preferences. But here is Bourdieu's punchline: while school success is officially seen to result from one's academic ability, it actually reflects schools' biased evaluations of cultural competence. Simple differences in students' class cultures get "misrecognized"—Bourdieu's term—as differences in native intelligence. Schools portray inequalities as unfortunate by-products of neutral academic standards, while Bourdieu traces them to invisible cultural biases that limit working-class success.

The concept of cultural capital has been refined by Annette Lareau (2011). Lareau places less emphasis on cultural affinities with the curriculum, and more on the aligning of parenting practices with school expectations. She sees the parenting styles of middle- and upper-class families as guided by what she calls "the logic of concerted cultivation." That is, these parents use a set of intensive cultural practices. They engage their children in expansive conversation, push them to succeed in school, and perform for adults under stress. They also learn which school programs are most prestigious, which teachers are most effective, and which schools send more graduates to universities, and how to place their children accordingly. This cultural repertoire is seen to allow concerted cultivators to "work" institutions like schools and maximize its rewards. Conversely, Lareau sees working-class parents who are less educated as guided by a "logic of natural growth." These parents grant their children more self-initiated play and unstructured time, and see educational matters as best left to teachers. This parenting style is easier for parents who must work shifts or multiple jobs, are less knowledgeable of school systems, and therefore have less opportunity to "cultivate" cultural capital in their children. These contrasting parenting styles, Lareau believes, transmit different advantages to children, and allow middle- and upper-class children to better align to the cultural climate of modern schooling.

Bourdieu and Lareau thus offer intriguing theories about relationships between family social class and educational success. However, identifying a theory and providing solid evidence are not one and the same. Bourdieu gets high marks for a bold theory, but when we examine evidence later in this book, we offer some warnings. Because Bourdieu's claims are based on class distinctions in France, one needs to caution whether the French case is generalizable to Canada. If French culture is more differentiated by social class, the direct influence of cultural capital may be weaker in Canada. For instance, Erickson (1996: 219) argues that in Canada, cultural variety, not cultural capital per se, is a most useful personal resource. The ability to access different cultural resources (e.g., knowledge of soap operas sometimes and familiarity with classical operas at others) can help accomplish what you want (see Garnett et al., 2005).

A second concept of Bourdieu's is "**social capital**." This idea has sparked a great deal of interest in North America over the past three decades (e.g., Coleman, 1988; Putnam, 2000). Social capital is about the power of social relationships, both positive and negative. When our social connections become durable, we become part of a network of people. These networks can bring social resources. If cultural capital refers to what you know, social capital refers to whom you know. The positive aspects of social capital are that personal ties can facilitate trust and mutual obligations among people. For instance, in educational settings families can draw on social capital to help navigate the schooling process, learning about the strongest teachers and the best learning opportunities while also avoiding the toughest hurdles. These networks can promote trust between teachers, students, and parents, and can thereby facilitate school success. But strong and dense ties can also have a downside. They can create both divisions among groups and loyalties that can stifle change. For instance, sometimes tightly knit groups, such as student **subcultures**, discourage their members from engaging with school (see Chapter 12). While these subcultures have much social capital—dense ties, reciprocal expectations, and mutual obligations—this form actually impedes their gathering of resources. Social capital is a double-edged sword.

Gender, Race, and Their Intersections

Several scholars have built on the ideas of Bowles and Gintis, and Bourdieu to examine whether selection differs by gender and race. As discussed earlier, feminist scholars contend that schools continue to reinforce a gendered division of labour. Drawing on educational history, and noting that early schools clearly segregated boys and girls and prepared them for different roles, these scholars contend that today's schools continue to do so, albeit in much subtler ways. Teachers may encourage girls to enter traditional fields of study and discourage them from STEM (science, technology, engineering, and math) fields; curricula writers may leave sexist messages in textbooks, lesson plans, and tests. Likewise, race scholars claim that selection processes are inherently biased against racial minorities, again with the result of reproducing racial inequalities in society. As we will see in a later chapter, these sociologists contend that several selection procedures are biased, such as interactions with teachers, curricula, testing, and so forth, all serving to disadvantage minority children.

These ideas have been further elaborated by an approach examining the "intersections" of race and gender (e.g., McMullin, 2010). From this vantage point, inequality is best understood and most readily experienced by people located at specific intersections of gender and race. The claim is that "multiple oppressions" create unique experiences in institutions like schools. The repeated assertion is that poor minority women are the most disadvantaged members of society, and thus have the odds most clearly stacked against them in schools and in all other facets of Canadian society. In a later chapter, we examine data on educational attainment and evaluate this and other perspectives.

Organizing and Legitimizing Knowledge

For Weber, modern schooling reflected the twin imperatives of the rising scientific world view with the organizational form of rationalized bureaucracy. Since Weber, contemporary theorists have examined how modern schools continue to legitimate themselves in an era of larger state bodies and expanded labour markets. As we outline below, **human capital theory** sees schools as organized largely to nurture productive skills needed in the economy. In contrast, credentialists purport that schooling has expanded in response to various forms of labour market competition, rather than as a reaction to greater skill demands. New institutional theory, in further contrast, sees modern schools as conforming to a legitimate organizational form that has only loose connections to economic imperatives.

Human Capital Theory: Schooling for Productive Skills

Two Nobel Prize–winning economists, Theodore Schultz (1961) and Gary Becker (1975), developed a theory similar to Davis and Moore. They focused on the role of education in creating skills and abilities that people need to be economically successful. Their "capital" metaphor signals that schooling is an investment: the time and effort devoted to schooling will improve one's skills, which will in turn be rewarded in the job market. Individuals are willing to endure school's time and effort requirements because these are likely to pay off in better jobs with higher lifetime earnings. In this way people "invest" in schooling—tuition costs, room and board, books and computers (often paid by an individual's family), and forgone earnings (i.e., the money they could have earned if they had worked rather than studied).

As a micro-level theory of how individuals are motivated to endure long periods of training for future financial rewards, this is very similar to Davis and

Moore. However, human capital theory sheds the idea that some jobs have a functional importance for societal survival. Instead, the theory simply operates on supply and demand, leaving it to employers to decide how much to reward people. However, as a middle-range theory of schooling, human capital is based on a brash premise: that the societal role of school is primarily economic. The theory assumes that individuals invest time, and governments spend billions, largely to reap financial prosperity down the road. It follows in human capital theory that schools are organized to maximize the production of skills needed in the economy. Schools in this sense are like factories. Their costs—books, buildings, teacher salaries—are "inputs." Student learning is the "output." If the yield from the output is greater than the costs of the input, then schooling is a worthy investment.

Some economists further argue that expanding schooling can create more societal equality. Looking back over the past 100 years—the "human capital century"—Goldin and Katz (2008) contend that as more people acquired higher-level skills in school, they were better able to utilize the latest technologies, and hence could handle those complex jobs that tend to pay higher wages. Recent rises in inequality, they contend, are due to the failure of the growing higher education expansion to match advances in new technologies. While the use of computers and automation has become ubiquitous across a range of economic sectors, many high-tech jobs remain vacant due to a shortage of qualified applicants, creating a new "skills mismatch." They advise policy-makers to encourage more youth to enter higher education, particularly in science and math, to keep pace with technological advances and reap its economic fruit. Taking this reasoning further, Nobel Prize winner James Heckman (2008) argues that because there is now less labour market demand for old-fashioned manual skills, broad cognitive skills like basic literacy can fetch a premium like never before. To reduce future skills mismatches, he calls for more programs to enhance foundational literacy and numeracy in early schooling so children can later acquire those higher-order skills that will be rewarded in future jobs.

Sociologists have a number of criticisms of human capital theory. First, do many young people really possess the ability to make rational investment choices based on expected lifetime rewards? Perhaps they have a rough idea, but it is a broad "guesstimate" at best. If one becomes a court judge, she or he will probably recoup the investment in law school tuition and forgone earnings, but this will be difficult to calculate in any detail while still a student. Furthermore, does everyone have the ability to turn educational "investments" into rewards? Sociologists have shown that many women earn less than men, even with comparable education in the same occupation (see, e.g., Kay and Hagan, 1998, on lawyers).

Second, does the labour market really reward skills as directly as human capital theory assumes? Professional associations and unions often bargain collectively on behalf of their members using various forms of "social closure" that restrict the numbers of people who can legally pursue their occupations.

As Weber implied, these bodies use educational certificates to regulate the supply of workers rather than to guarantee their actual skills and abilities. Likewise, owners of firms, stock investors, and corporate CEOs can reap incredible sums by manipulating their immediate market environments, rather than applying their productive skills per se. Skills thus have varying rates of payoff, and payoffs do not merely mirror the application of skills. Labour market structures can channel or impede flows of supply and demand in different ways. This is discussed further below.

Third, some sociologists are skeptical about the size of actual skill mismatches in today's economy. Harvard sociologist Barbara Kiviat (2012) cites data suggesting that widespread "skill mismatches" may barely exist (for a similar Canadian discussion, see McMahon, 2012). Today's public debates about "skills" often use the notion in multiple ways, referring variably to technological know-how, basic literacy, relevant experience, good attitudes, or just plain-old punctuality. Perhaps recent high school dropouts lack sufficient skills, she acknowledges, but her data suggest that most young workers are *over*-qualified for their jobs, and that many jobs go unfilled because they offer low wages! Today there is more of a pay mismatch, not a skills mismatch, she contends.

Fourth, just how tightly connected is the content of the curriculum to the workplace? Human capital theory is vague about the competencies that schools are supposed to teach and how these connect to what employers are rewarding. Many critics doubt that schools are organized to create skills with a factory-like efficiency, or that curricula simply mirror the demands of the workplace.

Credentialism: Schooling for Status Signals

This skepticism is embodied in a theory that draws a lineage directly from Weber. Randall Collins (1979) and his followers (e.g., Brown, 2001) have developed Weber's insight about the use of educational certificates to "monopolize" entry into occupations to develop a theory of "credentialing." At its most provocative, this theory sees schools more as credentialing bodies than as educating bodies. It asks: does schooling actually improve useful job-related skills, as presumed by human capital theorists, or does it mainly provide a piece of paper that serves as an occupational ticket? Asked another way, what exactly does an educational certificate certify?

Collins's argument is rooted in two observations. First, schools may be "over-educating" people. The economy may not have sufficient jobs for the number of educationally qualified graduates from high schools, colleges, and universities. For instance, faculties of education commonly graduate more teachers than can be realistically hired in schools. Such anomalies led Collins to describe **"credential inflation."** Just as monetary inflation means that a dollar today cannot purchase the same number of goods as could a dollar 30 years ago, a high school diploma today simply cannot land the same job it did 30 years ago.

This inflation occurs because of a growing gap between the abilities required in jobs and the levels of education job occupants possess. Employees are often over-qualified, with a growing gap between their learned skills and what their job actually requires.

Second, Collins doubted whether school content was as strongly connected to the workplace as human capital theorists imagined. For Collins, much of schooling—the hours of writing essays, solving quadratic equations, and practising the recorder—had precious little to do with the realities of most jobs. Take the standard high school curriculum. Except for a small number of vocational courses, Collins would challenge us to show how any of it—from English to math to music—connects directly to jobs. School curricula develop by their own dynamics, he argued, rather than in response to the needs of employers. Further, Collins notes, very few employers bother to look at student grades when hiring. Except for a few professional groups, course grades don't matter. Just show your piece of paper—diploma, certificate, degree—and that will suffice. If school content really was tightly connected to the job market, Collins reasons, employers would surely use school grades to choose suitable job candidates.

Historically, Collins traces pressures for credential inflation to social mechanisms that have intensified labour market competition. After the Second World War, urban job markets became flooded with competitors. With fewer North Americans working on farms, more people sought jobs in towns and cities. Simultaneously, as more women were employed for more years of their lives, they competed for jobs with men (though some occupational segregation remains). This struggle compels individuals to pursue their own interests, to seek a leg up on their rivals. One common competitive strategy is to obtain an educational credential. And, if employers find that many of their applicants have advanced diplomas and degrees, they may raise the credential requirements for some positions. If thousands of job candidates and employers adopt these strategies, an unintended consequence emerges: credential inflation.

Collins identifies other mechanisms that generate credential inflation. First, many occupational groups have a vested interest in inflating entry requirements. Professional associations, such as the Canadian Medical Association, aim to control occupational standards and set educational requirements necessary to practise their profession. This process is akin to Weber's notion that professions use educational certificates to "monopolize" or control entry into occupations. "Classic" professions such as medicine and law demand that their practitioners first obtain a general university education (i.e., BA or BSc) and then additional specialized training in a professional school. It is illegal for anyone to practise these professions without these credentials. By demanding higher and higher amounts of education, these occupations can reduce the number of their competitors in their field. For Collins, this process of "**professionalization**"—the efforts of an occupation to raise its standing in society—can fuel credential inflation.

Box 3.2 Credentialism in Action

In *The Wizard of Oz*, when Dorothy and her friends, the Lion, the Scarecrow, and the Tin Man, finally see the Wizard, he tells the Scarecrow:

> Why, anybody can have a brain. That's a very mediocre commodity. Every pusil-lanimous creature that crawls on the earth—or slinks through the slimy sea has a brain! . . . Back where I come from we have great universities, seats of great learning—where men go to become great thinkers. And when they come out, they think deep thoughts—and with no more brains than you have. . . . But! They have one thing you haven't got! A diploma!

The Wizard presents the Scarecrow with a diploma, and, of course, the Scarecrow is transformed. All the magic of schooling lies meekly in a simple, but powerful, piece of paper.

Source: *The Wizard of Oz*, screenplay by Noel Langley, Florence Ryerson, and Edgar Allen Woolf, Metro-Goldwyn-Mayer, 1939.

Professionalization has been emulated by many occupations. Think of all the requirements that didn't exist 40 years ago. Today to get ahead in social work, one needs an MSW. In business? Better get a BComm and then an MBA. In nursing, you need a BN. And, forget about teaching if you don't have a BA or BSc. What fascinates Collins is that these occupations easily survived in past generations without demanding these credentials. Each newly professionalized group, of course, claims that their heightened requirements are for "quality assurance"—whether in teaching, dental hygiene, or hairdressing. But Collins would challenge them to provide evidence for claiming their practice has become so much more complex and thus requires more schooling.

A second process that fuels credential inflation centres on the practice of employers. Managers are often flooded with applications when hiring, especially managers in large organizations. The sheer number of candidates makes careful and personal consideration of each applicant nearly impossible. Hence, managers need a "bureaucratic screening device" to reduce their applicant pool in ways that are legitimate, fair, and efficient. Employers have increasingly settled on screening via credentials. Even for jobs that are not particularly complex or demanding, employers will use education requirements to filter applicants.

Collins also contends that some employers prefer to hire employees with advanced credentials simply because they are prestigious. Historically, higher education has been associated with aristocratic culture, as Weber noted in his idea of the "cultured person." Think of how much of the traditional upper-secondary and university curriculum had medieval elements with little economic utility—the learning of ancient languages, thick volumes of speculative philosophy, and mythologies of classic Greece and Rome. Traditional universities had ceremony and pageantry that echoed religious rituals and monarchical courts, with caps, gowns, and gavels. While the association varied greatly across time and place, higher education has traditionally been associated with cultural prestige.

But small elite universities and aristocracies have long given way to mass universities and large middle classes. Universities have severed ties with old-style high culture, and are now associated with middle-class, white-collar, and professional work. A degree can mark status, signalling that its possessor deserves some sort of recognition. Businesses tap this signal, Collins observes, in order to gain trust from their clients and customers. In the business world, where transactions can be highly uncertain, clients seek signals of trustworthiness, reputation, and rank. Firms may spend thousands of dollars for such signals, sometimes decorating their reception areas with fine wood desks, nice lighting, and expensive carpets. This décor says, in effect, that the firm is serious, business-like, and not fly-by-night. For similar reasons, the firm may hire credentialed employees. For Collins, well-educated employees are the human equivalent to a nice piece of office furniture: they signal an honourable status. Advertising to customers a workforce with many letters trailing their names (e.g., BA, BSc, LLB, MBA, MA, PhD, etc.) can facilitate trust and repute in a highly uncertain marketplace.

A fourth and final logic also perpetuates credentialism. Here Collins (ibid., 194–5) points to the endemic problem of unemployment in advanced industrial societies. Any scaling back of education, he argues, would exacerbate unemployment. Education is itself a major employer; teachers are one of the largest occupational groups in Canada. Reducing the education labour force would boost unemployment. And, post-secondary education absorbs people who otherwise would be seeking jobs; if they sought work, unemployment rates would be even higher.

This logic has been recently extended into a more general theory of "rent." Rent refers to any social structure that boosts pay by manipulating forces of supply and demand. According to Weeden and Grusky (2011), there are many kinds of rents. At the lower end of society's pay scale, minimum wage laws legally protect salary floors. Welfare and unemployment benefits offer a basic income to individuals who lack jobs. Unions not only raise their members' wages through collective bargaining, but also boost rates for non-unionized workers in the same industry, as employers compete in order to attract desirable employees. In society's middle range, a variety of occupations use professionalization techniques such as credential requirements, certification, and licensing to maintain or raise their incomes, as discussed above. And, at the highest peaks of society's income scale, corporate executives and CEOs have devised ways to set their own salaries. Top executives have increasingly seized the power to determine the composition of the very bodies—boards of governors and consultants—who in turn set their salaries, bonuses, and stock options. As a result, CEO compensation has skyrocketed over recent decades, while workers' wages have stagnated.

This notion of rent offers a clear alternative to skill-based explanations of rising inequality. Instead of looking for widening skill imbalances, this alternative links rising inequality to new patterns of rent destruction and creation. Lower wage forms of rent have been eroded from cuts to welfare spending, unemployment insurance, minimum wages, and rates of unionized workers. In the middle range, existing forms of rent have been fortified, as some occupations have added new forms of credential certification and licensing to protect themselves from competition. And, at the loftiest reaches of society, corporate leaders, particularly those in the financial sector, have enjoyed new "mega-rents" by creating new financial channels, often byzantine and hidden, that give them incredible rewards. Some human capital theorists see this trend as due to the higher skills needed to run corporations in an ever-competitive global economy. But the rent perspective suggests that links between skills and pay can be weakened by various social structures. If correct, the rent perspective implies that society cannot simply educate its way out of inequality because labour market disparities are not simple reflections of skill disparities.

In later chapters we evaluate various arguments about the link between schooling and the labour force using sociological research. For now, we note that research consistently demonstrates two key facts: students do learn skills in schools, and education does pay in the labour market. As human capital theorists predict, people with more years of schooling have better cognitive skills on average, as measured by standardized tests, and they tend to earn higher wages and have better employment rates. But other facts are difficult to explain with human capital theory (e.g., the gender pay gap). Next, we turn to a final theory that offers a broader understanding of how schools gain legitimacy not only through their economic function, but also by promoting citizenship, supporting grassroots democracy, building community, and nurturing civic literacy.

New Institutionalism: Schools and World Culture

Schools have long been mandated to foster national citizenship. Governments created public schools as part of a nation-building effort. But in recent decades, schools have increasingly embodied trends on a worldwide scale. John Meyer and his colleagues link schooling to processes of globalization (see, e.g., Meyer et al., 1997). They begin with a simple observation: even though societies around the world differ culturally, politically, and economically, with each passing year their schools are becoming increasingly similar. Over the past half-century, the basic organizations of schools in quite diverse locales have slowly converged. Around the world, schools are age-graded, they are compulsory for both boys and girls, they share similar curricular categories such as "language," "math," and "science," and they demand that students spend a relatively similar number of hours in classrooms. This wasn't always the case. One hundred years ago, many societies didn't even have schools, and those that did, varied greatly in their structure.

For Meyer, the mechanism behind this convergence is the development of a broader "world society." Globalization is creating striking similarities between nation-state institutions. Since the emergence of such international bodies as the United Nations, all modern nations, Meyer argues, now must place some emphasis on citizenship, human rights, developing science, monetary policy, diplomatic exchanges, economic progress, and education. This leads them to develop institutions that are broadly similar, such as those that regulate labour markets, science, health, and, yes, education.

This theory breaks from common ways of thinking about how institutions develop. Typically, social scientists contend that an institution evolves in response to the needs of its surrounding society, reflecting local characteristics. For instance, we usually think that Canadian schools reflect our climate, or natural resources, or particular political arrangements such as Confederation. We commonly emphasize the uniqueness of Canadian history and reason that it should set the course for the development of our contemporary schools. And, both structural functionalists and neo-Marxists would agree, predicting that schools develop in direct response to either the technical imperatives of the economy (in the case of functionalists) or the particular needs of the local capitalist class (in the case of Marxists). But Meyer and his colleagues have documented that over the past few decades, school forms are converging across nations, such that their form is influenced less by local initiatives and internal forces than by a common **world culture** (ibid., 152).

How does this happen? According to Meyer, international bodies like the United Nations promote common templates for building state institutions. Professional groups meet internationally and design "best practices" that diffuse around the globe. Once in place in dominant nations, these institutions come to be seen as the "legitimate" way to design a school, hospital, or legal system. Developing nations then are encouraged and sometimes pressured to conform. Newly emerging nation-states especially want to ensure they are recognized by others and have some small voice and presence on the international stage, and they often seek membership in international bodies (e.g., United Nations, World Health Organization, World Bank, World Trade Organization). This process leads to a sharing of ideas, but also reinforces expectations about how nation-states should organize. This process in turn further entrenches **isomorphism**, for example, by requesting data on gender patterns in school enrolment.

To get a flavour of Meyer's reasoning, consider the following question: in which countries would you anticipate the greatest levels of female high school enrolment? Wouldn't the following ordering, from highest to lowest, make sense—Canada, France, Jordan, Botswana, and Colombia? In fact, the ratio of girls to boys is almost identical in each of these countries, and is slightly higher in Jordan, Botswana, and Colombia than in Canada and France. Despite substantial differences in religion, ethnicity, economic development, and region of the world, these countries have remarkably similar gender ratios in high school enrolments.

Why? "Common evolving world-society models, not a hundred different national trajectories, have led states to" exhibit stunning similarity in their standard education curricula, gender participation rates in schools, age-graded classes and promotion sequences, the training of teachers, systematic testing, and a stress on science education (ibid., 157). Two vital ideas need to be developed from this. First, a remarkably influential "world model" for schooling is accepted in virtually all countries. But it is a model with no legal authority. Few people question the value of schooling because education is recognized worldwide as a basic human right. Thus, for any nation-state to be recognized as part of the family of nations it is imperative that schooling be organized and students enrolled. Yet this very acceptance leads to what are often seemingly irrational results.

As Meyer et al. note, "the implementation of standard scripts for educational development in countries of all sorts . . . produces results that often seem quite bizarre. . . . Children who will become agricultural laborers study fractions; villagers in remote regions learn about chemical reactions" (ibid., 149). What makes this "bizarre?" Precious little evidence demonstrates that learning fractions or chemistry enhances the lives of these children or the prosperity of their societies. Yet, many people believe it does. In fact, in many quarters it is almost heresy to suggest otherwise even though persuasive evidence is in short supply. Legitimated beliefs about the good of education saturate our culture and that is why many people react in horror to the idea that standardized education may be a dubious benefit for these children.

A second strong focus of Meyer's work relates to a concept he calls "coupling," as in "**loose coupling**" or "de-coupling." Nation-states make many proclamations, but not all are lived up to. Gaps between proclamation and practice are legion. The values or ideals of a nation, as exemplified in its constitution, are often not well-coupled with actual practices. Almost every nation in the world claims to be a democracy, yet in many countries only a minority of people, if any, can vote (e.g., People's Republic of China, Kuwait).

This notion of coupling is important because it points to a feature of societies we highlighted in Chapter 1. Just like individuals, governments make claims about what they intend; however, the claim and its fulfillment are separate issues. Words and deeds, ideals and actions; these couplets are not always tightly correlated. For example, the Ministry of Education in British Columbia claims to promote school choice for families, but the vast majority of families can only realistically choose their local neighbourhood school. Or, to take a second example, what ministries of education may want to happen in the classroom (words or ideals) and what actually happens in the classroom (deeds or actions) may be only loosely coupled. Just as wary consumers are alert to false advertising, sociologists question whether bold claims are actually true.

Meyer's work is instructive because he highlights macro-level issues by comparing and contrasting entire societies. He illuminates powerful and deeply held cultural models about schooling while remaining agnostic on whether they actually materialize. His research program is a powerful illustration of a core sociological idea: what people define as real is real in its consequences. Ideas shape societies; beliefs have the power to legitimate and spread forms of schooling.

Conclusion: Consequences and Directions

Changing societal conditions over the past half-century pose several implications for sociological theories of education. In terms of socialization, debates have moved beyond considering only how schools deal with growing individualism in society to also examine if and how they socialize students differently by class, race, or gender. In terms of selection, the fact that good jobs increasingly require some sort of educational credential has increased pressure for youth to compete for the most prized credentials. Contemporary sociologists examine unequal attainments by class, race, gender, and Indigeneity, and offer various mechanisms to explain inequality and understand schools' role in this process. In terms of organization, more than in any previous era, schools today play the pivotal role of preparing young people for the labour force. But a key question looms: are schools organized to do this efficiently, or are there better ways to understand schooling?

Theories help us see aspects of social life that might otherwise remain invisible or taken for granted. They help us describe society in insightful ways and pose intriguing questions. However, to be compelling or persuasive, sociological theory also needs to fit the evidence of what actually occurs. In the following chapters we evaluate a variety of theories using research.

Questions for Critical Thought

1. What does the concept "individualism" mean? Thinking about your life decisions thus far, including your school decisions, are you more "individualistic" than your parents or grandparents? Did your school encourage or discourage this individualism? In what ways?

2. Did you have any favourite "interaction rituals" in high school? How did they promote collective effervescence and solidarity for you and/or others? Does your university or college have any comparable rituals? If not, has that changed your educational experience?

3. Think back to the various programs offered at your high school. In what ways, if any, did they reflect Bowles and Gintis's correspondence principle, and Collins's theory of credentialism, and notions of the hidden curriculum?

4. Within the bounds of the law, what would it take for a school today to be considered illegitimate? What might cause it to be closed down by a school board, and not just criticized by the public? Does this process relate to any of the theories discussed in this chapter?

5. Create a PowerPoint presentation outlining the strengths and weaknesses of human capital theory. Be certain to present the strongest case you can for the theory, making it as persuasive as possible, and then point to all issues that you think weaken the theory.

Suggested Readings

Bowles, Samuel, and Herbert Gintis. 1976. *Schooling in Capitalist America: Educational Reform and the Contradictions of Economic Life*. New York: Basic Books. This is a classic Marxist analysis of education.

Bromley, Patricia, Meyer, John W. and Francisco O. Ramirez. 2011. "Student Centrism in Social Science Textbooks: 1970–2005," *Social Forces* 90, 2: 1–24. This article is an application of neo-institutional theory to chart the centrality of students as focal actors in historical and comparative perspective.

Collins, Randall. 1979. *The Credential Society: An Historical Sociology of Education and Stratification*. New York: Academic Press. This is the classic opus from a credentialist perspective.

Drori, Gili, John Meyer, Francisco Ramirez, and Evan Schofer. 2003. *Science in the Modern World Polity: Institutionalization and Globalization*. Stanford, CA: Stanford University Press. This book provides an interesting analysis of globalization by the leading new institutional researchers.

Web Links

Sociological Theories and Perspectives
www.sociosite.net/topics/theory.php
This website has been created to offer students a wealth of resources on a wide range of sociological theories, both classical and contemporary.

The Sociological Eye
http://sociological-eye.blogspot.ca
This is a blog by Randall Collins, one of the most prolific and insightful scholars in contemporary sociology.

Part II

Selection: Inequality and Opportunity

4 Education Revolutionized

The Growth of Modern Schooling

|||||||||||||||||||||||||||||||||||||||||||||||||||||||||||||||||||||||||||||||||||||||||||||||||||||||||||||||||||||||||||||||||||||||||||||||||||||||||||||||||||||||||

Learning Objectives

- To understand the varying forms that schooling takes across time and space
- To discover how our notions of education have changed over the past century
- To see how school forms have evolved as a consequence of the changing values placed on education

|||||||||||||||||||||||||||||||||||||||||||||||||||||||||||||||||||||||||||||||||||||||||||||||||||||||||||||||||||||||||||||||||||||||||||||||||||||||||||||||||||||||||

Introduction

The twentieth century gave birth to a worldwide schooling revolution in most Western nations like Canada. Over the course of 100 years, formal education evolved from a patchwork of loosely connected practices into a universal institution embracing the entire citizenry. Deep changes in the economy, science, religion, family, culture, and politics all pushed formal education to mature as a major institution.

This chapter describes this schooling revolution, focusing mainly on Canada, outlining the early beginnings of education, the growth of enrolments and burgeoning expectations, the widening breadth of curricula, the expanding functions and forms of schools, and the exporting of school forms to other institutions. The sum of these trends has been a dramatic transformation. Schools and schooling are now central to our lives. Both at the individual level and at the institutional level, Canada has become a schooled society.

Beginnings of a Schooled Society

The origins of formal education, at least involving teachers and pupils, can be traced to the early Greeks. Aristotle, Plato, and Socrates all tutored pupils. However, prior to about the sixteenth century in Europe, most schooling was Church-based. As O'Day (1982: 25) argues, "for centuries academic learning [was] the preserve of the clergy . . . because only the clergy needed advanced literacy."

One way to trace the emergence of the modern form of Canadian schooling is to focus on the European roots of the school class. Philippe Ariès (1962: 176), a French historian, calls the school class the "constituent cell of the school system." In studying the first appearances of childhood as a recognizable phase of life, he shows that gradually, and in fits and starts, the school class emerged.

Consider the defining attributes of the modern school class. First, most students in a class are the same age. Second, classes are organized progressively by knowledge level. Third, classes meet in separate locations. Fourth, a class is often set off by a particular time period. In the history of schooling, which of these do you suppose came first—age grouping, knowledge or ability grouping, separate locations, or separate times?

The school class was first organized by level of knowledge (emerging around the sixteenth century). Students of varying ages, typically meeting in one large room, were drilled in the basics (e.g., the alphabet). Only once elementary material was mastered did students move to higher knowledge levels (e.g., grammar, followed by rhetoric and composition). "School classes . . . separate[d] students according to their capacities and the difficulty of the subject-matter, not . . . according to their ages" (ibid., 188). In other words, school classes were initially organized by ability.

Today's classes, almost without exception, are age-graded. The ages of students at any grade level typically span only two years, and most are born within months of one another. Age-grading started in the nineteenth century as educators began to worry about promoting young students too rapidly. Two worries were central: rushing students too fast and mixing students of different temperaments (e.g., the frivolity of younger students). At the same time, older students were discouraged from remaining too long at the same grade level. In an increasingly strict age-graded system older students were out of place and so they began dropping out of school.

This age patterning was typical of early education in Canada. By the early 1800s informal schooling was common in Upper Canada (now Ontario). Schooling occurred mainly through family tutoring, private schools, and religious schools, but slowly a public system emerged (government funded since 1807). "Children of all ages gathered together under one teacher for a few months or years, to learn the three Rs (reading, 'riting, and 'rithmetic) and a little religion and morals" (Prentice, 1977: 16).

By mid-century, however, a *system* of schooling emerged, centrally controlled and regulated. By 1871 children between seven and 12 were required to attend school for at least four months of the year. Teacher certification was mandated and school inspections were instituted. Gradually decisions about courses, books, and school rules became centralized under the control of the provincial Chief Superintendent of Common Schools.

As Prentice (ibid., 19) asks, what accounts for this "transition from the informal and largely voluntary, to formal, institutional, and compulsory education under the aegis of the state?" One can imagine a host of reasons for this transition. These could be hypothesized as follows:

1. *Economic/industrialization*: Schooling became essential to ensure a skilled and compliant labour force was available (e.g., Bowles and Gintis).

2. *Technical complexity*: Schooling was necessary to ensure young people had the rudimentary skills essential for success in a world growing more complex (e.g., Davis and Moore).

3. *Child susceptibility in a diverse world*: Schooling provided a venue to ensure children adopted a common value system (e.g., Durkheim).

4. *Nation-building*: Schooling was part of a larger process of building an independent country (e.g., Weber, Meyer).

Accountability, Old School

Contemporary notions of making Canadian schools accountable to the public mostly translate into having hundreds of thousands of children write standardized tests, and then having official websites and mass media report school-by-school average scores. But many educators criticize this regimen for providing little direction or support for their efforts to improve teaching.

The notion that schools should be accountable is hardly new; similar ideas have been around since the advent of public education. A century ago, when neither standardized tests nor electronic media existed, governments devised a different practice: they had inspectors physically travel from school to school to assess classrooms, grounds, curricula, and teachers. In theory, these inspections were to improve instruction by providing teachers with pedagogical support, encouragement, and advice. Inspectors were often the lone experienced professional with whom teachers in one-room schools had any contact.

But this old-school accountability was spotty, unsystematic, and not always warmly greeted by teachers (Gidney and Millar, 2012: 306). Why? Consider the challenge posed by the task of travelling rural Canada's vast and unwelcoming terrain one hundred years ago. Inspectors had to sometimes navigate huge expanses without modern roads, "roughing it" by carrying their own camping gear, bed, and cooking utensils. Piling up mileage was part of their job description, as was using every imaginable means—boat, rail, horse, bicycle, canoe, even toboggan. Fortunately, by the end of the 1920s, new technologies eased their burdens: automobiles began to replace teams of horses, inspectors could use telephones (at least in more settled parts of the country), and some could even take a small airplane to remote schools.

Yet, even with newly available technologies, the quality of inspections was questioned. The most remote schools were too far to be inspected annually. Long travel times necessitated that inspectors might visit a school for only two hours before needing to head off to another. Critics described such inspections as "superficial if not farcical," complaining that they generated few practical or constructive suggestions for improving classrooms, and did little to rectify the professional isolation of teachers in one-room school houses. Some teachers recollected: "What do I remember about teaching in a rural school? That I was entirely on my own. . . . You were entirely on your own. You were completely on your own" (ibid., 310).

When you get to Chapter 9's discussion of contemporary accountability practices, ask yourself: have teachers' reactions to them shifted much over the past century?

The first hypothesis for the rapid spread of public schooling proposes industrialization (and the rise of capitalism) as central. The problem here is causality. Mass schooling was in place well before large-scale industrialization. For example, Prentice (1977, 19) reports that by 1876 over 90 per cent of children aged five to 16 were *registered* as attending public school, yet the 1881 Canadian census shows that the majority of people still lived in rural areas and the percentage employed in non-agricultural jobs was just over 50 per cent. Indeed, until the 1950s, the Canadian economy, as well as schools, remained rooted in rural, non-industrial settings (Gidney and Millar, 2012). So, while schooling now plays an important role in labour force preparation, industrialization was not a primary cause for the beginnings of mass schooling.

Similar reasoning undermines the second proposition. With a still largely rural population in 1876, it is hard to explain the importance of the three Rs as a consequence of the technical demands of a complex society. No doubt reading and writing were seen as important, but there is little in the historical record suggesting that school promoters saw technical necessity as the prime educational motivator.

The third and especially the fourth hypotheses have more support. Prentice (1977: 34) argues that many educators promoted schooling because of "the weakness and incapacity of the young." Early school promoters like Alexander Forrester (Nova Scotia), Egerton Ryerson (Upper Canada), and John Jessop (BC) increasingly understood childhood as a separate phase in the transition to adulthood. It was a transition during which the young were understood to be susceptible to dangerous, amoral ideas. School was a place for the learning of foundational moral values, strict discipline, and proper deportment. However, even as staunch an advocate as Ryerson would not have been successful without powerful, organized support. That support came largely from the government.

A concern about diverse values helps to understand the importance of government action and nation-building (Curtis, 1988). First, political instability such as the 1837 Rebellion promoted fears of divisiveness and factionalism that could undermine the prosperity of a fledgling nation. Second, especially towards the end of the nineteenth century, the larger waves of immigration from various parts of Europe meant that attention had to be given to social cohesion. In this sense, the origins of schooling resonate with Émile Durkheim's arguments about moral education and socialization. What Durkheim did not stress, however, was the role of government power in creating an administrative educational system (as did Weber).

From the mid-nineteenth century in Canada, schooling became more centralized, with governments controlling who would teach and what they would teach and when. School inspection was prominent in the early days and truant officers were employed to ensure that everyone who was supposed to be there was there. Further, this was not simply an Upper Canada phenomenon. As Jean Barman (1995: 31) argues, by the mid-1860s British Columbians favoured a "free non-denominational education" system. This again depended on a central role for government, not only for funding but also in encouraging a school system that was distanced from religious instruction.

This latter issue raises the historic relation between church and state. Among the earliest educators in Canada were the Jesuits, Recollects, and others who sought to bring Christian values and ideals to the Indigenous peoples living in North America. As Ronald Manzer (1994) asked, "which great social institution, church or state, should exercise ultimate authority over the guidance of learning?" Complicating this history in Canada were various interest groups. These groups were mainly English, French, and Indigenous, and they differed principally along the lines of religion, language, ancestry, and provincial majority/minority status (i.e., French majority in Quebec and minorities elsewhere; English majority elsewhere but a minority in Quebec; Indigenous majority in none of the provinces).

Section 93 of the Constitution Act of 1867 (previously known as the British North America Act) delegated responsibility for education to the provinces. Nevertheless, subsections of the Act speak directly to the preservation of separate schooling for religious denominations. Effectively, the Act gave provinces the power to enact legislation and collect taxes for schools, with an important guarantee for separate denominational schools. Principally in Quebec and Newfoundland (which joined Canada in 1949), separate Roman Catholic and Protestant school authorities dominated K–12 education. In other provinces, provincial departments of education were more powerful, with various levels of support existing for separate religious schools. The majority of these provincial school systems were, at least in name, non-denominational, even though they were typically Christian schools and many really Protestant in character (e.g., up until the 1960s many Canadian schoolchildren began their day with Protestant reverence by reciting the Lord's Prayer and reading from the King James Bible, even in what were typically called common, or non-denominational, schools).

The reference to "common" schools came about via a strong social movement that rejected the European model of class-based or elitist education. The common school movement meant that all children could attend school, regardless of their social class (but in reality class divisions occurred, largely by neighbourhood; see Prentice, 1977: 138–69). The government saw schools as a method to build a nation and enhance citizenship. The school promoters saw schooling as an effective way to build a better society, instilling in everyone, no matter what their social class, common values and a strong work ethic.

Enrolments and Attendance: Creating a Universal Experience

The earliest Canadian public schools were humble. In the mid-1800s few schools were larger than a single house, employed more than a single teacher, or segregated children by age group. Most teachers were minimally educated. They rarely gave instruction beyond rudimentary literacy and mathematics. By 1900, and especially in rural locales, only a tiny fraction of students would complete high school. For the vast majority of young Canadians, school was something to attend intermittently

Figure 4.1 The One-Room Schoolhouse and the Modern School
Top: Eburne School, 1908. Eburne is now part of Vancouver. *Bottom*: Earl Haig Secondary School, Toronto, 2006.

for eight or so years of their lives, where they attained basic literacy and numeracy and received instruction in the rudiments of (Christian) religion and citizenship.

In the twentieth century, school populations exploded. As provinces established departments of education, one-room schoolhouses were gradually replaced with modern buildings of a far more bureaucratic, standardized character. This helped create a more uniform, "mass" form of schooling. The rationalized processes of the modern world were playing out as foretold by Max Weber. The average size of a Canadian school increased from 66 students in the 1920s to 156 in 1960 to 350 by 1970 (Manzer, 1994).

With the construction of these new buildings, enrolments soared. New norms emerged. It was now common for parents to enrol their children in local schools, although in rural areas not all did. But to capture the changing experience of schooling, we need to examine the historical record more deeply. As we implied above, enrolments are not the same as actual school attendance. In earlier eras, many children did not attend full-time because they worked on family farms or did other labour. For this reason, historians have given special attention to attendance rates (see Gidney and Millar, 2012; Katz and Mattingly, 1975). They estimate that in 1867, the year of Confederation, only about four in 10 registered pupils would attend on any given day. While some youngsters would have steady attendance for, say, six months of the year, they would disappear from schools when needed for farming, fishing, or trapping. Further, many schools did not offer instruction for children younger than seven. In the early 1930s, just over half of six-year-olds were in school and only 20 per cent of five-year-olds attended classes. Compulsory starting ages for schooling did not drop to ages five and six until later.

As shown in Figure 4.2, elementary schooling did not offer most young people a common experience until the 1930s. Only then was attendance more regular and predictable. Most students began school at age six, attending most days in non-summer months. The rate of change accelerated again after 1950, and by the 1960s full attendance in public elementary and high school was almost complete. However, even as late as 1951 more than half of Canada's population age 15 and older had not attained even a Grade 9 level of schooling, as seen in Figure 4.3.

Amid the economic boom of the post–Second World War a new mindset emerged among policy-makers in Canada and elsewhere. They actively promoted more schooling for longer periods of life. In this era the concept of education as an economic engine for the nation began in earnest (and this is when the human capital theory of educational investment was first proposed).

Assessing the immediate post–Second World War period, several trends emerge. First, the completion of elementary years had become nearly universal. By the mid-1960s, almost every Canadian-born youth completed at least the equivalent of Grade 8. Second, high school graduation became a benchmark of attainment. Rather than seeking full-time jobs in their mid-teens, most young people completed high school. The term "high school dropout" emerged as a new symbol of deviance. Whereas between 10 per cent and 20 per cent of current age cohorts

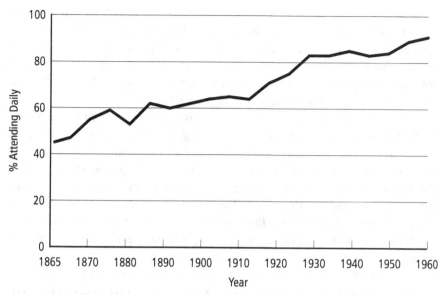

Figure 4.2 Percentage of Students Attending Daily in Public Elementary and Secondary Schools, Canada 1865–1960

Source: F.H. Leacy, ed., 1983, *Historical Statistics of Canada*, 2nd edn. Ottawa: Minister Responsible for Statistics Canada and the Social Science Federation of Canada, Catalogue no. 11–516E. Series W68.

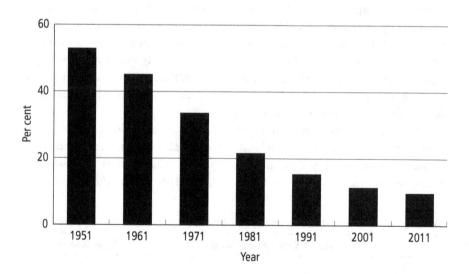

Figure 4.3 Percentage of Population 15 and Over with Less Than Grade 9 Education, 1951–2011

Source: F.H. Leacy, ed., 1983, *Historical Statistics of Canada*, 2nd edn. Ottawa: Minister Responsible for Statistics Canada and the Social Science Federation of Canada, Catalogue no. 11–516E (Series W68), http://www.statcan.gc.ca/bsolc/olc-cel/olc-cel?lang=eng&catno=11-516-X.

still fail to complete Grade 12 or its equivalent by the age of 20, these youth are no longer considered to be "normal." Various labels are used to denote this status, with the most common today being "at-risk youth."

Researchers now pinpoint the reasons for dropping out as both individual and institutional—poverty, a lack of parental education, a lack of intellectual nourishment at home (or at school), a lack of support programs for these youth, or a curriculum that is insensitive to their needs (all discussed in Chapter 6). High school graduation as a taken-for-granted expectation is novel in the grand sweep of human history. Now we expect all youth to complete high school.

Tracing money is another way to demonstrate expansion. After the Second World War the total funding for schooling surged. Table 4.1 shows this by tracking the total amount of money going to Canadian education and the amount of funding per student from 1950 to 1974. Over this 25-year period, total education funding increased 25-fold, while the amount of funding per student rose by a factor of 10, demonstrating that the increased funding (to $11 billion in 1974) was a function both of more students attending and more money supporting each student.

Here are two ways of demonstrating how profound these increases were. First, in the late 1960s the funding increase per pupil reached nearly 10 per cent *every year*. Contrast this with the funding constraints that have recently beset education in many provinces. Second, this was an era when more government money went to education than to health care. That has been subsequently reversed dramatically: governments now spend much more on health than on schooling, as shown in Figure 4.4. But this figure also highlights how spending growth on education has continued to outpace spending on social services and other government expenditures. The upward surge of public funding for schooling is not a mere artifact of overall boosts in government expenditures: it is instead a product of a growing priority on education. While rising health costs can be partly explained by our aging population, education spending continues to rise at the same time that the proportion of the population in the K–12 age-range has shrunk. This trend dramatizes the continuing emergence of our schooled society.

Three causal factors were behind this increased monetary support: one related to industry and science, another related to credential inflation, and a third related to equality of opportunity. First, as we saw in Chapter 3, the character of work has changed dramatically over the last 100 years. Science profoundly affected both what

Table 4.1 Total Expenditures on Canadian Education, 1950-74

Year	Total $ Expenditure (000s)	$ per Student
1950	438,751	166
1955	829,132	244
1960	1,705,986	389
1965	3,399,505	622
1970	7,676,049	1,207
1974	11,048,813	1,773

Source: F.H. Leacy, ed., 1983, *Historical Statistics of Canada*, 2nd edn. Ottawa: Minister Responsible for Statistics Canada and the Social Science Federation of Canada, Catalogue no. 11-516E (Series W61 & W66), www.statcan.gc.ca/bsolc/olc-cel/olc-cel?lang=eng&catno=11-516-X.

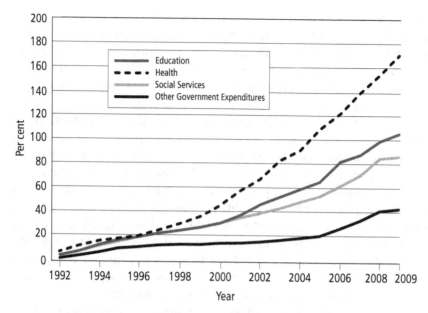

Figure 4.4 Percentage Change in Public Expenditures on Education and Other Government Programs, 1992-2009

Source: Authors' calculations from Statistics Canada, CANSIM data base, Table 385–0001.

we built (e.g., computers) and how we built (e.g., robotics). The cognitive know-how of the labour force had to be upgraded. Here, certain aspects of Davis and Moore's functional theory of stratification and of the human capital theorists make sense. Technical complexity was accelerating.

Remember, though, that more and more work was related to the service side of the economy and those jobs required a very different set of skills (e.g., leadership, communication, conflict avoidance, and resolution). While learning more about quarks and quadratics might take more years of schooling, it is not clear that learning civility and good graces demands much more extensive schooling. Randall Collins's arguments about credential inflation thus have some merit in explaining the historical record of school expansion, especially when considering the rise in educational requirements for jobs that have remained relatively similar through time (e.g., sales clerks).

Finally, from the perspective of industry, it is important to also remember schooling's socialization role. Durkheim saw that role as central to the maintenance of social solidarity and morality, while Bowles and Gintis saw it as a critical tool to pacify the workforce. School promoters have long vowed to develop students' work ethics, discipline, reliability, and willingness to follow orders. Being promoted from grade to grade requires that students, at least minimally, demonstrate these attributes.

School expansion was also fuelled, however, by goals of equality of opportunity. Modern schooling was not funded solely for the privilege of the upper social classes, though they may have benefited more (or less) from that funding. But common schools were made available to (almost) everyone, and the value of providing equal opportunity has been strengthened ever since. In more modern times, Prime Minister Pierre Elliott Trudeau hit a vibrant chord that resonated with many Canadians in the 1960s and 1970s when he spoke about creating a "just society." Providing educational opportunities for everyone was increasingly seen to be a basic human right, one that had profound public support. Internationally, notions of human rights were voiced and spread largely after the Second World War in which many million died fighting the tyranny and racial bigotry of the Nazi regime.

Further, as John Meyer and his colleagues (Chapter 3) have argued, this ideal emerged as part of a common world culture where the rights of individual citizens gradually ascended to new heights. Not only in Canada, but school expansion everywhere was fostered by this quickly diffusing new world model. Finally, the argument about expansion is based on the *idea* or *belief* about equality of opportunity, not necessarily upon its real existence (which will be examined in Chapter 6).

A final major trend in this post–Second World War period—again, one seen around the world—has been the emergence of a new era in higher education. In Canada, from the 1950s to the 1970s, a host of new universities were built. What were previously small religious colleges were transformed into modern universities. Institutions such as Brock, Cape Breton, Lakehead, Simon Fraser, and York appeared, and small religious colleges morphed into Brandon University, the University of Waterloo, and the University of Windsor. Canada was well on its way to becoming a schooled society.

Figure 4.5 illustrates the relentless rise of post-secondary graduation rates. The absolute numbers of graduates are rising year upon year. When this trend is coupled with the slowing growth of the young population, it highlights the

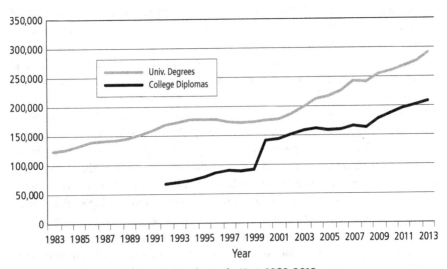

Figure 4.5 College and University Graduates by Year, 1983–2013

Source: Statistics Canada, Author's calculations: CANSIM 477-0020 and Education in Canada 1995.

growing proportion of young Canadians earning post-secondary credentials. Around 70 per cent of each new age cohort now moves on to post-secondary levels. Over 8 per cent are earning advanced degrees at the masters and doctorate level, which represents a doubling over the 30-year time span.

These trends are not unique to Canada. Participation in higher education is surging to unprecedented levels around the globe. Between 1900 and 2000, the worldwide enrolment in tertiary education grew a staggering 2,000 per cent (Schofer and Meyer, 2005). It is now common in many countries for more than half of an age cohort to be in some post-secondary schooling. To put this growth in perspective, Schofer and Meyer remind us that countries like Algeria, Kazakhstan, and Myanmar each now possess a similar number of tertiary students as could be found *in the entire world* at the start of the last century.

What is the impact of these enrolment trends? The expansion of secondary and then post-secondary education represents a profound transformation of people's lives. Although societies have built schools since ancient times, only over the past century has the student role emerged as a common experience. This revolution marks a fundamental shift in how young people are prepared for the adult world. It is reshaping the life course by altering our notions of growing up and maturing. We spend ever-longer hours and years in schools, rather than in full-time jobs. Only a few generations ago job preparation was done under the direct observation of adult family members or members of the broader community. Now modern schools segregate young people into a specialized institution, supervised by paid professionals. This creates what Ravanera et al. (2004) call a growing "standardization of the life course." Nevertheless, this model—having all Canadian youngsters formally educated in a publicly sanctioned school—has been a reality for only about 50 years. Only during this time frame have schools, more than any other institution, provided the shared experience of a "schooled society." If schooling has changed this rapidly in recent history, just how will it change in your lifetime and with what implications for you and your children?

The Revolution in Expectations

Recent decades have witnessed a dramatic revolution in expectations at the post-secondary level. Sixty years ago, "community colleges" barely existed. Universities were small "elite" institutions that housed about 7 per cent of the age cohort (i.e., of 18- to 21-year-olds; Leacy, 1983). But as commentators in the 1970s began to observe, university systems in nations like Canada were changing from an "elite" to a "mass" character. They shifted from catering to a small minority of young people seeking professional careers in a patchwork of mostly small institutions to a large system that catered to hundreds of thousands of youth seeking a variety of pathways into higher-end labour markets.

This expansion was accomplished by fostering relatively high educational aspirations among youth. In comparison to many other countries, Canada's high

Table 4.2 Parents' Academic Aspirations for Their Nine-Year-Old Child by Family Income (2006–7)

How far do you hope this child will go in school?	Lower-Income Families	Higher-Income Families
High school or less	23.8	9.4
Community college	13.1	9.6
Other post-secondary	12.9	18.8
University	50.2	62.2
Total	100%	100%

Source: Thomas (2009: Table E.)

schools sort students into only a few streams (e.g., academic, vocational). The majority of students enrol in the academic stream, a decision that is made relatively late in students' academic careers. This arrangement has promoted an "opportunity consciousness" among youth that sometimes encourages even mediocre secondary students to pursue further studies (Brint, 1998).

Current trends may be ushering in a new stage of higher education: an evolution from a "mass" to a "universal" system. As late as 1991, only 11 per cent of Canadians possessed a university degree, though over half of Canadian teens expected to attain a degree (Guppy and Davies, 1998; Bibby and Posterski, 1992). A 2006–7 survey, shown in Table 4.2, signals both a revolution of expectations and a perpetuation of social inequality. It displays how less than one-quarter of lower-income parents did *not* aspire to a post-secondary education for their children. Fully half hoped their children would attend university. These are remarkable figures considering that few of these parents would have attended such institutions. But the figures for higher-income parents—the most educated cohort of parents in history—are even more remarkable: over 90 per cent hoped their children would attend a post-secondary institution, with 62 per cent aiming for university. These and other data suggest that Canadian parents and youth have revolutionized their educational expectations.

One implication of this revolution is that many high school students who are relatively disengaged from their studies may nonetheless expect to prolong their educational careers. Youth who are keen and achieve well in school are very likely to continue into post-secondary levels. But even among parents who deem their children to be struggling in high school (as judged by their attitudes to school, achievement, and time spent on homework), most expect their children to attend a post-secondary institution (Butlin, 1999; Connolly, Hatchett, and McMaster, 1999). Post-secondary students have been portrayed historically as earning above-average grades, enjoying school to a moderate extent, and putting some effort in their studies. But this image may need revision. Whereas in previous eras students who disliked school, fared poorly, and did not do any homework would be rarely encouraged to pursue advanced studies, many are now expected at least to attend a community college. Increasingly community colleges take on all comers, even remedial students, with open admission policies to cater to these rising expectations.

Expanding Curricula

As higher education has grown, it has become increasingly central to societies around the world. This was not always the case. A century ago it was widely assumed that higher education served only specialized purposes, such as training elite professionals or civil servants. Today, however, most elite positions are accessed through universities. Traditional professions like law and medicine have long used universities as entry portals, but now more and more occupations can be entered only with post-secondary qualifications. For instance, the past few decades have seen a reorganization of business enterprises, with managerial positions increasingly requiring university degrees (e.g., the burgeoning demand for MBAs). Only a few decades ago it was considered absurd to require police, hairdressers, security guards, or salespeople to possess college or university educations. The notion that well over half of an age cohort would receive such schooling would have seemed not only ridiculous, but a huge waste of money. But now, higher credentials (recall both Weber's and Collins's arguments) have become a minimal criterion for elite selection in sector after sector. Schooling rationales are being resized for a new age. Whereas the original version of human capital theory, for instance, imagined a rather limited number of educated people fitting into a fairly static economy, now schooling is wanted for an unbridled expansion of economic and human potential.

"Curriculum" means something very different today than it did a century ago. The humble décor and physical surroundings of the "little red schoolhouse" were matched by equally humble school content. For most, elementary schooling largely meant covering basic literacy and mathematics, reading storybooks, and being introduced to civics and religious teaching. Secondary schooling broadened this through history and geography courses, with some basics from science. Higher education largely focused on philosophy (for theologians), law, and medicine. But the content of curricula has exploded in recent decades, with the largest changes being evident at the post-secondary level. We see two key areas: the expansion and absorption of vocational training for lower-level labour markets, and the knowledge explosion for technical subjects.

At higher levels, curricula have expanded in tandem with the knowledge revolution discussed in Chapter 3. For instance, whereas it was once common for upper-year high school students to take single courses in math and science, now there are multiple courses. This lateral expansion is even more visible at the post-secondary level. Fifty years ago most universities had a rather thin range of offerings, but now their course calendars bulge with hundreds of courses. For instance, the University of Toronto, typical of Canadian universities, boasts at least 700 different undergraduate programs and 200 graduate, with more planned. This is occurring around the globe, with universities and colleges stretching their offerings far beyond traditional fields, and continually multiplying into new realms of study (Frank and Gabler, 2006). It reflects Weberian processes of rationalization: increasing requirements for calculability and prediction require ever-finer and ever-higher levels of knowledge specialization.

Community colleges are especially distinctive in the ways that they have absorbed job training for various occupations. While in previous eras one might learn about hotel or restaurant management by working in a hotel or restaurant, or would learn about office security by working as a security guard, now there are college diplomas in these areas, and in many, many more. This is emblematic of a schooled society: schools at some level increasingly perform roles that in previous generations would have been performed elsewhere. Today, secondary schools are divesting themselves of much vocational education and are becoming more academic in orientation, and so colleges are increasingly embracing and absorbing job training. This process of bifurcation is one line of reasoning that Bowles and Gintis (1976) suggested in their correspondence theory of education and work.

Beyond job training, schools are taking on a variety of other social functions. In the next section we discuss how they are increasingly assuming a range of "social work" roles. There is an irony in this: as we hear more about the impending "knowledge economy" and the need to prepare young people for advanced jobs in high-tech sectors, schools are also being saddled with missions extending far beyond those cognitive goals.

Expanding Functions

Next we want to highlight other changes that may grow in significance in the coming decades.

First, the theme of "lifelong learning" is an increasing reality for many. Today, at the beginning of children's lives, advocates are calling for a variety of forms of "early learning." Publicly supported preschools and early learning centres are being opened in several provinces, with persistent calls to make them universally available. The rationales for early learning vary widely: some tout it as a form of universal daycare, and others hail its socialization benefits. But the rationale that is arguably most compelling to government is based on an emerging image of child cognitive development. For instance, a variety of Canadian organizations are pointing to preschool activity as vital for early brain development. They claim that success or failure in those years has lifelong consequences for health, behaviour, and cognitive functioning. Appealing to human capital theorists, they contend that any shortfall of public funding for preschool will eventually lead to staggering costs in the future for health care, lost productivity, and weakened citizenship. Their message is being heeded in some quarters. As one example, Ontario has implemented full-day learning for four- and five-year-olds, along with a comprehensive, continuous, and integrated system from birth to age 12.

At the other end of life's spectrum, adult education has grown in leaps and bounds in recent decades. Adult education consists of a variety of formal programs and subject matters, but is often identified with either job (re)training or a philosophy of community-based teaching that reflects students' own wants, needs, and responsibilities. Since the 1960s, more adults have spent more hours in formal programs of study. In the 1990s, 28 per cent of Canadian adults participated in such adult education and training programs (Statistics Canada, 2002). By 2003, this level of participation had grown to 48 per cent (Rubenson et al., 2007). Indeed, at post-secondary levels, the largest projected growth in enrolments is seen to be part-time university instruction for employed adults, what Clark Kerr has dubbed the "Market II." When this trend is viewed in tandem with growing participation in early learning and with upward enrolment trends in standard K–12 and post-secondary education, we see how schooling is thoroughly reshaping the life course.

But in addition, schooling is embracing a wider variety of roles and responsibilities. If you look at the website of any large urban school board, you'll see a bewildering variety of programs far beyond the three Rs. For instance, at the Toronto District School Board, typical of any large board, services are available that have little directly to do with biology, calculus, or geography. To support students, each school has access to a range of non-teaching professionals, such as occupational therapists, physiotherapists, psychologists, social workers, and speech pathologists. There are programs for child care, driver education, nutrition, parenting, and outdoor education. In short, modern schools now must perform a variety of roles beyond basic cognitive instruction and civic socialization.

This is indicative, we believe, of the new, more central role of schools in society: they are increasingly seen as principal vehicles for solving many contemporary social problems. Perceived problems in substance abuse lead to drug education programs. Fears of teen pregnancy or the spread of sexually transmitted diseases prompt sex education modules. The spectres of racism and intolerance have triggered huge growth in anti-racist and multicultural curricula. If it is believed that some children are malnourished at home, schools are asked to devise meal programs. If we want households to incorporate the modern three Rs (reduce, reuse, and recycle), schools are seen as avenues to nurture this "transferable" awareness (from school to home).

In fact, no other modern institution has been granted so much faith to address a multiplicity of social problems. Health-care institutions, for instance, are rarely called on to tackle problems beyond those of bodily and mental health. The criminal justice system deals almost entirely with lawbreakers; few expect that police and courts need other tasks in addition to keeping the peace, dealing with criminals, and rehabilitating inmates. Schools, in contrast, inspire much more of a religious-like fervour. Like no other institution, they are associated with a faith in progress and the redemptive power of modernity (see Egan, 1997 and 2008 for commentary on the negative consequences of this "multiple-mission" undercurrent in schooling).

Expanding Alternatives

Reflect again on the image of the "little red schoolhouse." So far in this chapter we've highlighted shifts from that school to the big brick box of the modern high school, and the massive expansion of offered curricula at all levels. But we are also seeing an expansion of alternatives in schooling. French immersion programming is one illustration of this trend. Begun in the 1970s to support bilingualism, French immersion programs now provide an alternative form of schooling for 300,000 Canadian students wishing to learn a second language (in this case French, but some provinces offer immersion in other languages as well, such as Mandarin in Alberta and British Columbia). This represents about 7 per cent of eligible students.

A second illustration of relatively new alternatives comes from the city of Edmonton (see Box 4.1), where public schools now boast a wide range of alternative programming for students. Not only famous in Canada as a school district promoting greater programming choice for students, it is receiving international attention as an exemplar for decentralized, "site-based" decision-making where more autonomy is given to teachers and school administrators in designing effective learning programs for students.

These curricular choices illustrate what we explore more fully in Chapters 8 and 9, namely, that programming in education continues to differentiate. Beyond alternative programs in K–12 public schools, there has also been recent growth in both home-schooling and private (or independent) schools. It would be easy to exaggerate the size of these schooling alternatives, but they have continually grown over the past few decades.

But the emerging alternative with arguably the most potential to radically alter the face of schooling comes from new online providers in higher education. For about 15 years, higher education has absorbed online provision, and has done so as yet without radically altering its standard practices. On the one hand, virtually all institutions supplement their instruction with online material, and many now offer online courses or "blended" forms of instruction. And, for-profit companies like the University of Phoenix have for 20 years captured a niche in higher education, often appealing to older adult students who already have careers and children. But on the other hand, the impact of this online provision has been limited so far. Our existing colleges and universities have incorporated online delivery without greatly changing their standard practices, and very few fear competition from the for-profit providers. These institutions have not only survived as we know them, but are also growing.

But today, some are proclaiming that a new kind of online higher education could soon challenge our standard institutions in more fundamental ways. In what we dub "Online Higher Ed 2.0," new providers are offering courses to the masses, without any in-person contact between students and instructors, without formal prerequisites or registrations, and in many courses, without any tuition fees. For

Box 4.1 Examples of Alternative Programs in Edmonton, 2016–17

- *Academic Alternative:* provides opportunities for motivated students who have achieved above-average performance.
- *Amiskwaciy Academy:* incorporates Indigenous culture into both the learning and school environments for junior and senior high school students.
- *Arabic Bilingual:* provides opportunities to acquire or maintain proficiency in both Arabic and English, and to obtain knowledge of related cultures.
- *Sports Alternative:* provides students with flexible programming and timetabling to facilitate their participation in sport-specific programs.
- *International Baccalaureate Primary Years:* provides an alternative, for students grades K through 6, that emphasizes the development of the whole person, as well as the inter-relatedness of knowledge and global awareness.
- *LearnNet Programming:* enables students to connect to their courses, learning resources, and online tools.
- *Meadowlark Christian School:* founded on the Christian worldview, teaches students how to live their Christian faith in the context of their local and broader communities.
- *Nellie McClung:* junior high programming for girls, emphasizes leadership, initiative, self-reliance, and independence in a single-gender setting.
- *Traditional:* focuses on traditional values and goals of education and citizenship, direct instruction of basic skills, and continuity of instruction and resources across the grade levels.
- *Victoria School of Performing and Visual Arts:* provides arts-oriented programming that emphasizes the performing and visual arts.

Source: Edmonton Public Schools Programs website, https://www.epsb.ca/schools/findaschool/fast/.

instance, EPIC 2020 (http://epic2020.org) claims that by the year 2020, these new modes of instruction will shatter existing models used by most universities and colleges. Tuition, degrees, and physical classrooms will be relics of the past, they declare. They cite Khan Academy as one example. Khan posts thousands of instructional videos on YouTube for free, has developed a series of chat rooms in which students can post questions, and has created an assessment system that provides instant feedback on learning. Most ominously, Khan and similar providers have abandoned the "degree-for-multiple-credit" model in favour of a system of awarding "badges," in which students get an award for showing competence in very specific skills, such as being able to use a particular kind of computer program or demonstrating facility with a statistical technique. As another example, in 2012 a Stanford professor launched "Udacity," an online instructional system that uses a variety of social media to help students teach difficult online material to each other. Udacity claims it is teaching hundreds of thousands of students using only a small handful of world-renowned "star" professors, each of whom is managing gigantic course enrolments in a solely virtual manner. In 2011 MIT opened "MITX," a stream of open-admission courses that use interactive technology that also claims to enrol hundreds of thousands of students. Several universities, including Canada's University of Alberta, joined "Coursera," a consortium of international universities that has built a similar platform for offering massive open online courses (MOOCs).

The radical challenge posed by these initiatives is, quite simply, efficiency: they claim to have the capacity to absorb incredibly expanded enrolments in an incredibly cheap manner. This comes at a time when some commentators, mostly in the US but some also in Canada, are decrying that higher education now simply costs too much in light of the small premium many degrees fetch in the job market. They warn that the higher education "bubble" is ready to burst, just like in an over-inflated housing market (for examples, see the essays posted at http://www.aei.org/publication/blog/higher-education/). Will these new innovations radically overhaul higher education as we know it, just as they boast? Certainly we need some healthy skepticism when hearing such audacious claims. One could reply that we've heard it all before. Prophets of new technologies have proclaimed the near extinction of traditional, face-to-face instruction since the invention of television. Claims that the higher education bubble is about to burst go back at least to the 1970s, when a famous Harvard economist wrote *The Over-Educated American* (Freeman, 1976). Another reply is that these new initiatives will greatly affect one sector of higher education, but not others. The kinds of course material offered by Udacity and Coursera are almost entirely technological in substance, dealing with computer science, statistics, and mechanics, but having very little to do with humanities, social sciences, natural sciences, and business—which have far larger enrolments in most universities. Perhaps those sectors will see some of their expansion channelled into these new forms, but other sectors may see their traditional forms survive.

Exporting the School Model

As a final example of the rise of our "schooled society," we briefly sketch a fascinating trend: the exporting of "school forms" to other social institutions. We offer greater detail in Chapter 13 but foreshadow our ideas here to illustrate how pervasive education, in all its forms, has become in our society.

A major trend in contemporary criminal justice has been the increasing use of diversion programs. For non-violent crimes, many justice officials now deem traditional penalties like incarceration and fines to be overly costly, inhumane, harsh, and even counterproductive. Research suggests that criminal penalties do not always serve as strong deterrents, and hence recidivism rates are relatively high. This has led to some reform movements, called in some places "restorative justice."

If you want wrongdoers to desist, so the reasoning goes, perhaps it is better to *educate* them about their toxic acts rather than merely punish them. Using this reasoning, recent years have witnessed great changes in criminal justice with the rising use of *diversion* programs. The rationale is that processing non-violent offenders, particularly youth, through the criminal justice system can be counterproductive. Diversion programs usually take the form of substituting penalties for some other program, such as treatment, community service, and—our interest—education. Many diversion programs now embrace a "school form." That is, their overt aim is to *educate* offenders through the use of instructors, curricula, and various school-like techniques. "Schools" are being used as an alternative to criminal sentencing for a variety of offences, including drinking and driving, drug use, harassment, shoplifting, and physical battery—the latter handled through "anger-management schools."

School forms are increasingly embraced elsewhere as well. Family life is now increasingly informed by parenting classes that cover, among other topics, child-birth procedures, toy safety, sibling management, financial investing for your child, and efficient management of family time. New conceptions of childhood combined with changing family practices push the schooling model downward into early childhood education and daycare. Leisure is being altered by the availability of courses in all areas of recreation, from learning how to play bridge to learning how to cycle around Europe. Corporations are increasingly turning to school-like forms to handle their training and apprenticeship needs—as witnessed in interesting ways by the explicit "campus" layouts of places like Microsoft and Sun Microsystems, and by "universities" created by General Motors, Dunkin' Donuts, and McDonald's. We return to this theme in Chapter 13.

Conclusion

This chapter has presented a series of interconnected themes. As modern schooling has grown, it has emerged as the lone institutional provider of a common experience for almost the entire populace. It does this in a form that is increasingly standardized, rationalized, and expanded. More and more aspects of social life are falling under the embrace of formal schooling, as it creates new curricula, assumes ever-more social functions, and gets exported to other institutions. More of our individual biographies are shaped by schooling of different sorts. We increasingly imagine our life histories as a series of educational completions—finishing high school, graduating with a diploma or degree, and so forth.

Furthermore, as schooling expands, the range of options *among* school types has grown considerably, from preschool, to diversifying high school alternatives, to an exponentially expanding range of post-secondary programs, and to a growing field of adult education and training options. All of this educational choice has had a net result: the "student" role has been gradually disconnected from the "child" role. Being a student is no longer age-specific. Whereas most "students" a century ago were aged seven to 16, people from almost all ages are now in school in a variety of capacities. Schooling is everywhere and it is increasingly done by everyone, at any place, at any pace, and at any time.

But with this expansion has come a new, more complicated connection between school and inequality. Coincident with post-secondary expansion, income and wealth inequality has worsened. The former represents a continuation of mid-twentieth-century trends; the latter represents a startling reversal. In the next chapter we build on our discussion of expansion by examining the structural transformation of schooling, focusing on new ways that schools are *accommodating* as many different types of students as possible, coupled with the growing *competitiveness* of some sectors of education. These are combining in many ways to make school provisions more *stratified* than in previous decades.

Questions for Critical Thought

1. Search the Internet for the course catalogue of a nearby community college. Then find a course catalogue in English from another country, such as Singapore, Hong Kong, or Dubai. Give examples of course programs that illustrate the arguments of this chapter. Do these compare well across countries?

2. Has post-secondary schooling expanded too much in recent decades? Or has it not expanded enough? Compare and contrast possible answers using perspectives from human capital theory, cultural capital theory, credentialist theory, and institutional theory.

3. Imagine that you are lobbying your provincial government to fund full-day, year-round universal preschool. Design an appeal that draws on human capital theory. Then design one that draws on Marxism; then feminism. Which appeal do you think stands the best chance of succeeding? Why?

Suggested Readings

Coates, Ken, and Bill Morrison. 2011. *Campus Confidential: 100 Startling Things You Don't Know about Canadian Universities*. Toronto: James Lorimer & Company. A Canadian university administrator offers an argument somewhat similar to Professor X (see below).

Cummings, William. 2003. *The Institutions of Education: A Comparative Study of Educational Development in the Six Core Nations*. Oxford: Symposium Books, Oxford Studies in Comparative Education. This is a bold attempt to theorize about the modernization of education using a comparative approach.

Gidney, R.D., and W.P.J. Millar. 2012. *How Schools Worked: Public Education in English Canada, 1900–1940*. Montreal and Kingston: McGill-Queen's University Press. Two of Canada's top educational historians map the contours of public school in the inter-war years of the twentieth century, examining its values, organization, and challenges.

Professor X. 2012. *In the Basement of the Ivory Tower: The Truth about College*. London: Penguin. An anonymous adjunct teacher in two US colleges takes a jaded look at the underbelly of credential inflation.

Wolf, Alison. 2002. *Does Education Matter? Myths about Education and Economic Growth*. New York: Penguin. This is a witty and skeptical examination of the expansion of British higher education.

Web Links

Edmonton Public Schools—Program Choices
http://districtsite.epsb.ca/root/index.cfm
For the Edmonton School Board, this link provides a taste of the variability in the school programs available.

Education Indicators in Canada
www.statcan.gc.ca/bsolc/olc-cel/olc-cel?catno=81-582-X&CHROPG=1&lang=eng
This regularly updated Statistics Canada website provides a wealth of indicators on the state of education in Canada.

Udacity
www.udacity.com
The home of a online provider that claims to offer a totally new learning experience, one in which students solve challenging problems and pursue "udacious" projects with world-renowned university instructors, not by watching "long, boring" lectures, but by putting students "at the center of the universe."

Coursera
www.coursera.org
The home of a publicly funded provider that is similar to Udacity.

5 The Structural Transformation of Schooling
Accommodation, Competition, and Stratification

||||||||||||||||||||||||||||||||||||||||||||||||||||||||||||||||||||||||||||||||||||||||||||||||||||||||||||||||||||||||||||||||||||||||

Learning Objectives

- To think structurally about the broad organization of school systems
- To compare changes in Canadian schooling to those in other nations, and understand why these changes are occurring
- To identify aspects of school organization that accommodate, stratify, or create competition among students

||||||||||||||||||||||||||||||||||||||||||||||||||||||||||||||||||||||||||||||||||||||||||||||||||||||||||||||||||||||||||||||||||||||||

Introduction

The previous chapter documented the expansion of schooling over the twentieth century. Before the Second World War, secondary schools prepared only tiny elites for university. But the past half-century has brought a sea of change, generating an almost tsunami-like expansion of post-secondary offerings. Thinking economically, policy-makers now regard upper-tier schooling as not only suitable but *necessary* for larger and larger numbers of people. Today's "knowledge economy" is said to demand skills that can be acquired only in post-secondary education. Thinking politically, more educators believe strongly in the rights of all children to attend inclusive schools, regardless of creed, colour, class, faith, or personal capacity. Thinking socially, more youth see that schooling will probably exert a strong impact on their eventual income, quality of job, and life chances. In tandem, these beliefs have triggered a "revolution of expectations" for higher education across Canada.

What impact has expansion had on the structure of school systems? This chapter begins by examining established forms of stratification in Canadian education over the past half-century. Comparing Canada to Europe and the United States, we describe **streaming** at secondary levels and differences among institutions and fields of study at the post-secondary level. We then argue that these structures are undergoing three transformations. First, pressured by egalitarian impulses, schools are accommodating more and more students, diversifying their offerings, and greatly expanding their range of programs, courses, and services. Second, pressured by selection impulses, segments of education that are able to generate the most demand are also becoming more competitive. Third, these crosscutting pressures are changing the form of stratification in Canadian education. While K–12 schools have long sorted students for different futures, that selection process is slowly moving upwards such that now higher education is doing more sorting.

Thinking Structurally: Established Stratification

The "common school" ideal (see Chapter 4) helped to organize and fund schools to be open and accessible. However, the "consumers" of education—students and their families—also influenced the education system, particularly when they sought advantages over others, or sought to preserve traditional social roles. These consumers have at times undermined the best laid plans of education policy-makers (see Labaree, 2010). Rhetoric often papered over uncommon experiences. The vast majority of girls and boys were indeed encouraged to attend schooling in the late 1800s and early 1900s. But sometimes, as seen in the first photograph in Figure 4.1 (Chapter 4), girls and boys were often segregated (and many older school buildings still have the separate entrances). And, many First Nations students attended residential schools. Some educational historians take issue with these images, arguing that girls and boys were mostly schooled together (Gidney and Millar, 2012), reminding us that many First Nations students did not attend residential schools, noting that in these schools many attendees were indeed non-native (Clifton, 2015). But nonetheless while access was promoted, advantages were not evenly distributed. Many girls and most First Nations children were channelled into limited education routes, and the effects of social class cut strongly across gender and ethnic categories.

Canadian high schools have for many years been organized as shown in Figure 5.1. Students are streamed. Streaming consists of splitting students into ability groups, and channelling these groups into an upper stream bound for post-secondary schooling and lower tiers offering vocational training. Our figure depicts three levels—the academic and vocational split (level "A"), the subject or field split (level "B"), and then what we call the placement or program split (level "C"). Curricula differ significantly between these streams. Students in upper tiers are exposed to advanced mathematics and acclaimed literary works, while those in lower tiers focus on the rudiments of literacy, numeracy, and practical workplace skills. These streams serve as institutional mechanisms that shape students' post-secondary options and eventual labour market opportunities. Most students reading this book will have navigated the upper tier; those in lower tiers have little chance of taking the courses necessary for direct entry to university.

How much streaming should exist? The number of streams and their permeability is a major policy issue. Some educators want to abandon this stratification, arguing that any form of streaming serves to stigmatize some students and reduce their aspirations (e.g., Clanfield and Martell, 2014). Others believe that streaming is necessary for students with modest academic abilities, and call for a simple sorting of students into academic or vocational streams, with the latter emerging only

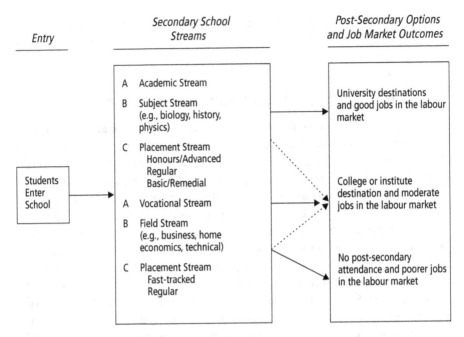

Figure 5.1 A Simplified Model of Streaming

in the final grades in secondary schools. Still others want to increasingly stratify high schools to benefit ambitious students, by creating programs like Advanced Placement, French immersion, and International Baccalaureate.

How did "common" schools become streamed? By and large, dominant families undermined the egalitarian rhetoric of early public schools by striving to protect their advantages. Most parents wanted their boys to become breadwinners. Most importantly, the middle classes wanted to provide superior opportunities for their offspring. Their lobbying efforts made school formally accessible to all, but also internally differentiated, giving some routes (i.e., streams) better opportunities than did others. Thus, ever since such data were amassed, youth from less advantaged backgrounds have been greatly over-represented in lower streams (e.g., those leading to less rewarding jobs) and under-represented in upper streams (Porter et al., 1982; Pike, 1970; Anisef et al., 2000). These patterns have largely remained stable (Krahn, 2017), not only in Canada, but also in the United States (Duncan and Murnane, 2011) and many other countries (Chmielewski, 2015).

We depict this in Figure 5.2. Students from wealthier and more advantaged family backgrounds tend to enter academic programs, which foster better higher education and labour market outcomes. Conversely, students from poorer and more disadvantaged families tend to enter vocational programs, which on average have humbler post-secondary paths and labour market outcomes. Note the correspondence between family background and stream is far from perfect—many students from poorer families enter academic streams and vice versa, but their probability

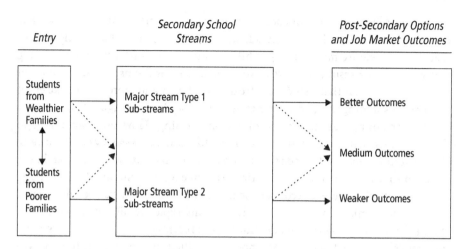

Figure 5.2 Different Entry Patterns into Secondary School Streams

of doing so is much less than for those from wealthier backgrounds (recall this argument from Bowles and Gintis in Chapter 3; a more recent illustration of this phenomena from Sweden is presented by Hällsten [2011]).

Modern schools eventually resembled "social selection machines." Based on a belief that not all students can benefit from the same curriculum, they channelled students into different types of schools and programs, assigning different badges of ability. Certain schools and programs were better or worse at providing opportunities for advanced education or for more exclusive jobs. Over time, the impact of school attainment on life chances grew stronger due to streaming (also known as "tracking" in the US; e.g., Baer, 2004).

Streaming is also controversial because of its potential impact on learning. Think of a hypothetical research project that compared the effects of school, streams, and student background on learning. If all students in a city were given a standard writing assignment, the quality of the compositions would surely vary, but would they vary more by students' school, their stream within a school, or by their family backgrounds and personal abilities? One of the consistently replicated, but counterintuitive, findings in the sociology of education is that differences between schools are minimal, and small relative to stream and individual background effects. There are two main reasons for this. First, most school structures, curricula, and teaching methods are similar. The 3,400 secondary schools in Canada do not differ greatly in their educational practices. As a result, school effects are not very big. Second, schools do differ markedly along social class and ethnic lines because they are located in different neighbourhoods. So, performance on the writing assignment would largely reflect student backgrounds, not school practices, as illustrated in Willms's (2004) study of student literary skills in Canada. Third, individuals differ from one another in their ability to write. This variation partly stems from family socio-economic status, ethnic background, gender, and mental ability, but even within any of these categories, there is a large amount of variation.

Streams, however, do impact students' writing performance because they shape opportunities for learning. Academic streams offer more challenging literary material and require more writing, while vocational streams demand less reading and writing. As a result, students in vocational streams are usually less proficient writers. Our point is that a student's stream has a larger and more immediate effect on her or his writing than does their wider school setting (see Figure 5.3).

So, streaming has important effects on learning. How does streaming in Canada compare internationally? In contrast to many European systems (Britain, France, and Germany), Canada's system has been relatively open (see Kerckhoff, 2002). European countries have historically channelled students at relatively young ages into entirely different secondary schools. These schools have been designated as either academic or vocational. These systems typically allocated students to these schools using major national exams. Until recently, this streaming was rigid; once students entered one type of school, few shifted to another. For those in vocational schools, opportunities for advancing to universities were essentially nil. If a British, French, or Japanese student failed an examination at age 15 or 16, he or she was effectively eliminated from further higher education. Standardized exams became watershed events in a young person's life. For instance, Britain's notorious "11-plus" exam sent a few high-scoring children at age 11 to elite "grammar" schools to prepare for university. The remainder mostly went to "comprehensive secondary" schools, which many promptly left at the legal minimum of age 16. In Germany, students are sorted into one of three types of schools, again differentiated by whether they prepare students for university or vocational careers (Lehmann, 2000, 2007). The demanding secondary school-leaving examination, the "Abitur," serves as a barrier for entry into university slots.

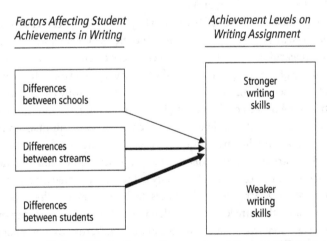

Figure 5.3 Impact of School Effects, Stream Placement, and Student Differences in Writing Achievement

Note: Arrow thickness depicts the biggest effect on writing achievement coming from individual student differences (e.g., family background, gender), followed by the stream students are in within a school, followed by the school in which they are enrolled.

Differences in Achievements on Standard Writing Assignment

These different systems ensured that, until recently, a far greater proportion of youth entered Canadian universities than did their European counterparts. Europe's legacy of a prestigious aristocratic culture encouraged its schools to emphasize traditional arts and science, classic literature, and philosophy, and to prepare elites, and filter the fortunate few using rigorous examinations. Thus, until recently it was inconceivable for French secondary students, for instance, to study electives such as business, accounting, or typing, or to have massive numbers of students enter higher education.

Canadian schools have been organized differently. Culturally, they have de-emphasized the cultivation of a high tradition, given our lack of an entrenched aristocracy. Canadian schools have instead largely promoted "practical" curricula and have not equated "excellence" and "quality" with high culture. Structurally, the Canadian system was not built to sharply designate a "gifted" minority from the rest via separate "streamed" schools (though trade schools were an exception; see Montt, 2011 for a cross-national comparison of how school organization influences student achievement). Thus, the Canadian system bears the imprint of the common school ethos, even though much inequality managed to emerge within that system. Partly for these reasons, many North American scholars have revised Bourdieu's ideas about cultural capital (see Chapters 3 and 9).

Virtually all Canadian secondary schools offer the same general credential—the high school diploma—regardless of stream. Most of our high school students encounter the same broad academic curriculum and emerge with the same credential. In an "all or nothing" contest, they can get one kind of credential—the diploma—or nothing at all. This homogeneity reflects the lack of direct job content in Canadian secondary school curricula. A diploma provides no guarantee about any particular skill for any specific job. It lacks vocational meaning. Canadian secondary schools channel many students to post-secondary levels, but prepare few for specific jobs.

Box 5.1 Linking National Traditions of Youth to School Structures

Chapter 1 discussed the role that schooling plays in the formation of youth subcultures. But as Brint (2017) argues, those subcultures vary across countries. Different nations nurture their own "traditions" of youth culture through their unique sets of educational demands and opportunities. For instance, in comparative perspective North American high schools are not particularly demanding, at least on youth who do not aspire to enter elite institutions in higher education. With less streaming in high schools, larger numbers of graduates, and larger proportions of post-secondary entrants, the Canadian education system serves to delay career choices for many

continued

youth to their twenties. By doing so, young people have the space to nurture their own autonomous cultures and social spheres, and to see their future as open-ended, even though many have restricted social possibilities.

Until recently, youth in many other nations faced different circumstances. For instance, Germany's tripartite school divisions make students "grow up" faster. At the lower end, apprenticeship programs make schooling more job-like. Similarly, high school performance matters more for later life success in Japan. Japanese youth wishing to enter prestigious universities and fields of study face a more intense secondary experience. Their scores on standardized tests determine admission to clearly ranked universities and fields, which in turn ultimately determine eligibility for desirable jobs. As a result, Japan's institutions pile greater pressure on its youth. Secondary classes are characterized by demanding, fact-laden drills. Most youth attend tutoring classes after school, and even on Saturdays, called *juku* (see Dierkes, 2013). Some claim these high-stake pressures and its institutionalized stress are responsible for the remarkable incidence of suicide among Japanese teens.

Britain's previous system of rigid streaming created polarized youth cultures. The chosen few who went to university shared a sense of entitlement, cultivation, and superiority. Elite schools, fed by the 11-plus exam, had an upper-class ambience, as did ancient universities like Oxford and Cambridge. In contrast, the majority of working-class youth faced a far more restricted set of educational opportunities, which nurtured a fatalistic class consciousness among them, and, in some cases, thriving anti-school subcultures (see Willis, 1977). With little chance of attending post-secondary institutions, the later years of secondary schooling seemed quite irrelevant to youth, many of whom wished only to leave school at the earliest possible age. They saw little to justify schools' discipline codes, uniforms, and expected deference to teachers. Our point is that national differences in the organization of schooling can shape students' cultural expressions, perceptions of status boundaries, willingness to exert intense effort, and senses of what is possible in life.

To understand international differences, Turner (1960) compared how nations structure educational competition. He saw the European model as offering "sponsored mobility:" a relative few (who were mostly already privileged) were selected early in their lives to enter an elite stream that ultimately led to university. In contrast, he characterized North America as offering "contest mobility": a majority was exposed to the same academic curriculum that graduated larger numbers to higher education. European systems were highly stratified by rigid tracking and restricted access to higher education, while North American systems had more unitary structures, flexible and limited streaming, and wider and more open competition to access higher education.

Figure 5.4 shows the consequence of these different policies. The white bars show that for people aged 25–64, just over 55 per cent of Canadian residents and about 45 per cent of US residents had a post-secondary diploma or degree in 2012. These were higher than the Organisation for Economic Co-operation and

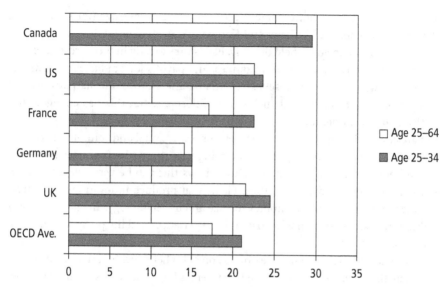

Figure 5.4 Percentage of Age Group Having a Post-Secondary Credential by Country, 2012
Source: Education at a Glance 2016: OECD Indicators (http://www.oecd.org)

Development (OECD) average (35 per cent) and the examples of France, Germany, and the United Kingdom. The dark bars focus more narrowly on the 25- to 34-year-old age group. Notice that France, the United Kingdom, and the OECD average are all accelerating relative to Canada. In contrast, the German system has not changed as quickly, although now growth is occurring there as well. We will discuss these changes later in this chapter. In the meantime, we next discuss stratification in higher education.

Stratification within Post-Secondary Education

Higher education is stratified along two main dimensions: selectivity or prestige of institution and field of study (Davies and Guppy, 1997; Gerber and Cheung, 2008). For centuries, elite universities around the world have provided their graduates with access to elite jobs, higher wages, contacts, and other advantages. Ancient universities in Europe such as Cambridge, Oxford, and the Sorbonne exemplify this elite nature.

The "Ivy League" (e.g., Harvard, Yale, and Princeton) and other major private universities (e.g., Stanford and Duke) have long had the grandest reputations in the United States. Next are large public state "flagship" universities (e.g., University of Texas), followed by several thousand smaller colleges and universities. At the bottom are two-year community, or junior, colleges.

In Canada, universities are not as strictly hierarchical although they demand greater entrance requirements than do community colleges, and are usually seen to be more academically intensive. Community colleges are mandated to serve job market niches that are both viable yet less lucrative on average (for Canada: see Dennison, 1995; for the US: Brint and Karabel, 1989; Dougherty, 2002).

The other dimension is field of study. Fields vary greatly in their prestige, exclusivity of their entrants, access to resources, and payoffs for graduates. Traditional hierarchies were based on closeness to aristocratic culture and its patrons, and brought prestige to humanistic fields like philosophy. But this has changed dramatically in recent decades. Today, status is increasingly flowing to fields of study that are closely linked to lucrative markets for professional and commercial careers in medicine, law, engineering, and increasingly, business. Their greater monetary return boosts their student demand, and allows them to be very selective in admissions (Frenette and Frank, 2016). Fields that produce innovations with great commercial potential, like computer science and biotechnology, are gaining power within universities. Thus, fields vary in the experiences and life prospects they can offer to students.

In some national systems, one dimension of higher education stratification can dominate the other. For instance, the US system is huge and diverse. It mixes an old private sector with a newer public sector, generalist universities with specialized institutions, including small, elite liberal arts colleges, state flagships, historically black universities, institutes of technology, and for-profit universities. But beyond its sheer size and variety, the US system is distinguished by its steep and entrenched prestige hierarchy. Movement up or down the top rungs is uncommon. Elite colleges and universities select among an increasingly exclusive national and international pool of applicants. This system encourages a greater number of American students to travel across the country for their undergraduate education, and persuades many US employers to value the "name brand" of elite institutions.

Canadian higher education is different. It lacks not only a notable private sector, but also a steep prestige hierarchy. Our system is comprised of mostly generalist public universities that, for the past half-century, have been formally recognized and funded as equals. The Canadian upper class has historically opted to send their children to high-status British and American institutions, and this has likely muted any demand to establish an elite Canadian university. Canada's flatter prestige ladder confers much less advantage to any particular university. These conditions have served to mute Canada's national market for undergraduate credentials; most applications for Canadian universities are at the local level, consisting largely of commuters. Only small numbers of undergraduates cross provincial borders, even for relatively prestigious universities like Toronto, McGill, and British Columbia.

These national differences are expressed in tuition fee and student expenditure patterns. Canadian provinces mostly strive to maintain parity across universities. Outside of Quebec, most Canadian universities charge about $6,000 for standard full-time tuition. US fees are typically much higher and vary more widely. Highly ranked private institutions will charge tens of thousands of dollars more than lower-ranked state institutions—room and board expenses not included. American institutions also vary far more in their operating expenditures and endowments

(Davies and Zarifa, 2012). Harvard's endowment of $36 billion (USD) in 2015 was 18 times larger than Canada's largest—the University of Toronto's $2.1 billion (CDN). But while Canadian institutions are less steeply stratified by selectivity, prestige, and wealth, their stratification across fields of study is similar to the American system. We return to these issues in a later section, and turn next to processes that are transforming the fundamental structure of schooling.

Accommodation

> *"It's a big job to make up a curriculum that everybody can do."*
>
> (Powell et al., 1985)

Over the course of the twentieth century, Canadian schools were mandated to teach a widening spectrum of youth. Teachers of yesteryear may have encouraged youth who seemed "different" or "indifferent" to drop out of school. But such thinking has been increasingly frowned upon since the late 1960s. The public, its elected politicians, and education bureaucrats now expect schools to retain as many youth for as long as possible. This mandate rests on two pillars.

One pillar is a pervasive understanding of the economic utility of schooling. For several decades human capital theorists have urged policy-makers to recognize schooling's role in the production of marketable skills, as discussed in Chapter 3. But that rationale has been resized for a new age. In the once-dominant image, schools were expected only to graduate a limited number of educated people because the economy was seen to be largely static. Human capital was deemed a waste in many sectors of that economy. But in the new image, schools are to produce greater numbers of graduates for an ever-changing economy. Human capital is now seen to possess a transformative power that can unleash an unbridled expansion of economic potential. This image is driving a slow evolution from "mass" to "universal" post-secondary systems. Policy-makers are calling for universities and colleges to enrol greater numbers of more diverse students to fuel the emerging knowledge economy (Ross, 2016).

The second pillar is a robust notion of educational equity. Since the Second World War, global norms have declared schooling to be a *human right*, needed to cultivate all sorts of human capacities, not only economic ones. In this world view, more children are capable of benefitting from schooling, regardless of their social origins or individual capacities. It downplays instrumental concerns in favour of calls for holistic education that is tailored to all learners. Virtually everyone is understood to be "educable," within "pedagogical reach," and deserving of academic instruction (Richardson, 2006). If prior to the Second World War the paradigm was "sink or swim," the new mantra is "success for all." And it has a new benchmark: virtually everyone ought to complete high school. Schools are being urged to respond to the unique needs of all categories of students, including sexual and religious minorities, and those with mental health challenges. Any lack of success of students in these categories is announced as a vital social problem in need of remedy.

Thus, in the public mind, contemporary schooling plays multiple roles: as a mainstay of societal development and indefinite economic growth, as a core enhancer of human potential, and as a rightful entitlement for all. These deep and pervasive norms raise a key question: what is their impact on the structure of education? We next examine the trend of greater diversity in school offerings.

How to Indigenize Public Education?

The Truth and Reconciliation Committee has urged educators across Canada to find ways to "Indigenize" their pedagogy, teaching, curricula, and school organization. This imperative is most pressing yet also quite ambiguous.

Indigenous peoples, unlike other ethnic, racial, linguistic, and religious minorities, claim sovereignty under both Canadian and international law. Our courts have repeatedly decreed their legal rights to partial autonomy and self-governance over certain territories and institutions, entitling them to nation-to-nation negotiation over funding and policy. So, sovereignty underlies the current politics of Indigenous education. But that education has two branches: reserve schools run by First Nations and overseen by the federal government, and provincially governed public schools. Each type has a different rationale. The former aims to simultaneously preserve native languages, repair local cultures, develop local economies, and ensure some measure of political autonomy. Finding ways to further Indigenize those schools are the responsibility of First Nations, who are by far the most knowledgeable authorities on their own traditions and needs.

But provincial public schools, attended by about 80 per cent of children who self-identify as Indigenous, are mandated to promote a diverse and inclusive image of Canadian nationhood, not a singular identity. So what exactly might it mean to "Indigenize" public schools in which the vast majority of teachers and pupils are not themselves Indigenous? What concretely might that entail?

The most direct answer is: no one knows for sure. Most educators share the goals of respecting Indigenous traditions, healing the cultural wounds inflicted by the residential school experience, and making schools more inclusive for Indigenous children. But any pursuit of those goals faces two key challenges. First, there is no singular Indigenous culture. Canada's original inhabitants lived across a great territory that stretched from sea to sea to sea, with many different nations and languages, religions, symbolism, and customs. To deal with this diversity, Indigenous educators are being asked to help mould school reforms, ensuring they do not gloss over important differences, and are sensitive to local traditions. Second, there are relatively few support systems to train Indigenous teachers and provide them with tools to design curriculum that is culturally appropriate, effective, and delivered in meaningful ways. This challenge is exacerbated by the relatively low numbers of Indigenous students in universities who are eligible to become teachers.

So, public school educators and students are being asked to each interpret "Indigenization" in their own ways, being mindful of the goals of truth and reconciliation. What common interpretations are emerging?

Some K–12 schools, colleges, and universities are actively recruiting First Nations students, teachers, and faculty in order to give themselves a stronger Indigenous presence. Others are creating new partnerships with First Nations in nearby areas, forging new cooperative links between those nations and schools. Still others are creating a new symbolism, one that mixes contemporary themes of multiculturalism and diversity with generic images of Indigeneity, which is sometimes presented as promoting more cooperative and less competitive relations among students. And finally, others, especially in universities, see Indigeneity as linked with a variety of post-colonial movements in various parts of the world. It remains to be seen if any of these forms of indigenization are having their intended impact.

From Factories to Shopping Malls to Accountability

One of the most poignant criticisms of modern schools is that they are overly bureaucratic, inhumane, and indifferent to the needs of students. This critical viewpoint has diverse origins, but the version that emerged in the 1960s and 1970s faulted schools for sacrificing youth's authentic development in favour of preparing them for post-secondary studies or the job market. These critics commonly portrayed schools as resembling nineteenth-century industrial factories more than contemporary human service organizations. The reasoning went something like this.

To adapt to the twentieth-century mandate of expansion, school authorities turned away from local forms of governance, and embraced instead more bureaucratic models. They interpreted the new mission to provide universal schooling as one in which they should serve all students a broadly comparable education. To ensure that everyone obtained a roughly similar experience, they worked to standardize schools' physical plants, teacher training, pedagogy, and curricula. To manage enrolment expansion, they organized schools into hierarchies of authority, starting from classroom teachers, extending through to the school principal, further upward to school boards, and ending with provincial departments or ministries of education.

Critics dubbed this the "one-best system" model of schooling (e.g., Tyack, 1974). This somewhat derisive label focused on how modern schools served up a "one-size-fits-all" style of education in a factory-like manner. Students were treated as anonymous and undifferentiated "inputs." Once in school, they were "processed" by curricula, pedagogy, and rules. By the end of the process, they had become "outputs" possessing cookie-cutter credentials. Critics implied that these highly bureaucratic schools were indifferent to the idiosyncratic needs of individual students.

This criticism informed a team of researchers who studied California schools in the mid-1980s (Powell et al., 1985). After visiting many schools, these researchers came to a quite opposite conclusion: rather than being like factories, schools since the late 1960s had become like "shopping malls!" These researchers reported that schools had been transformed into human service organizations, striving to accommodate as many students as possible.

According to their counter-reasoning, modern schools face a big challenge of translating new educational ideals into reality. In earlier eras, high schools could simply get rid of students who were uninterested in academic work and instead preferred jobs. They could regard high failure rates as marks of distinction and quality standards. But now schools were expected to retain the vast bulk of youth, including those with learning disabilities or with little academic ambition. The new motto was "there are no bad students, only bad teachers." Graduation rates became a standard metric to judge the efficacy of schooling, but student failure was now interpreted to indicate that *teachers* were failing. Yet secondary school teachers continued to encounter many youth who found academics neither appealing nor absorbing. They needed to somehow accommodate students who ranged in aptitude, preparedness, ability, and motivation more than those of their predecessors.

According to Powell et al. (ibid.), schools tackled this mission by becoming more "mall-like." They catered to the different needs and wants of students by diversifying their offerings in two ways. They first differentiated curriculum by degree of difficulty in order to retain students who could not handle tough academic material. As a current example of this "vertical" differentiation, math courses in most Canadian provinces are offered in pathways of varying difficulty (e.g., in Manitoba the following courses all provide graduation credit, but only the latter two allow direct entry to university: Accounting 40S, Essential Mathematics 40S, Applied Mathematics 40S, and Pre-Calculus Mathematics 40S). Schools also created "specialty shops" for students with different abilities. These included "gifted" classes for students both at the high and low ends of the ability spectrum, programs for English as a Second Language (ESL), for enrichment (e.g., Advanced Placement), and for specially able or vocational students. Second, schools made the curriculum more "horizontal" by creating new courses in the spirit of student choice. Secondary schools offered more electives, introducing subjects such as business and family studies, and expanded their extracurricular activities (e.g., sports teams, clubs) to unprecedented levels, aiming to entice students to feel part of a school community. Finally, schools offered more services than before to address a wide variety of social, physical, and emotional problems. Educators became sensitized to recognize different kinds of learning styles, as proclaimed by theories of "multiple intelligences" (e.g., Gardner, 1999).

The transition from factory to shopping mall also occurred in a more literal fashion. In the 1950s to the 1980s courses on woodworking, auto mechanics, sewing, and cooking were available in more Canadian schools than is now the case, both in middle schools (junior high schools) and high schools. These courses were expensive. Instruction was often in smaller groups that needed costly raw materials (e.g., textiles, auto parts) and machinery (e.g., stoves, sewing machines, lathes). Schools have since shifted much of their vocational orientation from manual, blue-collar skills to those commonly linked with the service economy, such as career and personal planning, management and marketing, and computer networking and digital media (in keeping with the expanded service economy discussed in Chapter 1).

Powell et al. (1985) concluded that these accommodations had a negative impact on academic standards. While they did not consider standards to have been lowered across the board, they saw these accommodations as encouraging a more "neutral" stance towards academic quality. The authors believed that previous secondary schools once championed academic effort for all, but the shopping-mall high school was demanding for only the most ambitious. Students aspiring to a more enriched curriculum could still find it. But expectations for others were eased. Low achievers could now pass from grade to grade by doing little more than attending in an orderly fashion. Modern high schools had evolved unwritten rules about the expected difficulty of certain courses. Informal "classroom treaties" and "effort bargains" unofficially designated some courses, particularly electives, to be easier, while others like advanced physics could still demand much effort and time-consuming preparation. Those teaching electives could face rebellion from students, parents, and even administrators if they dared to expect anything comparable. Why? The purpose of electives was to accommodate students, not to promote academic rigour and excellence (see also Sizer's [2004] "conspiracy of the least"). Many Canadian schools moved away from standardized provincial exams such as mandatory Grade 12 exams, and others like BC combine required and optional graduating exams.

Overall, this "mall-like" process successfully diversified school offerings while accommodating an ever-widening variety of "customers," but for Powell et al., these noble efforts also created new problems of quality and equity. New electives tended to be popular only by not being onerous, and expectations for many students were not high. One could argue that the vertical and horizontal diversification of the curriculum effectively reintroduced streaming into schools, even if more students could actively choose their own paths via course selections, rather than being explicitly assigned to tracks.

The Shopping Mall High School was written in the mid-1980s when schools were reducing requirements and offering more choice. But over the past four decades, the pendulum has swung back to make schools less mall-like in some important ways. The old emphasis on accommodating students is being blended with new concerns to ensure standards and accountability. In later chapters we discuss new accountability regimes in detail. We next examine how pressures to make schools more accommodating are being matched by those that are making some more competitive than ever.

Competition: Maintaining Inequality?

As discussed in Chapters 3 and 4, more kinds of jobs are requiring post-secondary credentials, including those that did not traditionally demand college diplomas or university degrees. Higher education is thus supplying workers for a larger portion of the job force than ever. Rising credential requirements encourage more families to view schooling as a competitive arena for getting ahead, and that in turn is triggering an unprecedented number of post-secondary applicants. But this enrolment expansion also fosters structural differentiation. Universities and colleges come to sort students for vastly different occupational and social opportunities. Greater numbers of credentialed fields make career destinations become increasingly variable. Some enter well-paying professional and executive positions, but others enter lesser-paying sectors. This differentiation sparks new pressures.

Sociologists reckon that as access to a certain tier of education widens, advantaged groups then pursue the next tier. For instance, high school graduation was a relatively rare achievement a century ago, and later, secondary levels were dominated by youth from middle- and upper-class families. But by the late twentieth century, youth from virtually all classes were earning high school diplomas. This universal access prompted large numbers from the upper and middle classes to head to post-secondary levels. And, now that post-secondary education has become popular across all classes, advantaged youth are increasingly seeking graduate and professional degrees. This vertical process of upward credential seeking has been dubbed "maximally maintained inequality" (or MMI; see Raftery and Hout, 1993).

MMI is also accompanied by a more "horizontal" process. In what has been dubbed "effectively maintained inequality" (or EMI; see Lucas, 2001), advantaged groups also tend to migrate to the more resourced, selective, or prestigious segments of any level of education. The premise of EMI is that educational organizations within any tier are often stratified by resources and prestige. Well-positioned schools, institutions, fields of study, and programs can confer to their graduates more social recognition, cognitive resources, and/or labour market advantages than can other entities. When this stratification congeals to a certain level, higher education institutions and fields can form a hierarchy. Clearly arrayed hierarchies encourage students to jockey for the most favourable positions.

The mechanisms of EMI and MMI explain a paradoxical effect of educational expansion. On the one hand, expansion has opened an unprecedented volume of student places for an unprecedented number of youth. But on the other hand, it has not meaningfully reduced SES (socio-economic status) inequalities in educational attainment. A large international literature shows that in most nations, links between socio-economic origins and access to higher education have remained largely constant (Shavit, Arum, and Gamoran, 2007; Walters et al., 2004; Wanner, 1999; Goldthorpe and Jackson, 2008). Despite decades of expansion, youth from affluent origins still tend to occupy the most advantageous segments of schooling.

EMI also highlights the uneven demand for higher education. Some programs and institutions attract a far larger volume of applicants than others. This unevenness generates competition for the most desired spots, particularly when high-demand programs become more exclusive and raise their tuition fees and/or admission standards. Lower-demand segments, often "second choices" for many students, sometimes react by becoming more accommodating. For instance, conditions may have polarized across different segments of American higher education in recent decades. The top-most colleges and universities have steadily raised their admission standards, and the most academically prolific students are concentrating themselves in those institutions. In contrast, lower-demand segments have adapted by lowering their admission requirements to attract applicants; some are now even less selective than they were 50 years ago (Hoxby, 2009). Some institutions and fields are rebranding themselves as "launching pads" for a second degree in professional or graduate studies (Collins, 2002; Wolf, 2002; Mullen et al., 2003).

The new competitiveness takes different forms in the United States and Canada. American higher education has shaped a distinctive "race to the top" on a national scale. Many students, particularly those from affluent backgrounds, perceive that choosing the "right" college is a crucial career move (Stevens, 2007). They have fuelled a "college choice industry" of published guides, special admissions workshops, and rankings of universities. The most prestigious universities are raising their admission standards and tuition fees to ever-higher levels while jockeying to lure "star" high school graduates at the same time. This spiralling competition in American higher education is also putting downward pressures on American secondary education. More high school educators feel compelled to deliver academically intensive programs and curricula by developing more diverse program offerings in an array of new school types. This "school choice" can come in the form of **magnet schools** and **charter schools** (both of these specialized schools are designed to attract students by offering unique programs) or can come in the form of specialty courses in calculus or physics. Among aspiring high school students, this competition is encouraging a series of competitive strategies. The push to earn top grades has created a sizeable private tutoring industry. The necessity of scoring well on the SAT—the standardized entrance exam for American colleges and universities—has created a large "test-prep" industry consisting of dozens of books and tutoring agencies that offer cram-courses. The desire for a further competitive edge has encouraged student enrolment in intensive secondary-level programs such as "dual enrolment," "Advanced Placement" (AP), and "International Baccalaureate" (IB) programs (the latter two with high-level curriculum that is globally recognized). And, families wishing help with their competitive tactics can now hire private "admissions management" consultants and advisors.

Many of these activities lack close parallels in Canada. With no equivalent to SATs, college portfolios, or early admissions to prestigious universities, Canadian high school students have less motivation to adopt similar strategies. The practice of ranking colleges, so established in the US, is relatively new to Canada. Further, Canadian secondary systems are much less differentiated. In the entire country there are only a handful of charter schools, all in the provinces of Alberta and British Columbia, and few magnet schools, though some urban school boards are diversifying their offerings. Thus, we see less of an American-style competition for placement in nationally renowned institutions, along with its associated strategies, north of the border.

But competition in Canada may be intensifying. The relatively flat hierarchy of Canadian universities by prestige, resource, and selectivity may mute institutional-level differences and hinder the development of a national market for undergraduate credentials, but it also shifts a greater weight of competition towards fields of study (e.g., computer science, psychology). Fields vary greatly in their volume of applications, admission standards, and payoffs (Walters, 2004). The saliency of fields appears to divert competition from Canada's high schools to its post-secondary institutions. Most Canadian students enter local institutions in general arts and science programs and then compete for entry into lucrative professional fields. While some similar processes occur in American institutions, the Canadian form redirects more pressure to fields of study, given the relatively weak pull of between-institution competition.

Consider Canadian tuition trends. Most provincial governments have allowed tuition for general undergraduate programs to rise substantially over the past 20 years, yet within each province, differences between universities are minimal, often within a few hundred dollars. But several provinces have deregulated fees for high-demand programs such as MBA, law, medicine, dentistry, engineering, and computer science. Some have risen 200 to 600 per cent, creating huge disparities between some professional programs and general arts programs. For instance, annual fees for undergraduate engineering at the University of Toronto were $14,330 for 2015, compared to the arts and science average of about $6,100. Tuition also varies between general BA versus professional fields within American universities, but that range is less than America's between-university range of fees. As advantageous fields of study in Canada set their own standards and tuition fees apart from the rest of the university, striking disparities *within* institutions are emerging.

Canada's form of competition is also illustrated by the practice of "recycling" (Walters et al., 2004). When denied entry into selective programs at well-known universities, many Canadian students transfer to a comparable field at a community college rather than remain in a university general arts program. In addition, many university *graduates* also earn community college diplomas in an effort to boost their job chances. It is estimated that between 10 and 15 per cent of Canadian bachelor's degree holders enrol in community colleges within five years, usually in applied fields like business or computer applications (Butlin, 2001). Note they are competing *not* by seeking a second, "higher" degree, but by earning what some might deem a "lower" credential. Few Harvard or Stanford graduates seek diplomas at their local community college. The "name brand" of a university appears to pay a lesser premium than does a marketable major in the Canadian job market.

Will Canadian universities ever form a hierarchy to parallel that of the United States? Some emerging pressures may steepen the currently flat ladder. A few universities are calling for more explicitly tiered funding that will designate them as "elite" institutions that will be semi-private and research-intensive. Governments may not support that reform in the near future, but market conditions are currently favouring older and larger research-intensive universities (see Guppy, Grabb, and Mollica, 2013). Their advantages—multiple professional schools, a core of wealthy alumni, corporate contacts—allow them to mount generously endowed academic programs, raise their admission requirements, and compete for the top students. Growing pressures on universities and colleges to generate their own revenue, whether through winning large research grants or luring corporate funds and alumni donations, may further stratify the system. And, if older and wealthier institutions are perceived by students and employers to offer a superior education, Canada's relatively mild "pecking order" of higher education institutions may be intensified. Much will pivot on whether students and employers view degrees from some universities as more valuable than others. We see little indication of this on a large scale, but there are signs of potential change. Over the past few decades, resources have been gradually allocated across Canadian universities in a more unequal manner (Davies and Zarifa, 2012). Well-publicized national rankings of Canadian universities continue to appear in major magazines and newspapers. University administrators, increasingly sensitive to their institutions' public image, are devising strategies to move up the ranks. As globalization continues apace, some Canadian universities are defining themselves as "world class" in an effort to differentiate themselves. Admission standards for universities may be widening. Queen's and McGill, for instance, are attracting a disproportionate number of high-achieving students, a trend that may be exacerbated by the shrinking cohort of 18- to 24-year-olds. Universities are increasingly competing to recruit top students from a smaller pool.

Other competitive strategies are emerging at elementary and secondary levels. Within public schools, enrolments in reputable AP and IB programs are growing. Private education is also growing. Larger proportions of Canadian students are enrolled in private schools (Davies and Aurini, 2011), though rates vary widely across provinces. Ontario alone has over 900 private schools (Figure 5.5), a rise of 50 per cent over 20 years. In Toronto, about 9 per cent of all students are enrolled in private schools and 13 per cent of all schools are private. In Quebec, private enrolments have risen substantially (Desjardins, 2009). This growth can be seen among both older and younger students, who are attending private elementary and even preschools in swelling numbers (Aurini and Quirke, 2011). And, another form of private education is growing, one more rarely recognized as such: tutoring businesses. This industry has undergone a staggering transformation. The number of businesses offering full tutoring services has grown 200 to 500 per cent in major Canadian cities over the past 30 years, despite shrinking cohorts of children. In 2007, about one-third of Canadian parents reported hiring tutors for their children (Canadian Council on Learning, 2007; Sweet and Roberts, 2009). Tutoring is expanding beyond traditional college prep for secondary students into elementary and even preschool levels (i.e., "Little Reader" programs), perhaps as a relatively inexpensive option for parents who cannot afford full-time private education. In sum, independent schools and private tutoring are two examples of markets powered by parents seeking to boost their children's school performance. Educational competition is filtering down to younger and younger age groups.

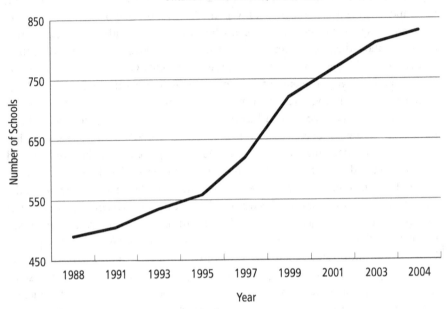

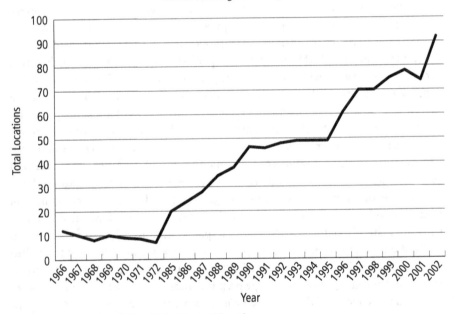

Figure 5.5 Examples of Growth in Private Education

A New Form of Stratification?

What is the full impact of simultaneous expansion, accommodation, and competition on education in Canada and elsewhere? Universities and colleges are expanding around the globe, serving to erode national differences in post-secondary enrolment (see Figure 5.4). Policy-makers everywhere want more young people to continue to post-secondary levels. In Europe, even the ancient, elite universities are slowly opening their doors to more students. Most European higher education systems are being modernized in a "contest mobility" model, dismantling barriers and opening opportunities. In a range of nations, de-streaming movements are encouraging more youth to enter academic programs. Informal streaming still exists, albeit in a less visible guise through course and program selection (Krahn and Taylor, 2007; see also Figure 5.1). But most secondary systems are "de-stratifying." Fewer are attempting to "cool out" youth by dissuading them to aspire to higher education, as they did decades ago. In fact, critics are faulting high schools for promoting a "college for all" ethos and its unrealistic expectations for an "easy" post-secondary workload (Côté and Allahar, 2007, 2011; Arum and Roksa, 2011). But beyond these critics, most policy-makers want high schools to channel more youth into universities and colleges, hoping that this process will ultimately generate wealth and enhance national economic competitiveness. Some youth are still being "cooled out" but, as we argue in the final section of this chapter, this process is increasingly moving to a new location: higher education.

Box 5.2 Is the Ivory Tower Accommodating a Crisis?

Are Canadian universities enrolling unprepared and unmotivated students? Is this situation new? If so, what are they doing about it? In their two influential books, *Ivory Tower Blues* and *Lowering Higher Education* sociologists James Côté and Anton Allahar address these questions by drawing on a variety of data as well as their own teaching experiences. They suggest that 40 per cent of all undergraduates are largely disengaged from their studies, yet many regularly earn As and Bs, despite minimal exertion or skill. In the past, many students may have coasted to a "gentlemen's C," but the authors contend that disengaged students are now more numerous and receive inflated grades for less effort. Administrators, they argue, not only tolerate this situation, but also welcome any student/consumer as long as they are willing to pay much-coveted tuition dollars. A potential crisis of legitimacy and integrity in universities may be looming, Côté and Allahar say.

Their argument has generated controversy. Supporters champion it as a fearless exposé of higher education's "dirty secret." Critics accuse it of exaggerating common problems, romanticizing yesteryear's students, and downplaying the possibility of new instructional methods that might better inspire today's students. While it is unclear whether Canada's universities have lost any legitimacy, Côté and Allahar are detecting

continued

an erosion of liberal ideals in higher education in favour of those oriented towards occupational training. The authors value universities for their capacity to transform students' hearts and minds, broaden their intellectual horizons, and create exemplary citizens, but others value them more for their human capital function, as in business schools or engineering. For a comparative argument regarding the US, see Arum and Roksa (2011).

Conclusion: The Upward Movement of Educational Selection

The increasingly powerful bond between education and scarce, desirable positions in society is transforming educational selection. That role is being performed less through overt exclusion, and more through enrolment expansion, credential inflation, and pressures to rank credentials. Secondary schools in past decades limited competition for university admission to a relatively narrow band of students. Today, as they accommodate more kinds of students and ease their streaming systems, more are advancing to the next tier. Historically, Canadian high schools have been less rigidly streamed than similar schools in most other nations, and now they are being "de-stratified" further. Processes of accommodation and competition are shifting towards post-secondary levels, where, perhaps not incidentally, resource distributions are far more unequal. Prestigious and endowed institutions, and fields that are firmly connected to lucrative commercial activities and labour markets, are becoming wealthier and more exclusive. In aggregate, these processes are further stratifying higher education. Post-secondary institutions are sorting their graduates for a wider variety of life opportunities than before. As they expand, these institutions are absorbing more of the selection roles previously performed by high schools. Selection mechanisms are migrating from one tier to the next.

This chapter has described important changes in schooling over recent decades. But who benefits from these changes? The next task is to track student fortunes within these transformed systems. Chapters 6 and 7 turn from this "macro" level analysis to a "micro" level examination of educational attainment by class, race, gender, and other categories of students.

Questions for Critical Thought

1. Download an undergraduate application form from an Ivy League university (e.g., Harvard, Princeton, Yale) in the United States. Reflect on how this application process is similar to or different from your own admission experience at your current university.

2. Could you apply the concept of the "shopping-mall high school" to your university? Give examples of how this would and would not work.

3. When you applied to university did you use the *Maclean's* rankings or any other guide to universities? Ten years from now will such rankings be more or less important? What would you look for? Do these rankings capture what you now think are important attributes of a post-secondary institution?

4. Fields of study may be highly unequal in Canadian universities. Through your personal networks, informally interview friends in other departments or faculties. How do they perceive different departments or faculties? Are some harder to enter or leave? Which offer better labour market outcomes? Which have the grandest public reputation? Ask your friends to explain why this stratification exists. Compare their responses to our ideas about stratification by field.

Suggested Readings

Côté, James, and Anton Allahar. 2011. *Lowering Higher Education: The Rise of Corporate Universities and the Fall of Liberal Education*. Toronto: University of Toronto Press. The authors argue that rising numbers of university students are disengaged from their studies, yet are awarded inflated grades. See also their earlier book *Ivory Tower Blues*.

Kirst, Michael, and Mitchell Stevens, eds. 2015. *Remaking College: The Changing Ecology of American Higher Education*. Stanford, CA: Stanford University Press. This book examines how a combination of pressures—a revolution in notions of accountability, wants for greater efficiency and productivity, and new technology—is changing the character of higher education.

Van de Werfhorst, Herman G., and Jonathan J.B. Mijs. 2010. "Achievement Inequality and the Institutional Structure of Educational Systems: A Comparative Perspective," *Annual Review of Sociology* 36: 407–28. This useful paper compares how schools are organized in different countries and the consequences of that organization for student outcomes.

Web Links

Sylvan Learning
http://tutoring.sylvanlearning.com
This is a commercial website highlighting how the private tutoring sector markets to students and families.

UNESCO Education
www.unesco.org/en/education
This United Nations website features many perspectives on a range of changing issues in world education.

Provincial Ministries of Education
www.edu.gov.on.ca/eng/research/projects.html
http://education.alberta.ca/department/ipr.aspx
The first link is Ontario's Ministry of Education research website, followed by a link to initiatives and projects at Education Alberta. These are useful as resources for issues that are germane in elementary and secondary education in two different provinces.

6 Unequal Student Attainments
Class and Socio-economic Status

Learning Objectives

- To understand patterns, trends, and explanations of social class disparities in school attainment
- To show how new research methods enter debates about causes of these disparities
- To comprehend the mechanisms of class inequality in education

Introduction: The Roles of Schooling in Societal Inequality

Processes of maximally maintained inequality (MMI) and effectively maintained inequality (EMI), described in the previous chapter, channel more affluent youth to higher tiers of schooling, and to relatively advantaged sectors within any particular tier. Decades of research show disparities in educational attainment persist despite a remarkable expansion of schooling options. This begs a question: how exactly is educational advantage inherited? No one can inherit their parents' medical licence, law degree, MBA, PhD, or teaching certificate. Because credentials must be earned, the transfer of advantage from parent to child must assume a form other than direct inheritance.

Think about how processes of inheritance differ across settings. In societies where land is the primary economic resource, affluent families pass property to their children. In societies where manufacturing and commerce are key economic assets, privileged children inherit business fortunes. But what is inherited in contemporary societies? Some claim that knowledge is becoming *the* prime asset and that the "knowledge economy" describes economic activity today. If they are correct, and if knowledge has become a focal economic resource and a primary personal asset, then how do advantaged families ensure that their children remain advantaged? One answer is that they will increasingly prize their children's pursuit of knowledge, and will direct their children's learning by continually stimulating and edifying their mental capacities. They might also choose schools that successfully impart cutting edge ideas and cognitive skills. A rather different answer, however, is that advantaged families may not increasingly value knowledge per se, but will instead strive to win the race for top badges of ability. They will learn to dominate access to those educational credentials that best offer prestige, power, and pay. Both answers suggest that nepotism occurs through an indirect process where some parents are more successful in actively intervening to improve their offspring's life chances. Whereas a few hereditary elites continue to convey their property and businesses (and in some nations, their political and military machinery) directly to their offspring, the vast majority can reproduce their status and advantage across generations only through personal achievement.

These answers connect to the contemporary theories discussed in Chapter 3. Each provided a different account of schools' role in (re)creating societal disparities, and each imagined future trends differently. For instance, the structural functionalists distinguished the role of "ascription" (e.g., mostly inherited demographics like sex, race, age, etc.) from "achievement" (e.g., what people actually do with their skills, abilities, performances, etc.) in determining whether or not the bulk of the populace was upwardly mobile. They noted that the principle of heredity ruled in traditional societies, such as India's traditional caste system or master-slave relations in slave economies, while advanced industrial countries such as Canada had shifted from ascription towards achievement. The functionalists believed that modern schools were key to that transition, serving as "great equalizers" that were increasingly promoting meritocracy by rewarding the best and the brightest students, regardless of their social origins, thus levelling the playing field and extending access to high-paying professional and managerial positions for all. Schools were seen to be a prime avenue for upward social mobility, one that would be increasingly fair and just as societies modernized. This viewpoint held sway in sociology throughout the 1950s and 1960s, and continues to be popular among many in the general public.

The neo-Marxists hold a starkly opposing position that has dominated academic circles for the past 30 years. They contend that schools "reproduce" social inequalities. The very design of mass public schooling, they argue, ensures that youth who are born disadvantaged remain disadvantaged. The central Marxist claim is that schools reinforce existing inequalities in the wider society by stereotyping disadvantaged youth, devaluing their cultures and skills, and steering them into lower streams. This class reproduction is said to occur through a variety of processes, some hidden and some overt.

Since these two theoretical positions were formed several decades ago, a mountain of empirical research on school inequalities has surfaced. From this mountain has emerged a more nuanced position: contemporary schools may actually succeed in reducing inequality, but fail to come close to totally eliminating it. In this account, children encounter huge inequality before they set foot in a school. In a society with great and rising disparities in income and wealth, young children live in very disparate home settings and neighbourhoods that offer very dissimilar resources, capacities, and mental horizons. Schools extend new learning opportunities to everyone, including the poor, but because affluent children are better positioned to exploit those opportunities, they fare better in school. According to this middle position, schools help disadvantaged youth, but cannot fully compensate for wider social inequalities that are beyond their control.

This chapter draws on research to examine inequalities in school attainment by social class and socio-economic status (SES). We devote this entire chapter to SES because, in many respects, it is more persistent than other forms of inequality in schooling. Further, most theorized causes and mechanisms were originally geared to explain class differences in attainment, and have been reworked and reapplied to other categories, such as gender, race and ethnicity, sexuality, and ancestry. Because research on class set many parameters for later writing, it is our focus here. The next chapter will examine disparities by these other student categories. This newer work focuses more on notions of "equity" than only on educational outcomes, and thus deserves extensive treatment in its own right.

Describing Class Inequalities: Rising Attainment and Persisting Disparities

As noted in Chapters 4 and 5, the twentieth century witnessed a pervasive institutionalization of K–12 schooling in Canada, and a more recent yet rapid expansion of its post-secondary levels. Indeed, just over a half-century ago, higher education was largely a small preserve for the upper and middle classes. Since then, educational attainments for youth from all class backgrounds have steadily risen. *Everyone* goes to school for more years of their lives. This expansion prompts a question: has it brought more equality?

When we examine social class, the short answer is "no." The attainments of affluent youth remain higher than those of poorer youth. Relative disparities along socio-economic lines have persisted. While less advantaged youth are attaining greater levels of schooling, advantaged youth have easily kept pace. Parental education, income, and occupational prestige remain strong predictors of children's school success, not only in Canada but also in most other Western nations (for reviews, see Davies, Maldonado, and Cyr, 2017; Malette and Guppy, 2017; Shavit, Arum, and Gamoran, 2007; Reardon, 2011).

The longevity of these disparities is remarkable. They surface at virtually all stages of schooling, from preschool to primary to secondary to post-secondary. For instance, preschool children from low-income households are far more likely to experience delays in vocabulary development than are more affluent children (Hertzman et al., 2010). By kindergarten, more low-income children are vulnerable due to their lower levels of language ability and cognitive reasoning (Janus and Duku, 2007). In general, socio-economic background shapes the readiness that young children have when they enter school (Duncan and Magnuson, 2011). These preschool disparities are soon manifested in elementary schools. SES disparities in literacy are evident from the first grade onwards (Davies and Aurini, 2013). Schools with larger proportions of students living in affluent and stable neighbourhoods fare much better on standardized tests (Johnson, 2005). By high school, teenagers with university-educated parents score considerably higher on reading, math, and science tests compared to their peers with less educated parents (Willms, 2002; Statistics Canada, 2010). These developmental gaps have an impact on later attainments. Youth from the lowest family income quartile are three times more likely to drop out of high school than those from the highest quartile (Frenette, 2007). While half (50.2 per cent) of youth hailing from the top income quartile of families attended university, only 31 per cent from the bottom quartile did so (Frenette, 2007). More recent data suggests this gap continues, although its size has shrunk modestly in the last decade (Finnie and Pavlic, 2013). Decades of educational expansion and reform have encouraged Canadians from all socio-economic strata to stay in school longer; yet longstanding patterns of educational inequality have persisted all the same.

The concept of the **socio-economic gradient** can deepen our understanding of these inequalities. It imagines inequality as a very elongated yet finely gradated social hierarchy. A family is positioned on that hierarchy according to their mix of economic resources like parental educational attainment, prestige of occupation, and income. One can graphically depict the gradient by plotting various measures of educational success across the full range of SES, as shown in Figure 6.1.

Steeply sloped gradients signify highly unequal attainments. For example, Figure 6.1 illustrates such a gradient among young children by plotting children's literacy levels by their family income, using data from the 1994–5 National

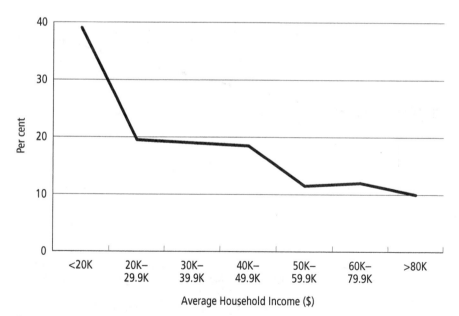

Figure 6.1 Percentage of Children with Delayed Vocabulary Development by Average Household Income

Source: Ross and Roberts (1999: Chart 19).

Longitudinal Survey of Children and Youth. It shows that approximately 40 per cent of children living in families with household incomes below $20,000 experienced delays in vocabulary development, while only about 10 per cent of children from the most affluent homes had any delay. As Hertzman (2000: 14) argues, this gradient indicates that children from wealthier families are better prepared for school from their very first day of class. Nothing in intervening years has changed enough to alter this pattern.

Similar gradients can be found among teenagers. Willms (2004) plots one for reading scores among 2,000 Canadian 15-year-olds. Figure 6.2 depicts how students in lower SES families have reading scores that are approximately 100 points lower than those from families with the highest SES (480 versus 580; for similar results in math and science, see Ma, 2001). When Willms's and Hertzman's findings are combined, they suggest that socio-economic gradients persist from kindergarten to age 15, and are neither erased nor noticeably diminished over time.

In Figure 6.3 we illustrate the socio-economic gradient in a third way. The graph uses data from several surveys of the educational attainment of Canadians aged 25–39 from 1986–2011. The socio-economic gradient is displayed by highlighting how the likelihood of having a university degree varies by your parents' educational background. The top two lines show a rising percentage for both women and men whose parents had at least one university degree. The bottom two lines, which are substantially below the top lines, show the percentages for women

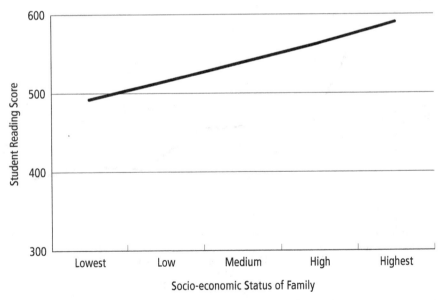

Figure 6.2 Socio-economic Gradient for Reading Scores of 15-Year-Olds

Source: J. Douglas Willms, 2004, *Variation in Literacy Skills among Canadian Provinces: Findings from the OECD PISA*. Ottawa: Statistics Canada, Catalogue no. 81 595-MIE2004012, www.statcan.gc.ca/bsolc/olc-cel/olc-cel?lang=eng&catno=81-595-M.

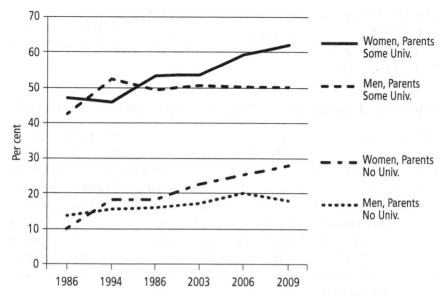

Figure 6.3 University Degree Attainment (in %) of Canadian-Born People 25–39 by Sex and Parents' Educational Background

Source: Author's calculations from Turcotte (2011); based on Statistics Canada national sample from the General Social Survey (original data cover 12 different surveys, we use only six for simplicity of presentation; see Turcotte for details).

Note: The survey dates are uneven so interpreting the annual rate of change is deceiving.

and men whose parents did not have a university degree. That comparison shows the substantial influence of socio-economic status on the likelihood of earning a university degree.

The figure also shows that the top lines and the bottom lines are rising at approximately the same slope (although notice the caution in the footnote to the graph). This demonstrates that the gap in the socio-economic gradient is not closing, at least not very much. Finally, the figure also shows that women have started to earn more university degrees than men and that this growth has occurred for women from both higher and lower socio-economic sectors.

SES gradients have four important characteristics. First, they occur at virtually all levels of schooling. Second, they persist no matter how many other demographic factors are taken into account, such as students' ethnicity, region, or family structure. In other words, these gradients represent a *causal* link between SES and educational attainment that cannot be explained away by other factors. Third, the gradient is *robust* across different measures of education and SES. Whether one examines academic readiness in preschool, literacy and numeracy at the elementary level, secondary school test scores, or post-secondary attendance rates, there is an SES gradient. These gradients reappear regardless of how one measures SES, whether by parental occupation, income, education, or class position. Fourth, the SES gradient has largely persisted over time and space. Despite great changes in school systems over the past century, it has endured. And, despite wide variations in societal conditions across nations, it exists virtually everywhere, although its steepness varies both cross-nationally and historically (see Davies and Janus, 2009; Shavit et al., 2007).

Causes of Inequality: Schools, Families, and Environments

Over fifty years ago, a young sociologist named James Coleman was commissioned to write a report on educational inequality in the United States (Coleman et al., 1966). In the 1960s, most commentators believed that unequal high school outcomes—grades, test scores, dropout rates—stemmed from resource inequalities that existed between *schools*. Due to a variety of funding regulations, American schools were (and still are) greatly unequal in terms of budgets, teacher salaries, class sizes, and library funds. People reasonably deduced that variations in student achievement stemmed largely from inequalities in school quality and resources. Coleman and his colleagues were commissioned to investigate. Their conclusion shocked many.

Coleman found that resource inequalities had some impact, but that student achievement was *much* better predicted by students' family socio-economic status—their parents' education, job status, income, and so forth. From this, Coleman concluded that student success was more powerfully caused by their family-based preparation for schooling rather than by variations in school resources. And in schools that housed families from a variety of socio-economic circumstances, large inequalities emerged *within* those schools. The lesson from the study is not only that socio-economic background is a powerful predictor of school attainment, but also that variations in school resources tend to have only a marginal impact (recall Chapter 5). While resources certainly can be important, their effects are rarely as strong as those of family background.

With the Coleman Report firmly in mind, more internationally oriented scholars turned to the world stage to further investigate this matter. Using very different data and methods, Steven Heyneman and William Loxley (1983) examined school attainment in dozens of countries. Among wealthier nations with more established school systems, family background mattered more for student achievement than did school variations, but among poorer nations with relatively new systems, school effects are actually stronger. Wherever schooling is strongly institutionalized, they reasoned, affluent families soon learn how to "play the game" and prepare their children for educational competitions. Wherever mass schooling is newer, schools can do more to level the playing field, since advantaged families are yet to develop strategies to pass on their advantages. This interpretation was bolstered by more recent findings showing growing family background effects in countries with mature and highly institutionalized school systems (Baker and LeTendre, 2005).

Returning to inequalities in Canadian schooling, these studies present a central question: what are the relative impacts of family background versus schools themselves? Do schools lessen, maintain, or actually worsen existing inequalities in society? Recall the contrast between functionalists who de-emphasized schools in favour of the primary role of unequal home environments, versus Marxists who tended to blame schools, depicting them as rife with prejudice and bigotry. A third position, hardened by decades of experience in school reform, contends that schools actually serve to reduce inequalities, but their efforts are greatly limited by powerful forces beyond their control.

Now, sorting through these different views *empirically* is quite difficult: *everyone* goes to school. If some groups of youth didn't go to school, researchers could, in principle, compare the fortunes of students versus non-students and see if the presence of education worsens or improves rates of inequality. But because compulsory school laws disallow this kind of a "natural experiment," researchers have to look elsewhere for variations in the provision of schooling. Fortunately, there is a time of year during which few are in school: summer! (See Burkam et al., 2004; Davies and Aruni, 2013; Downey and Pribesh, 2004; Alexander, Entwistle, and Olson, 2007.) Studies of "seasonal learning" are based on this reasoning: if schools treat middle-class children in a superior manner, learning gaps (as measured by standardized test scores) between them and poorer children would grow over the school year; alternatively, if those gaps grew over the summer, but narrowed during the school year, then schools may actually mitigate some of the disadvantages posed by unequal homes and neighbourhoods.

Recently, a large study from Ontario (Davies and Aurini, 2013) echoed key findings from American research on **seasonal learning design**: during the fall and winter months schools tend to reduce learning gaps along socio-economic lines, but during the summer when students are not in school, those gaps widen. For instance, Ontario children from lower SES backgrounds were found to suffer a "summer setback" in their literacy and numeracy skills between June and September; that is, what they learned during the school year tended to erode during the summer. In contrast, children from higher SES backgrounds, on average, continued to acquire literacy skills during the summer months. These twin trends served to widen the overall literacy gap between lower and higher SES children. If these patterns were compounded over just four summers, the gap would become an entire school year—a full grade level (see also Alexander et al., 2007).

Why is summer so consequential? The likeliest explanation is that not all families can provide children with equal learning opportunities once school is out of session. Highly educated parents have more time and resources to read to their children, expose them to sophisticated vocabulary, buy educational books and games, and encourage them with enriching activities, including foreign travel. Many poorer parents have less spare time and income for similar activities, and often lack confidence in their reading skills. Seasonal learning studies generally lead to the conclusion that schools do equalize learning opportunities for students from different backgrounds, at least in terms of measured learning, but those efforts are undermined by outside socio-economic forces.

This literature is useful for thinking about the causes of educational inequality. It suggests that schools can partly compensate for the lesser learning opportunities available to disadvantaged children, but do not come close to fully alleviating the vast disparities that children experience beyond the school gates. As long as socio-economic forces in society at large generate huge disparities—which are growing in Canada as elsewhere (Fortin et al., 2012)—there will be inequalities in school attainments. The great expansion of schooling over the past 50 years has greatly opened opportunities for poor children, yet more advantaged Canadians have kept pace by attaining even more education. Thinking about causality leads us to consider the varying influences of schools versus societal forces in producing educational outcomes. But regardless of their ultimate causes, outcomes are also produced through mechanisms that operate in families and schools. The next section points to key processes by which various causes have effects.

Mechanisms of Educational Inequality

We distinguish between "primary" versus "secondary" mechanisms. Primary mechanisms are social forces that create inequalities in education by directly affecting children's capacity to learn school curricula. "Secondary" mechanisms are processes that generate inequalities *within* the range of options afforded by students' performances, and that thus stem from their choices, motivations, and expectations (see Goldthorpe and Jackson, 2008). In other words, secondary mechanisms generate inequalities in ways that are independent of a student's capacity to learn. We borrow this distinction to organize a vast literature that proposes plausible mechanisms of educational inequality.

Primary Mechanisms: Sources of Ability

How does family background affect children's ability to learn school curricula? A logical place to begin a search for mechanisms is to think about intelligence. To open this chapter we asked, "Can knowledge be inherited?" We implied it could not. But anyone who believes that intelligence is inheritable, genetically passed from generation to generation, could disagree. Yet, one could counter: we *choose* to label some people as smarter than others. Further, schooling rewards some abilities over others, such as mathematical skill over musical ability, logic over intuition and spirituality, and abstract reasoning over hand–eye coordination. IQ tests, for instance, stress each of the former and none of the latter.

Yet, there is suggestive evidence that people differ in measured intelligence. Some radical egalitarians deny this, urging society to treat everyone equally and to assume that each person is as smart as the next. However, equal treatment and differential abilities are not the same. Just as some people are better athletes than others, some are smarter than others (and it does not matter if intelligence is measured by musical ability, abstract reasoning, or hand–eye coordination). People differ in abilities and social distinctions reinforce those differences. More important is the question about why people differ in intelligence.

One traditional debate about the causes of intelligence centres on nature versus nurture. Some emphasize the importance of genes and heredity, and contend that the genetic codes we inherit from our parents are consequential for our cognitive abilities. Those who understand nurture as the main cause emphasize the weight of family setting and environment, and contend that the social contexts in which we are raised are most influential for our mental abilities. And, according to some proponents of this view, genetic differences are the prime generator of class and racial inequalities in education (e.g., Herrnstein and Murray, 1994). We disagree with both arguments, and discuss why after noting a second fundamental issue.

This second issue relates to the meaning of intelligence and our measurement abilities. Research here has been especially clouded by a disreputable history. The first tests of intelligence were decidedly culturally biased. Then, unfounded claims that intelligence was inherited led many countries, including Canada, to sterilize people who had been labelled as mentally defective so that their genes would not be passed along. Finally, early scholars who examined the IQs of twins were subsequently charged with fraud, another taint on the research area.

Considerable evidence supports the conclusion that measured intelligence has an important hereditary or genetic component. The most persuasive evidence comes from studies of twins, especially comparisons between identical twins and fraternal twins (identical twins come from a single fertilized egg, while fraternal twins are non-identical, coming from two fertilized eggs). Identical twins reared apart have much more similar levels of measured intelligence than do fraternal twins reared apart. Furthermore, the measured intelligence of adopted children correlates more highly with their biological parents than with their foster parents. This evidence suggests that nature plays an important role in individual differences in measured intelligence. Brain matter, the neural networks of grey cells inside our skulls, is linked to genes—not to an intelligence gene—but to a bundle of interacting genes. How this evidence is interpreted is crucial.

Certain genes enhance athletic prowess, for instance, and often this translates into a desire to play sports. In the right environment—the competitive sports field—this genetic endowment can kick in. But notice that it is environment (i.e., context or nurture) interacting with heredity (i.e., genes or nature) to promote athleticism. Nature and nurture work together; it is *not* a matter of nature *versus* nurture (Ridley, 2003). Bright children who enjoy learning and are rewarded for learning will spend more time learning and become even smarter.

Nature influences individual differences in measured intelligence. But this does not mean that differences in the measured intelligence of groups (e.g., social classes) have a genetic component. At least four conditions would need to be met for that to occur. First, individual intelligence would have to have some genetic component (which we think occurs). Second, people would have to marry others of similar intelligence (which occurs, but is not a particularly strong association). Third, measured intelligence would have to be related to occupational attainment or other measures of social class (and here the relationship is generally weak). Fourth, intergenerational mobility between social classes would have to be minimal (for which there is some support). In our view, at most only a very small component of knowledge (as measured intelligence) may be inherited across generations by social classes.

In summary, individual differences in measured intelligence appear to have a modest genetic component, conditioned by social context, but this is far from a situation in which intelligence is inherited across generations in such a structured way that some sort of cognitive elite or an underclass has formed. The principle of heredity has, at best, a weak effect on the links between measured intelligence and structured social inequality.

One final note on intelligence is illustrative. The Flynn Effect refers to the rather remarkable fact that over the last few decades IQ scores have been rising (Flynn, 2016). These generational gains in IQ were initially unrecognized because IQ test results are constantly re-standardized to average 100 (so that proper norm comparisons are maintained). Explanations for the Flynn Effect remain contentious. It might be better nutrition, greater participation in schooling, or, most likely, a combination of several things. However, it is hard to see how this generational enhancement could be solely a hereditary effect or how it could explain the socio-economic gradient.

More evidence in favour of the role of social conditions is offered by examining achievement patterns among immigrants. Earlier in this chapter we noted that educational disparities have become very mixed and varied among Canadian racial and ethnic minorities. Some have searched for primary mechanisms to understand these patterns. Worswick (2004), for instance, has compared the test results for children of immigrant and non-immigrant families on three dimensions: vocabulary, reading, and mathematics. He concluded that "there is evidence of lower performance early in the school system by children of immigrant parents. . . . However, these children are found to have performance that is comparable to that of children of the Canadian-born by age fourteen" (ibid., 76). This is an exceedingly important result in that it demonstrates the education system is doing a remarkable job in enhancing the abilities of young immigrant students. More recent evidence supporting this comes from Hou and Bonikowska (2016). They compared high school graduation rates and university completion rates of children who are themselves immigrants (i.e., not born in Canada), who are second-generation immigrants (i.e., neither parent born in Canada but they are), 2.5-generation immigrants (one parent born in Canada) or third-generation or higher immigrants (i.e., like them, both parents are Canadian born). As you can see, people who have been in Canada the longest (bottom row of the table) have the lowest university completion rates and the highest high school dropout rates.

Table 6.1 High School Graduation Rates and University Completion Rates by Immigrant Status

Immigration Categories	High School Graduation Rate	University Completion Rate
Childhood immigrant	91.6	35.9
Second-generation immigrant	94.9	40.6
2.5-generation immigrant	93.3	33.8
Third-generation or higher immigrant	88.8	24.4

Source: Hou and Bonikowska (2016).

Immigration is not a disabling experience that sets back educational outcomes. If inherited intelligence is not the answer, and if immigrant experiences do not undermine learning, what other primary mechanisms can explain persistent socio-economic gradients in learning from young children to teens?

Primary Mechanisms: Family-Based Learning Opportunities

Let's begin with an obvious mechanism. Some students come to school hungry and are less ready to learn. The nine-to-three public school experience may be nominally free, but not every child has the same base level of preparation for the school day, whether in the form of a nutritious breakfast or a safe home environment. That is why many school districts offer free lunch programs, especially in poor locales. Beyond these base-level disparities, schooling still costs money. The most conservative estimates of additional costs associated with sending a single child to school are at least $1000 annually, excluding the costs of clothing, after-school child care, and the like (see e.g., https://yourfinanciallife.bmo.com/articles/cost-to-raise-a-child-550047/#.WCul4WYzV48 or use one of the "cost of raising a child" calculators easily found online). Other educational "boosters" that can accelerate children's learning readiness can be expensive as well, including tuition (university, private school), necessary supplies (e.g., binders, field trips), or extras like tutoring, summer camps, or educational games. Families with low SES have less income to provide material resources that stimulate reading, such as books, crayons, toys, etc. These financial costs can pose a barrier to less affluent children (see also Figure 6.4).

But here is an important message: class inequalities in schooling emerge regardless of whether the costs involved are large or small. Even in nominally free public schools, children from less affluent backgrounds earn lower grades and test scores (Figures 6.1 and 6.2) and have poorer graduation rates. Furthermore, even when some countries, such as France and Australia, had free university tuition and provided student grants, the socio-economic gradient persisted. Thus, "extra-monetary" processes obviously are occurring in schools, and most sociologists

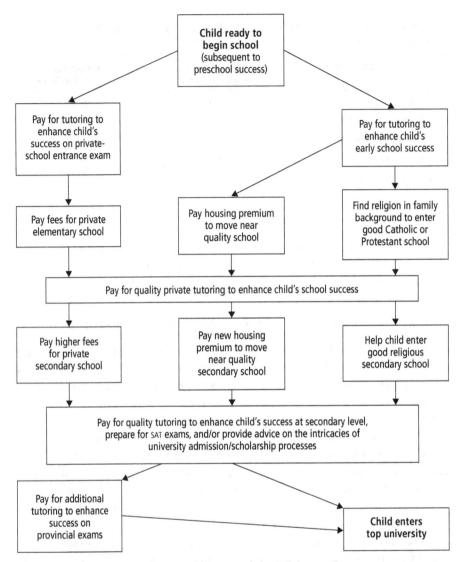

Figure 6.4 Strategies for Winning at "Enhance Your Child's Success"

believe these processes are far stronger than monetary factors. Over the decades, numerous theoretical approaches have been suggested.

Within families, parents are not equally positioned to provide stimulating learning environments for their children. Less educated parents are often less literate and numerate themselves, and are less familiar with schoolwork. Numerous studies have demonstrated startling differences between low- and high-educated parents in the level and richness of verbal interactions that they can provide for young children (e.g., www.earlylearning.ubc.ca/research-overview). Because children's language abilities develop early in life, parental interactions with their preschoolers can set foundations for later learning. Indeed, many longitudinal studies show that literacy and numeracy disparities in early years predict later student achievement (for a review of dozens of studies, see Davies and Janus, 2009). A large literature has shown that children are likely to be successful students when they hail from households that promote literary activities and conscientious study habits (Farkas and Hibel, 2008).

In this line of argument, middle-class households offer environments enriched by greater cognitive challenges, more dedicated work habits, and an assortment of literacy-enhancing activities. Many studies show that youth in poorer settings have less exposure to reading, to complex verbal reasoning, and to forms of high culture from their families and surrounding neighbourhoods. For instance, highly educated parents are far more likely to read to their children, regulate TV watching, and engage in the activities that make for effective home learning environments (Duncan and Murnane, 2011). Such environments have in turn been shown to be highly correlated with school grades, test scores, and attainment. Simply put, higher SES families produce more of the kinds of skills that schools reward.

These studies imply that policies are needed to compensate for inequalities in learning opportunities among families. For instance, programs for early learning (i.e., preschool) often aim to reduce early skill gaps among disadvantaged children. These policies aim to build early mastery of basic skills, ensuring that children from disadvantaged backgrounds do not fall behind their peers. A famous example is the popular children's television show *Sesame Street*, founded by an American program named "Headstart." *Sesame Street* uses television to teach inner-city children basic skills. Set in an urban, Brooklyn-esque backdrop, various friendly characters teach poor and largely minority children the alphabet and basic numeracy. In Canada, the importance of learning in early years is suggested by research based on the Early Development Instrument (EDI), developed by Dan Offord and Magdalena Janus. This research has shown sizeable SES gaps in many indicators of child development (Janus and Duku, 2007). Economists estimate that early learning programs offer the best return on investment among different policy interventions for skills, training, and education (e.g., Heckman, 2008; Trefler, 2009).

A second and related set of compensatory policies involve summer learning programs. Several studies show that the "summer setback" suffered by disadvantaged students accounts for a substantial portion of the achievement gap between advantaged and disadvantaged youth. Evaluations of Canadian and American summer programs suggest that some quite effectively reduce skill gaps (Borman et al., 2009; Davies and Aurini, 2013).

Socio-economic gradients may be lessened by reforming the school calendar. Our current September to June school calendar was adopted in an earlier era when child agricultural labour was useful. But today's "knowledge economy" has no such need for a long summer hiatus. Given the accelerating pace of modern life, more breaks of shorter duration might be an effective way to reorganize schooling. Finally, another alternative strategy to improve schooling outcomes for disadvantaged youth has been to raise the minimum school-leaving age to 18 years, for example. Various studies have demonstrated that this policy change can reduce the risk of unemployment and poor health, and increase lifetime earnings (Oreopoulos, 2005, 2007).

In sum, policies that increase (e.g., Headstart, higher leaving age) or shift (e.g., year-round schooling) "time on task" seem to promote more learning among dis-advantaged youth than do policies that restrict learning opportunities, such as grade retention, streaming, and perhaps even special education.

Primary Mechanisms: Stress

Economic circumstances can influence family functioning in other ways. Low SES can expose children to income-related stress. Financial difficulties affect parents' ability to pay bills and acquire goods (including services like child care or even medical care), and can cause separation, divorce, and family strife. Each of these stressors can affect parent–child relationships, whether by reducing quality inter-action time, by fostering harsh parental discipline, and even exposing children to parental mental health problems such as depression (which is related to SES). In these varied ways, poverty impacts socio-emotional adjustments among chil-dren (for a discussion of the "stress process" model, see Aneshensel, 2009) because income loss impacts parental psychological bonds and marital relationships, which, in turn, influence their parenting practices and, ultimately, impact children them-selves. Family conflict and support is more problematic in families with low SES because poverty generally creates more chaotic family lives.

These stressors provide the key mechanism by which inequality "gets under the skin" (Hertzman and Frank, 2006). That is, a family's socio-economic environment affects a child's basic functioning, even their central nervous system, through dif-ferent exposures to stress. Just as this pathway has been seen to create SES gradients in health, it is also seen to shape SES gradients in children's capacity to learn (see also The Council for Early Child Development, www.ecd-elcc.ca).

Sociologists have offered numerous explanations of racial disparities in education, with most focus on African-Americans. The dominant practice has been to tie racially based poverty to student disadvantages. US data suggest that low-income minorities like African-Americans, Latin-Americans, and Native-Americans enter kindergarten with lower levels of oral language, pre-reading, and pre-math, and less general knowledge than do Asian-Americans and white students (Farkas and Hibel, 2008). This circumstance is traced to their parents, who have lower educational levels and test scores, and to their neighbourhoods, where peers typically perform at a lower level (ibid.). In effect, this is explain-ing ethnic or racial disparities via the socio-economic gradient: low income—not skin colour—is the primary cause.

Primary Mechanisms: Contexts of Schools and Neighbourhoods

Schools and neighbourhoods can also shape children's capacity to learn. School composition, type, programs, and streaming can influence children's achievement through their distribution of learning opportunities. When they distribute resources equally among children, they can help diminish SES gaps. Alternatively, some studies suggest that schools that use ability grouping, grade retention, or tracking to deal with underperforming students do not necessarily help those students; they may even heighten SES gradients. Studies that attempt to estimate the causal impact of streaming (or "tracking"), ability grouping, special education, and grade retention generally conclude that youth in any of those programs probably have lower skill and achievement levels than if they were kept in mainstream learning environments (e.g., Burkham et al., 2004; Morgan et al., 2010). Their reasoning is that those practices serve to constrict the range of learning opportunities for low-performing students (among which low SES youth are over-represented) rather than expand opportunities for all, thereby creating more inequality among students. These researchers instead endorse interventions that compensate for unequal learning opportunities by extending mainstream opportunities rather than segregating weaker performers, such as early and summer learning programs.

Finally, some sociologists also emphasize the effects of neighbourhoods on children's learning opportunities. One plausible mechanism is that poor neighbourhoods can expose children to unsafe environments, and through that, to youth subcultures that are focused on immediate survival among peers. For instance, Elijah Anderson (1999) has written vividly about the "code of street" which emerges among youth in high-crime neighbourhoods. This code encourages teenagers, particularly boys, to adopt tough, aggressive personas as a survival strategy, and discourages them from taking their studies seriously (see also Paulle, 2013; Willis, 1977).

These three mechanisms—family learning opportunities, stress, and school-neighbourhood contexts—each provide a plausible route by which SES affects children's capacity to learn. However, sociologists have noted that in addition to these primary mechanisms, students and families from different origins make different educational choices, even when they have roughly the same level of ability and face similar options, at least on the surface. That is, research in Canada and the United States shows that youth from poorer backgrounds are far less likely to attend elite private schools or pursue post-secondary studies, even taking previous academic success and mental ability into account (Davies and Guppy, 1997; Karen, 2002; Mullen et al., 2003; Wolf, 2002; see also Frenette, 2005). Why? We next discuss secondary mechanisms that create persisting differentials in school attainment.

Secondary Mechanisms: Orientations to School and Cultural Mismatches

A branch of sociology called "status attainment" research has consistently shown that educational aspirations are good predictors of subsequent attainment (Beattie,

2002). While everyone "values" education, lower-class families have been found to be less aspiring of academic achievement. Not only do they face more hurdles ahead, but students from poorer backgrounds are less likely to even think about attending Harvard, Cambridge, the Sorbonne, or any other elite university. Why? Their "frames of reference" are narrower than those of middle- and upper-class youth. With a humbler cognitive horizon for judging what is possible to achieve, students from disadvantaged backgrounds are less likely to strive for great educational success.

However, observing that youth from different origins have different aspirations is one thing, but demonstrating their genesis and operation in schools is another. Several mechanisms have been proposed to understand how students come to adopt different frames of reference.

One approach is premised on the notion that the risks and benefits associated with schooling are unequally distributed in society. As discussed in Chapter 1, sociologists such as John Goldthorpe (e.g., Goldthorpe and Jackson, 2008) argue that youth's social class background shapes how they assess the risks and benefits of attaining further levels of education. For instance, high school graduates face several options: to seek employment, to go to community college, or to attend university (and some prefer none of the above!). Goldthorpe and his colleagues reckon that graduates rationally assess the risks and benefits of each option. Their judgments, Goldthorpe reasons, will be based on wishing to avoid downward mobility and overwhelming debt on the one hand, and preferring a well-paying, desirable job on the other. That seems straightforward.

But the hitch for Goldthorpe is that each assessment is shaped by one's socio-economic background. Each of us may fear downward mobility, but more affluent youth need to aspire to more ambitious paths in order to eventually match their parents' status. None of us want to be overwhelmed by debt, but youth from poorer origins may be overwhelmed by smaller monies than might youth from richer origins, who can often rely on the "Bank of Mom and Dad." For someone who cannot rely on their parents for financial assistance, university tuition fees may appear to be prohibitive. And what is considered to be a desirable job can vary too by social location. Someone whose parents are carpenters may deem being an auto mechanic a great gig, while someone whose parents are investment bankers may deem it a death sentence. Goldthorpe's "rational choice" framework thus offers a key secondary mechanism: socio-economic conditions shape educational expectations by determining how we perceive the risks and benefits of pursing another degree.

What other forces could possibly shape students' orientations to school? One simple idea is that poorer youth may simply lack role models. Without role models who have gone through higher education, many working-class families know little about how schools operate (see also Macleod, 1987). In contrast, other researchers look to schools as sources of dampened aspirations. Schools have been accused of "creating" inequalities by building them into their very structure. As discussed in previous chapters, schools often "stream" or "track" youth into hierarchically arrayed pathways. Because poorer youth are more often placed into lower streams, this practice can *generate* inequality by limiting their access to upper streams. The key issue is whether or not streaming is actually necessary. Critics have long called for schools to devise ways to broaden opportunities rather than limit them (see Guppy and Arai, 1993; Curtis et al., 1992; Rosenbaum, 1976). As discussed above, several studies suggest that streaming, grade retention, ability grouping, and perhaps even some forms of special education may not help children in ways that were intended but might instead create self-fulfilling processes in which youth disengage from school.

Another line of thinking about orientations to school switches the gaze from students and school structures to educators and the types of cultural practices they expect from parents. Some sociologists worry that middle-class practices often get defined as the norm. Using that norm, children from poorer families are seen to be less prepared for school. But using an ethic of cultural egalitarianism, many sociologists instead see working-class family practices not as inferior, but just different. Schools, they reckon, should attempt to better accommodate those youth. Hence, this theory posits that class disparities are rooted in a culture *mismatch*, not cultural deprivation (see Gamoran, 2001).

Perhaps the earliest claim for this approach was that teachers actively discriminate against lower-class students. The origins of this theory stem from a famous experiment called "The Pygmalion in the Classroom." Inspired by, of all things, rat-maze experiments, a psychologist and a school principal teamed up to explore if schooling has something analogous to the "observer bias" that occurs in scientific experiments. They hypothesized teachers' preconceived expectations of student abilities would lead to "self-fulfilling prophecies" or "observer bias." Their experiment aimed to test the power of positive labelling (see Box 6.1). Teachers are said to have low expectations for some students, particularly those from poor or minority backgrounds. These expectations are said to create self-fulfilling prophecies as those students internalize those labels, ultimately leading to underachievement (see also Rist, 1970).

Despite the enormous popularity of the Pygmalion experiment, and despite its intuitive appeal to a generation of educational advocates, claims of powerful effects from teacher expectations tend not to be supported by systematic research, at least not in recent years. The idea has an easy appeal because we all know our expectations do affect what we hear and see. However, the empirical evidence suggests teaching professionals are not so easily duped. This is not to imply that context does not matter, however. Teacher expectations alone are not so powerful, but placing children in school tracks labelled as remedial, with inferior resources and low expectations from their peers, parents, and professionals, will have effects. Context does matter, but expectations alone are not as consequential as many once believed (see, e.g., Weinstein, 2002).

Box 6.1 The Self-Fulfilling Prophecy of the Self-Fulfilling Prophecy?

One of the most famous experiments in social science was conducted as follows: students in a San Francisco elementary school were given IQ tests in September. The researchers identified 60 children to teachers as those who apparently, based on the IQ test, were "expected to bloom." However, those students actually had been selected at random. The researchers returned a year later to conduct a new IQ test. The results, they claimed, were startling. Those labelled "expected to bloom" were said to have enjoyed significant IQ gains, far above the control group. From this claim of finding powerful effects of positive expectations, many generalized these results to contend that negative labelling must also generate self-fulfilling prophecies and cause children to fail. They reasoned that teachers tend to interpret visual cues like dress, demeanour, vocabulary, and familiar appearances as badges of ability, when in fact they are artifacts of race or class background. Teachers use those visual cues to form negative expectations for certain children, who in turn internalize those labels and fare poorly in school.

It is no exaggeration to say that this experiment caused uproar in educational circles. For many, its proclaimed results confirmed their hunches that teachers, not students themselves, were responsible for student failure. They hoped the study would spark a wave of reform. Sociologists heralded it as classic study of socialization, and to this day it remains a staple in textbooks on education and sociology. However, after all of these years, it appears that few actually read the "fine print" of the study. The actual data themselves show a rather muted pattern (see Wineburg, 1987). For instance, though classes from Grades 1 to 6 participated in the study, significant teacher expectation effects emerged only in Grades 1 and 2, and only the effects among Grade 1 students were strong. Moreover, the mean effect among first graders was inflated by a single extreme case of a child who scored an initially abysmal low pre-test, only to improve later.

The bottom line, according to Wineburg, is that the Pygmalion experiment was misrepresented. Analyzing a host of subsequent studies, he found the average effect to be near zero. This led Wineburg to speculate that people continue to hold faith in the power of self-fulfilling prophecies because it resonates with the American faith in the "power of positive thinking" and because it fuels beliefs that intractable inequalities can be easily curbed simply through re-labelling. The failure of schooling to address issues of inequality does not lie in the minds of teachers (see also Weinstein, 2002).

A different approach, exemplified by the French sociologist Pierre Bourdieu (1990 [1977], 1988, as discussed in Chapter 3), centres on (mis)matches between students' cultural background and school content. His popular theory has two components.

The first component has affinities with Goldthorpe's thinking, but starts from a different premise. Bourdieu sees social action as less calculative, and instead emphasizes how people's socialization provides them with their mental norms, habits, and routines. Most people are often unconsciously guided by pre-existing norms and scripts. According to Bourdieu, we should not overstate the extent to which people rationally assess available information to judge costs and payoffs from various courses of action. For instance, he would place less emphasis on the idea that middle-class youth attend university because they engage in some sort of computation of risks and benefits. Instead, he would emphasize that many of these youth just "knew" they were going to attend since they were small children. Bourdieu would also emphasize how, in contrast, working-class youth would consider university to be a foreign territory; something that is simply off their mental radar screens. Qualitative researchers from Canada have used this thinking to argue that even when students from working-class backgrounds do attend university, they often feel less comfortable than others and sometimes drop out (Lehmann, 2009a, 2009b, 2014).

Second, and more boldly, Bourdieu offers a deeper "cultural mismatch" explanation of educational inequality. Focusing on social class, Bourdieu is famous for his contention that schools largely reward familiarity with middle-class culture. Presuming that social classes differ in their linguistic styles, cultural tastes, and organized activities, he reasons that schools reward various practices that are not really markers of intelligence, but are actually just the arbitrary cultural practices of middle-class people. Deploying his signature concept "cultural capital," he claims that seemingly "innocent" activities nurtured in the home can later pay off in school. Speaking to children using extensive vocabularies, exposing them to higher arts, and making them comfortable with structured lessons are all actually "investments" that are in tune with school curricula and practices—hence the "capital" metaphor. Teachers are said to perceive refined ways of speaking, ways of seeing, and familiarity with high culture as actual markers of talent, intelligence, and ability.

In fact, Bourdieu argues, these markers are just the arbitrary cultural tastes and styles of middle- and upper-class families, but are unrecognized as such by teachers who themselves come from similar backgrounds. Thus when advantaged parents speak to their children in formal tones, take them to art galleries and museums, and enrol them in all sorts of lessons (music, dance, or sports), Bourdieu believes they are nurturing unconscious habits that ultimately confer advantage in schooling, since educators regard them as signals of "ability" or "intelligence." Thus, this "cultural capital" is a possible secondary mechanism—Bourdieu reckons that working-class people are certainly capable of learning, but are short-changed in schools by a biased curriculum.

But what does research actually show? The North American evidence is equivocal at best. Importantly, little data suggests that teachers communicate more easily with students who participate in elite culture, or give them more attention and special assistance, or perceive them to be more gifted than others (e.g., Dumais, 2006). DiMaggio (1982), for instance, found that students' level of cultural capital matters only for non-technical subjects (e.g., the humanities). Kingston (2001), reviewing several studies, concludes that the only family cultural practices that are consistently associated with school success are reading (or any related practice that facilitates literacy) and monitoring of homework. Otherwise, student participation in various *beaux arts* activities—going to art galleries, museums, operas, and the like—does not fuel school success (see also Lareau and Weininger, 2003).

A somewhat more promising version of cultural mismatch theory focuses on racial minorities. Critics for several decades have noted the absence of minorities in literature and history texts. They reason that this is not only unjust, but also alienates minorities from school material. School boards have long sought to rectify this, and it is policy in many Canadian jurisdictions to ensure that curricular images are properly colour-coded, that curricula are multicultural, and that various ethnic heritages are suitably celebrated in events like Black History month. In this way, this version of cultural mismatch theory more closely corresponds to policy than does Bourdieu's version. But whether these reforms have been successfully implemented, and whether they are effective, are different questions. To our knowledge there are no systematic Canadian data on these issues.

Another type of "mismatch" explanation moves from the curriculum to relations between schools and families. The main idea behind this approach is that good family–school relations are important, particularly for effective interventions for at-risk youth. But if schools do not effectively facilitate such interactions with all parents, or expect certain kinds of interactions that differ from what families expect, problems may arise.

A renowned researcher in this area is Annette Lareau (2000, 2011). Her studies in a variety of American settings show that middle-class families, as compared to working-class families, have far more knowledge about schooling. Whereas poor and working-class parents are seen to be largely unfamiliar with the world of formal education, parents who themselves are highly educated are, in contrast, quite familiar with all of school's intricacies, and make strong connections between their home life and school. Middle-class parents interact confidently with educators, are less deferential to the professional authority of teachers, and are far more likely to attend parent-teacher meetings, volunteer with school activities, and go to school open houses. They know more about how schooling works and can act on it in ways that advantage their children. This middle-class "sense of entitlement" offers a sharp contrast to a working-class "sense of constraint" (Lareau, 2011).

Moreover, as Lareau and others are showing (see also Quirke, 2006), middle-class parents are scheduling their children's lives to ever greater degrees by enrolling them in structured activities such as music lessons, tutoring, dance, and organized sports. These activities have some affinity with school, which itself is a structured activity organized by adults. Social class differences come into play as teachers expect an interconnection between home and school. According to Lareau and Weininger (2003), social class shapes the ability of youth and parents to comply with the evaluative standards of schools. She argues that middle-class parents are able to strategically use their knowledge, skills, and competence to meet the institutionalized standards of evaluation used by schools. Those parents find it easier to conform to schools' expectations that parents be active, engaged, and assertive. Further, their children are more assertive in schools, and are more likely to be proactive and request assistance from teachers (Calarco, 2011).

Beyond cultural repertoires, Lareau also shows that life is structured in ways that make it easier for middle- and upper-class parents. The parents of working-class children often have longer commutes to work (often on public transit), frequently are engaged in shift work, can have problems arranging child care, sometimes have multiple jobs, and generally have far less flexibility in making arrangements with employers. The result is not only a cultural mismatch, but a structural constraint that limits effective engagement with their children's schools.

Race is also a focus of this research tradition. Lareau and others warn of alarmingly low levels of trust and support between some minority families and schools. For instance, Lareau examined relations between families and teachers in a midwestern US elementary school, and found that teachers *believed* they were warmly welcoming all forms of parental involvement. Teachers saw those beliefs as neutral and designed to promote achievement, and wanted parents to be positive, supportive, and to trust their professional judgment. Teachers repeatedly praised parents who had praised them, and liked those who were deferential, empathic, and had detailed information about their children's experience.

However, some black families found these expectations difficult to meet. These parents were highly critical of their schools and teachers, partly because their views were shaped by a backdrop of American race relations that had created legacies of distrust and distance between (mostly white) teachers and black parents. When black parents saw their children falling behind or being disciplined, they immediately sensed that an injustice was at play. But any angry displays of parental concern were deemed unacceptable and destructive by teachers. Lareau reckoned that white parents enjoyed relatively comfortable and trustful relationship with schools, while black parents had relations that were more suspicious, negative, and distant, and this process lessened their ability to intervene effectively for their children. These different relations were shaped partly by historical legacies of racial conquest, segregation, and inequality, far beyond the confines of any individual school.

Returning to social class, some sociologists have taken cultural mismatch even further. One of the most famous books in the history of sociology is Paul Willis's *Learning to Labour* (1977). Observing an all-boys secondary school in England's industrial north in the mid-1970s, Willis set out to study the interface between working-class students and schools. However, his focus was less on documenting the biases of school curricula or teachers than on the actions and reactions of students. His momentous claim was that traditional forms of working-class culture were entirely incompatible with the middle-class orientations of schools.

For Willis and his many followers, anti-school sentiment represents something more than a clash between working-class teens and their teachers: it was also a miniaturized expression of class conflict. Anti-school stances, Willis reasoned, paralleled the proletarian culture that was thriving in unionized factories during

Indigenizing Lareau

Sociologist Emily Milne (2016) recently applied Lareau's ideas to Southern Ontario, interviewing 50 parents and educators, most self-identifying as Haudenosaunee, Anishinaabe, Aboriginal, Métis, or Native. She came to a stark conclusion: that the legacy of residential schooling had undermined social bonds between these families and public educators, though it did so with important differences by social class.

Poorer parents were mostly disengaged from schools because of their negative experiences with educators during their own childhoods. An educator said "We have so many Indigenous parents that went through that residential school experience. They want their kids to have good lives but they don't see how education can help with that" (Milne, 2016: 278). Those parents had little trust and comfort with public educators, and did not see themselves as playing a lead role in their children's schooling. As one put it "I have the worst fears of teachers, to be honest with you. I'm nervous around them" (ibid., 276). Another said "I personally have not gone to my child's classroom. I didn't know that we could go in and watch a play or anything during school. I thought we were supposed to bring our kids to school and that's it" (ibid., 281). Unlike most "concerted cultivators" described by Lareau, one parent was completely surprised by news that both of her children were reading well below grade level.

Yet, family social class mattered. Middle-class Indigenous families had, if anything, an *intensified* relationship to schooling. These parents purchased educational materials and tutoring services. As one put it "My family is very academic. Math and science is what we focus on. Our kids have been surrounded by this their whole life. We read every day to them; reading's important" (ibid., 280). For these parents, their combination of experience with discrimination with deep beliefs in the importance of education motivated them to closely monitor their children's schooling. Some were quite forceful, comfortable to assert their children's rights. For instance, during a dispute, one parent said to a teacher "You're fired. I will find someone else who can work with my child. The teacher said 'you can't fire me.' And I said 'Watch. You will be fired. You will no longer be teaching my child'" (ibid., 278). Another parent wanted a Mohawk language program at her child's school. She initiated a parent petition and wrote to politicians and school board members, and shortly afterwards, her school launched a Mohawk program that has since grown every year.

This study illustrates the utility of Lareau's ideas: historical legacies of discrimination can weaken parents' willingness to fully engage in public education, though family social class can compensate, generating not trust per se, but an intensive overseeing of their children's schooling. Milne concludes that new policies are needed to allow public educators to better engage with Indigenous families.

the 1970s. For instance, just as factory workers rejected rate-busters and scabs, Willis believed that school rebels similarly condemned students who conformed to teachers' wishes. Just as industrial workers made life difficult for their supervisors and foremen, school delinquents opposed teachers' attempts to control them. And just as local workers would often act in solidarity in their struggles with management, schoolboy "lads" greatly valued their close friendships and refused to compete with one another for grades. For Willis, anti-school subcultures were broad reflections of the culture of the adult working class.

Willis's book was a major literary event in sociology, not only winning awards and accolades, but also spurring a mini-industry of imitation studies in a number of countries, including Canada. Some Canadian researchers, however, became skeptical about exporting wholesale Willis's claims across the Atlantic when they tested his ideas with a variety of methods. For example, Tanner's (1990, 1995) interviews with high school dropouts in Edmonton uncovered little of the thorough and confident rejection of school described in *Learning to Labour*. Rather, youth dropped out for very personal reasons and, disappointed with their meagre job prospects, retained hopes of returning to school one day. Baron (1989), conducting field research on delinquent youth in Victoria, found that they hailed from a variety of class backgrounds and were not "resistant" in Willis's political sense. Likewise, Davies (1994, 1995), using surveys of Ontario high school students and dropouts, found that students from working-class origins did not hold attitudes that were especially anti-school. Instead, those attitudes were more likely to be expressed along gender lines, with males and "at-risk" students voicing greater levels of anti-school sentiment. Finally, in a study of high school students in Alberta, Nakhaie et al. (2000) found no differences by social class among students resisting school.

There are several plausible reasons why Willis's working-class rebellion was not found in contemporary Canadian schools. One highlights the interplay between economic change and student attachment to school. The anti-school sentiment described by Willis was rooted in an industrial setting that offered many less educated youth relatively well-paying jobs in factories, a viable economic option that encouraged them to view school as irrelevant to their future. But such settings are on the wane; due to de-industrialization, the bulk of jobs are now found in the service sector, which fosters a different relation to schooling, one more instrumental and less dismissive. School rejection becomes costlier and rarer.

Another explanation highlights the interplay between national school systems and student attitudes. The older British system that Willis described closed off educational opportunities for most youth relatively early in their lives. By doing so, it fostered among most working-class youth a "class consciousness" (Brint, 1998), a fatalistic thinking in which they saw themselves as having a fixed station in life. In contrast, North American schools, with less rigid streaming and greater proportions in academic programs, foster an "opportunity consciousness" among youth in which many see open channels for upward mobility, and dream of upward mobility.

Conclusion

Despite a massive and international expansion of schooling over the twentieth century, educational attainment is still distributed along social class lines. Students from affluent backgrounds largely retained their advantages, despite rising levels of education for youth from all social classes. Through a process of "maximally maintained inequality," privileged populations retain their advantages by attaining more advanced levels of education. Expansion also triggers processes of "efficiently maintained inequality," as advantaged strata seek to monopolize the more prestigious institutions, and/or the more lucrative fields of study in any credential tier. These processes serve to devalue credentials attained by disadvantaged groups, as has happened with the high school diploma, which in turn generates a demand for further schooling, leading to a spiral of expansion as groups jockey to maintain or better their status. Yet, while socio-economic gradients tend to persist, evidence supports the "partial compensation" theory of education. Schools extend opportunities for youth from lower SES backgrounds, but are limited in their power to eliminate inequalities created by forces beyond. And, as we show in the next chapter, the evidence on school attainment is even more mixed for other categories of students.

Questions for Critical Thought

1. This chapter distinguished "primary" from "secondary" mechanisms of educational inequality. Anticipating the next chapter, under which category would you place a learning problem like attention deficit disorder (ADD/ADHD)? Could you place it under both? Neither? Discuss.

2. Go to a website that offers sample questions from a standardized test (e.g., PISA, PIRLS, EQAO, GRE, SAT, LSAT, etc.). Do you see examples of class, gender, or racial bias in any of these questions? Show examples as appropriate. If you don't see examples, suggest why not.

3. Willis described male peer groups known as "lads" and "ear 'oles" in his 1970s study, *Learning to Labour*. Are there modern-day equivalents, male or female, of "lads" and "ear 'oles" or are they racial in character? Discuss.

Suggested Readings

Calarco, Jessica McCrory. 2011. "'I Need Help!' Social Class and Children's Help-Seeking in Elementary School," *American Sociological Review* 76(6): 862–82. A former student of Annette Lareau observed elementary classrooms for an extended period of time, and found upper-middle-class children to be more assertive and confident when interacting with teachers.

Duncan, Greg J., and Richard J. Murnane (eds). 2011. *Whither Opportunity? Rising Inequality, Schools, and Children's Life Chances.* New York: Russell Sage. An examination documenting growing inequality in US society, and how that inequality has impacted children's home and school lives.

Khan, Shamus Rahman. 2011. *Privilege: The Making of an Adolescent Elite at St. Paul's School.* Princeton, NJ: Princeton University Press. This award-winning ethnography details how youth at an elite boarding school learn an evolving upper-class culture in which they eventually embody their advantages.

Lareau, Annette. 2011. *Unequal Childhoods: Class, Race, and Family Life, Second Edition with an Update a Decade Later.* Berkeley: University of California Press. Lareau revisited the same families she had studied 10 years earlier, and found that the lives of the now-grown-up children continued to be shaped by their social class origins.

Web Links

The Ontario Summer Literacy Learning Project
www.ontariodirectors.ca/Summer_Literacy/Summer_Literacy_Learning_Report.pdf
This link reports on Canada's largest summer learning study.

The Post-Secondary Pathways Project
www.yorku.ca/pathways
The site describes a large study of the educational paths taken (and not taken) by former students at the Toronto District School Board.

Frontier College
www.frontiercollege.ca/english_literacy.html
This is the website of a longstanding, non-profit organization that promotes literacy and lifelong learning among Canadian adults, mostly from disadvantaged backgrounds.

7 Attainments by Gender, Race, Sexuality, and Other Equity Categories

Learning Objectives

- To understand patterns of educational disparities by gender, racial/ethnic ancestry, sexuality, and other student categories
- To weigh arguments and evidence about the role schools play in generating patterns of attainment among various categories of students
- To analyze the ongoing institutionalization of equity categories, including those recognized only recently like sexuality and mental health

Introduction

Not all forms of social inequality in school attainment are invariant, as we saw for social class in the previous chapter. Other patterns of inequality have played out differently over recent decades. Some have reversed in particular ways (such as those by gender), some are highly uneven (such as those among Canada's ethnic and racial minorities), some have remained invariant like social class (such as for Indigenous students) and some are largely unknown (such as those by sexuality and some other student categories).

This chapter examines these "other" patterns of attainment and performs three tasks. First, it describes major patterns of disparity and explanations of them by gender, race, and sexuality. Second, it weighs the relative roles played by schools versus broader societal forces that reinforce or reduce those attainments. The previous chapter concluded that forces outside of school are particularly powerful engines of class inequalities. But is the situation similar for other kinds of disparities? Third, this chapter steps back and ponders the processes by which various student categories emerge and evolve in educational discourse, and become recognized and institutionalized. We begin with gender, and then examine race, sexuality, and other categories. Two caveats should be stated from the outset. First, the previous chapter set up many of the arguments in this chapter. Much theory and research in sociology of education initially focused on class inequalities, and so we use many of those tools to confront inequalities by gender, race, and other categories. Second, we focus this chapter on school attainment while remaining aware of other aspects of schooling—gaining social experiences, learning cultures, and being socialized. Chapters 11 and 12 will turn to these other topics.

Gender Inequalities

Describing Attainments: Equalizing in Fractal Form?

Males once dominated most levels of schooling. Higher education in particular was once a mainly male preserve. But that situation has changed over the past few decades.

Compare the relative fortunes of men and women on high school graduation rates, university attendance, grades, and test scores. Some of the old gender imbalance began to change in the late 1950s. By 1987 more women than men were enrolled full-time in undergraduate university studies. Among today's half-a-million full-time university undergraduates, there are about 80,000 more women than men (330,000 women as compared to 250,000 men). Table 7.1 shows the rapid growth of women attaining undergraduate and first professional degrees, with women receiving 60.4 per cent of all such degrees in 2013. Females now drop out of high school in fewer numbers, graduate more often, enter universities in greater numbers, and score higher on many standardized tests. Figure 7.1 shows that a century after the ratio of boys to girls equalized in common schools, the same ratio finally equalized and then changed to favour women at the university level. Women are also more likely than men to earn master's degrees; by 2010, 56 per cent of all master's students were female. Men still are the majority of PhD holders, but women are only slightly behind, and are expected to reach parity very soon (Association of Universities and Colleges of Canada [AUCC], 2011). In sum, men have been surpassed by young women on most measures of attainment (for a review, see DiPrete and Buchmann, 2013).

Change can also be seen in some fields of study. Table 7.1 shows the distribution of university graduates among 17 separate fields for 1961–2, 1992, and 2013. In 1961–2, just as the women's movement was gathering momentum, about one-quarter of university graduates were women (27.4 per cent). In some disciplines no women graduated (e.g., forestry), and in several others you could count the number of female or male graduates on one hand (e.g., for women, architecture, engineering, and veterinary medicine; for men, household science and nursing). But since the early 1960s, some fields have reached gender parity. For instance, only about one in 20 law graduates was a woman in the early 1960s, but 52 years later more women than men graduated from that field (57:43). Other professional fields have seen dramatic change as well, including commerce and medicine. The teaching profession is being re-feminized, with the percentage of female graduates having climbed from 38 in the early 1960s to 71.3 in 2013. These patterns of change are unmistakable.

In addition to these reversals are some instances of persistence. Some key fields of study have seen only modest change in their gender composition. Fields traditionally dominated by women, such as household science and nursing, still see few males. Women are still only a minority in STEM fields (sciences, technology, engineering, and math). Those fields are growing in most universities. Many STEM

Table 7.1 Undergraduate Degrees by Field of Study, Year, and Gender

Field of Study	1961–2			1992			2013		
	Total Degrees	Degrees to Women		Total Degrees	Degrees to Women		Total Degrees	Degrees to Women	
	N	N	%	N	N	%	N	N	%
Agriculture	351	9	2.6	549	261	47.5	690	453	48.9
Architecture	102	3	2.9	609	225	36.9	1,434	768	53.6
Arts	9,205	3,140	34.1	40,995	25,029	61.1	64,149	42,234	65.8
Commerce	1,144	52	4.5	15,510	7,428	47.9	41,250	21,348	51.8
Dentistry	229	8	3.5	507	192	37.9	372	213	57.3
Education	3,650	1,403	38.4	17,976	13,236	73.6	19,221	13,707	71.3
Engineering	2,437	4	0.2	7,389	1,026	13.9	13,986	2,628	18.8
Fine/applied arts	93	65	69.9	5,598	3,657	65.3	8,904	5,895	66.2
Forestry	110	0	0.0	705	225	31.9	2,094	1,251	59.7
Household science	303	303	100.0	1,104	1,020	92.4	3,603	3,081	85.5
Law	661	37	5.6	3,579	1,842	51.5	3,510	2,007	57.2
Medicine	846	86	10.2	1,887	831	44.0	1,962	1,221	62.2
Nursing	366	365	99.7	2,844	2,715	95.5	10,908	9,837	90.2
Pharmacy	275	77	28.0	774	498	64.3	1,338	840	62.8
Science	1,904	310	16.3	13,224	5,613	42.4	19,938	9,993	50.1
Social work	163	112	68.7	2,016	1,674	83.0	4,512	3,816	84.6
Veterinary medicine	72	3	4.2	285	177	62.1	324	258	79.6
Non-classified	877	260	29.6	5,088	3,036	59.7	9,408	5,994	63.7
Total	22,788	6,237	27.4	120,639	68,685	56.9	207,840	125,544	60.4
IQV	0.70			0.85			0.88		

Source: Data from Statistics Canada, Education in Canada (1973, 2000, 2013), Cat. No 81-229; www.statcan.gc.ca/bsolc/olc-cel/olc-cel?lang=eng&catno=81-229-X. Custom tabulations from Statistics Canada database "Classification of Instructional Programs."

Notes: IQV = index of qualitative variation. A higher number indicates a distribution more evenly spread among the categories; "Non-classified" includes degrees granted where field of study was not reported or is not included among the categories listed in the table. The data from 2013 is not strictly comparable to earlier data given new coding used by Statistics Canada. Our estimates show very minor differences where comparison is possible.

graduates do well in the labour market. They are extremely dynamic fields and have a large impact on our society. As we discuss later in this section, these persisting patterns across fields are important for understanding why women's sizeable gains in education have not been matched by comparable gains in the job market. For now, we highlight the reversal of many gender patterns of school attainment, noting some continued segregation among a few key university fields.

How can we describe this pattern of simultaneous change and persistence? One handy metaphor is the biological concept of "fractals," as used by sociologist Andrew Abbott (2001). A fractal is a living form that continually subdivides, creating new structures at different levels, while still resembling the original pattern. Fractals can expand, grow, and multiply, yet retain their basic appearance by replicating old distinctions in new ways. How can we apply this concept to gender patterns of school attainment? Let's begin with traditional conceptions of gender and work. Only a few decades ago males were commonly thought to be "naturally" suited for more technical fields such as math, science, and engineering. Masculinity was associated with a certain cold calculability, making men apt for technical pursuits. Females were thought to be inherently matched for "nurturing" fields such as teaching, nursing, and social work. Femininity was associated with child-rearing and other tasks involving personal care. And because such tasks were rarely seen to require a learned expertise, there was little perceived need for women to attend university.

As we saw above, gender traditionalism was challenged in powerful ways as women completed high school and then higher education in unprecedented numbers, while they achieved near-parity in some fields that were once male preserves, such as law, medicine, and social science. So at one level, this migration of women into uncharted territory represents a profound change. Yet, you can see vestiges of old distinctions if the particular specialties that women and men concentrate on within these fields are examined. In law, women enter family law, which deals with children and family relationships, in disproportionate numbers. Men, in contrast, continue to dominate lucrative specialties such as corporate law. In medicine, females now dominate general medicine, family medicine, and pediatrics—sub-fields that often deal with women and children. Men are far more numerous in surgical specialties. In social sciences, women are now the majority of students in so-called "soft" fields like psychology and sociology while highly quantified fields, such as economics, remain male dominated.

These gender patterns have a fractal quality. In one respect, they have undergone massive change as more women migrate to new fields. But in another respect, many old divisions persist. Few men have moved to traditionally feminine fields, and they still dominate in areas like engineering. So, as female enrolments expand and shift across fields, old gendered patterns still recur within many of those fields.

This fractal quality describes gender patterns of attainment in their full complexity. But explaining them and understanding schooling's role in generating them requires further inspection. We attempt this next.

Explaining Reversals in Attainment: Frames and Credentials

In one respect, the historic gender reversal in educational attainment is a story of a deep and profound cultural shift. It involves changing notions of typical career destinations for women (though not for men, as we discuss below), and about changing cultural frames of reference for girls and young women. In Chapter 6, we discussed how social class can shape expectations for schooling. Gender offers an interesting application of these secondary mechanisms. The broader feminist and women's movement in the 1960s struggled to change old gendered belief systems. They applied prevailing language about human rights and equality of opportunity to the realm of gender. Reporting in 1970, the Royal Commission on the Status of Women argued that "education opens the door to almost every life goal. Wherever women are denied equal access to education, they cannot be said to have equality" (1970: 161). In education, they nurtured cultural innovations gradually that altered imagined futures for girls (Gaskell, 2009). This new thinking was later institutionalized in schooling. Colleges and universities soon established special offices to promote gender equity, to encourage women applicants, and to rid campuses of sexist stereotyping and language. This promoted new forms of "opportunity consciousness" among women.

In another respect, this reversal also illustrates the lack of a comparable change in thinking about males. While female attainments have skyrocketed over the past few decades, male attainments have not kept pace, even as male attainments have grown, as illustrated in Figure 7.1; today's males "underachieve" compared to today's females, not compared to yesterday's males. Young men are not matching the rate of female increases, but their current attainment is historically unprecedented, nonetheless.

This is important to remember amid today's media depictions of male attainment. Some media largely invert stories from yesteryear about discrimination against girls. Critics see a "war against boys" in today's elementary and secondary schools, and blame an overly feminized teaching force that provide only poor role models for young boys, a curriculum that alienates them, and teaching styles that are too girl-friendly (for a popular example, see Hoff Somers, 2015). However, evidence to support claims about clear-cut discrimination against either girls or boys in schools is virtually non-existent (Davies and Aurini, 2011; Looker, 2011). Theories in previous decades that charged teachers with ignoring girls flew in the face of rapid rises in female achievement. Today, girls attain better grades than boys, and score higher on a range of reading and math tests, but this may be due to familial patterns of socialization. Milligan and Baker (2016) demonstrate that parents devote more time to educationally beneficial interactions with their daughters as compared to their sons. For example, parents are more likely to read and play educational games with their daughters than with their sons. The result, they suggest, could be better educational achievements for girls than for boys.

But in another respect, women's influx into higher education is less of a drama about toppling prevailing gender scripts than a mundane story of credentialism.

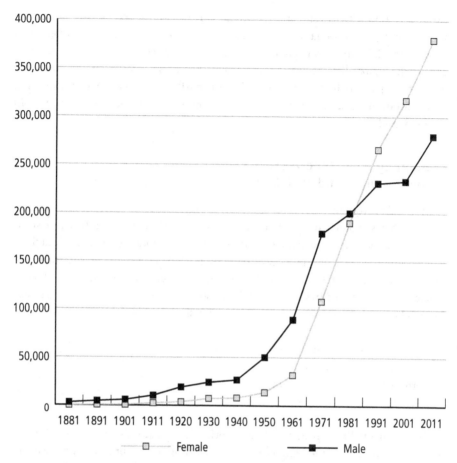

Figure 7.1 Full-Time Undergraduate University Enrolment, Canada, 1881–2011

Source: Data from 1881 to 1970: *Historical Statistics of Canada*, Series W455. Data from 1980 and 1990, Statistics Canada, *Education in Canada*. Data for 2001 and 2011: Statistics Canada, *Education Indicators in Canada*, Table D1.10, www.statcan. gc.ca/bsolc/olc-cel/olc-cel?lang=eng&catno=81-582-X.

Women have long dominated fields like teaching, nursing, social services, and secretarial work. But only over the past few decades have those fields moved their training into universities and colleges when those traditional occupations began to professionalize and upgrade their required educational certificates. This shift of credential requirements encouraged thousands of women who wished only to remain in those female-dominated fields to attend higher education. By altering the costs and benefits of higher education as per Goldthorpe's rational choice model, this credentialism fuelled much of the rise in female attainments *without* altering gender patterns in the labour market or traditional notions of feminine careers.

Another part of this story is the *lack* of a comparable shift in credential requirements among many male-dominated occupations. Many blue-collar jobs like mining, manufacturing, construction, and various skilled trades continue to *not* require any post-secondary credentials. Many of these occupations offer good wages, especially in unionized and/or high overtime settings. As such, the existence of these jobs allows many "underachieving" males to eschew higher education and yet not pay a hefty penalty in the labour market. The great gender reversal in school attainment has been fuelled in part—and oddly—by gender persistence in the job world.

Explaining Persistence across Fields: Indulging Our Gendered Selves?

Traditionally, women and men were seen to differ in their aptitudes for various kinds of tasks. Some saw gendered patterns of enrolment across fields of study as reflecting natural capacities. Others took a more moral stance, and imagined women and men as needing to have separate stations in life for the societal good. Many fields had cultures that were far from gender-neutral. A poem from Queen's University, reproduced in Cook and Mitchinson (1976: 167), illustrates the barriers women faced in gaining access to certain professional fields:

> I think all lawyers would agree
> On keeping our profession free
> From females whose admission would
> Result in anything but good.

Other fields like forestry and engineering have histories of being "chilly climates" for women. Crude sexual exploits and strong macho bravado were features of undergraduate hazing in both disciplines, a practice that only recently receded. Certainly these unwelcoming climates for women provided an explanation for old gender imbalances.

But both explanations are now limited in their power. Research on primary mechanisms (i.e., on different abilities to learn) largely concludes that males and females differ little in their cognitive capacities. Indeed, a leap of faith is required to assume social scientists can actually separate innate (i.e., genetically endowed) from learned abilities. Standard measures of student skills are products not only of our genes, but also of childhood experiences, ranging from those typically influenced by families to those influenced by schools. Both influences shape different experiences by gender when they segregate boys from girls. But even acknowledging this confounding of "nature" and "nurture" in measures of aptitudes and abilities, contemporary research typically detects small, if any, gender differences. For instance, Figure 7.2 reports a 2003 test of academic skills and knowledge among 28,000 15-year-olds. Similarly, discrimination explains only a shrinking portion of today's gender segregation across fields (for fuller discussions, see Charles, 2011; Wolf, 2013). For instance, Table 7.1 shows that the majority of today's students in law, medicine,

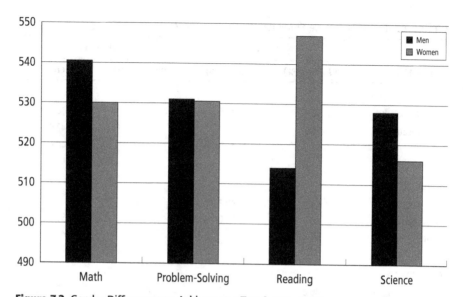

Figure 7.2 Gender Differences on Achievement Test Scores, 2003

Source: Bussiere et al., 2004, *Measuring Up: Canadian Results of the OECD Programme for International Student Assessment (PISA)*. Ottawa: Statistics Canada, Human Resources and Skills Development Canada, and Council of Ministers of Education, Cat. No. 81-590, www.statcan.gc.ca/bsolc/olc-cel/olc-cel?lang=eng&catno=81-590-X.

dentistry, and business are female. A more promising explanation examines how preferences for various fields are shaped before women enter higher education.

Consider women's and men's secondary course selection, as shown in Table 7.2. At first blush, the table suggests this explanation has relatively little merit because high school course selection is fairly balanced by gender. However, note that fewer women than men are likely to take Grade 12 physics, which is a key requirement for STEM fields in university. It is difficult to explain this early segregation with notions of chilly climates in university because these girls have little or no experience with those fields to begin with. This fact leads us to refocus our question: what causes gender differences in early course selection?

Maria Charles and her colleagues (Charles, 2011; Charles and Grusky, 2004; Charles and Bradley, 2009) offer a provocative cultural explanation. They see the rise of "post-material" values in affluent societies as having a two-fold effect on gender. On the one hand, post-materialism calls for a more egalitarian and equitable world, and refuses to justify discrimination on the bases of gender, race, religion, or sexuality. For decades it has been socially unacceptable to declare women to be inherently inferior to men, or undeserving of advanced educations and professional careers. But on the other hand, post-materialism also places great value on notions of self-realization, that is, the right *to choose* educational and occupational careers that are not only practical (i.e., yielding good salaries and job security), but also to allow us to express ourselves and our passions. In today's world, many are encouraged to "study what they love," not just what pays well.

Table 7.2 Grade 12 Course Enrolment by Gender and Year

Grade 12 Course	2003		2011–12	
	Women (%)	Men (%)	Women (%)	Men (%)
English				
British Columbia	52.4	46.8	51.7	48.3
Nova Scotia	50.0	50.0	53.0	47.0
Ontario	54.5	45.5	54.0	46.0
History				
British Columbia	50.3	49.7	50.0	49.0
Nova Scotia	49.0	51.0	49.0	51.0
Ontario	54.8	45.2	52.8	47.2
Mathematics				
British Columbia	46.2	53.8	46.8	53.2
Nova Scotia	50.3	49.7	50.7	49.3
Ontario	47.0	53.0	46.5	53.5
Physics				
British Columbia	29.8	70.2	32.0	68.0
Nova Scotia	39.0	61.0	34.7	65.3
Ontario	33.6	66.4	33.9	66.1

Most recent data: British Columbia 2010–11; Nova Scotia 2011–12; Ontario 2010–11.

Charles and her colleagues note that despite much cultural change, Western societies have retained strong vestiges of traditional masculinity and femininity, even in new sectors of employment. STEM fields like computer science, for instance, still carry strong connotations of masculinity, speaking to old ideals of tinkering with machinery (Villar and Guppy, 2016). But other cultures make different gender associations. Charles (2011) notes that in Malaysia, for instance, computer science is considered to be very suitable for women because its tasks require thought rather than brawn, and are usually performed in offices rather than outdoors. Taking a broader, cross-national view, Charles notes that many countries beyond North America actually enrol *more* women in science than in non-science fields. This occurs particularly in nations *not* known for gender progressivism or feminism, such as Iran, Oman, Saudi Arabia, Romania, and Azerbaijan.

What is going on? Charles pinpoints two things. First, relatively affluent nations like Canada have had a "social services revolution" that has transformed their job markets. New jobs now exist for a wide array of personal services, such as all kinds of therapy—for speech, mental health, physical ailments, occupational problems, marriage, family, relationships, and so on. Universities in Western nations now offer elaborate catalogues of courses in such fields. And most importantly, those fields attract practitioners who are overwhelmingly female. But in developing nations, where fewer people have large disposable incomes, those fields are far smaller or even unknown. Third World policy-makers place far more priority on STEM fields, which they deem essential for modernizing their economies. Second, STEM courses in those nations' secondary schools are often mandatory for everyone—male and female. Girls are exposed to science and math right through high school, whether they like it or not.

Charles (2011) concludes that despite the rise of gender egalitarianism, Western values of personal choice are reinventing gendered patterns of enrolment across fields. According to Charles, freedom of choice in secondary and post-secondary education allows us to affirm our inner selves, even those that remain stereotypically gendered. She speculates that many of us lean towards gender-conforming fields because we are subtly rewarded by peers and family for doing so, and are subtly discouraged from violating gender conventions. So, today's men and women can be "separate but equal;" equal in their rights and opportunities, but "separate" in many of their schooling and occupational choices, even new ones. And because STEM fields offer many labour market advantages, many outcomes are separate *and* unequal.

These patterns are also partly due to the choices of men, who rarely venture into what are seen to be female fields like nursing or early education. This lack of movement is partly due to the relatively lower rates of pay in such fields, but may be due to a lack of new ideologies that might celebrate such movement. Women who first entered former male bastions may have been seen to violate appropriate gender roles, but any stigma was often balanced by cultural innovations that celebrated such women as "pioneers," "trailblazers," or "breaths of fresh air." Do comparable innovations exist for trailblazing males? At this point in time, there are few. Such men can be stigmatized as not being "real men," effeminate non-breadwinners. Alternative interpretations of their career choices—helping people, serving society, or contributing to the economy—are yet to prevail.

Adapting our framing used in Chapter 6, we ask: do schools equalize opportunities for men and women, or do they actively reproduce traditional divisions? To think about this issue, we compare indicators of change across four different realms: schooling, job markets, family, and culture. Figure 7.3 illustrates changing gender "gaps" between 1976 and 2010 using several indicators.

Schooling gaps are represented by university degree attainment. Job market gaps are indicated by an index of occupational segregation (the extent to which males and females are employed in different jobs). Family gaps are represented by labour force participation rates, and "culture gaps" are indicated by polling data on proportions of men and women approving of single women having a child. The bottom line, representing education, shows the most dramatic

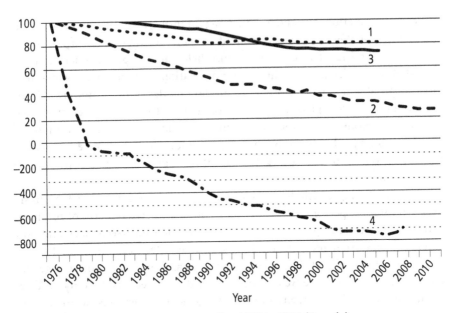

Figure 7.3 Four measures of Gender Inequality, 1976 to 2010 (Canada)

Notes:

1. Occupational Gender Segregation (data, 1976–2011, Canadian Census)
2. Gender Gap in Labour Force Participation (data, 1976–2008)
3. Per cent approving of single women having a child (World Values Survey—1982, 1990, 2000, 2006)
4. Gender Gap in Educational Attainment—ratio of male to female undergraduate university degrees, logged and normed (data, 1976–2008)
5. The first, second, and fourth measures are time series expressed as rates of change since 1976, standardized to a starting point of 100. The attitude question (approving single women having a child) is not standardized because the four data points do not correspond with the other time series.

change. Male advantage in 1976 gave way to parity by 1980 (as indicated by the zero line), and after 1980, a reverse gender gap emerged and continued to widen. The next lowest line—labour force participation—shows a continually declining gender gap. But the rate of change is far slower and remains far from parity. At a constant rate of decline, this line would reach parity in 25 years. The next line—occupational gender segregation—shows far less change; gender segregation declined by 20 per cent over the time period. Finally, the top-most line—the per cent approving of single women having children—shows slowly converging attitudes among men versus women.

What do these indicators all mean? First and foremost, they suggest education has undergone the most dramatic change by far; only schooling has a reverse gender gap. In contrast, change is far slower in other realms. Women continue to participate less in labour markets, occupational segregation remains substantial, and many men retain traditional attitudes towards mothering (see also Guppy and Luongo, 2015). This comparison suggests that education, as an institution, is relatively dynamic and fast-changing. Other spheres may even be impeding further change in schooling. It is possible that current levels of job segregation are "feeding back" and constraining students' choices of field of study, sometimes defying schools' attempts to promote new gender roles. All in all, we interpret this data as suggesting that schools, relative to other spheres, are "progressively gendered institutions." We further develop this argument in Chapters 11 and 12.

Racial and Ethnic Variations: Beyond Vertical Mosaic and Abella Images

Canada has been described as a mosaic. Starting with the diversity among the First Nations people who first populated the land, followed by the arrival of the French and the English, and finally through the explicit policies of the late nineteenth and early twentieth centuries to find immigrants to populate the West, the country has always been ethnically mixed. But today, Canadian schools are more diverse than ever. The immigration patterns of the past few decades have made our student bodies far more multiracial and multicultural. And, while Canada has always been diverse, it has also always been deeply stratified. Inequality has been a persistent quality of Canadian life. John Porter (1965), Canada's most famous sociologist, coined the term "**vertical mosaic**" over half a century ago to describe the intersection of class, ethnicity, and inequality, and he implicated schools as an active generator of disparities.

So how have inequality, diversity, and recent change affected school attainments? The functional perspective leads us to expect few differentials in attainment by race and ethnicity. According to this perspective, modern needs for a meritorious labour force, in tandem with "common" school ideals, ought to compel schools to be colour-blind and to reward everyone equally according to their efforts and talents. This model would predict that ascribable characteristics such as skin colour, linguistic accent, or ancestry should have a minimal impact on school success. In contrast, the Marxist model of *reproduction* predicts virtually no mobility among disadvantaged racial or ethnic groups. It instead imagines Canadian society as a caste system, where destinations are pre-ordered from birth, arrayed sharply by race, where schools are designed to channel minorities towards low-paying jobs in ethnic ghettos. Finally, the third position, which we label the "*limited compensation model*," predicts that schools can partly counteract some inequalities, but that legacies of societal disparities will constrain what they can do. From this point of view, schools offer new opportunities to many minority immigrant groups, but also reinforce some longstanding inequalities.

The reproduction model in education has been elaborated in two distinctly Canadian traditions. John Porter's (1965) seminal treatise, *The Vertical Mosaic*, portrayed Canada's numerous ethnic groups as being arrayed on an elaborate hierarchy of power and advantage. One indicator Porter used was education. His census data showed that those with the most education and who thus monopolized the school system were Canadians of British origin. Following directly behind were those of northern European ancestry, who were likely privileged by their physical and cultural resemblance to the British majority, Porter reasoned. Then, ranked accordingly, were those of central and southern Europe, French Canadians, various other minorities, and finally, Aboriginal Canadians. Porter's portrait of inequality in Canadian society depicted a multi-tiered ladder, a vertical mosaic with numerous ethnic groups ranked according to their resemblance (or not) to the British majority.

For many years Porter's work was hailed as a potent symbol that could galvanize efforts to fight inequality. But for the past quarter century, it has been criticized on both empirical and conceptual grounds (see Brym, 1989; Ogmundson, 2002). Empirically, researchers have either questioned his original methods or found much change among patterns of inequality since the 1960s. Conceptually, researchers have found glaring errors in how Porter linked census data to his claims about Canadian schools. In the 1960s Canada was recruiting workers from countries like Italy, Portugal, and Greece to enter manual labour jobs that required little formal education. But Porter incorrectly attributed those groups' meagre educational attainments to discrimination in Canadian schools rather than to immigration policy. Critics reasoned that a truer test of discrimination would be the school attainments in Canada of those immigrants' children. Subsequent research has found that Canadian-born children from southern Europe are in fact above the Canada-wide average (Davies and Guppy, 1998; Boyd, 2002, 2008).

Policy-makers soon changed how they conceived of inequality. Beginning in the 1980s, they looked south of the border for inspiration and implicitly discarded Porter's image of ethnic inequality as a multi-tiered ladder, replacing it with a more American-styled dichotomy. Groups in Canada, they now argued, were stratified into two massive camps: whites and visible minorities. We call this the "**Abella image**" because of the political influence of Judge Rosalie Abella's report for employment equity policy (Abella, 1984). In sociology, that report spurred the decline of the multi-tiered "ethnic" conception in place of a more dichotomous "race" model.

However, these two images of inequality are just that—conceptions to be tested with empirical data. For our purposes, the important question pivots on whether or not either image captures the complexity of educational attainment in contemporary Canada. Are school attainments still highly unequal, and if so, are they arrayed on a multi-tiered ladder with those of British origins at the top? Or are they sharply dichotomized, with white Canadians enjoying substantial advantages over visible minorities?

Figure 7.4 suggests that neither image fits today's complex patterns of educational attainment. We provide two tests of the imagery of Abella and the idea of Anglo-Canadian dominance in education. Figure 7.4 shows university degree attainment for Canadians between the ages of 25 and 39 born in this country. This figure divides this group into those who have both parents born in Canada versus those who have at least one parent foreign-born. While this is certainly not a perfect test, one would presume that if immigrant children were to struggle in the

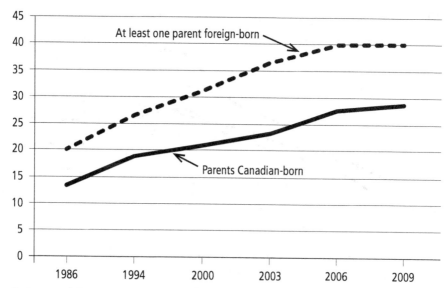

Figure 7.4 University Degree Attainment (in %) of Canadian-Born People Aged 25-39 by Birthplace of Parents, 1986-2009

Source: Author's calculations from Turcotte, 2011; based on Statistics Canada national sample from the General Social Survey (original data cover 12 different surveys, we use only six for simplicity of presentation).

Note: The survey dates are uneven so interpreting the annual rate of change is deceiving and is not the point of the figure (see text).

Canadian education system that people with two parents born in Canada would be more likely to graduate from university. The panel shows exactly the opposite. For six different years between 1986 and 2009, people with at least one parent foreign-born have been more likely to attain a university degree.

Figure 7.5 provides a second test of the same idea. Here the population of Canadians between 25 and 39 is divided by mother tongue (the first language a person learns). The figure shows that for six different data points, those whose mother tongue is neither English nor French are more likely to have university degrees. As Figures 7.4 and 7.5 suggest, this data is entirely inconsistent with the idea that people whose parents are foreign-born or whose first language is a foreign language are stigmatized and held back in the Canadian education system. They may face discrimination, but if they do they are still more successful academically than their peers who learned one of the official languages at birth or who had both parents born in Canada. (Recall that Table 6.1 reported very similar findings.)

Group variations in Canadian school attainment are difficult to depict in either Porter's or Abella's terms. There are great variations *within* both the visible minority and non-minority groups, with the clearest disadvantages being experienced by Aboriginals (for more evidence, see Boyd, 2008; Hou and Bonikowska, 2016; Thiessen, 2009). Patterns of attainment vary greatly among minority groups and among immigrants. Aboriginals are uniquely disadvantaged, while African-Canadian, Latino-Canadian, and other minority students are also underachieving.

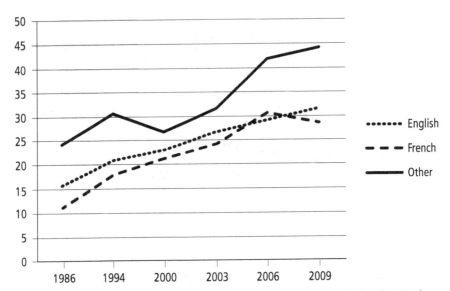

Figure 7.5 University Degree Attainment (in %) of Canadian-Born People Aged 25-39 by Mother Tongue, 1986–2009

Source: Author's calculations from Turcotte, 2011; based on Statistics Canada national sample from the General Social Survey (original data cover 12 different surveys, we use only six for simplicity of presentation).

Note: The survey dates are uneven so interpreting the annual rate of change is deceiving and is not the point of the figure (see text).

But if the form of inequality seems to take the shape of a multi-tiered ladder, there is little trace of the old British domination claimed by Porter 50 years ago. The existing data suggest that we need to look closely at the particular experiences of relatively unique groups.

What Is Schooling's Role in Change and Persistence?

Having described some evolving patterns of school attainment, our next task is to explain them. We next examine sociological efforts to sort out the various impacts of schools, families, and broader environments on racial, ethnic, and ancestral disparities.

Another vantage point on the "school versus society" debate comes from examining major legacies of race and ethnicity in Canadian history. School attainments vary markedly among racial and ethnic groups. Some scholars trace these variations to particular school processes, while others look to three legacies in Canadian history: differences in socio-economic status, colonization, and immigration policy.

Canada's ethnic groups, as in other diverse nations, differ greatly in their socio-economic and residential conditions. Compared to others, Indigenous people are more likely to live in rural areas, while immigrants cluster in urban areas. Some of those immigrants, but certainly not all, enter Canada with very few economic resources. For instance, some American scholars (e.g., Hao and Ma, 2011; Kao and

Thompson, 2003) have compared school attainment of various minorities over generations. They consistently find that socio-economic background is the most consistent predictor of school success for youth of any ethnic background. Aggregating to the group level, they assess the "predictability" of each ethnic group's attainment, that is, whether they attain levels of schooling that would be expected from their average socio-economic status. These researchers find that most immigrant groups have "predictable attainments." A few fare better than expected, yet even they converge towards the national average over subsequent generations. For instance, Asian and Jewish immigrants and their children have fared much better than would be expected from their SES. But in later generations, their attainments become far more "predictable;" their above-average attainments stem mainly from their higher-than-average socio-economic status, urban residence, and greater propensity to enrol in private schools. But some groups continue to fare worse than would be expected from their SES, such as African- and Latino-Americans. In Canada, SES is a far stronger predictor of attainment than is race/ethnic background, though some groups fare worse than would be expected from their SES, such as African- and Latino-Canadians and especially Aboriginal people, who are the most disadvantaged on all dimensions of social class.

But those SES patterns need to be understood in a historical context. Another legacy is the conquest of North American Indigenous people and their continuing economic subordination and residential segregation (see Chapters 3, 11, and 12). Rarely in world history have formerly enslaved minorities or conquered Indigenous people been fully integrated within the modern society and enjoyed full economic and political parity. In most international cases, including Canada, conquest and colonialism from previous centuries have continued to generate inequalities to this day. And, those stark inequalities in turn are reflected in education. These legacies continue to shape reforms aimed to enhance the educational levels of Indigenous people. It has not proven easy to reconcile the twin aims of boosting attainment while simultaneously ensuring that Indigenous identity and cultural heritage is respected and nurtured (see Frideres and Gadacz, 2011; St. Germain and Dyck, 2011).

Another legacy is mass immigration throughout Canadian history. Canada has had, historically, one of the world's highest rates of in-migration. But its sources and selection of immigrants have changed markedly over the past 50 years. Until the 1970s, immigration officials sought manual and skilled labourers from Europe, most of whom had relatively humble levels of schooling. Canada's immigration profile has since changed dramatically, luring far more immigrants from other continents, particularly Asia, and targeting many with advanced educational credentials. This shift has had consequences for ethnic patterns in Canadian school attainment. Some groups enter the country with the profiles that typically promote educational success—high levels of parental education, comfortable incomes, and urban residence—while others do not (Hou and Bonikowska, 2016).

Three legacies combine to make connections between race, ethnicity, and educational success quite variable in Canada. The history of colonization continues to generate patterns of low school attainment among First Nation, Métis, and Inuit youth. Changing selection processes in our immigration system have brought groups to Canada with greatly varying resources. Once a group is established within Canada, most eventually attain levels of schooling that are "predictable" from their current level of resources, though not all do so. Nonetheless, any understanding of attainment must acknowledge these legacies in addition to processes that are internal to schools themselves.

And, here's one final and important caveat: most forms of social disparity emerge *within* broad social categories like gender and race. This within-group inequality is growing (for US data, see Leicht, 2016; for British examples, see Wolf, 2013). Said another way, between ethnic and racial groups there are inequality differences, but within any ethnic group there is often great inequality in wealth or school achievement or morbidity. Likewise, among women (or men) one finds far greater ranges of income, educational attainment, and other indicators of life chances, than one finds between, say, the median woman and the median man. This understanding of inequality is not new (for older Canadian arguments, see Brym and Fox [1989], Liodakis [2002]), but it may have been forgotten in recent years. This caveat is important for educational policy: while most equity initiatives are pitched at easing group-level differences in schools, other policies are needed to understand students' needs at finer-grained, individual levels in order to be truly effective.

Sidebar: Thinking about Equity Categories

Let's step back and ponder what we have done so far in this chapter. To chart patterns of inequality, we categorized students by some broad demographic traits: economic conditions (class), social expressions of biological sex (gender), and ethnic ancestry (race). "Race, class, and gender" are categories with much social currency. They have a taken-for-granted quality. Educators (and sociologists) routinely invoke them. Few question whether they capture real social divides in people's life chances and experience. Ask someone to identify their gender or race, and most, with the exception of transgendered people, can quickly give a definitive answer. But asking someone about their social class is more complicated; while almost all "see" economic class, most people claim to be "middle class" regardless of their income and wealth. These categories form an implicit template by which officials count student enrolments, collect data, and devise equity policies.

The term "equity" offers a particular usage of such categories. It isn't precise; there is no consensus on its meaning. But it connotes something more than a special need or unique characteristic. Schools have long sorted students by religion, language, and ability (physical and mental) based on the rationale that each represents a distinct community (religious or linguistic), or have distinct teaching needs. But "equity" is a newer term that refers to a perceived social injustice to be rectified in institutions like schools. School equity aims to promote academic success by responding to unique student needs.

Changing Terminology for Indigenous Peoples

For the goal of Indigenizing Canadian education, what terms should be used? Advocates reject old labels that stem from legacies of racial insults, cultural hierarchies, and impositions of external authority. Advocates push for terms that show respect to Indigenous peoples, acknowledge their unique identities, and signal new partnerships with the rest of Canada. Today, businesses, governments, and activists are issuing guidelines on appropriate language. But choosing suitable terminology can be tricky. Many different terms are being used simultaneously, even among Indigenous peoples themselves. What could be considered to be apt varies by one's expressed purpose in different local, national, and international jurisdictions.

Some terms are rooted in particular ancestral lineages, histories, and traditions. For instance, some major groupings in Canada include the Kanien'kehá:ka (Mohawk), Mi'kmaq (Micmac), xʷməθkʷəy̓əm (Musqueam), and 'Irəkwɔl (Iroquois), among others. Other names for similar and overlapping groups include the Haudenosaunee and Anishinaabe peoples (see Milne, 2016). Often these terms imply clear connections to land and territory.

But other terms persist through their entrenchment in legislation. Centuries ago, the term "Indian" was coined after Columbus's voyages when he mistakenly believed he had found a new route to India. Despite that mistake, and despite its disrespectful connotation, it continues to have legal meaning. The term was embedded in Canada's Indian Act, which designated legal statuses with government-issued cards, permission to live on reserves, exemption from some taxes, and eligibility for certain government services. In 2011, there were 901,053 Registered Indians in Canada (according to Statistics Canada), while double that number reported having Indigenous ancestry, totalling about 6 per cent of the Canadian population. Though many fault the term "Indian" as a colonial imposition, some elders still use it because it was long institutionalized as an arbiter for legal statuses and rights.

Since the 1970s, the term "First Nation" has gained wide usage, referring to status Indians who are members of one of 600 recognized bands. The Assembly of First Nations, the largest and most established Indigenous political organization in Canada, is composed of elected chiefs from these nations. The term has a popular appeal because it clearly identifies Indigenous peoples as the original inhabitants of what is now Canada.

However, the term "First Nations" ignores two other Indigenous groups that were enshrined in the Canadian Constitution of 1982: the "Inuit"—an ethnic and linguistic group in the far north, and the "Métis"—people of mixed Indigenous and European ancestry. To deal with this inclusiveness issue, some governments coined the acronym FNMI, adding the terms "Métis" and "Inuit" to "First Nations". But this acronym still does not encompass those Indigenous people who have unclear connections to particular First Nation territories, such as survivors of residential schools who were removed from their home communities and never returned. Their identities became legally precarious: despite knowing they had an Indigenous ancestry, they could not demonstrate their status, and had to pass on that uncertainty to their descendants.

continued

To partly address this issue, the terms "Native" and "Aboriginal" were used to imply a general Indigenous ancestry that underlay claims to being among the "original" inhabitants of a land, while avoiding any reference to a particular community. But even those terms have been criticized for presuming that a group needs a primordial connection to a territory in order to be recognized. Some critics have called for a term that captures a variety of disenfranchised minorities in modern nation-states, beyond Canada, that have common experiences of colonial incursion, yet do not necessarily have an ancient claim to a geographical area.

Today, this term of choice is "Indigenous." It identifies peoples across a range of modern countries that endure colonized relations with various "settlers." The term has ascended throughout the world, championed by the United Nations. Yet, even this term is contentious. It was not invented by Indigenous peoples, but instead stems from a foreign and imperial language (Latin). Furthermore, it is a product of globalization, not localization. Its currency comes from drawing parallels between colonized peoples across far-flung jurisdictions, not from recognizing the distinct claims of any particular group. As such it glosses over huge differences in identity, language, and history among very different groups, particularly among those who descend from both settlers and the colonized. It also fails to recognize incursions among different Indigenous peoples in pre-modern times.

Using appropriate terminology can be challenging in Canada. Some have roots in racist slurs, yet remain enshrined in law; others speak to local traditions and practice yet are out of step with international trends, and still others enjoy currency in global institutions, yet are used only sporadically at grassroots levels. For a thoughtful and informed summary of these issues, see http://indigenousfoundations.arts.ubc .ca/home/identity/aboriginal-identity-terminology.html (accessed August 15, 2016).

Equity categories are not static. New categories are occasionally introduced, contested, and slowly institutionalized over time. Prevailing labels used to categorize students can change. Some stakeholders dispute various categories, saying they are an illegitimate lens for recognizing student differences. Others worry that categorizing students can bring stigma. Still others press strongly for some categories to have widespread recognition in schools. "Sexual and/or gender minority" is an equity category that provokes all three reactions.

Sexuality

In recent years, perhaps no other equity category has attracted as much attention as student sexuality. Sexuality continues to provoke a polarity of views. Some stakeholders, especially social movement activists, urge schools to recognize gay, lesbian, transgendered, and questioning youth, and do so in order to respond to the stigma, bullying, and harassment that confronts them in many schools. But other stakeholders, especially some religious conservatives, refuse to officially recognize this category at all.

Educators face pressures to thus recognize *and* overlook student sexuality. On the one hand, sexuality has been institutionalized as a legitimate category in human rights codes, workplace equity guidelines, and anti-discrimination policies. But on the other hand, equity policies for this group face several roadblocks. For starters, it is currently difficult to identify sexual minorities in schools. They face more risk than any other minority by becoming visible; virtually no other group has a comparable fear of being "outed." Further, because most youth are not sexually active until high school, many younger students may be unsure about their sexual identity. Nor is students' sexual orientation officially recorded in school administration records, unlike other categories such as gender, class (recorded by a proxy like free-lunch status), age, or disability status. Sexual minorities are not a clinical population that is treated by another profession, unlike some mental health or criminal categories. And despite ongoing reports of their bullying, beating, and harassment, some stakeholders refuse to grant sexual orientation legitimacy as an equity category. As a result of these roadblocks, school equity policies for sexual minorities are in their infancy; teacher awareness training, curricular material, codes of conduct, and special programs are relatively new and sparse. Nonetheless, there has been change. Policies aimed to confront peer bullying of gay and lesbian students have been drafted in recent years. Sex education curricula discuss sexual orientation, prompting criticism from some conservative quarters, yet prompting others to move those issues to human rights curricula. In some respects, this path of curricular revision follows those blazed for gender equity in the 1970s and 1980s, and for race and multicultural equity in the 1990s. Such revisionism signals how schools increasingly "do" equity using an increasingly standard template, as we discuss at the end of this chapter.

How do sexual minorities fare in Canadian schools? One consequence of their social stigma is a lack of systematic data on their attainments, at least compared to most other equity categories. Compiling such information would require surveys of students about their sexual orientation that were linked to their student records. But many students, parents, and educators are reluctant to gather such data. Nevertheless, there are some reports on other school experiences of sexual minorities (see Frohard-Dourlent, 2016). Figure 7.6 refers to one such study.

This 2009 survey of 1,500 high school students in an Ontario school board asked students to self-identify as one or more of the following: bisexual, gay, lesbian, queer, questioning, two-spirited, transgendered, or exclusively heterosexual. About 8.4 per cent self-identified as at least one sexual minority. Students were also asked to self-identify their gender, race, and religion, whether they had been bullied in school, and to judge their school's social climate. As Figure 7.6 shows, 55.4 per cent of sexual minority students reported having been bullied, compared to 27.5 per cent of those who self-identified as exclusively heterosexual. No other category—male, female, Aboriginal—had a comparable rate. When student grade, gender, ethnicity, and nation of birth were taken into account, sexual minorities reported being almost three times more likely to be bullied than did exclusive heterosexuals.

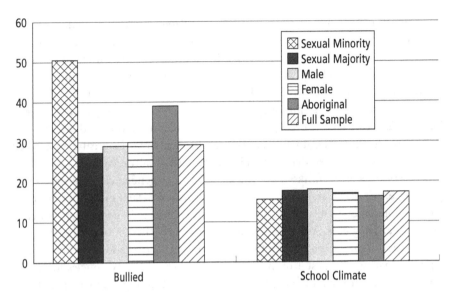

Figure 7.6 Reported Bullying and Negative School Climate among High School Students in One Ontario School Board (n = 1,500), Data Analyzed by Scott Davies, Denise Lamanna, and Tania Medieros

Notes: "Sexual minority" combines students who self-identified as any one of the following: bisexual, gay, lesbian, queer, questioning, two-spirited, or transgender. A few respondents who appeared to offer "prank" answers (based on their written statements in open-ended questions) were removed.

Sexual minorities rated their school's climate (feeling belonging, welcomed, respected, liked, and perceiving that teachers had high expectations for them) more negatively than others. These findings are similar to those in other North American studies (for a review, see Fetner et al., 2012). Overall, as many high-profile events have illustrated, sexual minority students continue to have negative experiences in schools, sometimes erupting into violent attacks. Those experiences are likely to reduce their school attainments, though definitive data is lacking.

Box 7.1 Gay-Straight Alliances in Canadian Schools: Progress and Controversy

Schools have long housed student associations that reflect equity categories, variously representing girls, boys, different nationalities, languages, religions, and ethnicities. But the clubs that have received the most attention in recent years have been Gay-Straight Alliance (GSA) organizations. These associations were formed in order to create safe spaces in schools for LGBTQ (lesbian, gay, bisexual, transgender, and questioning/queer) youth. They are generally student-run support groups for sexual- and gender-minority students who face personal difficulties or social hostilities, and aim to raise awareness of equity issues. They originated at a private boarding school in 1988 in Concord, Massachusetts, but have spread internationally. Canadian research suggests GSAs are effective vehicles for providing safe spaces in schools (see Fetner et al., 2012). Canadian students appear to strongly support them. Almost 88 per cent of 7,000 respondents to the 2011 Ontario Student Survey agreed students should be allowed to establish GSA organizations (www.peopleforeducation .ca/wp-content/uploads/2011/10/OSTA-P4E-Student-Parent-Survey-Final-Report. pdf). But not all stakeholders agree. Some Catholic school board officials have protested against explicitly naming clubs using terms that invoke sexuality, and instead prefer non-sexual names such as "Equity," "Open Arms," or "Respecting Differences" clubs. Some Catholic boards have since dropped their protests, but others are engaged in a standoff against ministries of education, who declare the establishing of GSA organizations to be a human right. This controversy underscores conflicting school mandates: some wish to uphold a particular faith, yet are expected to also comply with evolving notions of human rights.

Mental Health and Other Emerging Equity Categories

Schools have long offered "special education" to students deemed to have unique needs that require their own curricula and pedagogy. But today educators are being urged to recognize and accommodate other student needs within mainstream schooling. Mental health issues such as depression, anxiety, obsessive compulsive disorder, and Tourette's syndrome increasingly affect many high school students. Their teachers are increasingly expected to recognize these conditions, help students cope, and provide extra supports and accommodations.

But why might sociologists hesitate at this task? For decades, "labelling theorists" have focused on societal reactions to mental health conditions. Beginning in the 1960s, Erving Goffman, Thomas Scheff, and others drew attention to the social stigma surrounding mental health problems. Formal labelling, they contended, often worsened those conditions. Being socially recognized as "mentally ill" could limit job prospects, attract the stigma of being "different" and "strange," and might encourage labelled persons themselves to internalize that stigma and regard themselves as "different" and "strange." For many with a mental illness, facing their social stigma was worse than the illness itself.

Labelling theory has been very influential not only in sociology, but also in criminal justice, where it helped shape policies such as the Youth Criminal Justice Act. But social changes since the 1960s and 1970s may be altering the dynamics of labelling, at least in the realms of mental health and schools (for a discussion, see Deroche, 2012). Over the past decade, several anti-stigma campaigns are now attempting to transform public perceptions of mental health. The Canadian Mental Health Commission launched its "Opening Minds" campaign in 2009 to raise awareness of the real prevalence of mental health problems and the harm done by stigmatizing those problems. Further, since the 1960s, the number of mental health conditions recognized by psychiatrists and psychologists has greatly expanded. The DSM—the psychiatric "bible"—has expanded enormously since its inaugural edition 60 years ago: from 106 pages in 1952, to over 1,000 pages in 2013. This great proliferation of labels can certainly have the effect of expanding the influence of psychiatric professionals, but may also serve to "normalize" more mental health conditions by making them appear more prevalent, and hence less strange, threatening, and deviant. New kinds of supports and accommodations in schools, as discussed in Chapter 5, may allow students—at least sometimes—to be labelled with a mental health condition *without* being streamed downward, and instead receive accommodations such as extra time to complete assignments and exams. If some labels are no longer disadvantaging and stigmatizing, people's incentives for being labelled may change. As a study of parents in a highly competitive high school found, "At Wilton, Special Ed is a good thing" (Demerath, 2009).

But labelling still represents a dilemma for teachers (Ho, 2004). On the one hand, a label can serve, even unwittingly, to mark students as different, even deviant. On the other hand, it can be used to leverage additional supports that would be otherwise unavailable. Fully "de-labelling" a condition may reduce stigma, but may not bring needed supports. The dilemma hinges on whether recognizing a difference necessarily entails unequal treatment, or whether schools can treat students as "different but equal." This debate animates much diversity policy. Should schools institutionalize equity categories by offering distinct programming or by collecting data on these student categories? Or should schools just provide *symbols* of diversity—posters on walls, images in textbooks, themes in lesson plans—but go no further? Finding a tactic to recognize difference without bringing stigma and inequality is a challenge that comes with institutionalizing a relatively new equity category in schools. At this time, mental health is not a fully institutionalized category. Few schools have attempted to collect data on students with mental health problems, largely to avoid violations of privacy. As a result, the relation between mental health and educational attainment is not truly known. Some research suggests that students with officially recognized special needs greatly underachieve in Canadian schools (Sweet et al., 2012), but we do not know the fortunes of students with unrecognized emotional and behavioural problems. When an equity category is not yet fully institutionalized, many core questions about attainment remain unanswered.

Some advocates are trying to find answers by introducing new equity terms. One emerging term is "neuro-diversity," a fusion of thinking from neuroscience and multiculturalism—a rather unlikely pairing! Advocates want educators to view conditions such as autism and Asperger's syndrome as *differences* that occupy their own spots along a wide scale of neurological variation, but not as *deficits or problems* (Smagorinsky, 2011). They want mainstream schools to recognize and accommodate these differences by linking new scientific understandings of cognitive capacities and evolving notions of human rights. Advocates hope these new pairings can alter attributions for students' atypical actions and abilities. For instance, consider a teacher who has a student who utters strange grunts and phrases in their classroom. Without knowing anything further, the teacher may believe the student is being weird, strange, or wilfully annoying, and may even punish them. But if the teacher uses a scientific frame and sees the child as having Tourette's syndrome, they may better understand and help the child.

Why are mental health, sexuality, and neuro-diversity particularly important for sociology of education? They spotlight processes by which schools explicitly or implicitly judge certain types of students to be abnormal *and* necessarily problematic, or simply different but equal. They also highlight evolving notions of "educability"—judgments of whether students are suitable for mainstream academic instruction. Schools have long disqualified many students, particularly those seen to have cognitive deficits, but are being urged to see more and more students as educable.

Towards a Sociology of Educational Equity

How do equity categories emerge? We see a two-step process. First, much initial action occurs in political arenas outside of schooling. Social movements and political parties press equity issues to the fore, using what sociologists call "contentious politics." Equity-oriented social movements strive to confront established forms of thought and routines that can pose barriers to certain groups. The logic of contention includes a broad repertoire of tactics, ranging from violent forms like takeovers and hostage-taking, to conventional actions such as protests and rallies, to milder forms such as petitions, lobbying, and negotiations. The latter can sometimes indicate a taming of a movement, but can also be a successful end product of successful mobilization. Social movements take a keen interest in public schools because the latter offer a large and captive audience, representing a crucial opportunity to politically socialize the next generation. In their extreme forms, contentious politics can make schooling appear to be a battleground. But in their milder forms, they appear routine and uncontroversial.

Logics of contention can filter into schools through three channels. A top-down channel flows directly from political parties to schools. Public schools are, after all, ultimately governed by elected political parties that dictate policy to departments and ministries of education. Many policies follow this route, ranging from accountability to finances to bullying and discipline to equity policies. The latter include regional redistribution policies, funding formulas that direct extra funds to schools in poorer neighbourhoods with many ESL students, strategies to encourage girls to pursue STEM fields, and new legislation in response to high profile "bullycides." A bottom-up channel allows students, teachers, or parents to protest a policy and sometimes initiate change. A middle channel is more evolutionary. New teachers and students can slowly bring into schools new understandings of equity. Younger teachers, having been exposed to new equity thinking in their training, may connect contemporary understandings of equity to their notions of professional responsibility.

This latter channel represents a second step by which equity categories emerge, and involves a transformation of the logic of contention into the **logic of institutionalization**. But this transformation also involves a reciprocal influence between social movement and party politics and school routines and organization. Contentious politics can eventually alter the cognitive categories and organizational routines of schools. After a period of time, educators may begin to "see" sexual minorities and students with mental health needs, and increasingly see them as "equal." At first, a student club like a GSA organization may need to be established through logics of contention like protests, lobbying, and petition-gathering. But over time, GSA organizations can be established with far less political energy if they are seen to be legitimate organizations; as such, they become more widely adopted and diffused through time and space.

But external politics are also shaped, in turn, by schools' internal institutional processes. Public schools are run by a professional bureaucracy. Top-down school policies are ultimately implemented by school personnel. Historians like David Tyack and Larry Cuban (1995) have emphasized how, in a turn of phrase, "schools shape policies." Schools have their own routines, and reforms must be compatible with them to strongly take hold. Also, as David Labaree (2010) notes, top-down school policies often slowly fizzle away if they are unpopular with parents, while those that are popular can take a stronger hold.

This institutionalization process can be fuelled by the emergence of "equity professionals." Most large school boards have equity policies and specialized professionals that enforce those policies. These equity professionals work to transplant terms from political arenas into schools. Their impact can be subtle: to make equity categories and discourse appear normal, routine, and taken for granted.

Through this process, terms that were once products of activism eventually get institutionalized in schools. Former terms that were colloquial, insufficiently inclusive, and even insulting get replaced in order to signal new norms of inclusion. Think of a variety of shifts: from "coloured person" to "person of colour" to "race" to "racialized minority;" from "sex" to "gender" to "transgender," from "homosexual" to "gay and lesbian" to "LGBQ" to "LGBTQ"; and from "Indian and Eskimo" to "Aboriginal and First Nations" to "FNMI" (First Nations, Métis, and Inuit) to "Indigenous". These shifting terms mark the space where activism meets bureaucracy. The former embodies logics of contentious politics, the latter Weberian pressures to standardize and codify discourse into rules and procedures. Equity professionals work to align ongoing efforts of external social movements and evolving notions of human rights with schools' internal processes.

Most crucially, these professionals strive to spread logics of "seeing difference as equal" and expand the number of categories under the rubric of human rights. Whereas gender and race were once primary categories for equity, today's professionals are broadening that rubric to also cover sexuality and mental health.

As it spreads through society, their thinking becomes part of the logic of reforming institutions like schools. A great range of school jurisdictions are slowly converging on a similar set of equity categories that officially designate certain groups to be in need of remedy. The meaning and content of "equity" changes over time, yet becomes more standardized and universal in the process.

Conclusion

The previous chapter documented persisting class inequalities in school attainment, while this chapter documented the remaking of gender inequalities and the uneven patterning of racial inequalities. Similar patterns have been found in many other developed nations (for social class, see Breen et al., 2009; Shavit, Arum, and Gamoran, 2007; Sirin, 2005; for gender, see Breen et al., 2009; DiPrete and Buchmann, 2013; for race and ethnicity, see Rothon, Heath, and Lessard-Phillips, 2009; McAndrew, 2013). We also discussed the impact of sexuality, gender, and mental health on student experience in schools, particularly in the realm of bullying (see also Malette, 2017). Our thinking about equity categories leads us to ponder processes by which various categories are contended and institutionalized in schools, noting the dilemmas of labelling that accompany any effort to establish any category. This thinking prompts us to examine the contexts in which schools produce and reduce inequality. The next section examines the organization of schooling, focusing on forces that shape school structures, curricula, and teaching practices.

Questions for Critical Thought

1. In the previous chapter we asked you to ponder whether a learning problem like attention deficit disorder (ADD/ADHD) should be considered to be a "primary" or "secondary" mechanism of educational inequality. After reading this chapter, have you changed your mind? Discuss.

2. Can faith-based schools pursue their religious mandates while also providing equity to sexual and gender minorities? If so, what organizational strategies might they use?

3. Is special education more "equitable" now than it was in past? Refer to evidence in your answer.

Suggested Readings

Armstrong, Elizabeth A., and Laura T. Hamilton. 2013. *Paying for the Party: How College Maintains Inequality* Cambridge, MA: Harvard University Press. This case study of young women in an American university dorm began as a study of gender and sexuality, but ended as an exploration of the continuing power of social class in higher education.

Jimenez, Tomas R., and Adam L. Horowitz. 2013. "When White Is Just Alright: How Immigrants Redefine Achievement and Reconfigure the Ethnoracial Hierarchy," *American Sociological Review* 78(5): 849–71. This article is based on field work in a Silicon Valley high school, where children of Asian immigrants were enforcing new racial norms. They granted whites less status, associating them with lesser academic achievement, laziness, and mediocrity, while linking Asian-ness to higher achievement, hard work, and success. Are there similar trends in schools in and around Vancouver, Victoria, Toronto, Calgary, Edmonton, Winnipeg, Ottawa, Montreal, or Halifax?

Pascoe, C.J. 2011. *Dude, You're a Fag: Masculinity and Sexuality in High School.* University of California Press. The author finds that the "specter of the fag" serves to regulate heterosexual as well as homosexual boys and how their "fag discourse" is tied to both gender and sexuality.

Web Links

Ontario Ministry of Children and Youth Services
www.children.gov.on.ca/htdocs/English/topics/specialneeds/mentalhealth/strategy.
aspx
This website gives details on "Moving on Mental Health," a new Government of Ontario initiative designed for children, youth, and families in need of support.

Assembly of First Nations
www.afn.ca/index.php/en/policy-areas/education
The Assembly of First Nations website is dedicated to improving the schooling of First Nations people.

Martin Family Initiative and Indigenous Youth
www.maei-ieam.ca/about.html
This initiative hopes to enhance education for Indigenous students. It consists of partnerships between Indigenous organizations, businesses, provinces and territories, and educational institutions.

Part III
Social Organization and Legitimation

8 The Changing Organization of Schooling

Learning Objectives

- To use organizational concepts to compare educational organizations to other types of enterprises and highlight the unique character of schools

- To examine changes in the interpersonal relations between students and teachers, and link those changes to various experiments to engage students with academic work

- To be able to alternate between middle-range theories and micro- and macro-levels of analysis in studying the sociology of education

Introduction

For some social scientists, schooling's main contribution is to build a stockpile of skilled workers for the economy. As discussed in Chapter 3, for economists—and for human capital theorists in particular—this role is integral in the knowledge economy. Others are skeptical, believing "credentialing" to be the vital contribution of schooling (Collins, 1979). Still others believe that schooling's prime power comes from the "charter"—its authority to confer a socially recognized status on graduates—rather than its ability to create skills (e.g., Meyer, 1977).

In a schooled society, these phenomena are all at work. More jobs now require higher-order cognitive skills. Credentialing is increasingly unquestioned as a method to ration access to scarce occupational positions. But graduates exit schools with a tremendous variation in their abilities. No school guarantees skill levels among its graduates. This raises a key question: what is the goal of school organizations: to produce requisite talents or to appear legitimate? What shapes the way schools are structured?

In this chapter we examine schools as organizations, highlighting changes over the past century in how they have exerted authority, motivated students, and bureaucratized. We outline key theories, highlight various experiments in school organization, and end with a glimpse at contemporary "market-based" schools. Our goal is not to repeat what we did in Chapter 4, where we examined alternative schooling forms, but instead to understand how the dominant organizational form that now prevails has come into being. This examination leads us to conclude that current trends are serving to strengthen some of schools' organizational constraints.

From Traditional to Legal Authority

The way Canadian schools are structured has changed substantially during the last 150 years (see Prentice, 1977; Gidney and Millar, 2012). Pre-modern schools were small and informal. Educational authority was highly decentralized. Canada had thousands of school boards, most controlling only a few small schools. Most teachers had great discretion over how to carry out tasks, usually with little formal training. Lessons were taught as they had been taught years before, without a raft of formal guidelines or background studies. Schooling was not guided by large-scale planning and rule-bound execution. Rather, schools operated more via what Max Weber called "**traditional authority**."

Teachers were proclaimed to be, along with religious authorities, moral trustees of society. More prestigious teachers had a priestly aura (and indeed in many schools, teachers were priests!). They had **in loco parentis** or parent-like authority over students. They could discipline students largely as they pleased, often resorting to corporal punishment (e.g., the strap). Students obeyed teachers through a sense of loyalty and social bond with authority; they did not see themselves as signatories to any kind of social contract. Teachers and their school material commanded public deference. The curriculum was justified by its association with time-honoured values, moral precepts, dominant religions, and treasured cultural traditions. But gradually government authority rationalized schooling even in the late 1800s. This is what school promoters were effectively doing (Axelrod, 1997; Prentice, 1977).

Both the pace and intensity of this early rationalization have changed. Over the course of the twentieth century, a sense of citizen duty to obey authority figures and institutions gradually weakened. In its place, more contractual understandings emerged that stressed mutual obligations and individual rights. Any reading of legislation affecting education shows the gradual growth of regulatory language. More recently, the student role has been redefined. Today's youth culture is less deferential, and their parents, acting as their supporters, are far more challenging towards educators, even litigious. In Weber's terms, modern schools have gradually altered their relations to students and families, embracing a more "legal-rational" authority.

A central feature of legal-rational institutions is their rationalized character (see Chapters 2 and 3). Modern organizations are alert to remove the arbitrary, to provide a clear and sufficient reason for every social act. Over time, this justification has been expressed less in older moral terms and more in terms of social utility and newer notions of rights. Public education is hailed less as a vehicle to pass on traditions and more one to build nations and develop economies. This trend can be seen in rudimentary changes in curricula. Over the late twentieth century, Canadian schools cut "irrelevant" courses, such as ancient languages, and adopted new ones that were seen to be necessary for daily living (e.g., computing). Course material was selected less according to humanistic ideals and more according to pragmatic visions of personal, societal, and economic development.

This rationalization altered society's essential image of teachers. Teachers were seen less as moral exemplars and trustees of the common good, and more as professionals who were responsible for skill development. This shift to legal-rational authority can be seen also in student discipline. Particularly since the 1970s, schools have de-emphasized rigid forms of personal discipline, proclaimed the rights of students, and taken seriously their need to be accountable to parents.

New modes of authority also changed the governance of schooling. Administration became centralized, with power moving up to board and provincial levels. Some, perhaps token, forms of influence were also directed to parents and students. Since the 1960s, conceptions of educational "stakeholders" have broadened to make room for student government and, more recently, parent councils. Importantly, as power has both "moved up" to provincial levels and to some extent "moved down" to parents and students, educators have felt their influence squeezed. Teachers, for example, report feeling less "appreciated" (see Guppy et al., 2005).

This movement from traditional to legal-rational authority was accompanied by a change in organizational form. Schools grew in size and looked less like little houses and more like office buildings or factories (see Box 8.1). They were increasingly governed by general rules. Lines of control were formalized from top to bottom, with hierarchical chains of command and clearly defined responsibilities. Regulations delegated authority to credentialed officials in a more specialized division of labour, particularly at upper grade levels. Personnel were selected for their advanced training, rather than for personal ties to high-ranking officials. Increasingly, public schools hired teachers that were certified with university credentials. Curricula were standardized, increasingly approved by higher-ranking bodies. Schools adopted near-uniform age-graded levels from kindergarten through Grade 12, using generic course categories like mathematics, literature, science, and history. This is a story of standardization.

This modernization also altered social relationships. Students were increasingly seen as "clients." Revised ethics of teaching proclaimed the individuality of the student, championing the importance of tailoring education to each unique pupil. The role of the educator shifted from providing moral leadership towards diagnosing particular learning difficulties and recommending solutions, akin to how a doctor or lawyer works with clients.

In short, modern schools became more *bureaucratic*. Schools became a world of rules, regulations, flow charts, and timetables, resembling modern hospitals, corporations, and governments. In some respects schools are exemplars of Weber's ideal-typical bureaucracy. They rationalize their activities, produce mountains of paper trails, create universalistic rules, and so on. However, they diverge from Weber's ideal type in one fundamental respect: they are not necessarily organized to be efficient or effective. This does not mean they are "wasteful," but rather that they are "institutional" organizations with peculiar traits, as detailed in the next section.

Box 8.1 School Size and Class Size

Have schools become super-sized? As with many stories, this one has different angles. If we look at size historically, and from the angle Ariès took (Chapter 4), we find a trend towards smaller classes. That is, the actual number of students per educator has reduced dramatically over the last century (see Figure 8.1). But from a different angle some will argue that schools have become top-heavy with administrators. We now have more superintendents, financial officers, principals, and on and on (i.e., rationalization). Official statistics classify these administrators as educators although they spend little time in the classroom. But even with this minor caveat, over the century the size of classes has declined.

What we see from yet another angle is that schools themselves have grown dramatically larger (see Figure 8.2). Research suggests that school size matters—too small and schools do not have adequate facilities such as labs or gyms, but too big and schools lose any sense of community (Lee and Loeb, 2000). Finally, we want to reiterate two key points. First, relative to other factors, and in particular family background, school differences have relatively modest effects on student achievement. Second, more challenging than class or school size is the diversity of abilities within classrooms and schools.

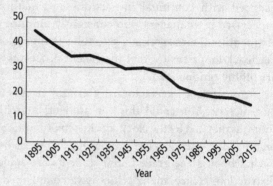

Figure 8.1 Ratio of Students to Educators in Public Elementary and Secondary Schools, 1895-2015

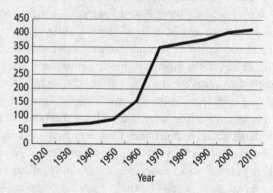

Figure 8.2 Average Size (# of Students) of Public Elementary and Secondary Schools, 1920-2010

Institutional Theory: Schools as Loosely Coupled Bureaucracies

When thinking of their organizational character, it is useful to compare schools to very different kinds of bureaucratic enterprises. Consider an automobile factory. Its goal is relatively clear—to manufacture a profitable car. To meet a bottom line of production quotas and costs, factories carefully select "inputs"—reasonable quality steel/plastic, machinery, rubber, workers, and so on. They discard defective inputs. Factories then employ a complex and well-coordinated technology to transform inputs into a clear output—a car. Processes are sequenced with continual inspections and quality controls. Work is directly supervised by managers who constantly monitor procedures. When problems are identified, managers strive to solve them because faulty cars reduce profits. Feedback loops ensure that inefficient processes are retooled. These activities are highly rationalized.

Are schools like factories? Certainly many school attributes are rigidly bureaucratic. You could think of students marching from classroom to classroom, as dictated by the clock. Lock-step promotion from grade to grade is rigidly organized. All schools use standardized courses in math, English, and sciences. Each school is age-graded, and students are subjected to a sequenced plan of instruction. Hence, many critics have complained that schools are too factory-like, inhumanely processing students, treating them as inanimate "inputs" and "outputs."

But in crucial ways, schools differ from factories. Consider the complex relation of school "inputs" and "outputs." Unlike factories, public schools cannot easily discard any "defective" inputs. Their mission is to teach all children. They are forbidden from choosing among students, and certainly cannot flatly reject any, except in the most extreme circumstances. As discussed in Chapter 4, this organizational reality compels public schools to accommodate an astounding array of student talents, aptitudes, motivations, and abilities. This compulsion produces a persistent finding: ever since educational data has been collected, measures of students' social backgrounds have been better predictors of their achievement than have measures of schools' technical processes. In other words, student "inputs," their parents' socio-economic status, cultural capital, and level of education, are powerfully connected to their eventual "outputs"—school achievement. School "processes"—teaching methods, financial expenditures, instructional resources—certainly influence learning, as shown in the literature on seasonal learning discussed in Chapter 6. But the impact of school processes on many student outcomes is relatively weaker than is the impact of student background. The coupling of the huge variability in students' conditions outside of schools with public schools' inability to select their students makes it incredibly challenging not only for schools to equalize their outputs (say to guarantee that all of their graduates have a specific level of skills) but also to demonstrate their effects on students that are independent of students' prior characteristics. We discuss the large literature on "school effects" in Chapter 11 (for Canadian examples, see Davies and Aurini, 2013; Johnson, 2009).

Consider other aspects of school outputs. For starters, there is no consensus over the goals of schooling. Just what is the purpose of a school? Car factories have a singular aim—build profitable cars—but schools have multiple aims, ranging from imparting cognitive skills, to nurturing citizenship, developing character, and creating a spirit of community. These multiple goals complicate any evaluation of school "outputs." Many are hard to measure. Can we accurately gauge school success at nurturing citizenship? And, even if everyone agrees that schools should improve children's cognitive skills, methods of defining and measuring that output are not fully agreed upon. Educators continue to debate whether standardized tests are valid indicators of learning.

Moreover, consider the "process" or "technical activity" of schooling. Factories can use assembly-line methods to convert inputs into outputs. Assembly lines are the epitome of a highly rationalized technical process. Engineers carefully design these systems, creating exceedingly coordinated procedures that are subject to continual monitoring. But classroom "technology" is far less rationalized. There are no "engineers" that pre-design standard learning procedures; instruction is rarely subject to continual monitoring and retooling by supervisors. Instead, teachers are granted a significant degree of discretion in relatively isolated classrooms, quite unlike factory hands on the assembly line. Few teaching methods are exactly defined, systematically designed, and universally applied. While teachers are given broad instructional goals, they are expected to apply their own discretion, unique skills, and personal talents. Supervisors (i.e., principals) rarely inspect teachers' instructional strategies. And, when they do monitor teachers, those inspections are usually quite subjective, rarely based on exact measures of performance. Teachers are told what they should accomplish in the classroom, but are then left to their own devices, and are rarely sanctioned for deviating from some kind of standard procedure.

But many aspects of schooling are rationalized. Standardized course labels are routine—"math," "science," and "history." Teachers must be certified, at least in public schools. They must record enrolments and grades using standard procedures. They must broadly follow an approved curriculum. And students typically progress through a sequence of grade levels, from elementary to secondary. If and when they graduate, they receive a universally recognized credential—a high school diploma. All of these formalities are highly structured, standardized, and controlled. They comprise the essential image of a "school."

So, schools are bureaucracies with a twist: some of their activities are highly rationalized (age-grading, hours of instruction), others are not. Instructional activity varies considerably from classroom to classroom, school to school, board to board, and province to province. Every Canadian high school has something called "Grade 10 English," but the innards of that course can vary from province to province, board to board, school to school, and even teacher to teacher.

For these reasons, institutional theorists such as John Meyer describe schools as "loosely coupled;" their formal structures are highly rationalized, but their technical activities—instruction—are not. This loose coupling ensures that schools are bureaucratic, but not always efficient.

Now, why would a school want to be loosely coupled? There are two essential reasons. On the one hand, any attempts to rationalize instruction could create all sorts of problems. Pedagogy is more art than science. Instruction is a very uncertain technology; methods that work for one student may not work for another. Teachers work with large groups of students, and can only individualize their techniques to a limited degree. Further, most teachers would resist overly intrusive regulations. Many are guided by their professional discretion and experience, rather than the dictates of distant bureaucrats. Few want their classrooms to be monitored by a supervisor. While teachers are often required to broadly follow a curriculum, they regard any routine check of their performance as a violation of professional autonomy. So, rather than closely monitoring their technical activities, schools have instead adopted a "logic of confidence," a norm that respects the professional autonomy of teachers.

On the other hand, schools are rewarded when they conform to formal structures, and are punished when they deviate. These formal structures are products of an evolving image of what comprises a legitimate "school." One century ago, school forms varied markedly from town to town, region to region, and nation to nation. But over the twentieth century, standard school forms were institutionalized, not only across North America but around the world (Meyer et al., 1992; Meyer and Ramirez, 2000). There is far less variability now in school organization. Today, "real schools" are recognized as having certified teachers, age-grading, recognized course labels, and so on. Any school that lacks these formalities appears to be illegitimate. Imagine an elementary school without grade levels, or an English/French course, or a qualified teacher. That school would be ordered to change or face possible closure. But if that same school conformed to standard formal structures of schooling, yet was not particularly successful in teaching reading to children, it would face criticism, but not the threat of closure. Our point is that public schools can usually survive as long as they comply with standard rules, regardless of whether their practices are demonstrably effective. This reality gives schools a peculiar reward structure. In one instance, they are allowed considerable latitude when arranging their technical/instructional activities. But in another instance, they must rigidly conform to standard formal structures or face possible sanction. This motivates public schools to conform to formal structures in order to appear *legitimate*. They closely monitor things like teacher certification, administrative paperwork, properly formatted grades, officially approved texts, and other practices that maintain a facade of legitimacy. Yet they remain loosely coupled by leaving technical activities—instruction—to the discretion of teachers.

Institutional theory builds on this analysis by showing that schools have become "isomorphic" over time. Isomorphism refers to the process by which organizations become more similar in form. Because schools can enhance their legitimacy by conforming to standard organizational forms, newly opened schools, anywhere in the world, usually copy successful existing schools or correspond to directives from higher authorities. This process of isomorphism makes schools resemble one another to an amazing degree. And, it is driven by their need to appear legitimate, not by any need to rationalize their technical processes, as would be true in a factory.

PISA PANIC!

Who is the most influential figure in global education policy today? John Dewey? Paolo Friere? Bill Gates? Some commentators point not to those figures, nor to a great classroom teacher or popular minister of education, but instead to Andreas Schleicher, a relatively unknown German statistician. Why? Schleicher oversees the Program for International Student Assessment (PISA). Despite his anonymity, he has become a de facto broker of international school policy. PISA tests thousands of 15-year-olds on math, reading, and science every three years in 60 countries around the world. Other similar tests exist, but PISA is *the* international measure of school effectiveness.

Through the lens of world culture theory (Chapter 3), PISA embodies "global rationalization," a process by which national leaders reshape their institutions according to evolving international norms of efficiency and effectiveness. PISA is a standardized metric used to measure performance. Its focus on basic literacy, math, and science speaks to human capital rationales that see those subjects as the rudiments of the new economy. And, the scoring of PISA into international rankings is compatible with prevailing images of global competition.

But is this rationalization always a good thing? The practice of ranking necessarily creates winners and losers. Policy-makers look to PISA to rate their schools, interpreting high international rank as evidence of success, and drops in rank as cause for concern. Finland, topping many recent PISA rankings, hosts foreign educators searching for lessons to improve their schools (a phenomenon known as "The Finnish Fetish"). Ranking also triggers "PISA panic" in many countries. Intensely negative media coverage usually follows disappointing PISA results, along with warnings of a looming crisis of skills and employability among youth. Critics blame mediocre teaching and curricula. Policy-makers devise a series of school reforms aimed at shoring up basic skills and boosting scores in the next round of PISA.

continued

Some educators worry that this panic has made PISA too influential. To rank well, schools probably need to teach curricula compatible with PISA content. PISA may be promoting a curricular standardization across national school systems, one that is insensitive to local needs, and may be narrowing the scope of curricula. Subjects untested by PISA—history, music, art, physical education, even sociology—may be de-prioritized in schools (see Meyer and Benavot, 2013). Incidentally, Canada has fared quite well on PISA (see Chapter 9), but recent drops in math scores have sparked our own panic, prompting reforms to the teaching of math. Should Canadians use PISA to guide our schools?

Schooling as Work: Motivating Students

Yet, even loosely coupled schools encourage students to do *something*. Schools are work organizations. Work detail varies from school to school and remains endlessly contested. Nevertheless, students are expected to actively study in some way. Schools must therefore attempt to motivate students. But in doing so, they face many barriers. There is a yawning gap between professional ideals and the realities of schooling. Teachers want voluntary clients, but modern public schools are "custodial institutions" whose clients are mostly captives, compelled to attend by truancy laws. Students are assigned teachers—they rarely choose them. Teachers have authority to sanction and to judge students. The sheer number of students in most classes creates distance in teacher–student relationships, straining professional ideals of individualized instruction. Large classes also compel teachers to adopt various control strategies in order to prevent some students from becoming overly disruptive. Much of schooling is about coercing students to comply with school directives.

The challenge for today's teachers is to make students engaged and enthusiastic, yet play a policing role when necessary. But today's "legal-rational" teachers lack many of the options of yesteryear's teachers to deal with wayward students. They no longer exert a "parent-like" authority, nor possess an arsenal of disciplinary tactics like corporal punishment, humiliation, or dunce caps. Today, those tactics can bring reprisals. Many teachers now believe that any undue "policing" can subvert their professional ideals and distract them from their real aims. Strict discipline codes, for instance, can be self-defeating when they generate resentment and stifle independent desires to learn (see Hurn, 1993). While many schools still have "zero tolerance" for extreme forms of deviance, few contemporary educators want to be the kinds of disciplinarians found in prisons or mental institutions. Yet, because teaching is still akin to workplace supervision, teachers need to motivate their captive students in less-than-optimal settings.

Another problem is that teachers offer incentives to students that are weaker than those in employing organizations. Schools typically elicit student compliance by dispensing grades. While grades are a valuable currency for entering higher education, they can be meaningless "funny money" to youth who do not pursue post-secondary studies. As a result, many educators want to motivate their students to have not only an instrumental tie to schooling, but to also be *intrinsically* motivated to learn. Many theories of pedagogy encourage students to engage and gravitate voluntarily towards educational material. They strive to entice students to work not just for grades or to evade sanction, but out of a true interest and fascination. But achieving this goal also faces several constraints.

Progressive Pedagogy in the Mainstream: Less Structure Is Better

The previous section noted a series of hurdles that confront teachers. Most teachers would love to have fully voluntary enrolees, but most youth are legally compelled to attend school. Many would love to work with students on an individual basis, but school funding levels make that impossible. Some would like to select which students enter their classes, but public schools are mandated to serve everyone. Rather than working in ideal settings, teachers must teach sizeable classes of captive students that vary greatly by ability and motivation. Dealing with this reality is their principal challenge.

Over the past century, **progressive education** reformers have discussed ways to optimize teaching and learning given these constraints. "Progressive pedagogy," rooted in the intellectual efforts of John Dewey early in the twentieth century, has been a force in Canadian schools since the 1960s (see Davies, 2002; and Chapter 10). Dewey proclaimed the need to make learning child-centred, an engaging activity directed as much by the student as by the teacher. Teachers should cater to students' interests, not vice versa (see Box 8.2 below). This re-centring of education, he argued, would unleash students' motivation for learning. This reasoning has underlined decades of reforms aimed at engaging students in modern school organizations (see Tyack and Cuban, 1995).

Mainstream schools have pursued this progressive agenda by de-structuring some aspects of the learning experience. Beginning substantially in the 1960s, progressives called for schools to be less regimented, arguing that strict rules and procedures could stifle rather than focus student imaginations. Over the past 40 years, fewer curricula have had rote- and memory-based exercises. Fewer teachers have demanded rigid discipline. Corporal punishment has been largely replaced with notions of student rights. More teachers encouraged some interaction among students, allowing them to chat and move freely in the classroom. Fewer teachers arranged student desks into straight rows while more adorned their walls with colourful posters and student artwork, often next to traditional

Box 8.2 Montessori and Waldorf

Montessori and Waldorf are leading brands among alternative schools. Maria Montessori (1870–1952) first opened her "house for children," her *Casa dei Bambini*," in Rome in 1907. In 1919 Rudolf Steiner founded the Waldorf School in Germany, a school dedicated to the children of the employees of the Waldorf Astoria Cigarette Company. Both schools have been hugely successful, both in terms of sustainability and spread. Now parents can send their children to either a Montessori or Waldorf school in most of the great cities in the world. Indeed Waldorf (www.iaswece.org) now reports having over 2,000 schools in more than 70 countries, while at least 22,000 Montessori schools can be found in over 114 countries (www.ami-global.org).

Similar to Summerhill (Box 8.3), both schools are rooted in a child-first, nurturing pedagogy. They stress all aspects of child development, from emotional through spiritual, physical, and psychological to intellectual. Computers and televisions are banned, natural materials as opposed to synthetics are stressed, and the creative and performing arts are central. In both approaches children are encouraged to be the active authors of their own development. Where differences begin to emerge is first with timing—Waldorf schools leave the three Rs of reading, 'riting, and 'rithmetic until at least age seven, whereas in Montessori students can choose to pursue this at much earlier ages. In Waldorf schools imitation and imagination are central at the earliest ages, with a premium placed on oral listening and memory. In contrast, the Montessori approach is more structured, with children grouped by age-ranges. As the teacher senses a willingness to learn new things, academic lessons are offered (see Edwards, 2002 and Nuhoglu, 2013 for comparisons of these two programs).

emblems such as the flag or the Canadian landscape. Each of these measures, progressives hoped, would encourage students to feel more at home, relaxed, and motivated.

Another trend has been to integrate learning. Many educators feel constrained by teaching discrete subjects that rarely connect with each other. For instance, they believe that less is learned if students follow a rotary system, taking a math class, then English, then science, and so on, without any attempt to discover any mutual relevance between these different topics. Many progressives advocated forms of "de-coursing" and the "project method" to promote a greater integration among topics. For instance, a Grade 5 class may begin a project on Africa, and devise a coordinated series of holistic lessons that combine elements of art, history, geography, literature, and even math. Progressives reason that such lessons are more enticing to students because they better illustrate the relevance of each subject, and create a more meaningful whole learning experience.

Finally, a repeated priority in progressive pedagogy has ing." While a notoriously slippery concept that has been t ways, "critical thinking" refers to the continual re-examinati that often are implicit in school topics. For progressives, le about memorizing facts, such as names or dates in history. I more about the processes of thinking—observing, analyzin_,_, about a fact-based end product.

Open Schools, Free Schools, and Deschooling in the 1970s

By the end of the 1960s, these progressive reforms filtered into many Canadian schools. The typical mainstream classroom became less regimented than it had been in the 1950s, at least in some respects. Nevertheless, some educators in the 1960s and 1970s felt these reforms did not go far enough. To further unleash intrinsic motivation and make educational experiences deeper and more meaningful, they wanted more radical departures from traditional school organization. They launched a series of experiments across North America, some of which live on today.

One such experiment was "open-concept" schools. These schools attempted to realize progressive ideals largely by altering their physical environment. Classroom walls were removed, replaced by large open spaces called "pods." Resembling contemporary kindergartens and Montessori schools, students were encouraged to move freely between various "activity areas" that offered semi-structured assignments and tasks. Students would work at randomly arranged tables, not in rows of desks, and were encouraged to interact freely. Overall, open-concept schools embodied many progressive ideals by attempting to motivate students with a freer and less regimented physical landscape.

Free schools took this experimental attitude further. Not content with de-structuring the physical aspects of schooling, free schools aimed to motivate students by de-structuring *all* aspects of schooling. The prototype for contemporary free schools was Summerhill, an English private school founded in the 1920s by A.S. Neill (see Box 8.3). In the 1960s and early 1970s, hundreds of free schools opened across North America, hailed by their advocates as the only humane way to organize learning. Most were closed in the 1970s, though some continue to this day in some versions of alternative schools and home-schooling.

Free schools were founded on an unshakeable belief in "authentic learning" as something that must be self-motivated, self-regulated, and self-evaluated, hence deeply personal to each learner, and ultimately non-measureable. Formal evaluations of students were seen to create unwanted power differentials between staff and students. While free schools varied in how they implemented this vision, many embraced the following features. Daily activities were voted on by the entire school community. No student would be forced to do lessons. Attendance was not mandatory, and all school exercises were optional. The educational experience was almost entirely unstructured, unless a student wanted to structure it by him- or herself.

Box 8.3 Summerhill

England's Summerhill is widely regarded as the first free school (see www. summerhillschool.co.uk). A.S. Neill, a charismatic educator, founded the school in 1921, wanting something quite unlike any other school that was in England at that time. He aimed to allow children to discover their identities and interests in a safe, self-governing, democratic community. All of its lessons were optional. Teachers and classes were available at specific times, but children themselves were free to choose whether or not to attend. Students of all ages were mixed together under the reasoning that everyone should be free to learn from everyone else in the school community. School laws and rules were made by majority vote; pupils and staff alike had equal votes. But has Summerhill survived in today's era of standardized testing and accountability? While Summerhill is still open, it has run into regulatory trouble for its low test scores. Nevertheless, it retains its unique philosophy of child freedom.

No grades or report cards were issued. Students were encouraged to develop their own ideas, interests, and talents without being compelled to compete with others or to measure up to some external standard.

While free schools represented some of the boldest experiments ever conducted in education, they were inherently unstable organizations. Most enjoyed a rapid rise and an equally meteoric demise within a few short years, perhaps due to two traits that made their survival precarious.

The first trait affected their external legitimacy. As we argued earlier in this chapter, mainstream schools derive much legitimacy by conforming to well-established "formal structures." But free schools, fascinating as they are, removed most of that structure. Many hired non-certified teachers, unimpressed by formal credentials. Many expunged structured courses, standard curricula, and rigid timetables. Some harkened back to traditional forms of organization by mixing students of all ages. These attributes made free schools unique, but also stripped them of organizational attributes by which schools garner legitimacy. Free schools' thin formal structures made them highly anomalous. If a school gets rid of teacher roles, credentials, curricula, marks, courses, and a daily time-table, is it still a school? Because free schools did not formally evaluate students, employers and post-secondary institutions were not sure if they could accept their graduates (see Box 8.4).

The second trait centred on their unstable internal dynamics. While free schools were part of a broader trend that replaced traditional forms of authority, made rules less arbitrary, and recognized the rights of all school community members, they went much further by dismantling teacher authority altogether. But without such authority, how could teachers motivate students to work?

Box 8.4 Free Schooling Taken to the Extreme: Illich's *Deschooling Society*

When free schools were sprouting up all over the continent, Ivan Illich (1970) published *Deschooling Society*, a literary phenomenon seldom seen in education. Illich, a radical theologian, relentlessly indicted contemporary schools. He portrayed schools, prisons, and asylums alike as worsening the very social problems they proclaimed to fix, wastefully and self-servingly expanding their influence over people. In older times, he wrote, people could perform literate occupations—teaching, journalism, and business—with little formal schooling by learning skills through their families or local communities. But modern mass schooling has equated "education" with enrolling in school, sitting through required classroom hours, covering modules, and passing courses—regardless of the real quality of learning. This institutionalization discourages self-taught learning, he argued, making ordinary people dependent on school credentials.

The solution to this problem, Illich argued, was to dismantle modern schooling. His verdict was based on a series of progressive assumptions: that all learners are driven by a natural curiosity, that schools alienate this natural desire, triggering apathy and rebellion among students. His cure was to allow learners, rather than "experts," to control teaching. Formal credentials would be banned, replaced with publicly funded vouchers that could be redeemed in "learning webs," networks where people exchange instruction in whatever skill they want to learn. Decades later, his proposal seems impractical. Today in our schooled society, almost no one is against school per se. Those with particular qualms want to reform schools, not dismantle them. But *Deschooling Society* is still worth reading as a barometer of social change, a glimpse to a time when the consensus over schooling was less complete, when anti-school treatises were less rare. And, while Illich's solution may be utopian, his sentiment about intrinsic motivation is still voiced by many educators today.

As seen in Illich's *Deschooling Society* (1970: P1):

> Many students intuitively know what schools do for them. They school them to confuse process and substance. Once these become blurred, a new logic is assumed: the more treatment there is the better the results; or, escalation leads to success. The pupil is "schooled" to confuse teaching with learning, grade advancement with education, a diploma with competence, and fluency with the ability to say something new. His imagination is "schooled" to accept service in place of value. Medical treatment is mistaken for health care, social work for the improvement of community life, police protection for safety, military poise for national security, the rat race for productive work. Health, learning, dignity, independence, and creative endeavour are defined as little more than the performance of the institutions which claim to serve these ends, and are "improved" by allocating more resources to their management.

This issue guided Ann Swidler's (1979) intriguing study of two free schools in Berkeley, California during the mid-1970s. Those schools lacked explicit rules, and instead promoted whatever students considered fun, exciting, casual, and unusual. The teachers were young, energetic, and idealistic, and loved to experiment with unorthodox lessons. Yet, most wanted their students to occasionally switch tack and do routine activities, such as participate in conventional lessons, do assignments, and work quietly on tasks. These unexciting things make teachers' jobs much easier; always being "on" is tiring, even for a radical pedagogue. But these teachers needed to motivate students without resorting to the formal authority wielded by mainstream teachers, who could reward students with grades or threaten them with penalties. How could free school teachers muster a minimum level of social control without having any sanctioning power over their students?

At first, Swidler noticed a particular tactic. Many teachers strove to cultivate a personal mystique. They aimed to appear cool, unpredictable, exotic, and complicated. In Weber's words, they worked to be charismatic. This image-conscious teaching had a purpose: it helped forge emotional bonds with students and coax them to work. This was an art of friendly persuasion.

But after a period of time, Swidler observed that many students stopped cooperating, even with the coolest teachers. Charisma seemed to have its limits, like a scarce commodity whose reserve is depleted with repeated use. So the teachers reacted with a new strategy: to entice students through personal revelations, pleas, and reminiscences that would expose their vulnerability. Teachers hoped that intimacy would bring them sympathy. For instance, if students were being disrespectful, a teacher might "open up" and express his or her personal feelings of betrayal or disappointment. But even this strategy was far from foolproof. While useful in the short term, Swidler observed that its impact weakened over time. Charisma was not a long-term substitute for formal authority.

Free schools illustrate both macro-level and micro-level features of modern schools. At the macro-level, mainstream schools need to appear legitimate by embracing predictable structural forms, regardless of whether educators believe them to be effective. This legitimacy creates trust in the community, allowing schools to send their graduates to workplaces and post-secondary institutions. By not complying with that organizational practice, free schools ceded a key source of legitimacy. At the micro-level, teachers face a key dilemma. On the one hand, they do not want to alienate students and quash their intrinsic motivation. In today's culture, overly rigid exercises of discipline will generate resentment and can ultimately backfire. But on the other hand, most teachers must brandish some level of authority in order to maintain levels of order needed to accomplish their tasks. Teachers walk a tightrope: they need to build personal ties with students, yet wield authority when needed. By not granting some legal-rational authority to its teachers, free schools lost a key source of organizational stability.

In retrospect, free schools and open schools were examples of a short-lived cultural expression of unhappiness with traditional schools. Today we see a contemporary movement with some eerie parallels. These newer reformers also want schools to shed some of their old organizational forms and transform themselves into something different, something more catering, and student-oriented. But far from sharing a hippie-inspired, anti-materialist ethos, these current-day radicals are taking their inspiration from the world of business.

School Choice and Market Reforms in Education

These new critics of public education partly resemble their progressive forebears. As did critics in the 1960s, today's reformers portray public schools as antiquated, call for new pedagogies, and lament educators as aloof and slow to change. But rather than claiming that today's public schools are de-humanizing, today's reformers see them as underperforming.

Over the past 20 years, "market" reformers have hailed school choice arrangements as the key tool for reforming public education. For over 30 years, advocates like Chubb and Moe (1990) have wanted to subject public schools to market forces. Why? According to these critics, public governance motivates schools to conform to legal conventions, rather than to provide effective service. Unions demand the hiring of certified teachers. Boards force compliance to curricular guidelines. Governments leverage school practices by various funding formulas. These bureaucratic shackles, they argue, make public schools like any inefficient monopoly: they become unresponsive to their clients. Market reformers aim to pry schools from the grip of bureaucracy, and instead expose them to competitive pressures similar to those faced by for-profit businesses.

One of their fundamental principles is to shift funding power from central bodies to parents. Current funding arrangements, they claim, trigger processes of isomorphism by rewarding schools for conforming to standard organizational forms. School choice reforms that placed funds directly in the hands of parents would, they claim, reverse these tendencies. These reforms would allow schools to survive only if they attracted fee-paying clients, and would thereby create an imperative for schools to cater to their clients. Further, they tout these market mechanisms as providing a better medium for matching the wants of parents and schools. Parents want a greater variety of school choices, they reason, and so they believe that choice arrangements would encourage the entry of new and innovative schools, and inject far more "breakthrough thinking" into schooling.

Choice reformers also champion market forces as a key lever to raise the quality of schooling. They reason that market forces can motivate schools to perform at higher levels by imposing real sanctions on schools (i.e., by depriving them of the funds needed to survive). Their prime mechanism for raising standards is the ranking of schools by their test scores, a common practice in Canadian media and think tanks. Choice reformers reason that "customers" can judge school quality only by comparing them according to some kind of "gold standard." Standardized test scores, they reason, provide one such benchmark. If parents can clearly see that a school is underperforming by such benchmarks, that school will either boost its performance or lose its clients, according to this theory.

Are more Canadians thinking along these lines? Research suggests that many Canadians share some sympathy with the broad sentiment of "choice," but far fewer embrace full-fledged market reforms (Davies and Aurini, 2011). School choice is currently growing in Canada, but much of it involves the creation of more choices *within* public school systems. Many urban public school boards have expanded their school programming in an effort to provide a wider menu of choice for families. Alberta has taken this creed the furthest, moving beyond standard school offerings with a range of educational innovations (recall the Edmonton Public School Board example highlighted in Box 4.1).

But other models of choice have shown less growth. Another Alberta initiative has been to create 13 "charter schools," based mostly in Calgary (Bosetti and Gereluk, 2016). These are independently run public schools that mostly pursue a special pedagogical theme. They are not private schools, since they operate on public funds and are regulated by the province. But their existence does inject market thinking into education, as they encourage parents to choose among a range of school themes, ranging from ESL, traditional academics, Suzuki music and philosophy, science and math, and programs aimed specifically at gifted, Indigenous, female, and at-risk students. But since emerging in the 1990s to much fanfare, the charter school movement has largely stalled in Alberta, and has failed to take root elsewhere in Canada. Similarly, the proportion of Canadian students enrolled in private schools has grown over the past 20 years, but mostly in affluent urban locales. For instance, the number of private schools grew by 40 per cent in Ontario over the past decade. In Toronto, almost 10 per cent of all students are enrolled in private schools, much higher than the national average of 6 per cent (Pizaro Milian and Davies, 2017). Similarly, Montreal now has a wide range of schools, many of which are semi-private, and receive only partial public funding (Desjardins, 2009). Yet, without further public subsidy, it appears that there are real limits to the growth of the private-school market, especially since most Canadians support greater funding for public schools (Davies and Aurini, 2011).

This limited impact of the school choice movement in Canada prompts a key question: do market forces have the impact on schools that are proclaimed by their advocates? As we have seen before, theory is one thing, empirical reality another. Studies of Toronto's private-school sector, a fast-growing educational market, are informative. This sector has many newly formed schools that are financially precarious and constantly need to attract clients to survive. Such schools epitomize the "lean and mean" market-driven schools, and make for a good test of the claims of market advocates. And indeed, as several scholars have found (e.g., Aurini and Quirke, 2011; Pizarro Milian and Davies, 2017; Quirke, 2013), market conditions had some expected effects. To attract clients, these schools developed specialty programs, offering small classes in an astonishing array of programs, mandates, and philosophies of teaching, ranging from intensive academics to woman-centred instruction to liberal arts, social justice and environment issues, museum-based studies, multiple languages, "core knowledge," accelerated learning, and even a few "alternative" schools. Some also offered alternate hours and part-time or per-credit courses. A few catered to diverse student populations, such as gifted students, athletes, dancers, those with Caribbean origins, or students with learning disabilities or special needs. Many have intimate classes of about 10 students, creating niches in an otherwise competitive marketplace.

But contrary to the predictions of market advocates, these schools did not compete via other forms of quality. Almost none reported their test scores, university placement rates, or compared their rank to other schools. Market competition did not drive them to improve their test score rankings. In fact, their precarious finances motivate them to avoid such competition, and instead seek specialized niches. Despite market competition, they had a loosely coupled organization.

These findings illustrate a key issue in school choice: on the one hand, schools are supposed to evaluate their students, and yet a key commercial credo is that the customer is king. When a for-profit school must assign student grades, is the customer still always right? Some Toronto private schools have been accused of "selling" inflated grades to attract students. Likewise, for-profit universities and colleges are not known for their academic rigour; indeed they are seen to relax their standards to retain struggling students (for discussions, see Aurini, 2012; Ruch, 2001).

The point is that markets have some unexpected impacts in education. Alberta's "quasi-market" of a variety of schools thrives through strong government regulation and generous public funding. In contrast, "purer" markets that lack government regulations and subsidies, such as Toronto's private-school sector or Canada's private tutoring industry, can unleash a greater variety of educational themes, but do not encourage schools to compete via high performance. Market forces by themselves may inspire schools to cater to student and family whims, but government oversight may be needed to nudge them to boost their quality. But most importantly, without public funding, private schools are accessible only to those who can afford them. As such, they cannot offer equity to the overwhelming majority of Canadians.

Conclusion

In contemporary times, schools' legal-rational organization has pushed them to experiment with different types of authority structures in order to accommodate their clients in more ways. In the 1970s, this involved transferring some power from teachers to students. Today, this sometimes involves using market mechanisms to make students analogous to customers. Both of these initiatives presume that students need to be treated as unique individuals. Both remain contentious. Whether students are seen to be equal voters in a school democracy or as customers in a school market, strong currents push schools to act authoritatively and guarantee some modicum of quality. As more and more jobs require educational degrees and diplomas, this role becomes more imperative, and can constrain schools' capacity to experiment with innovative pedagogy. The next two chapters examine two other aspects of school organization: curriculum and teaching.

Questions for Critical Thought

1. Many schools today have explicit codes of conduct that outline the rights and responsibilities for students and teachers alike. Do these codes illustrate Weber's types of authority? Or do they represent a breakdown of authority?

2. Provide examples of loose coupling among your current university courses. Can you see counter-instances of universities moving towards tighter coupling?

3. Given your own experience in school, how would you motivate students to be effective learners? What reforms actually work? Which backfire? Be brutally honest, with examples.

Suggested Readings

Aurini, Janice. 2012. "Patterns of Tight and Loose Coupling in a Competitive Marketplace: The Case of Learning Center Franchises," *Sociology of Education* 85(4): 373–87. This article discusses an application of new institutional analysis to private tutoring organizations. Despite the presence of tough market forces, Aurini finds that private education organizations retain loosely coupled forms.

Mehta, Jal. 2013. *The Allure of Order: High Hopes, Dashed Expectations, and the Troubled Quest to Remake American Schooling*. New York: Oxford University Press. This book recounts a century of attempts to apply principles of rational administration and control from above. Each reform wave gradually discovers that schooling is not easy to "order" from afar: policy-makers are too distant to know what schools need; teachers resist top-down mandates; and the practice of good teaching is too complex to be externally standardized.

Meyer, Heinz-Dieter, and Aaron Benavot, eds. 2013. PISA, *Power and Policy: The Emergence of Global Educational Governance*. Oxford, UK: Symposium Books. A series of contributors argue that PISA influence over global education has become excessive, concurrently serving as diagnostician, appraiser, and policy council to school systems all over the world.

Web Links

A.S. Neill's Summerhill
www.summerhillschool.co.uk
This is the official website for the world's longest running free school.

Education Reform
www.ctf-fce.ca/publications/Briefs/Report_EducationReform2012_EN_web.pdf
Prepared for the Canadian Teachers' Federation, and written by Andy Hargreaves and Dennis Shirley, this 2011 brief looks at reform initiatives and the role teachers might play in changing how schools operate.

Canadian Education Blog
http://educhatter.wordpress.com
This blog offers a very useful discussion on a range of topical issues in Canadian education, including topics such as alternative schools, charter schools, faith-based schooling, and school choice.

9 Curriculum
The Content of Schooling

||||||||||||||||||||||||||||||||||||||||||||||||||||||||||||||||||||||||||||||||||||||||||||||||||||||||||||||||||||||||||||||||||||||||||||||||||||||||||||

Learning Objectives

- To describe changing and enduring curricular forms and content
- To recognize reciprocal influences between society and the curriculum
- To detect mechanisms that standardize, rationalize, and stabilize curricula

||||||||||||||||||||||||||||||||||||||||||||||||||||||||||||||||||||||||||||||||||||||||||||||||||||||||||||||||||||||||||||||||||||||||||||||||||||||||||||

Introduction

Curriculum is the "stuffing" of school. It includes not only formal programs of instruction, learning material, course content, and lesson plans, but also school rules, procedures, and routines. Because schools are the primary institution responsible for socializing youngsters, curricular designers are mandated to nurture personal traits and technical competencies that will allow future citizens to contribute to both civic and economic realms. This mandate stretches curricular content to include teaching facts; promoting technical abilities such as arithmetic and grammar; boosting skills like debating, persuading, and critical reasoning; and promoting fundamental values and virtues such as civility, fairness, responsibility, and tolerance.

This broad mission makes the curriculum a lightning rod for intense debate. Curriculum controversy is fuelled by the complexity of knowledge in today's world. Scientific and technical knowledge is growing exponentially, world cultures are increasingly interlinked, yet school content can only represent a slim slice of all human knowledge. Even if one takes a restrictive view of knowledge as meaning just known facts, schooling can capture only a slice of what is known. The sum of human knowledge could never be condensed into one curriculum. A myriad of possible competencies, skills, and values could be stressed in schools. Not everything can fit. Further, if one takes a more expansive view of knowledge, recognizing competing systems of thought—scientific, religious, aesthetic, and even common sense—then it is doubly clear that not everyone's favourite slice can be fully included. Some groups will inevitably feel their understanding of the world has been given short shrift. Educators thus need to make countless decisions about school material in terms of what to include, how to sequence it, and how to optimize its breadth and coherence.

Sociologists probe these decision points. They seek to understand and explain how the curriculum is constructed and evaluated. They examine how schools prioritize some content over others, and hence "stratify" knowledge itself, defining what does and does not count as "official" knowledge (Apple, 1997; Young, 1998: 16–21). For instance, schools have been instrumental in promoting the cultural authority of science in the modern world, often privileging that cognitive model over others, such as religious or spiritual knowledge.

Consider the following two examples. First, Darwinian evolution is central to most school curricula, even though many people in the world, perhaps even a majority, believe strongly in other explanations for the origins of life. Second, conclusions based on the coherent, logical assembling of information and evidence are mostly favoured in schools over conclusions based on intuition, meditation, or a "sixth sense." Again, however, a great many people rely more on the latter types of reasoning than on the former in making decisions. Darwinian evolution and rational logic are simply two examples of the "official knowledge" that most school curriculum legitimates.

Schools also use the curriculum to sort and select students. Schools have the institutional authority to rate someone's ability and intellectual worthiness. With this responsibility comes more controversy. First, schools often create curricular tracks and decide which students should be assigned to which tracks (see Chapter 5). Second, the evaluation of a student's comprehension of the curriculum also generates social stratification. School success is tied to most people's eventual occupational attainment.

Finally, beyond imparting know-how and evaluating learning, schools also socialize students and aim to mould competent members of society. Through this process schools reinforce and legitimate some cultural standards and world views, helping them become "second nature." It is useful to pause here. "Legitimating" is a central feature of what schools do, and the curriculum serves to effectively affirm the legitimacy of some cognitive models and cultural systems over others (Egan, 1997). This legitimating function is often taken for granted and routinely ignored.

One further concept is important. Sociologists often distinguish between the manifest (overt) and latent (hidden) processes that operate in schools. This applies to the curriculum as well. Curriculum guidelines do not, for example, explicitly highlight competition and badges of ability, but these are important features of schooling. As such they constitute part of a "hidden curriculum" that may not be explicitly and officially designed by educators.

This chapter uses a variety of theoretical lenses and research traditions to examine the curriculum. We describe major trends in its content and form, investigate mutual influences between curriculum and society, and identify key mechanisms by which the curriculum is constructed and delivered.

Content: The Multiple Dimensions of Modern Progressivism

The curriculum has changed continuously over the past century and a half. Conceptions of effective teaching and learning have been transformed. In the earliest days of Canadian public schooling, school promoters such as Jessop and Ryerson stressed moral values. They conceived of children as vessels into which teachers could pour proper values. Strict discipline and rote memorization were staples of teaching. Instruction centred on the teacher. Students endured endless memory drills (e.g., spell "stork," spell "quark," spell "quart").

Gradually, over the last century, educators embraced a more nuanced view of teaching and learning. With schools increasingly mandated to accommodate more and more students with diverse skills, philosophies of pedagogy changed towards what Canadians call "progressive education." Progressives aim to make schooling more egalitarian, humanistic, and child-centred, and usually contrast this approach with more traditional subject-centred and teacher-centred styles (Davies, 2002). The educational emphasis shifts from "covering content" towards "facilitating learning," hoping to make the needs and interests of the student paramount (see Bromley, Meyer, and Ramirez, 2011).

What are some key elements of this shift from traditional to progressive curriculum? We can point to four examples. First, some subjects have withered, particularly ancient languages like Greek and Latin. Dropping those courses reflected the modern belief that courses should be "useful." A second key change is revealed by curriculum aimed to accommodate a growing diversity of learners, especially at the secondary level. With more students staying longer in school, educators have tailored curriculum to a wider variety of abilities and motivations. This has created a tension: some commentators deplore the "dumbing down" of the curriculum while at the same time others remark on its rising level of sophistication (along with rising student IQ scores, noted in Chapter 5). Third, the curriculum has become mostly more diverse within broad subject categories, typical of the "mall-ing" of high schools discussed in Chapter 5. More schools offer selection among core courses, such as in gifted or international baccalaureate programs or among science electives. Consider that in 2017 New Brunswick high school graduates could satisfy the science requirement by passing one of nine upper-level courses: Auto Electrical Systems, Biology, Chemistry, Environmental Science, Introductory Electronics, Micro Electronics, Physics, Physical Geography, or Robotics and Automated Technology.

Box 9.1 Teaching Prejudice Any Longer?

In the 1960s two university scholars, Garnet McDiarmid and David Pratt, undertook a study of the Ontario high school curriculum. In launching the study, William Davis, the Conservative party's Minister of Education, said:

> We are about to make a thorough examination of all school textbooks, not just for the purpose of removing material which may be offensive, but more

continued

important, to make sure that our textbooks . . . [do] full justice to the contributions of many peoples to the development of our Province and Nation. (McDiarmid and Pratt, 1971: vii)

The resulting book, aptly titled *Teaching Prejudice*, relied on a detailed content analysis of 143 English- and French-language texts used in social studies in the 1960s (e.g., history, geography, civics). McDiarmid and Pratt (1971: 45) concluded that students were "most likely to encounter in textbooks devoted Christians, great Jews, hardworking immigrants, infidel Moslems, primitive Negroes, and savage Indians." Using a smaller sample of only 14 textbooks, Guppy and Lyon (2012) reassessed the earlier findings (fewer books are now approved for use in the curriculum which is the main reason for the smaller sample). Following McDiarmid and Pratt they looked for "evaluative assertions" (i.e., judgmental claims invoking emotive terms) regarding the same target groups. Their findings were dramatically different. Modern textbooks have virtually none of the judgmental representations found in the books of earlier decades.

Why has the distortion that permeated the textbooks of the 1960s been reduced so dramatically? Guppy and Lyon point to a variety of interest groups who now play a more prominent role in the textbook publishing process. As they argue (ibid., 126):

Textbooks are now subject to close reviews at various levels, including Ministries of Education and textbook publishers. As an illustration, Nelson Education published *Canada: Face of a Nation* in 2000 and used four consultants (including Ed Swain of the Métis National Council) and 12 reviewers (including seven students).

The modern review process and the criteria ministries of education now use to vet textbooks minimize the old bias that permeated the books examined in McDiarmid and Pratt's *Teaching Prejudice* study. Relatively similar guidelines for the approval of textbooks are now a place in all provinces. For example, the Ontario Ministry of Education (2008: 7) guidelines require the following of all textbooks:

The content must be free from racial, ethnocultural, religious, regional, gender-related, or age-related bias; bias based on disability, sexual orientation, socioeconomic background, occupation, political affiliation, or membership in a specific group; and bias by omission. The material should present more than one point of view, and be free from discriminatory, exclusionary, or inappropriately value-laden language, photographs, and illustrations.

This approach demands that publishers and authors work to be "inclusive." Certainly there has been a major change in the reduction of old forms curriculum bias over the last half-century. Indeed, with new forms of politicization emerging in education, we might ask: are new forms of bias emerging?

Fourth, subject-based "book" knowledge continues to be regarded as superior to more generalized or integrated curriculum, and is more valued than practical and vocational training. Thus, contemporary curricula remain stratified. "Official knowledge," to repeat Apple's phrase, is subject-based, book-based academic study.

Nonetheless, if we think about these combined trends, and compare the top academic students in the 1950s with the top academic students in the 2010s, the latter are likelier to have been exposed to a richer, more challenging curriculum. Today's students have more options, whether through honours' programs, accelerated gifted classes, or the Advanced Placement/International Baccalaureate curricula. They may be no brighter than those of the 1950s, but they learn a more complex array of knowledge at an earlier age (e.g., compare a good senior-level math textbook from the 1950s and the 2010s).

Digital Learning 2.0: Now the Fun Really Begins?

If progressive educators have one priority, it is to engage students. Progressives want classrooms to be exciting, intrinsically interesting, fun, and enjoyable. Learning, they say, should not be drudgery but should be voluntary, not be coerced by rules or the lure of grades. To meet these goals, progressives have long looked to broader cultural scripts in order to make classrooms appeal to the sensibilities of their students. In earlier eras, progressives reckoned that many students watched game shows on TV, and so they incorporated games like "Jeopardy" into their lessons, aiming to motivate students with the lure of winning a contest that had some school material smuggled into its format. But today's students have grown up in a very different culture, one that has changed the "rules of engagement." How can today's educators meet the same goals in a new age?

No one can doubt the ascendency of digital technology in contemporary life. Almost everyone uses laptops, tablets, and smart phones for work, leisure, or school. Today's classrooms are stocked with smart boards and tablets; many institutions offer online courses and use digital platforms. Digital technology has largely suffused schooling. But many progressives are calling for more, wanting this technology to not merely serve as a convenience or curricular supplement, but to *transform* the very process of learning.

Progressives did not always think this way. The first wave of digital technology in the 1990s had only a limited impact on conventional classrooms. Larry Cuban (2001) rated those early efforts as thin, facile, and ineffective. He described classroom computers as "underused and oversold," employed largely as souped-up typewriters. Most teachers retained their traditional instruction styles because they were unfamiliar with the technology and had little support from administrators. Digital Learning 1.0 was deemed largely a failure because it did not significantly alter the classroom experience.

But much has changed. Over the past 15 years, students and teachers have become much more conversant with an ever-wider variety of software and platforms. There is far more "buy-in" for the use of technology among stakeholders. As a result, some educators are calling for a broader range of hi-tech tools for their classrooms, including interactive software, robotics, and digital games. They hope that by making lessons resemble contemporary forms of leisure, learning will be more engrossing and captivating. For instance, some are "gamifying" their lessons, structuring them into layered steps that incentivize students to explore a series of gratifying rewards. Their goal is to promote not only deep learning, but also positive traits like creativity, initiative, and determination. For a discussion of the emerging twenty-first century classroom, see Rizk (2017).

Table 9.1 Average Percentage of Total Instruction Time Allocated to Subjects in Primary School Curriculum, 1945–86

Subject	1945–69 (%)	1969–86 (%)	Number of Countries
Languages	36.0	33.9	70
Mathematics	16.5	18.2	80
Natural sciences	7.1	7.9	75
Social studies	8.1	8.1	73
Performing arts	10.0	10.2	71
Religious/moral	6.4	5.2	68
Physical education	6.9	7.1	72
Hygiene/health	1.4	1.2	70
Practical/vocational	6.3	5.1	73
Other	1.6	3.1	

Source: Adapted from Benavot et al. (1991: 91).

But change has been slow in other respects. Core subjects in primary school curricula have been remarkably stable over Canadian history, and throughout the world. A surprisingly similar amount of time is devoted to teaching national languages, mathematics, natural science, social studies, and performing arts. As Table 9.1 shows, the time allocated to specific elementary school subjects has been consistent, with languages receiving about 35 per cent of instructional time, mathematics between 15 and 20 per cent, natural science between 5 and 8 per cent, social studies about 8 per cent, and performing arts subjects about 10 per cent (slightly more change has occurred in the high school curriculum, in part to cater to the diversity we noted; see Kamens et al., 1996).

Change has not been as massive as one might imagine from intense debates over curriculum. There is very modest evidence of more "academic" learning over the last half-century, with less instruction time devoted both to national/local and foreign languages, slightly more devoted to mathematics and natural science, a real decline in practical and vocational teaching, and a slight rise in the performing arts. Baker and LeTendre (2005: 150–68) replicate this basic finding using international data from the Third International Math and Science Study (TIMSS). Comparing mathematics curricula in 30 countries in 1995, they conclude that the average amount of instructional time per topic did not vary greatly across these nations (ibid., 161).

Form: Rationalizing and "Blocking" Knowledge

While many theories speculate broadly on the content of school knowledge, fewer examine its broad form. Our starting point is to observe that schools have delivered an increasingly rationalized and bureaucratic curriculum. Only a small handful of alternative schools, such as "free schools" (described in Chapter 8), truly organize learning in a de-structured and unbureaucratic form. Otherwise, the form of the curriculum appears to vary little among mainstream schools (and this may be a principal reason that "school effects" are relatively small—Chapter 4). We next examine key elements of this form.

The modern curriculum involves a division of labour. Think about how workplaces, for instance, separate tasks into increasingly specialized segments. We can use segmentation to illustrate the rationalization of school curricula. Time is a scarce resource in schools. With too few hours to accomplish all that is expected, educators have responded by "parcelling" knowledge into an intellectual division of labour. For instance, in the mid-1800s, school curriculum was thought to encompass a traditional trilogy—reading, 'riting, and 'rithmetic, the "3Rs." Since then, it has differentiated enormously. While schools at the start of the twentieth century offered only a single course called "science," contemporary curriculum contains not only biology, chemistry, and physics, but also environmental science, microelectronics, and many others. This illustrates a key concept: school knowledge has been increasingly taking the form of discrete chunks, known as **curricular blocks** (see Bernstein, 1975). Several features of blocks are notable.

Administrators carefully regulate the number of instruction days and hours per year. They must decide about length, sequencing, and interconnections among chunks of knowledge, dividing activities into formal timetables, separate subject lessons, and grade levels. In a block system, knowledge is sliced into subject "silos." As students move through schools from earlier to later grades, the curriculum is increasingly organized by such blocks. Over time, schools have been using the block system in earlier and earlier grades, often implicitly through "time on task" allocations. Many elementary schools now use block organization to ensure they cover basic tasks in literacy and numeracy.

One consequence of blocking is that schooling can feel like an assembly line. The English block is over, and now it's physics, and then history, and then physical education. The school bell rules! The more insular each block is the more learning is crammed into inelastic time windows. This silo-like insularity thickens as students move from kindergarten through to their final high school year. In elementary years, teachers may devote a block to a particular country or region (e.g., Brazil), and within this block, will create a variety of linked lessons to, say, folktales, geography, history, and math, a technique known as "the project method." Here, boundaries between subject areas are relatively permeable. But in senior years, blocks tend to be isolated, creating a situation in which what happens in English, for instance, has little bearing on physics. Also, learning activity can be similar or different across blocks. The English teacher rewards you for voicing an opinion, but the physics teacher resents being interrupted by questions.

Blocks highlight certain education dilemmas. When they are relatively insulated, students become progressively separated one from another, and this is exacerbated when coupled with greater teacher-centred activity. Where blocks have tightly controlled boundaries, students are rewarded for thinking "inside the block." They learn what questions are appropriate and which are not. Questions transcending blocks tend to be ignored, ruled out as beyond the domain of that particular block. According to Bowles and Gintis and other critical scholars, this process alienates students, and helps prepare compliant workers.

Yet, blocks have their benefits. Working "inside the block" provides teachers with a much easier sense of student mastery of subject material. Furthermore, although many real-world problems may transcend the boundaries of subject blocks, blocks can promote specialized skills. Being a Jack- or Jill-of-all-trades—and a master of none—is of limited use since solutions to most problems still require some specialized skill and knowledge. Blocks foster specific skills, though they may not nurture broad and deeper comprehension. This is the stress of human capital theory and functionalism—the need to develop specific and relevant skills.

Finally, subject blocks are not all equally valued. Some subjects, such as physics, are "serious," while other blocks are less so. This is the stratification of knowledge, the differential valuation of subjects. Students labelled as "smart" excel in math and physics, while students who excel in drama or physical education are considered good citizens but not necessarily "smart." As per our discussion of the "shopping mall high school" in Chapter 5, each level of this stratification is associated with a distinct "effort bargain," with higher levels being permitted to legitimately demand greater efforts from students.

Demographics represent an important rationalizing pressure on the curriculum. The expansion and diversification of students attending school for longer periods have presented school systems a huge range of academic competencies, preparedness, and motivations, and administrators have responded with standardized, manageable timetables. Here we see a mix of progressivism and rationalization. Students may seem like cogs in well-oiled bureaucratic machines that repeat scripted labs in chemistry or well-rehearsed lessons on the First World War year upon year. Yet this bureaucracy also has a focus on the whole child and her particular needs, and so we have seen the emergence of a range of upper-year courses such as journalism, law, Native studies (now labelled "Indigenous Studies"), each part of the Saskatchewan Grade 11/12 curriculum, to cater to student interest.

In sum, blocks represent a particular rationalized form of modern, progressive curricula. They are useful for administrators, and enable some things like subject mastery, but constrain others like subject integration. Blocks also facilitate another form of school rationalization, one that has risen to great prominence: scheduled time for assessment and testing.

More Rationalized Form: Types of Evaluation, Assessment, and Testing

Modern schools do a lot of assessing, evaluating, examining, grading, marking, quizzing, and testing. Pundits of various persuasions hotly argue the merits and demerits of this. Their debates range widely from statistical intricacies about validity and reliability, to philosophical discourses about the desirability of measuring learning, to political arguments about the appropriateness of performance indicators, to the psychology of test-taking, to the economics of the value-added nature of assessment, and on and on. A jungle with much heat but less light!

Different sociological theories also understand evaluation in their own way. For functionalists and human capital theorists, evaluation underlines the schools' merit-detecting role, ensuring that the most able are allocated to the most demanding occupations. For the Marxist, evaluation is a tool to thwart the mobility of the lower classes and to impose degrading "badges of inability" that justifies class reproduction throughout society. For the institutional theorist, assessments are about legitimating schools' "chartering" authority, which underlies the use of credentials in rationing access to sought-after positions in the labour market. However, since these theories were originally established in the 1970s, the role of assessment has been heightened by growing political pressures for school accountability, a topic we turn to next.

Testing as Sorting and Selecting

Tests sort learners into different ability levels and streams. In awarding badges of ability, schools declare who are the best and the brightest. Typically, grades are the underlying currency used in awarding badges. Those tests that are most consequential for future opportunities are known as "high-stakes" tests. They would include Grade 12 provincial examinations or, in the United States, SAT exams. A lot rides on success or failure with high-stakes testing.

Sorting and selecting decisions are often based on "summative" tests which attempt to capture, in summary form, what has been learned over some time interval. Such testing can also include "norm-referenced" standards. Norm-referenced testing compares students—one person is better than another or is above or below the "norm." The "norm" is the typical, average, or normal performance in a group. IQ tests are norm-referenced, with a score of 100 constituting the norm.

Concerns about testing often centre on accuracy (or, more technically, validity). Dispute rages over how adequately a few exam questions can tap a large subject domain. Exams may dwell too much on some issues while ignoring others, and fail to systematically probe the full range of a subject. They may promote "teaching to the test" and encourage educators to pay more attention to curricular material that is likely to be examined, with less attention to breadth and depth. They may reflect preconceived assumptions of the test-makers more than the test-takers.

In principle, these concerns can be remedied. One could, in theory, devise a valid test that covered the full range of a subject domain. However, a second and potentially more worrying complaint is that testing can only scratch the surface of what a student knows and understands. Some argue that testing is overly focused on fact or information recall, and not on deeper, more complex, nuanced comprehension.

For example, Davies might recite basic information about quarks and get a good mark, but lack an appreciation of the connections between quarks and the fundamental particles of nature. Or Guppy may score well in literature by knowing James Joyce wrote *Ulysses* but lack an appreciation that quarks were named after a character mentioned in that novel (English meets physics!). Deeper appreciation and creativity are things that tests simply cannot measure, so the argument runs.

This latter line of argument has troubles, however, at least in its strongest version. While testing may often be crude or blunt, does this mean that it can *never* probe a deeper, more nuanced realm? The problem with an extreme anti-testing argument is that it implies that schools should teach students things that cannot or should not be tested. In other words, how can anyone know if learning has taken place? As Carr (2003: 160) argues, "it is difficult to see how anything that could *not* be tested might count as genuine knowledge." Just as there cannot be a private language unique to one individual, it is hard to conceive of knowledge that is shared among people but that cannot be evaluated or examined.

A weaker version of the anti-testing argument is that tests can be superficial. Creating quality evaluation methods is more difficult than politicians and parents often assume. And, many worry that the trend towards "more testing" is not clearly creating "greater learning." As Ungerleider (2003: 249) notes, "if [testing] worked in the simplistic way that some politicians seem to think, kids today would be the most learned students ever." Testing is more helpful when it serves a more diagnostic purpose.

Testing as Diagnostic

Some testing can be used to assist, and indeed motivate, student learning. By monitoring students continuously and closely, teachers can guide learning. As concepts and skills are mastered, new ideas and abilities can be introduced. Think of this as a simple wheel: introduce new material, evaluate student knowledge and understanding, then proceed by either reviewing or introducing new material. From the student's perspective, and with the right pacing, learning is reinforced by success on tests that signal expertise in new areas.

Educators refer to this as "formative" evaluation. Designed to highlight levels of comprehension, formative testing typically occurs throughout a course, with summative testing at the course's conclusion. Diagnostic testing is also often referred to as "criterion-referenced" since it compares student accomplishments to a standard. The "criterion" is understood as what a student ought to know or understand. Driving licence tests are criterion-referenced. If you meet a pre-defined standard, you pass. Teachers typically put far more weight on diagnostic evaluation, whereas politicians and parents tend to stress standardized testing of the sorting-and-selecting type.

Confounding this situation further is the assumption that standardized examinations are more objective and scientific than are the appraisals of teachers. Many politicians presume that teachers' own assessments are more subjective and thus less reliable. While some articulate this as an either/or choice, others feel that since all testing involves human judgment, the best approach is to combine testing based on explicit competency requirements with the wise assessment of those teachers who have worked regularly with the same students. While some deride this familiarity for being open to the whims of teacher biases, others note that sound decisions often come from first-hand experience, whether one is a teacher, stockbroker, or priest. Constructing a false trade-off between objective and subjective has more appeal to the politician than it does to the educator. But this debate over objectivity versus subjectivity is linked to a rising tide in testing—testing aimed to enhance accountability.

Testing as Accountability

Education has a political character, if for no other reason than its status as a public, tax-supported institution. In democracies, publicly funded institutions are seen to be accountable to elected officials. Yet, understandings of accountability have changed in the past decade. Before, provincial governments left policy largely to education professionals, especially in areas such as the curriculum and teaching methods. But increasingly, the political has begun to intrude on the professional, especially in the area of student achievement. Today's politicians are actively trumpeting standards-based accountability. Their message is simple—student achievement ought to meet some pre-set standard, and schools must ensure that students attain that standard.

Performance indicators are front and centre in debates about accountability. In many provinces, ministries are asking schools to show improvements over time on selected indicators. Table 9.2 provides a stylized summary of how this works.

Table 9.2 Performance Indicators and Accountability (Hypothetical Targets)

| | | Trendline Data | | |
Performance Measure	Baseline Data	2013	2017	2021
High school graduation rate				
Overall	80%	82%	84%	85%
Aboriginal youth	60%	64%	68%	72%
ESL	80%	82%	84%	85%
French immersion	85%	86%	87%	88%
Standardized test scores (average score)				
Reading (Grade 5)	80%	82%	84%	86%
Mathematics (Grade 8)	84%	85%	86%	87%
Writing (Grade 10)	85%	87%	88%	89%
Science (Grade 12)	85%	87%	88%	89%

Source: Loosely based on provincial ministry statistics from Alberta, British Columbia, and Ontario (see current websites for changes).

Provincial education ministries establish performance measures, such as student achievement, that they believe reflect broad quality education. To encourage positive change, policy-makers typically focus on improvement over time. This focus on increased performance has made phrases like "value added," "improvement over baseline," and "annual yearly progress" ubiquitous in education. Throughout North America, although more in the US than in Canada, some officials want to tie school funds and budgets to measures such as student success rates on standardized examinations. This practice is creating controversy, since it directly links test scores to school budgets, and effectively penalizes low-performing schools while using a method whose validity is widely questioned (for a discussion and empirical examination, see Downey et al., 2008).

In some respects, accountability is moving to the international domain. The Programme for International Student Assessment (PISA), discussed in the previous chapter, attempts to measure student competencies, such as reasoning abilities, rather than measure mastery of any particular curriculum. How Canadian provinces rank in this international context has often been used to prod change at both the provincial and national levels, even though Canada fares reasonably well compared with many other nations (Table 9.3). The relatively lower ranking of American students has led to an explosion of "education accountability offices" in every US state and they also appear in many Canadian provinces (for example, Ontario established the Education Quality and Accountability Office [EQAO] almost 20 years ago).

As we discussed in the previous chapter, the very existence of international bodies that monitor student assessment is consistent with Meyer's institutional

Table 9.3 Estimated Math, Reading, and Science Scores for 15-Year-Olds, Canada and Selected International Countries, 2015

Country	Average Math Score	Average Reading Score	Average Science Score
1 Singapore	564	535	556
2 Japan	532	516	538
5 Finland	511	526	531
7 Canada	516	527	528
15 Germany	506	509	509
15 United Kingdom	492	498	509
24 United States	470	497	496
31 Russia	494	495	487
62 Brazil	377	407	401

Notes: Countries ranked by science scores. Seventy-two countries participated, including about 540,000 students. Testing was done in many different languages, including both French and English in Canada.

Data Source: http://www.oecd.org/pisa/pisa-2015-results-in-focus.pdf.

arguments about an evolving world model for education (see Davies and Guppy, 1997: 446–7). Such bodies further rationalize schooling. This important trend prompts a key question: *where* do these pressures come from? What are the social influences on the curriculum?

Social Influences on the Curriculum

Let's revisit a question that we raised earlier in this chapter: why are some topics included in the school curriculum, but not others? Why do some entire subjects rise and others fall over time? For example, why have social studies and business emerged as core features of curricula, while Greek and Latin, once the mark of a truly cultivated individual, waned over time? And why are some subjects widely popular, while others are not? While almost every modern school teaches language, math, science, and social studies, many do not offer courses in commerce, computing, ethics, or psychology, at least not as broadly or deeply.

A major dispute centres on identifying external groups that help construct the curriculum, and determining their degree of influence. Theories differ sharply on this issue. Functionalist reasoning, as previously described focuses on moral elements of schooling (Durkheim) and its role in meritocratic selection (Davis and Moore). They see curricular form and content as broadly sculpted by forces of modernization. Dreeben (1968), for instance, saw an array of modernizing pressures that act on schools, from new forms of morality to economic requirements. Rather than recognizing any particular group as exerting pressure on the curriculum, he believed that a wide societal consensus backed what should be taught.

Critical theorists see things differently. They contend that curricula are the outcome of battles among antagonistic actors, with powerful interests usually winning out. In particular, some critical scholars assert that business agendas and powerful interest groups ultimately prevail in determining what gets taught in school (e.g., Molnar, 2001). Other critical scholars focus on pressures emanating from the capitalist system, as opposed to specific actors, arguing that the current neo-liberal economic climate is dictating school reform (e.g., Rezai-Rashti, 2009). These approaches commonly view schools as highly susceptible to the influence of outside powerful actors and forces.

A very different sociological approach builds on Weber's notion of bureaucracy, and emphasizes the degree by which curricula may be increasingly *insulated* from wider pressures. That is, they argue that the solidification of legal-rational bureaucracy in schooling (discussed in the previous chapter), along with the professionalization of educators (discussed in the next chapter) has combined to erect a bureaucratic wall around most school content. For instance, they would point to the lengthy vetting that curricula now go through in ministries and school boards before their approval and implementation. The gatekeepers in this process are usually salaried bureaucrats with educational backgrounds, and are rarely business people or social movement activists. Further, educators' professional norms prize their own expertise over outsiders, and portray outside influences as illegitimate. This may sound strange today, when more and more people call for schooling that is relevant for the "real world." But many case studies reveal instances of school officials successfully fending off curricular challenges from a variety of groups (e.g., Binder, 2002).

Are there ways to reconcile these divergent views? While schools may indeed deflect many curricular challenges that emanate from outside their gates, we can certainly point to many successful efforts, such as anti-racist education, sex education, anti-drug education, and revisionist history, to name a few. And, while corporate leaders and business groups may have little direct access to school curriculum, they appear to have considerable indirect influence. Educators are sensitive to job market realities, and want their graduates to be employable. Calls to make curricula more "relevant" often entail the creation of courses that are marketable and appealing to employers. Over the decades, we have seen a steady rise in business-oriented courses and apprenticeships, and more applied and commercially oriented studies. These trends are quite stark in higher education, where business programs (BComm, MBA, Executive MBA, Commercial Studies) are ever-pervasive, and in some instances, are crowding out the traditional liberal arts (Brint et al., 2005; Kraatz and Zajac, 1996; Polster, 2009). To reconcile these diverging views, we encourage five ways to think about social impacts on the curriculum.

First, it makes sense to view the permeability of the curriculum as highly uneven. Some curricular areas are more susceptible to outside influence than are others. For instance, material that addresses social problems such as discrimination, violence, or substance abuse, which are often developed in tandem with social activists and social movements, tend to be incorporated as "add-ons" to the regular academic curriculum. Like other forms of extracurriculum, they tend to lack permanence, and are subject to being repeatedly adopted, revised, cut, and sometimes re-adopted. Within the regular academic curriculum, some courses are more permeable to outside influence than others. For instance, social studies and humanities courses tend to be more contested than natural science and mathematics. One can easily recognize how the colonial character of much early education in Canada reflected this country's close connection to Britain and to British values. A century later, some argue that despite considerable change, the curriculum tended to privilege a European orientation to history and literature (e.g., Barakett and Naseem, 2009; Carter, 2006) although recent evidence suggests this claim is greatly overstated (see Guppy and Lyon, 2012 and Box 9.1). Today, one could argue that the curriculum privileges a cosmopolitan, globalizing, "post-national" outlook on the world. Social movements have made some inroads in revising history, literature, and social studies curriculum (think of multiculturalism), but have been far less successful when challenging "core" science and math courses (see Binder, 2002).

Second, it is important to distinguish between "direct" influence, where particular group representatives play an immediate role in shaping curricula, and "indirect" influence, where educators themselves design curriculum in ways that cater to the perceived wants of a group. Business groups exert a powerful indirect influence, for instance. As we discussed above, teachers and parents want students to be employable, and so educators cater courses to the perceived wants of employers. Also, education is ultimately governed by provincial political parties, and many listen to business lobbyists.

Third, it helps to recognize that curricula are products of compromises among various rivals. For instance, the curriculum can be seen as having several major thrusts, each subject to influence by different groups (e.g., Kliebard, 1995). Multiple actors, not just business and professional educators, can be influential. Consider the case of classical literature. In past eras, great literary traditions were the products of aristocracies, gentries, and upper classes. In modern times, they survive (barely) in schools when they are championed by literary specialists and bibliophiles, many of whom are teachers or writers or professors. In contrast, more vocational curricula are usually popular with business lobby groups, while pressures for schools to be more inclusive and accommodating are pushed by social reformers and progressive politicians.

Fourth, it is useful to recognize that regardless which group and which component of the curriculum is subject to outside influence, modern public schools face relentless pressures to rationalize their offerings. Because they are mandated to retain millions of students for most of their youth, and because accountability pressures are likely endemic to any institution that receives billions and billions of taxpayer dollars, it is hard to imagine curriculum taking a non-bureaucratic form.

Because each of these four pressures is simultaneous, the resulting curriculum is a compromise, reflecting a plurality of interests, thrusts, and concerns. This quality ensures both enduring and recurring battles between more or less utilitarian images of education. Some stress occupational training and labour force preparation, others prize ideals such as the broadening and deepening of the human mind. Different interest groups take differing perspectives. Many industrialists and business proponents stress the utilitarian view, echoing human capital calls to develop skills conducive to workplace productivity. Often coupled with this more practical, skills-based training is an emphasis on the sorting of individuals via achievement testing. In contrast, liberals and more libertarian thinkers stress generalized education that is open to all and that encourages broad conceptual skills and abilities. Cultivation of the imagination and of the critical faculties is prioritized, along with social justice, citizenship, and a broader range of socio-emotional abilities. The "common" curriculum with relatively little tracking, especially compared to Europe, can be seen as a by-product of these democratizing forces. Thus, in important ways the modern curriculum is a continuing balance between these contending pressures—one stressing selection and stratification, and the other emphasizing evolving understandings of citizenship and human rights.

Fifth, and finally, it makes sense to distinguish between the form and content of the curriculum, and to distinguish between local, national, and global levels. Consider an approach that emphasizes not local politics, but instead, broad global forces. Institutional theorists such as John Meyer partly *invert* the assumption that school curricula reflect their surrounding society. This argument is based on an examination of the *form* of the curriculum rather than its content. Their prime argument is that curricular forms have become increasingly *disconnected* from schools' local conditions (for a thorough statement, see McEneaney and Meyer, 2000). That is, as formal schooling spread around the globe, it formed a broad "template" for the curriculum. While the particular content of schooling still varies across schools, boards, provinces, and countries, educators increasingly adopt a standardized template consisting of similar emphases on languages, mathematics, science, and co-ed organization.

This trend embodies a historic shift from traditional to legal-rational forms of organization, in that school knowledge has increasingly shed the imprint of religious orders and aristocratic traditions, and adopted universal norms of science, societal inclusiveness, and economic utility. The source of this template is a world body of professional educators who transcend any nation-state and who value portable and generic skills over local traditions. As evidence, an analysis of textbooks in dozens of countries around the world over many decades found that many increasingly adopted this standard template (Bromley, Meyer, and Ramirez, 2011). This diffusion is most striking in developing nations. Many countries, following the precepts of the United Nations, have implemented co-ed schooling, even in countries where women and men continue to perform sharply segregated roles in the rest of their society. Fewer schools anywhere are now mandated to serve only certain categories of people (except for those designated to serve Indigenous Canadians, and even these are justified through the language of equity). As a result, the imprint of local actors becomes increasingly faint on curricular forms. As more countries in different corners of the globe adopt these standardized templates, a sociologist can no longer predict a nation's curricular form by knowing its type of economy, political system, or cultural traditions.

In sum, several social forces influence the curriculum. Some affect its form, others affect its content, and these influences vary by sectors of the curriculum. At any moment of time, the content of modern curricula is a compromise among competing actors. Its form is increasingly rationalized and global in reach. Each theory has mixed success when we examine the historical record. Functionalists can be faulted for paying insufficient attention to the social origins of the curriculum. More critical scholars are right to portray schools as battlegrounds with contending rivals, but have overestimated the direct impact of business groups on the curriculum. Feminists and anti-racists have focused on historical biases in the curriculum but have been slower to recognize changes that have occurred in recent decades. Institutional theorists focus on broad international shifts in the form of the curriculum, while neglecting local variations in its content.

With these social influences on the curriculum in mind, we next reverse the causal arrow and examine a different question: what is the impact of the curriculum on students and society?

Schooling Ghosts in the Hidden Curriculum?

Benson Snyder (1971) popularized the idea of the "hidden" curriculum. He argued that schools affect children not only through their content, but also through their tacit assumptions, implicit rules, and informal routines. This notion of curriculum includes not just lesson plans, but also physical architecture, classroom layouts, intramural sports and extracurricular activities, time schedules, and beyond. The hidden components of the curriculum, both in the form and content of schooling, was said to have a profound socializing impact on students. For instance, high school classrooms are typically arranged to facilitate teachers' controlling discussion, with student-to-teacher exchanges easier than student-to-student interactions. For Benson, what is "hidden" in this arrangement is an implicit lesson that students should naturally cede authority to teachers.

Sociological theorists have since elaborated this concept in bold ways. Functionalists such as Dreeben (1968) used it to understand how schools teach a range of contemporary skills, ideals, and beliefs and prepare youth for the increasingly complex modern roles. For him, curriculum faces three acute challenges. First, schools must compensate for the waning moral power of religion and extended families, but, rather than remaining mired in tradition, schools must teach modern values. Second, schools must impart cognitive skills for upgraded, post-industrial economies. Third, modern schools need youth to identify with the modern nation-state and increasingly global notions of society, and not only with local groups. How do schools accomplish these tasks?

For functionalists, a benevolent "hidden curriculum" is at work. Students are seen to learn modern values such as universalism, democracy, and competitive achievement—not through overt lessons, but rather through school routines and procedures. As David Labaree (2010: 224) claims, "the system has never been so much about education as about schooling." In the curriculum, form trumps content. Students learn to embrace competitive status-striving not by reading any particular book or attending any particular lecture but through the repetitive format of schooling. The endless process of testing, awarding grades, and ranking students against each other, functionalists argue, instils competitive ethics in students. Status-striving is made to appear natural and taken for granted. Students may never hear a teacher cajole them to compete with one another, but they don't need to because competition is embedded in the most basic of school routines (and constantly reinforced by parents enquiring about test results).

Marxists such as Bowles and Gintis also recognize a powerful hidden curriculum, but see it as far less benevolent. They claim that what is "hidden" is actually the culture of capitalism, and the values that are subtly promoted are passivity and docility. The purpose of this hidden curriculum, they argue, is to prepare students, particularly those from working-class origins, to take orders and accept subordination in alienating workplaces (see Bowles and Gintis, 2002). Further, schools' endless testing and grading is seen to condition students to act as competitive individuals, not in collective solidarity with one another. According to Bowles and Gintis, schools *could* use other plausible arrangements, such as awarding group grades, or not awarding grades at all (as in free schools). These arrangements, they note, could form very different habits among youth.

Other versions of the hidden curriculum concept focus more on subtle messages that may be embedded in the content rather than form of curriculum. One hundred years ago, Max Weber stressed the power of dominant **status groups** to assert their priorities in the curriculum. More recently, this argument has been re-adopted by those that contend that the curriculum values some cultures over others, particularly those connected to advantaged social groups. There are four contemporary forms of this status group argument.

First, class-oriented researchers such as Bourdieu (Bourdieu and Passeron, 1990 [1977]) claim that curricula tend to reflect, celebrate, and reward the culture of the highly educated upper-middle classes. By doing so, curricula implicitly denigrate other cultures. As reviewed in Chapter 3, Bourdieu claimed that schools reward the sophisticated taste and style of privileged classes, though this unequal process was "hidden" by the guises of meritocratic contest and equality of opportunity.

The science fair highlights this advantage. Well-educated parents with deeper financial pockets are much more adept at helping their children construct a project showing, for example, how capacitors might replace batteries as powerful electrical storage devices. This same child is far more likely to have been to Paris and visited the Musée des Arts et Métiers which preserves, since the 1790s, scientific instruments and inventions. In contrast, children from working-class backgrounds are less likely to have travelled internationally and are more likely relegated by financial pressures to showing the capillary action of celery stalks.

Second, critical race scholars contend that curricular content is racialized, promoting the cultural superiority of dominant racial-ethnic groups, harming the identities of minority youth (e.g., Dei, 2009). With growing migration of peoples around the world, Canada has become a more racially diverse society, and this has sparked considerable changes in course content. But these scholars claim that Canadian institutions still celebrate the "Western canon" and its roster of authors like Austen, Balzac, and Shakespeare. But as discussed above, research has shown that much has changed. The curriculum that Ryerson, Jessop, and others fostered in the early Canadian schools is a far cry from today's schools that teach about ethnocentrism, feminism, racism, transphobia, homophobia, and xenophobia. Today Canadian history is told very differently in English Canada, Quebec, and First Nations schools (McAndrew, 2013).

Third, feminists lamented the lack of female role models in schoolbooks and their trivialization of women's work in the home and in places of employment. For example, some contend that James Watson and Francis Crick may not have discovered the helix structure of DNA had it not been for the path-breaking imaging work of Rosalind Franklin. Nevertheless here too change has occurred, with much greater attention now given to ensuring the curriculum is more gender representative (Villar and Guppy, 2016).

Fourth, and in contrast, conservative social critics invert each of the above arguments. Inspired by an ongoing debate over the "culture wars," they see a very different reality in today's schools. They point to curricular revisions over the past 25 years in areas of sexuality, gender and multiculturalism, and worry about a possible de-institutionalizing of free speech. These trends, they argue, are not neutral, but are promoting the authority of secular, post-national progressives over established cultural traditions and values.

A final version of the hidden curriculum argument comes from new institutional theory (e.g., Meyer, 1977). Here the curriculum is seen as having its impact *not* by providing any distinct, consistent, or lasting experience for students. On that point, Meyer is skeptical, arguing that schools affect different students in varying ways. Further, any such effects generally dissipate with time. He argues that the impact of the curriculum is instead wrapped up with schools' "chartering" authority, that is, its power to confer a social status to graduates that becomes a basis to allocate them to jobs. Notice this idea is very similar to the credentialist arguments of Randall Collins (Chapter 3), where the piece of paper, not the actual curricular content, is most important for employment. Students, Meyer reasons, are affected more by this new status than by their past school experiences. Any new attitudes and beliefs that they adopt reflects a process of anticipatory socialization for new roles, instead of prior conditioning. Meyer contends that the institutionalization of credentials in labour markets affects students more than do the particulars of curricular content or form.

Empirical Research: Socialization Messages, Status Cultures, and Skill Sets

Despite its popularity in sociology, the hidden curriculum concept is double-edged. On the one side, its inclusive image of curriculum incorporates the full experience of student learning. It draws attention to taken-for-granted or implicit aspects of schooling. It links to longstanding sociological research on the unintended consequences of informal organization operating within bureaucracies. But on the other side it makes the notion of curriculum more amorphous and harder to pin down. It is easy to assert the impact of a "hidden curriculum" in a lazy way. Because everyone goes to school, it is tempting to simply infer that curricula must have certain effects, and *assume* its power without supporting evidence. Further, use of the concept can ignore action or agency, and treat students as dupes or dunces who are unaware of surrounding forces. And, now that warnings of the "hidden curriculum" are routinely discussed in schools of education, it is harder to pinpoint what exactly teachers are supposedly unaware of. Schooling is a dynamic interplay between students, teachers, and school structure, and neglecting that interplay can exaggerate the power of the hidden curriculum.

Is there actual evidence of a hidden curriculum? For empirical researchers, this is a tough and thorny question. It is easy to point to this or that classroom feature as having a strong hidden power, but harder to demonstrate its actual effects on students. Indeed, a major theme of this book is that such effects are hard to detect. Laws that compel all students to attend school leave no control group for comparison, creating uncertainty over whether schools themselves create abilities in students, or whether the same people would have developed them even if they were not in school. Assuming that causal claims should be backed by evidence, below we assess the empirical strengths and weaknesses of the hidden curriculum concept, with the hope of sharpening its utility.

For starters, it is very difficult to adjudicate among functionalist, Marxist, and new institutional versions of the hidden curriculum argument. Functionalist arguments are pitched at a grand historical level. They contrast the kinds of values and orientations that are needed in traditional versus modern societies, and tend to assume that contemporary schools tacitly transmit those needed in modernity. As such, one would need to have a grand historical comparison of school effects to provide support for functionalist theory, and we do not know of any such comparisons that would meet the standards of today's empirical researcher. Marxist depictions of the hidden curriculum hinge on the assumption that workers would be inherently rebellious in capitalist societies if no institutions were at work to contain conflict. When working-class insurgency and militancy began to decline in the mid-twentieth century, Marxists reasoned that modern institutions must operate as pacifying forces in society. Bowles and Gintis identified schools as culprits in this process. Again, an empirical challenge to this kind of analysis is that there is no control group for comparison, and thus we do not know if unschooled youth would act any differently once they were in jobs. Over the years, many commentators have noted that in contemporary times, radical politics are much more likely to be embraced by youth with greater rather than lesser amounts of schooling, such as university graduates (a feature for example of protests associated with the Arab Spring). And for similar reasons, Meyer's institutional argument is very difficult to assess empirically. Because it is pitched at a societal level, one would need to compare groups in societies in which the use of credentials was institutionalized, versus groups under the opposite condition. We do not know of any studies that have tested this version of new institutional theory. In general, these kinds of "hidden curriculum" arguments are difficult to assess empirically.

However, using different methods, we can assess variants of the hidden curriculum argument that focus on status groups. For instance, in a noteworthy study of "socialization messages" in schools, Steven Brint and his team of researchers (Brint et al., 2001) went into dozens of primary school classrooms and searched for implicit messages that could be embedded in textbooks, rules, discussions, posters, assignments, tests, and physical surroundings. In terms of curricular forms, they found that schools mainly focused on mundane matters of personal conduct. Students were implicitly encouraged to be courteous to others, to not be disruptive, and to get along with their schoolmates. But as we elaborate in Chapter 11, this was accomplished in a loose and indulgent fashion, rather than one that encouraged passivity and docility. In terms of content, they saw few messages that were recognizably political, either from a left-wing or right-wing perspective. Rather than uncovering any kind of "culture war" in the classroom, they found little content that could be connected to any recognizable status group. Thus, while dominant classes and ethnic groups clearly influenced literature and historical writings in past eras, today's school content is difficult to associate with those status groups (recall Box 9.1).

Consider next Bourdieu's argument: one would need to clearly identify the arbitrary culture of the dominant classes, find curricular content that expresses that culture, and then show it to clearly benefit some children over others. Research on "cultural capital," (DiMaggio, 1982; Kingston, 2001) casts doubt on the first assumption, finding that few people of *any* class participate in "high-brow" or "beaux arts" culture. As Kingston (2001: 90) puts it:

> [T]he distinctive class cultures that Bourdieu claimed to exist in France do not have clear parallels in the United States. Consider, for example, the class patterning of musical taste: Appreciating "elite" genres, cultural capital theory would suggest, is a valuable cultural resource. True, audiences at classical music concerts are primarily composed of affluent managers and professionals. Yet this crucial matter is also true: only a small minority of any class goes regularly to these concerts. Mahler—who? Or who cares?

If today's curriculum contains little traditional "high-brow" or upper-class culture, this change likely reflects a key finding from the sociology of culture: the changing of cultural hierarchies (Khan, 2012; but see Veenstra, 2015). Cultural prestige has become less tied to classic European traditions and increasingly tied to international influences. New "cultural omnivores" are *au courant* with a wide range of cultural matters, from Internet soap operas to classical operas to hip hop to Bollywood to Drake. This cultural agility is said to have more social currency than old-fashioned European snobbery (Garnett et al., 2005). In education, high schools have long developed multicultural curricula. Even elite universities, once bastions of aristocratic culture, are now prioritizing cultural innovation over tradition (Lehmann, 2000; Ramirez, 2004; Khan, 2012). Hidden in the curriculum is often an arbitrary valuation of what history is worth relating and what was not.

Curricula in past eras have also been highly gendered, though little of this was "hidden." Once in high school, boys and girls were often groomed for very different family and workplace roles, since this was considered part of the natural social order. Many older history books could be read as implying that women played no central role in shaping the past, but as discussed above, many curricula have since been partly rewritten.

These examples also remind us that areas of the curriculum such as humanities and social studies are particularly susceptible to status group influence, while others are less so. It stretches logic to connect natural sciences and mathematics to any one ethnic group. Those disciplines arose in an international context, and Canadian curriculum designers followed global norms when adopting them. This helps explain an empirical finding: schools mostly reward practices that nurture literacy and work habits (Kingston, 2001). Basic activities such as having books in the house, being read to, and reserving regular hours for study are not the arbitrary property of any class or ethnic group, and schools tend to reward activities regardless of student origin (see Farkas et al., 1990). Good evidence also implies that, for all students, staying in school longer increases reasoning abilities, cognitive skills, and civic attitudes (Heckman, 2008; Kingston et al., 2003). To summarize, it is difficult to empirically detect many hidden and status cultural effects of curriculum. The final section of this chapter examines the mechanisms that promote change and stability in the curriculum.

Mechanisms of Stability: Rationalization

The curriculum seems to embody a paradox: there is a remarkable similarity in some aspects of the curriculum across nations, and yet local curricula are reformed regularly. How can this paradox be understood? One mechanism that can both change and stabilize curricula is rationalization. As Weber predicted, teaching over the last century has been gradually more specialized, especially at the secondary school level. Over time, only people trained at universities in mathematics were recruited to teach math and only teachers trained in physical education hired to conduct PE classes. This practice entrenches disciplinary advocates within the school system, with teachers championing their own subject specialties where discrete curriculum blocks such as math, biology, and chemistry still appear, although slightly greater subject integration now characterizes social studies. Characteristic of all bureaucracies, schools developed departments based on disciplinary specialties, and this became another source of inertia that resisted more integrated curricula.

Another way to understand the paradox is to view local change in the context of ever-widening global organizational circles, what Meyer calls "world-society" (Chapter 3). The societal importance of education is magnified over time through its link to national agendas for progress, justice, and economic development. This process builds "reform" into the institutional fabric of modern schooling. At the world level, continuous reform cycles emerge. International professional organizations meet regularly to devise ways to improve curricula, teacher training, testing, equity provisions, to name but a few. The institutionalization of international testing reinforces this logic of reform by providing a forum for country-by-country comparisons of test scores.

Another pressure for rationalization comes from worries about quality assurance. Are schools doing a good job of educating people? Consider here the complaints about students who are said to graduate from high school unable to spell, or compose a grammatically correct sentence, or calculate the surface area of a pizza. Certainly, as more and more students of differing ability levels have gone further and further in school, there is some relative dilution of skill among lower-ranked graduates. As Nagy (2000) argues, whenever issues of quality become prominent, the use of standardized exams tends to follow in a well-established historical pattern.

Why are calls for accountability voiced with such urgency? In part, they reflect the political governance of schooling. Parties on all sides of the political spectrum have mandated or reinforced centralized testing, whether they be New Democrats in British Columbia, the Conservatives in Alberta, or the Liberals in Ontario. Other pressures come from parents. As the race to the top in education intensifies, parents are increasingly concerned to ensure success for their children. Fairness and transparency are important parts of competition. Standardized testing gives the selection system an important stamp of legitimacy. Any possible favouritism that teachers might have is eclipsed by standardized examinations. Because the tests are the same for everyone, success must reflect merit, or so the argument runs.

In sum, there are three forms of testing—selective, diagnostic, and accountability-driven—while sociological theories largely emphasize only selective testing. Functionalists saw it as necessary for identifying meritorious students; Marxists viewed it as a tool to legitimize the blocking of opportunity to less fortunate youth; while institutional theorists regarded it as a way for schools to claim their chartering authority. Since those theories were originally crafted in the 1970s, governments have placed far greater emphases on school accountability, perhaps in conjunction with the rising numbers of students pursuing post-secondary studies. The changing context of schooling has tended to promote all three forms of testing.

Mechanisms: Legitimating Curricula

"Legitimation" processes can also create change and stability in the curriculum despite changing political and cultural currents. Take for instance the changing meaning of "progressive" pedagogy. While these ideals have been repeatedly invoked in Canadian schools, exactly what they entail has changed repeatedly. Davies (2002) arrived at this conclusion after examining three Royal Commission reports on education from the province of Ontario. Published between 1950 and 1995, each report used the language of "progressive" education to call for improvements in the system. All three rejected rote learning, championed "educating the whole child," and advocated "critical thinking." Beyond that, however, each report "framed" progressive themes in ways that reflected its own surrounding political and cultural climate. The 1950 report called for more curriculum tracking and IQ testing. The 1968 report then *condemned* those very same practices in the name of progressivism. The 1995 report then lauded more tailored programs and standardized tests, again under the same banner. These inconsistencies beg the question: why is there so often a disconnection between policy rhetoric and actual practice?

Mechanisms: Loose Coupling

The previous chapter described schools as "loosely coupled," noting that while many formal aspects of schooling are standardized and tightly controlled, the actual practice of teaching itself has little monitoring, and takes place largely behind closed doors. This organizational reality extends to the curriculum.

Think of the *dispersal* of power to construct Canadian curriculum. Education is the responsibility of the provinces where ministries and departments authorize the curriculum, providing guidelines and instructional resources for different subjects at each grade level. Boards, typically working with experienced teachers, further outline guidelines, recommending textbooks, and providing other teaching resources. Classroom teachers are then expected to use these resources to create detailed lesson plans. At the end of this lengthy process, students encounter these learning materials. But note what happens along the way. Teachers need to interpret this curriculum in their own ways, drawing on their own thinking patterns, habits, interests, and strengths. Students in turn will translate teachers' interpretations to generate their own understandings of the curriculum. Some students will be attentive, but others will tune out and turn off, or will select content they like while ignoring the rest. What is eventually learned will hardly be an exact replica of the intentions of high-level curriculum planners.

Conclusion

School curriculum is created by historical choices about which knowledge to include. Pedagogy has become broadly more progressive, and has been increasingly rationalized. The content of curriculum is shaped by several social influences, including group competition and accountability pressures that prioritize standardized student assessments. In turn, curriculum likely has important effects on students, but debate rages over whether its impact stems from its hidden or overt content. The dynamics of curricular implementation are shaped by legitimating processes and loose coupling. With increasingly standardized, rationalized, and accountable curriculum, our next chapter turns to another central issue: what happens to the status of teachers? Are teachers also influenced by relentless rationalization and globalization, or are they gaining professional power from these forces?

Questions for Critical Thought

1. Find examples of textbooks used in schools 40 or more years ago. Compare these older texts to more recent books in the same subject. Comment on changes in their content, organizational structure, and kinds of learning exercises.

2. Most students reading this book have written one or more standardized test. Reflect on the role of this testing in your educational career—was it focused on diagnostics,

selection, or system accountability? Given current trends, which role(s) will such testing play for your children?

3.   Thinking back on your school experience, what would you cite as the most prevalent form of "hidden" curriculum? Give examples. Reflect on the degree to which it was hidden, and from whom it was hidden.

Suggested Readings

Baker, David, and Gerald LeTendre. 2005. *National Differences, Global Similarities: World Culture and the Future of Schooling*. Stanford, CA: Stanford University Press. Baker and LeTendre have presented an international view of school curriculum trends from advocates of new institutional theory.

Binder, Amy J. 2002. *Contentious Curricula: Afrocentrism and Creationism in American Public Schools*. Princeton, NJ: Princeton University Press. Binder's text is an award-winning analysis of two very different reform movements in American public schools.

Council of Ministers of Education Canada. 2016. *Measuring Up: Canadian Results of the OECD PISA Study: Performance of Canada's Youth in Reading, Mathematics, and Science*. http://cmec.ca/Publications/Lists/Publications/Attachments/365/Book_PISA2015_EN_Dec5.pdf. This book detail results for Canadian youth in the 2015 PISA assessment.

Koretz, Daniel. 2008. *Measuring Up: What Educational Testing Really Tells Us*. Cambridge, MA: Harvard University Press. Koretz provides a thorough overview of complex issues involved in promoting, interpreting, and using results from different kinds of standardized tests.

Web Links

Mental Health and High School Curriculum Guide
www.cmha.ca/highschoolcurriculum
This website promotes a type of "social problems curriculum" for use in Canadian secondary schools.

Home School Curriculum
https://diyhomeschooler.com/
What might a "do-it-yourself" curriculum look like? This website offers resources for the would-be homeschooler.

Organisation for Economic Co-Operation and Development (OECD) and Programme for International Student Assessment (PISA)
www.oecd.org/pisa
Run by the Organisation for Economic Co-operation and Development (OECD), PISA measures the competencies of 15-year-olds in reading, mathematics, and science every three years.

10 The Sociology of Teaching

Learning Objectives

- To understand schools as workplaces
- To be able to compare and contrast schools with other types of occupational settings
- To use concepts from the sociology of professions to understand trends in teaching

Introduction: The Paradoxes of Teaching in a Schooled Society

By definition, schooled societies give high priority to education. A by-product is a large occupation devoted to instruction. It is inconceivable to think of a mass school system that processes millions of youth without a well-developed teaching corps. Indeed, teaching now is one of the largest occupations in Canada and represents the single most likely career for educated women. As of 2012, Statistics Canada estimated there were about 342,000 full-time elementary and secondary teachers in the Canadian public system. Including full-time teachers in independent (private) schools, colleges, and universities, the total workforce would be well in excess of 420,000.

Schooling was not always accorded such priority in Canada. Before the 1960s, teaching was not a particularly good job. Nineteenth-century education was rife with examples of teachers—particularly female teachers—who had meagre pay, unstable contracts, and hazardous working conditions. Many teachers at elementary levels were barely educated themselves, at least by today's standards (Gidney and Millar, 2012).

These humble origins reflect the type of system built by the original Canadian "school promoters" (Prentice, 1977). Like their American counterparts, these administrators desired a universal system to "democratically uplift" the populace (Brint et al., 2001; Cummings, 2003). The massive size of the public system created a large demand for teachers, and sometimes it was difficult to find well-qualified recruits, particularly in rural areas. School officials typically lowered teaching requirements to solve labour shortages, a solution that did not help the early status of Canadian teachers. Many were teaching rudimentary lessons and had to seek recognition through their moral role. In church-backed schools, teaching was akin to a priestly calling, and even as schools secularized, teachers continued to be seen as "social trustees" (Brint, 1994) because they had the responsibility of socializing children. Nineteenth-century public school teaching was dominated by the need to shape the moral fibre and character of the next generation more than any need to pass on esoteric knowledge.

This practice contrasts sharply with many European systems. Those systems were oriented to cultivate elites. Until well into the twentieth century, European secondary schools mainly groomed small numbers of affluent youth to enter a tiny collection of prestigious universities (e.g., in France, they were groomed for *les Grandes écoles*). This association with societal elites enhanced the status of European teachers. But over the past half-century, public school systems changed both in Europe and in North America. Since the 1960s especially, the conditions for most Canadian teachers improved. With governments directing millions of dollars to modernize schooling, teaching jobs were upgraded. New teachers were required to obtain a university degree and existing teachers without degrees were encouraged to get one. Teacher training was absorbed by universities. From this institutional base, educational research became a huge enterprise, with hundreds of professors hired to train novice teachers and to conduct research. Teachers themselves became more specialized. Secondary teachers needed credentials to demonstrate competence in specialized courses, or to work with unique student populations. As teachers gradually downplayed their moral role, they assumed a "legal-rational" role of "course specialist," who managed large classes and facilitated subject-based knowledge. Finally, teachers unionized and through collective bargaining, their pay was raised. In a relatively brief period of time, teaching was transformed from an occupation with below-average pay to one with well-above-average pay. This transformation benefitted female teachers in particular.

In the 1920s, women held over 80 per cent of all elementary and secondary teaching jobs. But as conditions and pay improved between 1960 and 1980, men's proportion of these positions grew to almost 50 per cent. Yet, female representation in teaching has since rebounded (recall from Table 7.1 that over 70 per cent of recent education graduates were women). Importantly, the modern organization of teaching has protected women from pressures that spoil women's status in other occupations. The emergence of a highly rationalized hiring, pay, and security structure has permitted female teachers to largely match their male counterparts who have similar qualifications. Collective bargaining and detailed rules have allowed them to raise and maintain status over recent decades. This social circumstance is rather unique—that a female-dominated occupation can actually upgrade relative to others. Most occupations with a majority of female members suffer from relatively low pay, a lack of public recognition, and devaluation of their skills. In essence female-dominated occupations tend to absorb a "status hit"—especially if they are stereotyped as "nurturing" jobs like nursing or child care. Caring for others is often seen as "natural" for women, and hence these skills are assumed to be in abundant supply (Krahn, Lowe, and Hughes, 2015). But teaching in its modern, rationalized form has buffered these pressures, maintaining its levels of salary and job security. In general, the transformation of schooling from a humble system for democratically uplifting the masses through basic literacy to a complex organization of professionals for socializing the masses has served to upgrade the status of teachers. But the full story is not quite that simple.

The past decade has witnessed many challenges to teachers' authority. Reforms to promote accountability through standardized testing and curricula and school rankings have been implemented despite strong opposition from teachers. Provincial governments have dealt aggressively with teachers, sometimes declaring them to be unproductive. Parents, too, are now less deferential towards teachers, with some, particularly those who are highly educated themselves, demanding a greater voice in the running of schools.

These pressures can be glimpsed in media images of teachers. Many portrayals of teachers are unflattering. At best, a Hollywood movie will portray a heroic and inspirational mentor who struggles to set tough, inner-city youth on the straight and narrow path. But too often teachers are seen as dull and rule-obsessed bunglers who are barely tolerated by their hipper yet captive students. On the TV news teachers are shown on strike or protesting funding cuts. It is rare to see a public image of a teacher as a consummate professional.

Moreover, recent years are marked by episodes where journalists, politicians, and parents blame teachers for all sorts of societal ills, such as illiteracy, moral decay, and youth unemployment. Few other occupations stand similarly accused. For instance, doctors are rarely deemed incompetent when a disease breaks out; firefighters are seldom targeted as scapegoats during an arson spree. But teachers are typically held responsible for reports of rising dropout rates or falling student test scores, despite ample evidence that these problems are predicted far more powerfully by student background than by teacher attributes. For today's educators, teaching is a great career but a difficult job. Despite attracting many dedicated practitioners, and despite enjoying upgraded conditions, teaching has a surprisingly high rate of attrition (Guppy and Davies, 1996). Many teachers love working with children and regard teaching as their vocation, but they face serious workplace strains that come from needing to balance the competing demands of administrators, parents, students, and politicians.

Teaching today entails two paradoxes. First, our schooled society has raised the status of teaching while at the same time subjecting it to greater critical scrutiny. Teachers today hear louder criticism than before, despite being educated and qualified as never before. For instance, in 2001, most Canadian teachers described their job as more stressful than a decade before (Canadian Teachers Federation, 2001), and in the early 1990s only half felt their profession was respected in their community (King and Peart, 1992). Ontario surveys suggest that most adults are satisfied with teachers' job performance (Hart and Kempf, 2015). But the irony is that as schooling is increasingly prioritized in society, teachers collectively feel *less* valued and respected than before.

Second, as politicians continue to pour monies into education, they are more likely to challenge teachers' authority. The dominant thrust of Canadian school reform over the past two decades has been for provinces to seize greater control of education, sometimes at the expense of teachers' input. It is unclear whether the public or the law supports this trend. A recent poll showed that many Ontarians stated that the province has too much control over education (Hart and Kempf, 2015). In BC, teachers won a 2016 legal battle that forced the BC government to hire more teachers after the province had unlawfully cut the workforce and unfairly altered class size caps.

This chapter presents a sociological framework to address several paradoxes (see Box 10.1 for another paradox). First, we argue that organizing schooling in modern legal-rational forms offers teachers several *professional* traits and grants them a **semi-monopoly** in public schools. Second, governments' higher priority for schooling encourages them to subject teaching to greater *control* and to challenge teachers' authority. Further, the modern, societal mandate of schooling—to retain and accommodate the majority of youth through high school—inhibits

Box 10.1 Unionist or Capitalist?

Teaching is a paradoxical profession/job/occupation. Canadian teachers are simultaneously members of powerful unions and substantial owners of private corporations. Normally one thinks of union members opposing the interest of corporate owners, or vice versa. However, as one of the largest unionized occupations in the country, teachers are very influential both in the union movement and within some political parties. Simultaneously, via their large pension funds, teachers have a large ownership stake in commercial markets.

Ontario teachers, for example, have a pension fund with assets of approximately $171 billion (2016; see www.otpp.com). Since 1990 the plan has averaged earnings of 10 per cent every year. They have substantial funds invested in two European airports (Brussels and Copenhagen) and own Imperial Parking Corporation (Impark) which controls over 400,000 parking spaces in major Canadian and US cities. They own both the Toronto Eaton Centre and the Pacific Centre in Vancouver. The Ontario teachers' pension fund is the largest in the country, but in the other provinces teachers have substantial fund investments as well.

At the same time, through their unions, most teachers are affiliated either directly with the Canadian Labour Congress (CLC), as is the case with most Ontario teachers, or with provincial labour federations, which are members of the CLC. For example, the British Columbia Teachers Federation is a member of the BC Federation of Labour, the latter representing approximately 500,000 union members in the province.

This dual role, at one and the same time powerful corporate investors and strong union members, highlights yet another of the ambiguities among teachers and their labour force ties.

teachers from developing a specialized, cognitively based style of pedagogy, and instead reinforces their role as motivators and classroom managers. Combining these two points, we contend that this mandate, along with the emergence of various accountability procedures, is serving to reinforce teachers' **semi-professional** status.

While the two previous chapters examined broader organizational changes in schooling, highlighting bureaucratization, rationalization, and changes in authority relations, this chapter highlights how those changes have shaped teaching.

Teaching and the Sociology of Professions

Through the study of medicine, law, and similar occupations, sociologists have developed concepts to analyze how some occupations acquire more prestige and exercise more autonomy than others. Three particular concepts are of interest when examining teachers: traits and processes, jurisdictions, and logics of control.

Traits and Processes: Upgrading the Profession

The "trait and process" approach to the professions examines how some occupations pursue strategies and acquire characteristics that give them power, prestige, and control over their work (see Leicht and Fennell, 2001). This literature highlights medicine and law as "classic professions," characterized by knowledge that requires lengthy and elaborate training, high pay, the autonomy to set professional standards, the ability to discipline members, and task autonomy. These traits, according

Some of today's challenges to teacher authority are rooted in broad cultural shifts in society.

Source: © Copyright 2010 Daryl Cagle. Reprinted with permission of Cagle Cartoons Inc.

to this reasoning, allow such occupations to achieve "professional" status. The process of acquiring such status is known as **professionalization** and is used by lower-status occupations to raise their collective standing. Professionalization involves organizing an occupational association to serve as a collective voice, developing a code of ethics (after medicine's Hippocratic Oath), housing training in universities, creating a credential, and most importantly, getting the state to recognize that credential.

Using these criteria, sociologists have long deemed teaching to be a "semi-profession" (e.g., Etzioni, 1969). On the one hand, teachers possess several professional traits, such as university training, required credentials, and some degree of task autonomy, as indicated by their lack of supervision in the classroom. These achievements have come in part from the union-style actions of past generations of teachers, marked by the occasional episode of labour militancy. But this professionalism also stems from society's growing need for educational standardization. As schooling became a prime basis to ration jobs, pressures mounted to ensure that the credentials obtained by students at different schools could roughly represent a comparable level of cognitive and attitudinal development. Hence, over time schools increasingly standardized their practice, adopting common course labels, grading standards, and, of course, teacher qualifications, albeit in loosely coupled forms. The adoption of professional traits by teachers was quite compatible with the role of schooling in rationing access to higher-end labour markets.

On the other hand, teachers are subordinates in a vast bureaucratic hierarchy. Provinces and school boards design curricula and standardized tests. That hierarchy also determines the conditions of teacher training, which is of relatively short duration compared to other professions. Further, the utility and necessity of this training have been questioned. Thus, teachers may lack a key professional trait—training that is specialized and widely recognized (see Box 10.2).

For instance, one hidden source of "de-professionalization" in teaching comes from administrative decision-making. Principals will often engage in "out-of-field assignments" and give courses to teachers despite their lack of particular qualifications, such as when a math course is assigned to a teacher without mathematics training. Such a practice arguably implies that anyone can teach and thereby devalues the trained expertise that goes into teaching. As Ingersoll (2003: 166–7), a former teacher turned sociologist, puts it:

This assumes that teachers are interchangeable blocks that can be placed in any empty slot. Treating teachers like low-skill workers makes them useful to administrators as generalists able to teach a wide range of subjects, justifying less rigorous and costly training, lower salaries, and making replacement easy. Yet this managerial habit is not defined as malpractice, as it would in other professions. . . .

For Ingersoll, one consequence of this non-recognition of expertise is that teachers' professionalism is understood in overly personal or public service terms.

Box 10.2 Preparing Teachers

Teacher certification requires a Bachelor of Education (or equivalent). Sixty-two Canadian universities enrolled about 50,000 students in teacher certification programs in 2016, with nearly 20,000 graduates. Unlike most self-governing professions, such as law or medicine, certification requires no additional examinations or work (e.g., articling) beyond the university level (see Crocker and Dibbon, 2008, Van Nuland, 2011).

Teacher education programs migrated to universities in the second half of the twentieth century, a shift with both pros and cons. In the process of professionalizing any job, university training has become a hallmark of occupational distinction. Further, the housing of teacher education in universities served to elevate "education theory" to a greater intellectual footing (at least by association) and enhance the belief that university research could inform effective classroom practice. Certainly teaching would have suffered as a professionalizing occupation had its training remained outside higher education.

Migration to the university was not without costs though (Young, 2004). Because universities emphasize scholarship over teaching, professors in faculties of education were pulled into the orbit of scholarly research, needing to publish books and articles and secure grants. These activities tend to isolate education professors further and further from elementary and secondary schools and their teachers. So while the university has been beneficial for the professional aspirations of teachers, it has simultaneously widened the "theory/practice" divide.

A related tension focuses upon the best preparation for teachers. One route has new teachers becoming subject experts by specializing in a disciplinary major (e.g., English, mathematics) as a first degree and then obtaining tailored courses devoted to teacher education as a second degree (a "consecutive" program). A second route has prospective teachers enrolling in professional teacher education courses at the same time as disciplinary majors courses (e.g., English) within a single university degree. Most elementary teachers take this latter "concurrent" program, while most secondary teachers follow the consecutive model. In part this program difference explains why elementary and secondary teachers have rather distinct identities, with elementary teachers more devoted to teaching practices than their secondary school counterparts, who often focus more on discipline-based practices. In many jurisdictions, this elementary–secondary divide is reinforced not just by separate teacher preparation programs but also by separate schools and separate unions. No natural age-divide among students separates teachers in this manner. Notice too that this dual model of teacher training is unlike what occurs in other professions where, for example, everyone in a faculty of medicine follows a similar path.

Finally, teachers are strategic actors in the eyes of policy-makers. As Rivkin, Hanushek, and Kain (2005) argue, teacher quality is a very important factor influencing student achievement, a factor more readily altered than class size and more efficacious than incremental changes in class size. Raising teacher quality is a policy direction most likely to enhance student learning. This realization is likely to strengthen calls to reform teacher education.

Teachers are judged for their "commitment," "sense of duty," "diligence," and "warmth" rather than their expertise. While such characteristics are certainly desirable and valued in all professions, few professions claim them as the essence of their practice. No physician would declare that simply caring about a patient or being their inspiration qualifies him or her to practice. To doctors, engineers, or lawyers such attitudes are necessary but hardly sufficient for performing their tasks. Can you imagine a non-specialist doctor, analogous to a substitute teacher, stepping in at the last minute to perform surgery? This difference occurs in large part because physicians have much greater control of the organization of their work. We next elaborate further on this gap between teaching and "classic professionalism."

Jurisdiction: Monopoly without Esoteric Knowledge

The study of "**professional jurisdictions**" (Abbott, 1988) focuses on "turf battles" among occupations. This approach examines how occupations vie for the right to monopolize a certain task area. It complements the "trait and process" approach by emphasizing three things: that monopolies are the result of competition between occupations; that an occupation's success is enhanced by a rare and complex knowledge base; and that professions suffer when their tasks and modes of evaluation are not clearly defined.

Monopoly

Historically, physicians have claimed a monopoly over government-recognized health care, successfully fending off the challenges of chiropractors, naturopaths, and other health-care workers. By losing these battles, chiropractors and naturopaths can rarely obtain health insurance claims because those are monopolized by licensed physicians. This history also shows how doctors have worked to subordinate groups like nurses and orderlies. Nurses, paramedics, and orderlies cannot perform many simple procedures without the permission, oversight, and consent of a doctor. Further, the "classic professions" enjoy a strong monopoly throughout society. For instance, certified doctors not only have a monopoly of practice in hospitals, but also in other realms. Any corporation or sports team that wants a medical expert on its staff must hire a certified doctor, since it is illegal for anyone else to perform surgery, prescribe drugs, or engage in many other forms of medical practice. Lawyers similarly enjoy a strong monopoly. Corporations must hire certified lawyers to protect themselves even if others could dispense similar advice or carry out specialized contractual duties.

Teachers in Canada are peculiar from this vantage point. They have a near-monopoly in the public system, where schools can hire only certified graduates with the requisite training from an accredited university. This requirement gives teachers a "labour market shelter" from other possible competitors. Yet, this monopoly does not extend beyond the public system. In most provinces, private schools are not compelled to hire certified teachers. Indeed, a study of the growing private-school market in Toronto found that *most* new schools lack rules requiring the exclusive hiring of certified teachers (Quirke and Aurini, 2016). Nor do teachers monopolize other emerging forms of education. For instance, home-schooling can be legally practised by anyone, regardless of their qualifications or educational background. Private tutoring companies freely hire instructors who have no teacher training (Aurini, 2012). Corporations that hire formal instructors to train their employees are not required to hire certified teachers (Scott and Meyer, 1994: Ch. 11). Universities do not hire certified teachers without PhDs.

This lack of a monopoly can be justified by beliefs that "effective teachers are born, not trained," products of personal charisma more than learned skills (Quirke and Aurini, 2016). Home-schoolers, for instance, typically appeal to their parental authority and love when justifying their right to teach their children (Stevens, 2001). Imagine parents making the same claims to argue that they are qualified to perform surgery! But public recognition of teaching as necessitating elaborate training is highly contested. Outside of public schools, anyone can teach, quite literally (see also Glazer, 2008).

Knowledge

Does teaching excellence come from an arduous and indispensable training in technical knowledge, as in medical, dental, law, or engineering schools? Or are the abilities teaching requires of a different nature, rooted in personal experience and "people skills" rather than theory-based training? Teacher training has been bolstered over the decades, with some calling for even lengthier and more elaborate periods of training. All public school teachers today are trained in a university major, such as history, English, or sociology, and receive instruction in pedagogy in faculties of education. But some question the nature of teacher training. Bachelor degrees are no longer uncommon; millions have been earned in Canada. Further, except for technical subjects in high school, school content is rarely complex; the challenge for instructors is less to master their material than to *teach* it.

Studies have long suggested that teachers see their experience and personal qualities as more crucial to their performance than their training (e.g., compare Lortie, 1975 to Paulle, 2013). They admit to rarely invoking formal theories of pedagogy on the job, and regard classroom management abilities to be rooted in charisma rather than in a set of trainable skills. They also emphasize that training is useless for any teacher who does not like or cannot inspire children. Given these job requirements, it is unsurprising that teachers report that the most enjoyable aspect of their job is making a difference in children's lives, not their particular subject areas (Brint, 2017; Canadian Teachers Federation, 2001).

Recalling your own high school experiences you will likely recognize why teachers are required to take on disciplinarian and classroom managerial roles. Over 85 years ago, Willard Waller (1965 [1932]) described how large and diverse classrooms create an inherent conflict between children's spontaneity in social settings and teachers' needs to maintain some degree of control. In ways that still ring true, Waller described how a teacher strives to strike a precarious balance between having a friendly rapport with students and remaining an authority figure (see also Clifton and Roberts, 1993).

Such conditions do not promote professionalism. The potential for developing a more systematic practice of pedagogy may lie in more personalized settings. Many breakthroughs in the contemporary study of learning are emerging in special education, such as for the teaching of autistic and dyslexic children. These advances have been facilitated by one-on-one conditions that are more like private practice or private tutoring than standard classroom schooling. As long as teaching is associated with a "warehousing" role, it will be difficult to develop a more "professional" model of instruction. Without the ability to develop more individualized forms of instruction, there now exist no agreed-on principles for group-based teaching. Despite the existence of thousands of books on teaching, basic principles remain in dispute, and no one can claim that any one particular set of techniques is consistently more effective than others. Hence, many contemporary theories of pedagogy centre on elaborating their philosophical roots or political intentions rather than developing clearly defined techniques (Rowan, 2002; Glazer, 2008).

To understand this quandary further, we need to recall theories of school organization discussed in previous chapters and examine how bureaucratic hierarchies constrain what teachers do.

Logics of Control: Loose Coupling within a Bureaucratic Hierarchy

The ultimate authority for Canadian schooling lies in provincial ministries and departments of education. Authority flows down to school boards, then to principals, and finally to the classroom teacher. A major issue in education rests on the balance of power between these stakeholders. For advocates of teacher professionalism, ministries and boards are useful for playing coordinating roles and supplying classrooms with funds and resources, but the bulk of direct education—from content to evaluation—ought to rest with teachers. For advocates of central control, public accountability in education is possible only when important decisions are made by high-ranking provincial bureaucrats who answer to elected politicians, who themselves answer ultimately to voters. To understand this debate over control of education, we begin by examining how teachers are evaluated.

Most Canadian teachers are evaluated rather sporadically and, when they are inspected, the methods are often disputed. For instance, most teachers are periodically assessed using "peer evaluation" in which an administrator such as the principal observes the teacher's classroom for a few hours. Between inspections, evaluation is very impressionistic. Most schools implicitly use a "911" approach, intervening only in response to an emergency or complaint. Otherwise, schools rely on impressions of teachers' general reputation and popularity.

Why is the evaluation of teaching so loose? Typical public schools, according to new institutional theory, are loosely coupled organizations, and as such, they are more readily rewarded for seeking legitimacy than for demonstrating their effectiveness. This loose coupling encourages schools to conform to educational conventions such as hiring credentialed teachers. This practice, discussed in Chapter 7, is based on a "logic of confidence" whereby certifications are assumed to guarantee a minimum standard of teaching quality, and justify the granting of considerable discretion to practitioners. So, rather than having their instructional effectiveness continually inspected and assessed, teachers are largely unsupervised on a day-to-day basis (see Guppy et al., 2005).

Turmoil in Costen Elementary

"The school's been through a lot of turmoil. A lot." (teacher interviewee)

Many policy-makers champion notions of school accountability. In organizational terms, accountability often translates into efforts to "recouple" schools. This recoupling can include tightening links between assessments of teachers and student performance, standardizing courses and evaluation procedures, and closely monitoring the actions of teachers. Many teachers oppose these forms of recoupling, seeing them as infringements on their autonomy. So what exactly happens when administrators attempt to recouple schools, doing things such as using students' test score data to judge teachers, conducting random spot checks in classrooms, and expecting teachers to use principal's lesson plans and grading rubrics? How do teachers react?

Not very well, according to sociologist Tim Hallett. Hallett conducted intense field work in an elementary school in the American Midwest between 1999 and 2001. His timing was strategic. City officials were just beginning to implement a new accountability policy for their schools. They deemed many prevailing educational practices to be wasteful, inefficient, and disorganized. They began to hire educators who shared their priorities for higher test scores, faithful implementations of their policies, and a new culture of education. The administrator who was hired to oversee this program had a finance background, not a background in education. He wanted schools run more like well-oiled businesses than like social services organizations. And, he had just hired a new principal, Ms Kox, to implement his ideals at "Costen Elementary," a fairly large public school.

Ms Kox took pride in her tough, no-nonsense approach to school management. While she appreciated that "some good teaching" had already occurred at Costen, she also believed that too many teachers wasted their classroom time, lacking a sufficient focus on instruction. She touted classroom management techniques aimed at boosting "time on task" and eventually, test scores. She told faculty that "if we monitor the students constantly, they don't have time to act up." Because Costen teachers had praised their previous principals for "hiring good people and letting them do their jobs," Ms Kox wanted teachers to know that she was the new sheriff in town. She set out to shake things up, becoming a formidable presence in the school by regularly popping into classrooms unannounced. Here are some excerpts from Hallett's field notes:

> Kox heads to Room 124 and stands inside the doorway. Students sit quietly as the teacher does something at her desk. Kox observes for a few seconds but does not say anything. Then we head to Room 224, and Kox does the same thing. Kox opens the door, and students scurry around their desks. The noise rises, and Kox asks the teacher, "Why are they running?" The teacher responds, "They're running to get their books." Kox says, "That's unacceptable" and makes them settle down, telling students, "Show me your learning position." Once students are sitting quietly, Kox says, "Stand up, get what you need for science, and put your book bags away. You have five seconds. Five . . . Four . . . Three . . . " Students move quickly but quietly and return to their seats. Kox says, "Straighten up the books around you." Then she walks around, checks their homework, and instructs, "Raise your hand before you speak." When they settle down, Kox says, "OK, we are ready for learning? Have a good day."

> Kox and the assistant principal review report cards, and Kox wonders aloud, "If they are all using the same materials, do the teachers assign the same grades? It's the same curriculum" (implying they should). Kox continues, saying, "We should standardize." Looking at a report card she sighs, "Oh, I don't like it." Kox looks at a report card and says in disbelief, "Oh, come on! Recognizing numbers 1 through 10 is not introduced [during the first quarter] in kindergarten?" Looking at another report card, she comments, "No, this is more than I can handle. Why is it [Rooms] 231 and 232 have different criteria? Are we teaching the same things to students?"

As these examples attest, Ms Kox rejected much of the "logic of confidence" that had long prevailed in the school. She enacted a new "recoupled" logic that regulated teacher's daily duties and monitored if they were complying. For example, previous principals had always "rubberstamped" report card grades, but Kox scrutinized them, even as some teachers "panicked," disbelieving that someone was actually reviewing their grade books. To monitor instruction and ensure teachers aligned with the city's formal academic standards, Kox required teachers to submit daily lesson plans, and organized an instructional review in which she examined examples of students' work. Hallett then examined the impact of this recoupling among teachers. He recorded this typical conversation between two teachers, along with some field notes, shortly after Kox arrived at Costen:

> Maggie: (In a choked voice) It seems like every time we're told to do something, this is gonna happen and this gonna happen, then the whole thing just falls apart and there's no continuity in this school.

> Brenda: (Trying not to cry) That's right.

continued

Maggie: I try, I really have, but I've just had it, I'm in a bad place right now.

Brenda: If we did a survey, I bet 75 percent would agree with you, the lack of continuity, the ambiguity.

Fieldnotes: Anxiety increased as teachers received feedback from Ms Kox. A kindergarten teacher had submitted an exercise where students practiced writing letters. Kox wrote: "What's the grading rubric?" Baffled, by this surveillance, the teacher told me "this is bullshit," because "this is kindergarten" and students are "just learning this letter."

Ironically, Ms Kox's changes did not have their desired effect. Whereas the school's average reading scores had previously risen over eight years, they dropped slightly during Kox's tenure. Further, many veteran colleagues chose to leave rather than comply with her changes. Topping it off, one teacher compiled complaints from her colleagues in a 119-page volume titled *Turmoil at "KOX"sten School*. The volume included 36 letters from 27 teachers and eight letters from six staff members. The letters decried the rate of recoupling and Kox's tough approach, describing the school as in "turmoil." The teacher sent copies to district, regional, and central offices, the teachers' union, and almost anyone else she could think of. Just as Ms Kox dismissed teachers' previous practices as unaccountable and inefficient, teachers rejected Kox's reign, believing she had tampered with their professionalism. This rebellion prompted the central office to conduct an official investigation into Kox's tenure at Costen, even though she did not break any formal rules or overstep her authority.

For Hallett, Costen's story reveals a hidden irony in large organizations. Accountability regimes typically involved recoupling school systems, creating transparent and common standards. Common standards are assumed to boost certainty and trust among a range of stakeholders. But if recoupling clashes with older, loosely coupled practices, the opposite can ensue: distress, turmoil, conflict, and heightened levels of distrust. This irony speaks to John Meyer's (1977) thoughts about loose coupling and the logic of confidence: for all of their inefficiencies, they often maintain peace among a range of actors, and allow organizations like schools to get on with their core tasks.

Why do schools evaluate their core task of instruction so casually? Institutional theorists look to the very nature of education. Teaching, they argue, is a human service fraught with uncertainty. Unlike working on a physical product, it requires cooperation with *people*. Because effective teaching rests partly on the efforts of the student, teachers have only limited control over their ultimate product: student learning. The skills required in teaching are relatively intangible and indeterminate, at least compared to production-oriented professions such as engineering.

Institutionalists also emphasize that schools have multiple goals. Educators often bristle at the increasingly popular notion that learning can be captured adequately by standardized tests. Debates have raged for decades over whether those tests are valid measures of learning and whether schools can ignore their other missions, such as promoting citizenship, nurturing creativity, building community, and moulding character. But how does one assess a teacher's effectiveness in achieving these less determinate goals?

Given the uncertainty of learning and schools' multiple goals, advocates of teacher professionalism argue that education is enhanced when teachers are granted more professional autonomy (Ingersoll, 2003). Good teaching requires flexibility, they argue, because its "clients" are neither mature nor voluntary (for a discussion, see Dooner et al., 2009). Schools, they argue, benefit from lessening bureaucracy and making education more like a professional community. Having administrators assume more control over evaluation and curricula only alienates teachers, they argue, without truly improving learning. Standardized testing, say its critics, promotes "teaching to the test" rather than innovation, and provides misleading measures of any student's ability. Many teachers argue that they are in the best position to evaluate their students because they have daily, detailed, and direct interactions with those students, and can measure their learning with their own tests and assignments, which they believe provide more valid indicators of any student's talent. Advocates such as Michael Fullan (2011) further argue that eroding teacher's discretion will only de-motivate them and make it more difficult to recruit into the profession. Put in organizational terms, the combination of immature and involuntary clients, uncertain instructional techniques, and multiple goals serves to place real limits on how much teachers' work should be bureaucratized.

However, many reforms that have emerged over the past 25 years, such as standardized tests and curricula and teacher re-accreditation procedures, tend to threaten teacher autonomy (Mehta, 2013). Claiming that too much of schooling goes unmonitored, many administrators see such reforms as tools for injecting more rigour and accountability in education. In the language of institutional theory, these reforms serve to "recouple" schools by imposing stronger supervisory regulations on classrooms. That is, when ministry or board officials control more aspects of schooling, they expect teachers to merely execute these initiatives, rather than use their own expertise, granting teachers leeway only to carry out tasks designed by management.

Another managerial initiative to control classrooms indirectly comes in schemes for paying and incentivizing teachers. According to critics, present arrangements do not motivate teachers. Canadian public school teachers are mostly paid on a salary schedule or "grid" that takes into account years of service and education credentials (i.e., BA, MEd., etc.). A new teacher with a BA typically starts at the salary provided in year one for a BA, and each year afterwards moves up the pay scale by seniority. Each year brings an automatic annual pay increase until year 12 or so, when most salary schedules peak. Further, this system tends to grant teachers "tenure" or job security after a probationary period.

To its critics, this system has a crucial shortfall: by recognizing only years of service and credentials, it disconnects pay from performance (see Raham et al., 2008).

Grids, critics say, fail to financially reward superlative teaching or punish poor teaching, cannot financially motivate those teachers whose salaries have already peaked, and have no reference to the grade level or subject matter taught, even though some, such as math and science teachers, are in greater demand. Uniform salary schedules, according to their critics, reward only experience and credential acquisition, and thereby discourage teachers to be concerned with student performance. Furthermore, grid systems are more characteristic of union workplaces than of professional occupations (even if the distinction is blurring in some places).

To solve these perceived problems, critics have promoted new kinds of incentives. Some want teachers' pay to have a large merit-based component that would factor in their students' performance on standardized tests, or evaluations by students or parents. These critics want to use such performance indicators to widen salary differentials because they presume that differentials will motivate teachers. Some point to university professors, who have sizeable merit-based components to their salaries stemming from their research and teaching performance. Teachers highlight several difficulties with this proposal, however. One is that student and parent evaluations are more like "satisfaction surveys" than measures of learning or teaching effectiveness. This problem is especially acute for elementary teachers whose students are young children that lack the maturity to judge them properly. Further, parent judgments can be highly inaccurate as they are rarely in the classroom.

Others wish to link teacher pay to their students' performance on standardized tests, reasoning that since standardized tests are designed by outside educators, they represent objective measures of learning. Teachers who better prepare their students for these tests will have their efforts reflected in higher test scores. To control for greatly disparate student compositions across schools (test scores are highly correlated with students' socio-economic backgrounds), reformers recommend "valued-added" measures that attempt to identify teachers' unique impact on their students' test scores over a year. Indeed, a famous American study claims that the best teachers can boost their students' lifetime earnings by over a quarter million dollars (Chetty, Friedman, and Rockoff, 2014).

Needless to say, these proposals are controversial among Canadian teachers. Few appear to currently support them, doubting that student test scores truly reflect their teaching competence, and worrying that such proposals rely on unreliable estimates of their real influence over students. Teachers contend that school-based instruction can be reinforced only by having students faithfully complete their assigned homework and engage in literary activities with their families. Teachers can control what goes on in the classroom, but have far less influence beyond it.

More broadly, these various proposals speak to issues of professional control in education. By regularly scheduling teachers' salary increases, "grids" weaken central administrators leverage over teachers once they have been hired, granting teachers a modicum of autonomy. Merit-pay schemes would bolster administrators' influence over what teachers do in the classroom: reformers see them

as offering incentives to good teachers; critics fear they will dilute teacher
tonomy. Currently, control over teaching is at a crossroads. Over the decades
teachers have won concessions and status largely through union-style actions of
collective bargaining, strikes, and political lobbying, rather than having their
professional authority recognized and valued by administrators. Union tactics
stem from their need to counterbalance the greater decision-making power
of high-level administrators in governments. As long as political influence in
education remains concentrated in those bureaucracies rather than dispersed
among individual teachers, teachers will use union tactics to press their wishes
beyond the classroom.

Conclusion: How a Noble Task Reinforces Semi-Professionalism

This chapter began by highlighting a striking paradox: the high priority that
Canadian parents and policy-makers place on education makes teachers feel
undervalued and under siege. Critics accuse teachers of wanting to be treated as full
professionals while shying from being accountable for student outcomes. As some
put it, if medical doctors botch their surgeries, they can be sued for malpractice.
If an engineer designs a bridge that soon collapses, the engineer will be forced to
accept blame. Yet teachers are seldom, if ever, held responsible for student illiteracy.
Is this fair?

This issue hinges on determining a suitable reference group for teachers. If one
believes that they can be validly compared to professions who work on physical
objects, such as bridges or bodies, then it may be fair. But if one compares them to
human service professions, then it may be unfair, since client compliance in those
areas of work is seen as the primary responsibility of the client, not of the practi-
tioner. If a fitness instructor designs a diet and exercise plan and a client fails to
adhere to that regimen, few blame the instructor. Likewise, it may be unfair to
blame teachers for students who exert little effort or even fail to show up on a regular basis (for an entertaining take on this debate, see Box 10.3).

To understand this paradox, this chapter used concepts from the sociology
of professions. Canadian teachers made gains in the 1960s through the 1980s by
adopting many traits held by classic professions and by winning a semi-monopoly
in public schools. However, since public education is governed through a vast
bureaucratic hierarchy, there are limits to teachers' autonomy. Today's accountability agendas have allowed administrators to seize some further control over education. The pressing need to control costs while accommodating millions of students
serves to inhibit the development of cognitive-based pedagogies that might facilitate further professionalism. As long as schooling is conducted in large and mostly
involuntary classrooms rather than individualized settings, teachers will need to
play custodial roles, manage classroom discipline, and motivate youth, too many of
whom are disinterested in school.

High-Stakes Testing for Dentists?

eat! He sends me reminders so I don't forget checkups. He uses the latest techniques. He never hurts me, and I've got all my teeth, so when I ran into him the other day, I was eager to see if he'd heard about a new program. I knew he'd think it was great. I said, "Did you hear about the new program to measure the effectiveness of dentists with their young patients?"

"No," he said. He didn't seem too thrilled. "How will they do that?"

"It's quite simple," I said. "They will just count the number of cavities each patient has at age 10, 14, and 18 and average that to determine a dentist's rating. Dentists will be rated as Excellent, Good, Average, Below Average, and Unsatisfactory. That way parents will know who are the best dentists. It will also encourage less-effective dentists to get better," I said.

"That's terrible," he said. "That's not a fair way to determine who is practising good dentistry." "Why not?" I said. "It makes perfect sense to me." "Well, it's so obvious," he said. "Don't you see that dentists don't all work with the same clientele; so much depends on things we can't control? For example, I work in a rural area with a high percentage of patients from deprived homes, while some of my colleagues work in upper-middle-class neighbourhoods. Many of the parents I work with don't bring their children to see me until there is some kind of problem. Also, many of the parents I serve let their kids eat way too much candy from a young age, unlike more educated parents who understand the relationship between sugar and decay."

"It sounds like you're making excuses," I said. I couldn't believe my dentist would be so defensive. He does a great job.

"I am not!" he said. "My best patients are as good as anyone's, my work is as good as anyone's, but my average cavity count is going to be higher than a lot of other dentists because I chose to work where I am needed most."

"Don't get touchy," I said.

"Touchy?" he said. "Try furious. In a system like this, I will end up being rated average, below average, or worse. My more educated patients who see these ratings may believe this so-called rating actually is a measure of my proficiency. They may leave me, and I'll be left with only the neediest patients. And my cavity average score will get even worse. On top of that, how will I attract good dental hygienists and other excellent dentists to my practice if it is labelled below average?"

"I think you're overreacting," I said. "Aren't you a professional?"

"You don't get it," he said. "Doing this would be like grading schools and teachers on an average score on a test of children's progress without regard to influences outside the school, the home, the community served, and stuff like that. Why would they do something so unfair to dentists? No one would ever think of doing that to schools."

I just shook my head sadly, but he had brightened. "I'm going to write my representatives," he said. "I'll use the school analogy; surely they'll see my point." He walked off with that look of hope mixed with fear and suppressed anger.

Source: Reprinted with permission from the June 2000 issue of School Administrator magazine, published by AASA, the School Superintendents Association.

This reality leaves educators with some quandaries. Should teacher training become more research based, guided by studies and formal theories, or should faculties of education mainly select their students by looking for personal traits? As it stands, education faculties do both. They demand solid university grades from their applicants, which imply a strong cognitive component to teaching, yet also seek applicants who have experience working with children and a commitment to the equitable welfare of youth. Both are entirely reasonable practices and illustrate how teaching is a human service that requires both personal qualities and cognitive abilities.

Teachers' professional dilemmas showcase some ideas we discussed in previous chapters. The historic transformation of schools into legal-rational bureaucracies has expanded teachers' capacity to gain professional status, but it also has created a hierarchy of authority that increasingly challenges their autonomy. Rationalized schooling facilitates credential-based monopolies, but by also inhibiting individualized pedagogies, it pushes teachers towards modern "social trusteeship," based not on commanding traditional forms of deference but on offering a contractual relationship.

All of this suggests that teachers are best seen as "semi-professionals," and that current trends are reinforcing this status. The use of standardized testing and curricula to make classroom practices more uniform from school to school and from board to board makes it difficult for teachers to devise their own curriculum or deviate from test material. As competition to enter universities becomes keener, students want assurance that their courses are recognized. This fuels further pressures to standardize courses, and perhaps even make grading standards uniform—a concern taken further in the US in the guise of the SAT. Pressures for schools to be accountable usually entail some centralization of decision-making in provincial ministries or departments of education. These pressures may reflect a neo-liberal ideology held by conservative politicians, but *any* society with large numbers of youth that pursue higher education will face pressures to centralize control over education. An essential irony is that the truly noble task of uplifting the masses through schooling is serving to solidify teachers' semi-professionalism. This irony reinforces a central theme of this book, namely that schools' effectiveness is limited by broader inequalities in society. Schools do partially compensate for such inequalities, but wider social forces constrain them. This chapter has offered a variation on this theme: that the structure of modern schooling limits teachers' professional status.

Nonetheless, teaching continues to recruit well-educated and dedicated men and women who welcome the challenge of working with youth. It continues to offer educated women a viable career option. Despite all of today's challenges, teachers still strive to make a difference in children's lives. Our evidence suggests that in the face of substantial societal inequalities, they do make that difference.

Questions for Critical Thought

1. Interview a teacher. Use the concepts of "professional" and "semi-professional" to probe the teacher's understanding of their job. Discuss the teacher's responses.

2. Can teachers legitimately claim to possess esoteric, professional knowledge? Is pedagogy currently a science? Can it become one?

3. Who is in the best position to evaluate a student: a teacher who has daily contact or a professional bureaucrat who uses a standardized test? Give examples to support both positions. Think of the implications of your answer for teacher professionalization.

4. There is currently a glut of qualified teachers in the labour market. What can be done about it? Discuss various options.

Suggested Readings

Chetty, Raj, John N. Friedman, and Jonah E. Rockoff. 2014. "Measuring the Impacts of Teachers II: Teacher Value-Added and Student Outcomes in Adulthood," *American Economic Review* 104(9): 2633–79. This article claims that high quality teachers have substantial impacts on their students' life chances.

Ingersoll, Richard. 2003. *Who Controls Teachers' Work: Power and Accountability in America's Schools.* Cambridge, MA: Harvard University Press. This is an insightful analysis of how school organization affects teachers' work and professionalism.

Lortie, Dan C. 1975. *Schoolteacher: A Sociological Study.* Chicago: University of Chicago Press. Lortie's *Schoolteacher* is considered one of the classic sociological analyses of teaching.

Van Nuland, Shirley. 2011. "Teacher Education in Canada," *Journal of Education for Teaching* 37(4): 409–21. Van Nuland provides a useful overview of provincial differences in teacher training, while highlighting some of the key issues facing all programs (e.g., enrolments, technology, and equity).

Web Links

Canadian Federation of Teachers
www.ctf-fce.ca
This is the official site of Canada's largest professional organization for teachers.

Canadian Society for the Study of Education
www.csse-scee.ca/csse
The CSSE is composed of professors, students, researchers, and practitioners who contribute to educational knowledge, prepare teachers and educational leaders, and apply research in the schools and classrooms. There is also a link to the *Canadian Journal of Education*.

Transitions to Teaching 2015
http://www.oct.ca//media/PDF/Transition%20to%20Teaching%202015/EN/2015_T2T_main_report_web_en.pdf
This is an updated report by the Ontario College of Teachers on the teaching profession in Ontario.

Part IV
Socialization

11

Socialization
The Changing Influence of Schools on Students

llllllllllllllllllllllllllllllllllllllllllllllllllllllllllllllllllllllllllllllllllllllllllllllllllllllllllllllllllllllllllllll

Learning Objectives

- To understand changing impacts of Canadian schools on youth, including new forms of morality and identity formation
- To explore methods to assess "school effects:" how sociologists distinguish the influences of schools versus their surrounding communities on youth

llllllllllllllllllllllllllllllllllllllllllllllllllllllllllllllllllllllllllllllllllllllllllllllllllllllllllllllllllllllllllllll

Introduction: The Continuum of School's Socializing Power

Reflecting on the influence of schools, Pierre Bourdieu (1988) describes a unique student in French history, the "oblate." Oblates were students from impoverished backgrounds, adopted as charity cases by church-run boarding schools. The brightest were trained as either clergy or academics. What is sociologically fascinating about the oblates is that having been cut off from their family roots and having been educated, clothed, fed, and housed by a single school, they represent rare examples of pupils who were almost entirely socialized via schooling. Not surprisingly, these students grew to identify strongly with their school and its teachings, were deeply grateful to the institution, and dedicated their lives to scholarship and academic learning.

Bourdieu's vignette helps us think of school socialization along a continuum. At the one extreme are famed boarding schools, where the institution regulates virtually every facet of life. It controls where, how, and when students sleep, eat, dress, and conduct their leisure time. Friends are chosen from within the school; the school becomes the entire social universe for its inhabitants. Connections among people are dense: everyone knows each other and knows about each other. Reputations circulate widely. Boundaries between insiders and outsiders can be thick and strong. These schools resemble what Erving Goffman has called "total institutions"—organizations, such as prisons and monasteries, which shape people's entire identity by controlling almost all facets of life. In boarding schools, teachers are powerful socializing agents, forging the identities of their pupils, having an almost singular impact on how they speak, look, and act.

At the other extreme of the socialization continuum is home-schooling using online education. If one's education consists solely of online courses, then school intrudes in these students' lives in an extremely piecemeal fashion. Rather than being a physical entity that surrounds the senses, "school" merely appears on one's laptop, phone, or tablet, to be engaged or ignored at one's wish. Education does not strongly shape one's social ties and interactions, or demarcate insiders from outsiders. School is simply one minor socializing force among many, like a television program to be turned on or off.

Most Canadian students experience school socialization somewhere between these extremes. Relatively few attend boarding schools or enrol solely in online education from home. Most attend public schools full-time, Monday to Friday. Using this perspective, this chapter explores the varying ways in which schools socialize students. We approach this topic largely from a historical vantage point, contrasting the ways school-based socialization has changed over the past 150 years. This chapter poses three fundamental questions. In what ways has the moral influence of regular public schooling been transformed, in what ways do schools shape different identities, and what are the most consistent "school effects" on students?

Morality: The Marginalization of Religious Schooling

As discussed in Chapter 2, Durkheim assigned schools the mission of providing modern society with the moral glue that could compensate for the declining authority of religion. The structural functionalists similarly assumed that schools provide crucial socialization, seeing schools as substitutes both for families and for traditional churches. Functionalists, and then neo-Marxists, portrayed schools as focusing on the inculcation of modern, or capitalist, values. With this theoretical legacy in mind, we first examine how religious education has changed in Canada.

The history of Canadian schools is one of changing forms of religious and moral influence. The earliest public schools in the mid-1800s were nominally secular (i.e., not religious), but their religious character was clear and overt. Schools were mandated to provide moral teachings. The father of public schooling in Canada West (what is now mainly Southern Ontario), Egerton Ryerson, was a Methodist minister who aimed to create a literate, religious, and devout citizenry. He argued in 1847 that Christianity ought to be the "basis and cement of the structure of public education" and that it "was central to social order." By 1850 he ensured that all common schools had to open and close with prayers, teach the Ten Commandments, and have scripture readings (Prentice, 1977: 128). This was part of a powerful belief that religion-infused schooling could morally "perfect" children and curb perceived problems such as excessive materialism, rising incidences of youth crime, societal ignorance, and dwindling community spirit.

Religion was also institutionalized via constitutional obligations, with Roman Catholics being granted separate schools in Ontario and Protestants being granted schools in Quebec. While denomination-based arrangements differed by province (see Manzer, 1994), the compromises of Confederation and later provincial politics clearly enshrined a religious basis into Canada's schools.

The central place of religion in public school missions lasted a century. Even to 1950, in what was known as the Hope Commission (1950), the leaders of Ontario schools were calling for schools to teach "cardinal virtues" and "Christian ideals, as personified and exemplified by Jesus, which have an appeal to all persons of good will, and are the surest common ground for an education program" (Government of Ontario, 1950: 36–7). This report urged Ontario schools to "prepare children to live in a democratic society which bases its way of life upon the Christian ideal" (ibid.) and to promote "respect for religion and the principles of Christian morality" (ibid., 123–4). Even nominally secular schools had clear religious and moral overtones. While this sort of language may sound incredibly creaky and "uptight" to many contemporary ears, it strongly resonated among older generations.

Cultivating Social Boundaries in Private Religious Schools

"Social boundaries" refer to any group's feeling of distinctiveness from others in society. Boundaries can be fortified by distinct practices and enacted beliefs that demarcate a group and forge its distinct identity. For individuals, successful rituals can create sensations by which they feel to be part of a "we," one that differs from a "them." Rituals can also guard against norms or practices that threaten group identities and erode social boundaries. Modern societies like Canada have myriad and overlapping social boundaries. Most Canadians have multiple and fluid identities, rooted simultaneously in their sense of ethnic ancestry, race, gender, nationality, and so on. Public schools, through both hidden and overt curriculum, are places where children encounter a rather porous set of social boundaries, ones that can create, enforce, break down, and/or reassemble their identities. Families that embrace most of today's secular norms will feel little tension between their values and those taught in public schools, and might welcome the eroding of some old boundaries. But among children from families with strong bonds to a religious faith, particularly those that provide a "master identity," public schooling can threaten some of their established social boundaries, and may even become an unviable option.

For instance, today's public schools take progressive stances on issues ranging from the origins of the earth to appropriate gender and sexual norms. These stances can clash with some religious norms. For instance, some British Columbia Christians have opposed the teaching of evolutionary theory in public schools. Several Ontario religious groups have objected to that province's sex education curriculum, claiming its conceptions of gender and sexuality are inappropriate for young children. Both controversies have triggered spikes in private-school enrolments; thousands of religious families have left their provincial public system.

Private religious schools shine a spotlight on schools' socialization role because they need to balance mandates of teaching common norms while also imparting a particular religious faith and identity. To witness how these schools walk this tightrope, sociologist Jeff Guhin (2016) conducted field work among two of North America's fastest growing religious private-school sectors: those for Sunni Muslims and those for Evangelical Christians. Over one and a half years of field work around

New York City, Guhin found few differences between those private schools and local public schools, except for two key practices: Sunni schools had distinct gender norms, and Evangelical schools utilized a unique form of "Biblical literalism."

Like their counterparts at nearby public schools, Evangelical teachers taught most academic topics, and their students worried about social dangers like drugs and gangs. But their understandings of academic topics and social norms were infused by this proviso: that the Bible was literally true, and provided *the* lens through which Evangelicals experienced the world. Accordingly, Evangelical teachers did not teach evolution, believing that doing so would weaken the Bible's authority and corrode their faith. A teacher said to his students: "Guys, I'm sorry but Satan has used the evolution philosophy to deceive mankind . . . a big giant lie that we evolved from this primordial soup with absolutely no purpose in life. . . . The Bible may not be not a science textbook, but everything it says about science is true." His students agreed. When asked about a hypothetical Christian scientist who might teach evolution, several said at once "Then he's not a Christian." Discussing a friend who planned to attend a college that taught evolutionary theory, several students spoke as if one of her family members had just died.

In contrast, the Muslim schools saw more compatibility between their religion and science, despite also believing in their scripture's literal truth. Their most distinctive beliefs instead centred on Islamic rules for gender. Signs near the schools' entrance called for "Proper Islamic Attire" and featured a stick figure woman in a hijab and abaya, a modest full-body dress. Females always wore that clothing during school hours, though not always at home, in order to demarcate Sunni schools from public schools. They defended the hijab as a symbol of living peacefully in the surrounding society, and as a positive source of identity, one that provided a refuge from the objectification of women and sexual promiscuity they saw as rampant in secular societies. One student asked Guhin "Ever see that show *16 and Pregnant*? I see it and think, 'Thank God I'm a Muslim, I don't have to worry about things like that'." Christians also believed that women needed to act in certain traditional ways at school, but for them, the enactment of gender was a far less distinctive aspect of their religious identity.

The two school communities also saw their relation to the rest of society quite differently. Muslims compared themselves to other historical minorities that had to overcome prejudice. One teacher said "We have to do what the Italians, Irish, and African Americans all did before us, and challenge stereotypes . . . for some people Muslim means terrorist, and we have to challenge this." Muslims worried about their portrait in the broader society as being sexist and violent. Evangelicals, in contrast, were clearly defensive about having a public image that deemed them ignorant and intolerant. One teacher told his class, "The media does a number on Christians and makes us look like buffoons every chance they get."

Guhin's field work uncovered how religious schools create social boundaries by giving key issues a heightened moral salience. Evangelicals focused on Biblical authority and avoiding evolutionary science. Sunni Muslims emphasized traditional gender roles and wearing the hijab. These practices demarcated religious schools from public schools. They also remind us of complex issues pertaining to diversity and tolerance. Can public schools fully accommodate all faiths without also promoting secular science and gender progressivism?

The historical record suggests that a purely secular approach to public schooling is a relatively recent creation in Canada. But once the momentum shifted, schools changed fast. By the late 1960s educators had very different ideas about moral teachings. A more "modern" moral agenda emerged. Starting in the late 1960s and 1970s, Canadian public schools gradually removed the Lord's Prayer and Bible readings. By 1968, the next major Ontario commission after the Hope Commission made little mention of "cardinal virtues" or Jesus. In what became known as the Hall-Dennis report (Government of Ontario, 1968: 27), educators were told:

> Ontario is caught in a severe dislocation of values. . . . The existence and effectiveness of God is openly and widely challenged. The changing standards of sexual morality, the position of the church on birth control, its involvement in issues of social justice—the raising of all these issues indicates that people in Ontario are questioning many basic religious beliefs.

Fewer teachers in the 1970s understood their role as one of promoting a traditional sense of moral duty. By that time, learning came to be viewed as a much more individualistic quest (ibid., 49):

> Learning is by its nature a very personal matter. There is virtually a metabolism of learning which is as unique to the individual as the metabolism of digestion. Parents and teachers may create conditions for learning in mind, but the actual learning experience is intimate and subjective, for each human being reaches out to the world in his own idiosyncratic way.

New educators wanted a new way of teaching for a new age. Their understanding of truth and morality was becoming more individualistic and less overtly religious. Roll over Durkheim!

This shift can be seen in the governance of Canadian public education. Over time, fewer religion-based school boards existed. It has been many decades since any province *added* religious boards. Some, like Quebec and Newfoundland, abolished their religious boards and removed religious schools from their provincial public systems. This shift in governance had a key impact: it motivated Canadian families who want religious education to seek alternatives outside of the public system. While not overly large in number, Canada has seen a growing number and variety of private religious schools (Alison, Hasan, and Van Pelt, 2016; Pizarro Milian and Davies, 2017), as well as growth in religious home-schooling (Basham et al., 2007). Some of these Canadians believe contemporary public schools are too secular. Indeed, the secularization of public education has helped fuel an international "school choice" movement. In Canada, this movement has assumed a few forms. Several Alberta charter schools have religious themes; Edmonton religious schools get some public funds, as do some religious schools in British Columbia and Quebec. Ontario briefly offered a tax credit for private schools in response to religious lobbyists.

Over time, therefore, religious schooling has moved from the centre of Canadian public education to its periphery. It continues to survive, but in altered forms: in separate environments that are fully funded by some provinces (e.g., Roman Catholic separate schools in Ontario), partly funded by other provinces (as in Quebec), or financed jointly through market mechanisms and subsidies from religious groups. Religious schooling is now something to be chosen by individual families, not something to be dictated by governments. Provinces continue to fund religious schools in various forms. But they do so to accord with contemporary understandings of individual rights and entitlements, not to accord with older understandings of moral duty.

A New Morality? Codes of Conduct, Human Rights, and Social Problems

The peripheral place of religion in public schools raises two questions: do public schools still promote some sort of morality, and if so, what is its nature? Today's public schools tend to understate their moral aims in comparison to cognitive goals like providing skills and narrowing achievement gaps. Nonetheless, schools continue to be regarded as forums for thinking about moral issues, but with a new style and character.

The new morality has not simply replaced religious edicts with secular edicts. Instead, it has multiple reference points, suiting a culturally diverse society with many religions and with many people who declare no religion at all. It celebrates fewer exemplars of righteousness. It tolerates more ambiguity. And, this morality is taught in a new fashion. Moral education is now about exposing students to a fuller range of contemporary controversies, beliefs, and ideals, and encouraging informed choices. It is less likely to portray certain, unambiguous truths. It uses fewer authoritative methods like rote repetition, and more pedagogical tools that promote discovery. The new style of pedagogy relies less on moral indoctrination and more on criticizing society, questioning dominant values, and illuminating social problems.

This new morality, rooted in the 1960s, reflects contemporary notions of human rights, critical thinking, and multiculturalism. It reflects the influence of "world culture" in John Meyer's sense, spreading evolving understandings of human rights and equity. It reflects a shift from traditional forms of moral authority, founded in religious imagery and ethics, to legal-rational forms that have a more contractual quality, as exemplified in school codes of conduct. Students are to abide by clearly articulated rules, as are teachers and parents.

Now, this is the "theory." What is the "practice?" That is, what do empirical studies (inspired by the "hidden curriculum" concept discussed in previous chapters) tell us about the *actual* socializing processes in schools? As discussed in Chapter 3, Collins's "interaction ritual" framework offers a useful lens for interpreting classroom socializing processes. This framework examines the varying

Box 11.1 Faith-Based Schooling

The pull of religion is less powerful now than in the past for a growing number of Canadians. Church attendance is down, fewer women and men become nuns or priests, and religious edicts have far less impact nowadays. Religion is no longer central to the Canadian public school system. Gone are opening and closing prayers in schools. King James bibles are no longer prominent on teachers' desks. The singing of religious hymns is rarely, if ever, heard in public schools. Religion has become more private, de-centred from schooling.

Yet simultaneously religion remains a notable feature of modern schooling. Catholic schools remain prominent in many provinces and are a choice educational institution for many parents. Religious independent schools are the most prolific form of private schooling in the country (Alison, Hasan, and Van Pelt, 2016). For these Canadians, a secular school system is both a curse and a blessing. It is a curse because moral teachings and spiritual inspiration have been removed from the public school. It is a blessing though because it allows space for schools with inclusive faith-based curricula and a concentrated focus on the teachings of a single faith, whether it be Evangelical Christianity, Judaism, Islam, or Sikhism.

These kinds of faith-based schools have grown in recent years in Canada, despite declines in the size of the youth cohort. This growth has been fuelled in part by the school choice movement, described in Chapter 8, and also large waves of immigration with families wanting to preserve some form of cultural heritage. This new wave of faith-based schooling has also benefitted from Canadian ideals that support multiculturalism, which some groups use when lobbying for cultural protections and rights (see Davies, 1999).

There is much debate around the merits of faith-based schooling. Proponents laud the diversity that faith-based schools can generate through their support of views and practices that rarely exist in public schools, and thus broaden the range of students' exposure to cultural traditions and practices. Opponents see religion as something best left at home, and as something that diverts public money from public schools. Why, opponents in various provinces argue, should Catholic schools receive public monies while other faith-based schools receive little or none? Catholic school funding is a constitutional legacy that some want changed.

power of school symbols and interactions for generating a sense of collective effervescence among students that may—or may not—get them to feel part of a group and energize them with feelings of moral purpose.

With these ideas in mind, Steven Brint and his team (Brint et al., 2001) conducted a study in which they recorded the implicit "messages" that could be detected in textbooks, rules, classroom discussions, and physical surroundings of several California primary schools. They found that schools indeed attempted to socialize their students, but only into a rather mundane set of moral tenets.

First and foremost, teachers urged students to work in an orderly fashion, respect others, participate in class, and cooperate with staff and classmates. They expected students to be punctual, neat, clean, and patient, and accept adult directives, and rewarded those who completed their tasks. Brint et al. interpreted these messages as simple ones of organizational control: teachers provided clear guides for daily conduct because they felt that classrooms, like any other kind of organization, need to be safe and orderly. Because elementary schools have clients that are less mature than those in most other kinds of organizations, teachers probably asserted their control more firmly than they might have with a class of adults. Brint et al. saw nothing that they thought to be authoritarian.

One could interpret this finding as confirming Bowles and Gintis's notion of a "hidden curriculum" that fosters obedience to authority. But Brint and his colleagues witnessed very few episodes of strictly enforced obedience. Teachers instead relied on participatory methods to encourage student compliance, methods that were less common during the heyday of Bowles and Gintis. They used token economies to reward children for completing duties. They offered children choice among tasks. They rotated children between activity centres. They maintained control with a mostly light touch, mixing dictates with frequent classroom celebrations. They deployed these methods in flexible, unregimented, and even indulgent manners to "capture" rather than "command" children's interests. So, they interpreted any "message" embedded in these methods as one that was preparing children for the fast-paced task environments of contemporary workplaces, fewer and fewer of which resemble old-style factories.

Another message spoke to modern values like social justice and diversity. But these values were rarely taught explicitly, and when they were, they were delivered in a strikingly indulgent manner. Remarkably, teachers strove to motivate *all* students. Whereas schools in the past would have given up on students deemed too poor, too troubled, or too slow, Brint et al.'s schools worked hard to engage the entire student body, even the least able. Teachers regarded self-esteem to be essential for learning. "Justice" revolved around a contemporary notion of "respect," not an older version that pivoted on moral respectability and duty, but one that prioritized getting along with others while being careful to acknowledge their self-esteem and sense of self-worth.

Also using an observation method, Jackson et al. (1998) similarly found that schools promoted notions of interpersonal respect, but embedded them into a variety of social causes, such as protecting the environment, helping the homeless, fighting racism, or fundraising for overseas children's assistance. Yet, they were struck by the way in which this activism was pursued in an individualistic fashion. Students were encouraged to relate their own experience and venture their own opinions. Teachers rarely had an explicit, hard-edged, and prescriptive moral tone, and instead wanted students to simply understand key issues. They adorned their classrooms with "feel-good" posters that exhorted a host of catchphrases, urging children to read, be respectful of others, or stay in school. This "bumper-sticker morality" was designed for quick consumption rather than deep discussion or reflection. The teaching of ethics, the authors concluded, tended to adopt the kinds of symbols used in mass entertainment and marketing.

These studies also illustrate another component of contemporary schoolings' socializing agenda: to address social problems. Today's schools have a fast-changing, multi-faceted "social problems curriculum" that variously aims to curb drug use, unsafe sex, racism, cyber-bullying, and so on. It consists of an array of classroom modules and exercises that can spark controversy when it crowds into the three Rs. Teachers report being stressed by having to "cram" these social problems modules into their regular curriculum. Some have questioned the actual impact of this curriculum (e.g., Labaree, 2010), and evaluation studies offer mixed assessment (Calear and Christensen, 2009; Rosenbaum and Hanson, 1998). We return to this issue in the final section of this chapter.

In sum, religion-based morality has been largely replaced in public schools by a new moral education. This morality is informed by modern notions of human rights and individual needs. It relies on a taken-for-granted cognitive schema in which all students are active agents who are responsible for their own actions, and need not rely on an anointed religious precept for guidance. This may represent a new "hidden curriculum" that is sensitive to student self-esteem and individual learning styles, and broaches notions of social responsibility through an ever-shifting "social problems curriculum" that responds to a variety of emerging societal issues.

Shaping Identities: Gender and Race

Public schools may now be more secularized and individualized, but in reality students have greatly diverging experiences in school. Sociologists have long contended that any focus on common socialization can obscure significant differences. This is where studies of socialization merge with those of inequality.

Historically, "common schools" prepared girls and boys for different roles, and did so overtly. As discussed in Chapter 4, education leaders in the mid-1800s encouraged citizens to pay new taxes to fund compulsory schooling for both boys and girls by appealing to the need for a common moral education. But "common" did not mean "the same." Prentice (1977: 111–12) notes that both sexes had roughly equal access to education, but were segregated in a variety of ways (though, see Gidney and Millar [2012] for a different emphasis). In Upper Canada in 1865, girls could enter grammar school by passing an examination, but were excluded from the classical course which was a prerequisite for entry into the university or the professions. Further, the Education Office insisted that common schools have separate entrances, separate playgrounds, separate seating, and even separate recitations for boys and girls.

Boys and girls were registered in elementary and secondary schools in almost equal numbers, though more boys than girls typically attended. In the early 1850s, ratios in Upper Canada were in the order of 125 boys for every 100 girls (Davey, 1978: 240). The 1865 ruling to exclude girls from classical courses must have met with some displeasure, because only a year later a new regulation "provided that a girl taking the classical course could be counted as half a boy, for the purposes of the provincial grant" (ibid.). Effectively, girls were permitted to take courses leading to university and the professions, but schools were penalized financially for providing such opportunity.

Thus, while both sexes attended school, their experiences differed. Females were seen to benefit from moral education and from basic literacy, but were otherwise given little priority. Importantly, this curriculum was not "hidden." School programs openly mirrored existing gender roles in society at large, and assumed their necessity to be self-evident. Until the past half-century, few ideologies challenged gender traditionalism.

As a result, fewer women than men attended university. A century ago most Canadians would have scoffed at the idea of a woman's "needing" a university degree. Given her station in life, a degree would have been deemed a waste of money and support that could be better spent on a male breadwinner. Indeed, a good university was a "female-free" university. In 1881 only 42 women were reported enrolled in Canadian universities, as compared to 2,964 men. Not until the 1980s did the ratio of female-to-male university undergraduates reach parity.

At least two consequences follow from women's relative lack of access to university in the late 1800s and the early 1900s. First, and most importantly, only men qualified to enter professions such as dentistry, engineering, law, and medicine, and thus they reaped the money, stature, and influence that accrued to these positions. Women's exclusion from these fields limited their chances of occupying significant leadership roles in the building of Canada. Second, very few women became faculty members in Canadian universities. While school teaching has always had a significant number of women, the professional employment of females in universities remains to this day lower than for men, though more in STEM (science, technology, engineering, and mathematics) fields than others.

Yet otherwise, women's representation and attainment has clearly changed greatly (Guppy and Luongo, 2015). Many stations in life, both inside schools and beyond, are freer of gendered gates. But in what ways are schools still gendered? Where do we still see vestiges of traditional femininity and masculinity and even their reinvention?

First, some educational hierarchies are still gendered. Teachers in preschools and elementary schools are almost entirely women (over 80 per cent). But further up the hierarchy, in secondary and post-secondary teaching and in upper levels of educational administration, more high-level positions are held by men. Elementary schools have been likened to "academic harems" when they have been staffed entirely by women, save for the most powerful position—the principal (Tyack, 1974). Nonetheless, women have increased their share of positions of authority, becoming principals, superintendents, and ministers for K–12 schools, as well as professors and administrators in higher education. But though hierarchies in educational administration are changing, most elite positions remain male-dominated.

Gender may still make its way into the curriculum. For several decades, feminists charged school textbooks with being loaded with old stereotypes and tacit messages of female inferiority. Elementary-level texts often used sexist language (i.e., "he" as the universal pronoun) and depicted males as the lone active characters in illustrations. Stories often depicted gendered stereotypes, such as stay-at-home moms or women in nurturing careers. High school literature courses had few female authors; history texts disregarded the contributions of women. Curricula have changed much since the 1970s, especially when provincial governments set curricular guidelines that monitored gender representation in most course material (Villar and Guppy, 2016). As a result, most of the attention in this area has shifted towards race, which we discuss further below.

Another form of gender inequity occurs in extracurricular programs. Schools have long funded men's sports teams at higher levels than female teams, giving them more priority and recognition, particularly in higher education. This imbalance is clear in most schools; the question is its source: whether it is deeply structured in school thinking, or whether it stems from a reluctant tendency to please communities, funders, and the broader public.

But today, many equity professionals are feeling pressured to reinvent rather than remove gender in schools. As boys continue to underachieve relative to girls, often from the earliest grade levels, educators are increasingly accused of having developed curricula and teaching styles that are insufficiently "boy-friendly." Whether or not this charge holds up to scrutiny (for skepticism, see Davies and Aurini, 2011 and Looker, 2011), some schools are responding by hiring more males to teach the primary grades and by revising curricula to make reading "cooler," such as using stories based on sports and by embedding lessons in activities, games, and competitions.

Taking a more empirical approach, Legewie and DiPrete (2012) trace today's achievement gaps to gender orientations in school. They note that gendered identities begin to form in early childhood, and are reinforced by peer groups once children enter school. Boys soon learn to value competitiveness, activity, and aggression, while girls are viewed as cooperative and conciliatory. Girls' peer groups, they claim, rarely stigmatize academic engagement as un-feminine. But young males sometimes associate anti-school stances with masculine traits like toughness, bravado, and independence. These stances can weaken boys' orientation to academic achievement. Disruptive boys can gain pride by being uncooperative, expending little effort and resisting school authority if doing so brings status among their peers. But these authors also find schools that are high-performing schools and have student bodies with high SES have smaller gender achievement gaps, namely because boys in those environments had pro-school work habits and attitudes. The trick, Legewie and DiPrete argue, is to help less advantaged schools encourage their boys to develop cultures that associate academic learning with masculinity.

Studies like Legewie and DiPrete's reveal the nuanced relationship between schools and gender identities. Historically, public schools were among the few places in society where for a few years of their lives, boys and girls were grouped together and actually performed the same role. Harrigan (1990: 805) comments that "by placing boys and girls in common buildings with a common curriculum in the early years, schools were a force for decreasing gender differences at a time when churches and independent organizations continued to differentiate them sharply." In many respects, school organization has promoted forms of gender integration, though gender clearly continues to permeate peer life and thereby enter the classroom. Why? Charles and Bradley (2009) contend that gender continues to be a fundamental axis of human identity. Contemporary Western culture celebrates gender equality *and* gender difference. Children enter schools with already well-developed conceptions of appropriate masculine and feminine traits, and gender seeps into schooling as students affirm their essential femininity or masculinity.

But the subtle point pivots on the extent to which contemporary schools reinforce or reshape gendered roles. Gender scripts are clearly imported into schools from neighbourhoods and families, the media is jam-packed with gendered images, and labour markets remain fairly segregated by gender. In light of these potent sources of socialization, one could argue that schools, if anything, partly counteract them. For many years, schools have actively recruited girls to enter scientific fields, sometimes with success. Virtually all well-known feminists in Canada are themselves products of our universities. Female gains in post-secondary enrolments have greatly outpaced their gains in the labour market. Thus, schools have taken a leading role in creating equality, and have fuelled much of women's collective economic mobility in recent decades. Yet, in other ways, schools continue to be gendered, at least when we consider boys. Schools may not *create* traditional notions of masculinity, but they provide staging grounds for their youthful displays and shape their varying expressions. As we saw in Chapter 7, conceptions of gender and sexuality in peer groups too often converge to victimize students with homophobic bullying, and those virulent forms of masculinity are unlikely to disappear in the foreseeable future. In a twist of equity reasoning, educators are now being urged to find ways to accommodate traditional masculinity in order to boost male achievement, with some calling for the return of all-boy classrooms, which can only "re-gender" some aspects of schooling.

Race and Its Canadian Legacies

Among nations, Canada is one of the most ethnically and racially diverse. Even though 80 per cent of Canadians are native-born, most of us have ancestral pedigrees from elsewhere. In part because of this greater diversity, Canada has legacies of blunt racism and ethnic inequality. Some observers use the term "racialization" to assert that schools, along with other social institutions, institutionalize "race" as a living experience, imposing negative identities that make racial minorities feel different and subordinate (Dei, 2009). In another version of this theory, the concept of "intersectionality" is used to assert that social life is always experienced through combinations or "intersections" of race, gender, sexuality, and Indigeneity, and that people in multiple minority positions are always the most disadvantaged.

Canadian education has plenty of historical examples of "racialization," the most blatant being the episode of residential schools for Indigenous children, as described in previous chapters. The Canadian government explicitly set out to mould Native identities by sending up to half of all Indigenous children to these schools, which acted as total institutions, replacing Native rhythms of life with a bureaucratic regimen. Their purpose was to sever Native children's bonds to their families and communities, and create "modern Indians" who would speak English or French, convert to Christianity, and train for menial jobs. Today's politicians now express deep regret for the residential schools, and have new educational policies that strive to retain Indigenous cultural and linguistic heritages. But residential schools left a legacy of economic, political, and cultural damage that is felt in Indigenous communities to this day. Likewise, access to common schools for young black children was also the exception in earlier eras, not the rule. As Axelrod (1997: 79) argues, in the face of prejudice in both Ontario and Nova Scotia, "coloured" children were sometimes unwelcome in public schools and were segregated in black-only schools. Some segregated schools were imposed by the white majority, while others were promoted by blacks themselves who supported American notions of "black uplift" (Winks, 2005). Specific laws that created those separate schools for these children have been long removed. Today, critics still see colonial stereotypes in school curricula and promote cultural sensitivity training and anti-racism curricula (e.g., Dei, 2009), but it is otherwise difficult to ignore change in schooling practices (Lyon and Guppy, 2018).

As a result, the process by which today's schools shape racial identities is likely quite subtle and mixed, and dependent on its interaction with other social categories such as class and gender. In the US, Carter's (2006) ethnography of Latino- and African-American students in New York found larger gender achievement gaps among these minorities than among white-Americans, and traced them to the strong presence of anti-school subcultures among minority males. Those subcultures encouraged black and Latino males to develop a "hard" posture characterized by mental, physical, and emotional toughness, one that was at odds with "soft" presentations of self that schools rewarded. The subculture rewarded its members' status when they retained a stance of cultural authenticity, creating what Carter called "non-dominant cultural capital," something that was rarely rewarded by their teachers. But some black and Latino males in her sample were academically successful. Carter dubbed those boys as "multicultural navigators" who managed to balance the demands of their peer groups with the demands of school. Carter reasoned that too many male students struggled to maintain their cultural identity while embracing dominant standards of achievement, and thus had their intellectual abilities underestimated by their educational institutions. Schools, she reasoned, need to employ "cultural navigators" who, possessing both dominant and non-dominant cultural capital, can help minority youth seize educational opportunities without having to compromise their sense of self.

Somewhat similar processes may be occurring in some Canadian cities, at least among underachieving immigrant minorities and Indigenous people. As educators change their priorities from assimilating minorities to recognizing pluralism and diversity (Guppy and Lyon, 2012), some have established separate Afro-centric and Indigenous public schools in cities like Toronto. Because these schools are yet to demonstrate any better outcomes for their students, their futures teeter on different understandings of equity. Some worry that they are promoting their own version of racialization by segregating children and branding them as different from the mainstream. They want instead to continue to integrate minorities into public schools. Future research on this issue will need to recall data presented in Chapter 7 showing that in aggregate, Canadian minorities have higher rates of achievement than the majority, and that the 2015 PISA results show that Canada does a better job of educating immigrant children than almost any other nation.

School Effects: Cognitive, Social, and Political

Political liberals and sociological functionalists alike have long celebrated schools as places that can nurture democracy and produce literate citizens. As discussed in Chapter 6, studies overwhelmingly suggest that schools help develop cognitive skills like vocabulary, reasoning, literacy, math abilities, logical and abstract reason, organizing information, and thinking hypothetically about events that are removed from daily experience. But what other socializing effects do schools have, such as political and social attitudes and financial outcomes?

It is tough to empirically test the impact of schooling on these realms. Ideally, a researcher can successfully sort out school impacts from the influences of families, neighbourhoods, labour markets, the media, and peers, because these antecedent factors might otherwise explain associations between education and later outcomes. The research tradition on "school effects" has developed empirical methods to test the influence of schooling. The reasoning goes like this.

It is well established that people with more years of education tend to earn more money, participate more in civic and political arenas, and have more liberal attitudes. Schools may actively create these outcomes. But people with certain predispositions and pre-existing resources may attain those outcomes anyways, even without going to school. We know, for instance, that school attainment is strongly influenced by students' socio-economic background, pre-existing cognitive abilities, and parental education, but those same factors also influence labour market success as well as political and social attitudes. So, rather than profoundly changing students, schools may be merely sorting and selecting individuals who already possess advantageous characteristics. If so, any outcome may be due not to a "school effect," but instead to what is known as a "selection effect." The trick for establishing if schooling actually changes attitudes, dispositions, and resources is to take account of any other factors that affect student outcomes. When selection effects are ruled out, schools are said to "add value."

Using advanced statistical methods, researchers find a variety of school effects. Those who are more educated are healthier and live longer. They tend to be more knowledgeable. They are involved in politics and civic events, and are more liberal, tolerant, "open-minded," and progressive on issues of gender and racial equality, minority rights, and civil liberties. They are less likely to rely on custom and tradition to guide their thinking. And, they tend to earn more money than peers that are otherwise similar but have less education (for reviews see Gross and Fosse, 2012; Hout, 2012; Kingston et al., 2003; Pallas, 2000; Raudenbush and Eschmann, 2015). Research largely concludes that schooling does more than merely "certify" the cultural dispositions that are bred in the home, and instead actively promotes healthier and more civic-minded living. Surely this suggests that schools deeply socialize and transform students. Or does it?

Institutional theorists have their doubts. John Meyer (1977) has argued that many school effects are really "chartering" effects. In his view, education influences people not so much by imposing consistently powerful experiences, but instead by conferring a socially recognized status, such as a high school graduate, BA holder, PhD, and so on. Many people quickly forget what they learned in school, and many later acquire skills and values in the workplace. But because society *recognizes* credentials, people with the status of "graduate" are entitled to certain things, such as higher-level jobs. For Meyer, this socially recognized status is the key. Some graduates may have learned useful skills and values, others may have not, but all acquired a social status and the perks that come with it. Meyer reasons that conferring a new status on people shapes their attitudes and actions in a process of "anticipatory socialization." People learn to grow into their role, and adopt the mindsets of people in similar positions.

This certainly sounds pessimistic and cynical, and for good reason: research clearly shows that schooling, on average, has positive effects on students, as we have seen. But this research can be reconciled with Meyer's theory by remembering two central ideas. One is that effects observed in research are *averages* that often have a significant amount of variability. Attending school can produce more liberal attitudes and political participation in many people, but not in all. Variation is the key. Another idea involves loose coupling: schools only weakly control their core processes, rarely measuring, monitoring, or assessing their impacts on students, yet in any given year, hundreds of thousands graduate from Canadian high schools, colleges, and universities with a single, uniform credential—a high school diploma, college certificate, or university degree. A great variety of aptitudes and convictions are papered over by those singular credentials.

This loose coupling stems from schools' toleration of great variations in student engagement. Many students are actively engrossed and energized by their studies, and are deeply transformed in the process. But some students are clearly disengaged, rarely participating in class, doing little if any work. Yet, such students can take advantage of "social promotion" at the K–12 level, and if they make it, inflated grades at the post-secondary level (Arum and Roska, 2011; Côté and Allahar, 2011). It stands to reason that school effects on highly disengaged students are likely to be quite weak. Another process comes from progressive styles of teaching moral and political values. Progressives strive to expose students to alternate ways of thinking rather than to dictate and impose uniform beliefs. As a consequence, this form of pedagogy facilitates a wide range of impacts on students. In sum, schools may effectively socialize many of their charges, but their loose coupling permits a great deal of variation among graduates.

Conclusion

To understand how schools socialize students, this chapter began by tracing shifts in the content of moral education in Canadian public schools, noting the increasingly peripheral place of religion. Moral pedagogy has become less authoritative and more progressive, encouraging students to learn moral lessons by doing and reflecting, not only by listening and reciting. Schools' impact on student identities has also changed. School organization, teaching, and curricula may be less overtly encoded with traditional gender and racial messages, but aspects of student peer life remain strongly gendered and "raced." The challenge for sociologists is to sort out the extent that schools create, reinforce, or counteract traditional identities. Research on school "effects" offers some hints. Public schools appear to promote relatively liberal social and political views, and have cognitive and financial benefits, particularly for graduates from disadvantaged backgrounds. Revisiting a theme from previous chapters, schools appear to partially compensate for inequalities that have roots beyond their gates.

But this equalizing is only partial, and reminds us of the limits of schooling's socializing power. Paradoxically, that power may actually become *weaker* in a schooled society. Today there are fewer and fewer "oblates" in Canadian society whose selves are cast by schools. As more students commute long distances to school or learn online, fewer schools have the qualities of a "total institution." More than before, today's schools must compete with other socializing agents. Many older youths are employed part-time, play sports, have dense social networks, and are immersed in popular culture and entertainment. The "student" role is just one of many that they juggle simultaneously. If many post-secondary students are studying less than in past eras and are gaining fewer cognitive skills, as some evidence suggests (Arum and Roska, 2011; Côté and Allahar, 2011), the transformative power of higher education may be weakening. Conversely, at elementary levels, today's parents are spending more time on developmental activities (Sayer et al., 2004), are hiring more tutors (Aurini, 2008; Hart and Kempf, 2015), and are purchasing more extracurricular lessons for their children (Daly, 2004; Quirke, 2006). These trends are weakening schools' monopoly on structured lessons, at least among the middle class. The upshot of both trends is that educators must work harder to have a "net" impact on their students. Educational socialization may be edging towards the weaker end of the continuum.

With this issue in mind, the next chapter evaluates the limits of schools' socializing power. It examines competitors for students' hearts and minds and explores the impact of social scripts that are written beyond the school gates.

Questions for Critical Thought

1. Design a research study that sorts out the socializing influences of schools, families, neighbourhoods, labour markets, media, and peer groups.

2. Research shows that highly educated people tend to be more supportive of civil liberties, non-traditional roles for women, and rights of minorities. Why? Does schooling have a primary causal influence? Is it mostly a selection effect? Or do educated people have their biases that aren't measured by social scientists?

3. Observe an elementary-level classroom. Do you see "socializing messages" in operation? Cite examples with reference to arguments in this chapter.

4. Most universities have policies promoting inclusion, equity, and diversity based on race, gender, and sexuality. But those policies almost never mention social class. Ask some of your classmates how they feel about this omission in light of data presented in this book.

5. Are home-schooled children socialized differently than are children in regular public school environments? Can you design a research study that could compare each milieu?

Suggested Readings

Dillabough, Jo-Anne, and Jacqueline Kennelly. 2010. *Lost Youth in the Global City: Class, Culture and the Urban Imaginary*. New York: Routledge Falmer. This book is an examination of youth at the edges of urban centres, defined by marginalized statuses via low income, immigration, and so forth.

Kahn, Shamus Rahman. 2012. *Privilege: The Making of an Adolescent Elite at St. Paul's School*. Princeton, NJ: Princeton University Press. This book is a good account of the socialization effects of an elite private school in preparing children for upper-class adulthood.

Kirp, David. L. 2007. *The Sandbox Investment: The Preschool Movement and Kids-First Politics*. Cambridge, MA: Harvard University Press. The Sandbox Investment is an engaging example of the broadening of schooling's reach towards younger and younger children.

Web Links

The Atkinson Centre
www.oise.utoronto.ca/atkinson/Main/index.html
Housed at the University of Toronto, this centre promotes research on early child development, with a good focus on policies and practices.

Human Rights of Children
www.international.gc.ca/rights-droits/kids-enfants/index.aspx?view=d
This site is for the Government of Canada's focus on the rights of children. It has useful links to other relevant sites.

Socialization: How to Deal with It
http://homeschooling.about.com/od/socialization/Socialization_How_to_deal_with_it.htm
This is an interesting debate about the merits of school socialization from the perspective of home-schooling parents.

12 The Limits of School Socialization
Competing Influences on Students

|||||||||||||||||||||||||||||||||||||||||||||||||||||||||||||||||||||||||||||||||||||||||||||||||||||||||||||||||||||||||||||||||||||||||||||||||||||||||||

Learning Objectives

- To understand the limitations that schools face when they socialize students, including competing influences on students, macro forces such as entrenched inequality and rising youth culture, and micro forces such as peer hierarchies

- To recognize manifestations of these forces in schools, student subcultures, bullying, and crime

- To detect variations in the reciprocal impacts of student and school organizations

|||||||||||||||||||||||||||||||||||||||||||||||||||||||||||||||||||||||||||||||||||||||||||||||||||||||||||||||||||||||||||||||||||||||||||||||||||||||||||

Introduction: Emphasizing Limits

To put it mildly, school is not the only thing in children's lives. As children grow into teenagers, their peers and other institutions (e.g., the media) grow ever larger in importance. The previous chapter discussed schools' traditional and contemporary attempts to socialize youth. This chapter takes hints from previous chapters to emphasize important *limits* to this socializing power. It emphasizes the convergence of environmental and internal processes that compete for students' attention and sometimes counteract educational objectives. This chapter begins by discussing societal influences that can promote forms of student disengagement, ranging from entrenched forms of social inequality to colourful expression of youth culture, and then examines the formation of peer hierarchies in schools. To borrow a term from Chapter 6, these reactions can be considered to be rather visible "secondary mechanisms" that affect achievement. This chapter then examines manifestations of these forces in schools, describing processes that form student subcultures and promote bullying and school crime. Finally, we end by re-examining important variations within and between schools in the power to socialize youth.

Macro-Level Competitors: Forms of Entrenched Inequality

As discussed in Chapter 6, students enter schools with hugely disparate home conditions. Their homes are their prime socializers, and just beyond are their local neighbourhoods. Local rates of poverty, unemployment, and crime can affect students' behaviour at school, shaping their aspirations and expectations for the future. Importantly, entrenched forms of social inequality can greatly alter student orientations to school.

One form of entrenched inequality can be found in traditional working-class communities. These communities were products of industrial and factory economies that created stable and cohesive, though not wealthy, neighbourhoods. These kinds of locales could be found in a variety of Canadian cities, such as the Junction, South Riverdale, and Mimico in Toronto; North and East Hamilton, Verdun in Montreal, and East Vancouver. In England, "Hammertown" (actually the city of Wolverhampton, the setting for Willis, 1977) is often held as the quintessential working-class community. In such settings, jobs in unionized companies were often handed down across generations. Jobs in heavy manual labour were stable, though few offered routes of upward mobility. A half-century ago, many sociologists were interested in whether emerging norms of high school completion and post-secondary attendance would filter down to those communities. Their immediate answer was no. They found that relatively few youth from working-class backgrounds aspired to higher education. Advanced schooling was not on their mental radar screens. David Downes (1966), for instance, found that traditional working-class communities in England nurtured few dreams of upward mobility among their youth. Most pupils, he reasoned, had little interest in school because they didn't imagine themselves pursuing higher-level studies. This lack of aspiration took on a particular cultural expression. With few initial hopes of using schooling to climb a social ladder, and yet being too young to begin full-time employment, older students were in a state of limbo. School was boring for them, and so they engaged in pranks simply for fun, as a cure for their restlessness. Sometimes their mild rebellion was expressed in fashions from the world of popular music and movies, which provided an alternative identity for students who were disengaging from their studies (see Tanner, 2015).

As discussed in Chapter 6, Paul Willis largely reiterated this thesis, but gave it a distinctively Marxist flavour. In *Learning to Labour* Willis offered rich and entertaining descriptions of the classroom antics of working-class boys. But the book won fame for its interpretation of the "lads" subculture. For Willis, those antics were not mere teen hijinks, but were cultural expressions of class politics, though much of this conflict was unarticulated by the lads themselves. Their belief that school activities were largely irrelevant for the workplace skills was an insight into credentialism and deskilling. Their denigrating of teachers' advice represented a penetration into the capitalist hidden curriculum. And their refusal to exert effort in school resembled a fledgling attempt to control their own labour power. Subsequent research has cast doubt on the degree to which Willis's ideas can be generalized to contemporary Canada, and whether school rebellion is essentially about social class. But many researchers remain fascinated with his depiction of male peer groups' bravado and aggression, and much research does confirm some of the masculine quality of opposition to school. Other scholarship examines a neglected topic in Willis's work—the academic success of some working-class boys (see Ingram, 2011). Further, the rebellion depicted in *Learning to Labour* has led others to explore the gendered nature of student peer groups.

Another form of entrenched inequality can be found in areas that some sociologists refer to as "socially disorganized;" mainly urban locals in which poverty and crime combine to divert many youth from conventional norms and careers. Elijah Anderson (1999) offers a particularly vivid account of social disorganization in his ethnography of a neighbourhood in Philadelphia. In a ghetto known as "North Philly," economic change and racial discrimination weakened local businesses, families, police forces, and sanitation services. These conditions encouraged the emergence of new norms to guide interpersonal behaviour. Whereas social interaction in affluent areas is guided by norms of politeness and civility, Anderson describes how youth in that low-income and high-crime area were instead socialized into the "code of the street." With only a sporadic police presence, norms of toughness and aggression prevailed. Youth had to signal their ability to "handle themselves" or else be preyed upon. If someone was openly disrespected in public, they had to react aggressively or lose face and be subject to further intimidation. The code also regarded public displays of polite and respectable behaviour as signals of weakness and vulnerability. Now, Anderson knew that most youth in North Philly abided by conventional norms when in private or at work. But to survive, they had to "code switch" and act tough when necessary. What impact does this street code have on schools? According to Anderson, the code of the street diverted youth from formal education, making school seem irrelevant for their futures. To keep the code from intruding into the school, the local high school developed a series of security policies, including a dress code that outlawed the street-wear that signalled gang membership, and used elaborate security monitoring systems, including video cameras, metal detectors, security guards, and mandatory student ID cards. But that school continues to have high dropout rates in its battle against the code of the street.

A third type of entrenched inequality comes in lasting forms of racial subordination. Cultural orientations to school can be powerfully shaped by segregated workplaces and neighbourhoods, which themselves are historical legacies of racial inequality. But such circumstances vary among groups. Building on an old idea in sociology (Lieberson, 1961), John Ogbu (1992), and Signithia Fordham (Fordham and Ogbu, 1986) observed that minority groups experience school differently and that the same ethno-racial groups can perform differently in different national contexts. For instance, Asian immigrants have almost invariably performed very well in North American schools, enjoying high achievement and educational expectations, while African-Americans in the United States and Indigenous Canadians have had much less success (Goyette and Xie, 1999; Boyd, 2002; Thiessen, 2009). Similar patterns have surfaced in other nations (Rothon et al., 2009). Yet, some Asian immigrants elsewhere have had a rather different experience. For instance, Koreans in Japan have endured a long history of slavery and enforced servitude, and have historically fared poorly in Japanese schools. To Ogbu and Fordham, what needs to be grasped is why minority students *vary* so much in their educational attainment and attachment to school. These variations, they argue, cannot be understood either by blaming North American educators or by celebrating "model minorities" that have been successful in schools. The same schools and the same ethnic "cultures" can elicit widely varying responses in different contexts.

Ogbu and Fordham claim that any understanding of minority student subcultures must account for the particular history of minority–majority relations in any society. One can understand the reluctance of some groups to abide by the dominant school culture only by turning to history. Their reasoning goes like this. Racial minorities have different collective experiences of incorporation in each host nation. If they entered a country voluntarily through immigration, they are more likely to view public schools as offering opportunities to get ahead. In contrast, if their incorporation occurred involuntarily through historical conquest or forced migration, they are likely to view schools rather differently. In this framework African-Americans who were coerced to North America through slavery and First Nations peoples whose territories were forcibly seized by European settlers would be considered **involuntary minorities**. In contrast, most other racial minorities were **voluntary minorities** who willingly came to North America through modern immigration. In further contrast, whites are the dominant group in North America.

These histories shape each group's views of public schools. As the majority, whites largely see schools as neutral institutions that offer opportunities and pose few barriers. They regard expectations to learn standard forms of grammar, vocabulary, and decorum as reasonable. Likewise, voluntary minorities see schools as vehicles for upward mobility, a main route for the economic opportunities they sought through immigration. Immigrants expect to encounter linguistic or cultural challenges in school, and see them as temporary barriers that can be surmounted with effort.

Involuntary minorities see educational institutions very differently. Because of the historic role of government institutions in collective oppression, they regard those institutions with suspicion. North American governments typically aimed to sever any links of both African slaves and Indigenous people to their ancestral origins. For these involuntary minorities some linguistic and religious traditions carry on, but most have dwindled. For instance, African-Americans, historically barred from controlling their own schools, were almost entirely distanced from African languages, religions, and other cultural inheritances. Indigenous children and their families experienced residential schooling largely as an act of cultural aggression and as a disintegrating force on Native communities (see Wotherspoon, 2014). Public schooling, until recently, served to eradicate their local languages, customs, and traditions in favour of the English or French language and Christian religion. According to Ogbu and Fordham, such legacies can encourage involuntary minorities to view cultural or linguistic barriers in school as unjustifiable. Because of their cultural insecurity, conformity to white culture can threaten their group identity. They will approach mass public education with more suspicion. Many will interpret the standard curriculum as an imposition, not as an opportunity, and perhaps even a veiled attempt to neutralize their distinctive cultural practices. They might equate school with the culture and language of the "enemy" or "oppressor."

Immigrant minorities take a different approach to the same curriculum, according to this reasoning, because their cultural heritage is more secure. They voluntarily enter host nations with traditions, languages, and religions that are both intact and distinct from the majority. If they wish to maintain those traditions, they can choose to do so. Adopting the language and cultural practices of the majority is less threatening because they have a secure tradition to fall back on if they so wish, and because these practices can offer economic and social opportunities. These legacies can nurture student subcultures. Ogbu and Fordham's fieldwork in American schools led them to claim that many African-American youth associate school effort and success with "whiteness." Just as Willis's lads stigmatized their peers who embraced the student role, African-Americans were seen to denigrate similar peers as "acting white." Black youth, they claimed, associated school learning with white culture, and thus a threat to their social identity, self-worth, and community. Furthermore, they saw effort in school as unlikely to pay off, believing that well-educated blacks would not be fully accepted by whites anyway, and would not receive equal rewards for their schooling. Ogbu and Fordham became renowned for claiming that an anti-school subculture was pressuring African-American youth to equate any pursuit of academic success as disloyalty to their cultural identity and community.

This "acting white" thesis became highly influential in sociology after it was originally formulated in the 1970s and 1980s. But is it true today? Several sociologists have put the theory to the test using a variety of research methods. American studies offer mixed results, but the bulk of evidence casts some doubt on its continuing applicability (for an example of conflicting conclusions, see Downey, 2008 and Harris, 2011 versus Farkas, 2003; Carter, 2006 takes a middling position). Most conclude that only a small portion of African-American students adopt that oppositional stance. Tyson et al. (2005) visited eight schools in North Carolina and found only two high-achieving black students who felt a peer stigma for "acting white." Otherwise, most African-American youth valued school achievement as much as anyone else. But *all* high-achieving students feel *some* peer stigma. Regardless of race, earners of top grades usually get branded as "geeks," "nerds," or "brainiacs." Only in some schools, such as those with highly unequal achievement by race, does this pressure become racial and expressed in taunts of acting white, they concluded. Otherwise, most youth value school achievement. Linking to our discussion of Carter (2006) in the previous chapter, cultural conflicts may rise when there are particularly large gaps between practices that breed school success and those of some groups. Problems occur when schools fail to fully accommodate those practices. For instance, Downey and Pribesh (2004) found that white teachers in the United States interpreted *different* student behaviour as oppositional *misbehaviour,* and consistently rated black students as poorer classroom citizens than white students. Black teachers did not rate students in the same pattern.

Does the "acting white" phenomenon exist in Canadian schools? Far less systematic research on the topic exists here, perhaps due to the difficulties of importing an idea rooted in American realities. One difficulty is that Canadian school achievement has more mixed ethnic and racial patterns, and does not form a sharp white–black dichotomy, as discussed in Chapter 7. Another is that histories of different minorities differ north of the border. The majority of black Canadians are "voluntary minorities" who have been immigrating since the 1960s. Indigenous Canadians comprise the main involuntary minority. Yet another difficulty is that histories of conquest in Canada are different. Quebecers who trace their ancestral roots to France may see themselves as an "involuntary minority" within Canada as a whole, though a majority within Quebec. But unlike other involuntary minorities, *Québécois* have administrative authority over their own schools, as guaranteed in the Constitution Act, which grants them more self-government and institutional autonomy than either First Nations people or any immigrant group. As a result, their educational attainment, especially in recent decades, has matched that of English-Canadians (for example, almost an identical percentage of younger French- and English-Canadians have a university degree). Yet, while many immigrant groups perform very well in Canadian schools, Chapter 7 showed unmistakably lower attainments for First Nations, African-Canadians, and Latino-Canadians. Do these lesser attainments spark oppositional subcultures in our schools?

Recommendations for better accommodating minority identities also vary. Much educational policy aims to integrate all Canadians into mainstream schools via inclusive, multicultural curricula. But some want stronger school alternatives such as "black focus" schools in order to promote a more positive cultural identity for African-Canadians. These critics charge "colour-blind" policies and meritocratic ideologies with ignoring the real salience of race in children's lives and with adopting reforms that do not truly address minority needs. Critics refer to school multiculturalism as "tourist curricula" that only superficially address historical legacies of racism. They fault teacher sensitivity training for allowing teachers to remain insufficiently aware of their own identities and biases, and to remain blind to practices that may be colour-coded. But to bring this reasoning to a full circle, others may counter that granting too much attention to race and ethnicity may unintentionally lower expectations for some students. In a Canadian study, Riley and Ungerleider (2012) had experienced teachers making recommendations for student placements—either remedial, standard, or advanced—based on information from scholastic performance in grades 4 to 7 as well as information on student social class, ethnicity and ancestry, gender, and English language proficiency. Of the 21 teachers they interviewed, only one made judgments about Indigenous students based solely on scholastic performance. The other 20 made judgments that incorporated their own expectations about the role of social background in shaping Indigenous student futures.

Common Competitors: The Rise of Youth Cultures

While entrenched inequality mainly impacts students at the bottom end of the socio-economic ladder, a very different competing influence affects almost all students. Perhaps the loudest distraction for students over the past half-century has been the rise of youth culture. When most people ponder how youth differ from adults, they think about biology and emotional maturation. And of course, people certainly change physically during their teens. But biological development offers a limited explanation of rapid cultural changes among youth. Human biology, we must remember, evolves very slowly over generations. In a historical time span such as a few decades, for instance, biology effectively becomes a constant, not a variable. Social expressions of this maturation can, in contrast, change much more rapidly and repeatedly over time, and they vary across nations and among different social groups, as we will show. The term "adolescence" is a social construct with widespread usage for only the past 60 years. Only recently has "youth" been widely recognized as a major life stage between childhood and adulthood.

Sociology provides the analytic tools to understand how and why expressions of youth culture continue to change. Here we discuss two concepts. The first traces how social segregation produces distinct cultures. For instance, African-Americans have proclaimed their unique forms of music, slang, accent, and traditions that are highly distinct from the white majority. This culture emerged through centuries-long practices of enforced segregation, in which most black Americans had little daily interaction with whites, at least in forms that involved respectful reciprocity. Similarly, Eastern European Jews developed their own language (Yiddish) and customs in ghettos in cities like Prague and Warsaw. Second, when groups are relatively similar, small differences can loom large and become badges of distinction. The term "narcissism of small differences" refers to tiny cultural peculiarities that can assume great social importance. For instance, many cultural differences between Canadians and Americans seem rather insignificant to people from other continents. Outside of Quebec, Canadians and Americans largely share the same language, religions, and popular culture. Yet Canadians feel a need to distinguish themselves, and point proudly to unique "Canadianisms," such as preferring hockey, peppering sentences with "eh," or using terms like "pop" instead of "soda" or calling wool hats "toques." They may seem trivial to the rest of the world, but can be important to English-Canadians.

Both segregation and the amplification of small differences can be applied to youth in schools. One result of the historic extension of education, described in Chapter 4, is that it forced more people to spend longer durations of their lives in schools, and thereby helped create distinct youth cultures. How? Extended schooling usually prolongs youth's economic dependence on their guardians and postpones their plans to start their own families. Age-graded classrooms also create an incredible amount of social homogeneity. As Seeley et al. (1956: 93) phrased it in their classic ethnography of a post–Second World War Canadian community, *Crestwood Heights* (actually, Toronto's Forest Hill), a student's "grade" powerfully shapes their "definition of self." Think about it: where else in society do people spend theirs day with peers that are almost exactly the same age? Workplaces, families, and leisure institutions mix people of a variety of ages. But age-grading in schools creates a bounded social world that is unnaturally homogeneous and rather exceptional. Today, almost all Canadians are in school until the age of 17, and around three-quarters continue in school into their 20s. These attributes of schooling interact with other modern trends: smaller families put more attention on children's individuality, and greater material affluence fuels consumer industries that cater to young people, including clothing, popular music, television, and movies. Each helps to forge identities that are age-distinct.

In many respects, modern youth culture was born in the 1950s and has continued to evolve since. The early post–Second World War era saw the emergence of a novel social expectation—that youth ought to stay in school longer and graduate from high school. That expectation, coupled with a post-war prosperity that raised family disposable incomes, created a new social space for teenagers. For the first time in history a sizeable number of teens were without full-time jobs, family responsibilities, or full independence from their parents. Older high school students could now reach physical maturity without assuming adult roles and privileges. High schools were being slowly transformed into "custodial" institutions that "warehoused" many non-academically inclined youth.

It is no accident that during the same decade, police and government authorities announced the existence of a new "youth problem." Too many young people had too much time on their hands, they claimed. Police departments formed new youth squads. The term "juvenile delinquency" described their encounter with new, senseless antics. Schools, for the first time, became widespread targets of vandalism. Classic popular movies of the day, such as *Blackboard Jungle* and *Rebel without a Cause*, often depicted schools as hostile places, as jail-like institutions that bred alienation and aimlessness.

These social conditions allowed for the expression of new cultural forms in which youth assumed particular clothing, hair, and musical tastes associated with alternate lifestyles, or as termed by sociologists, "subcultures." Over the decades, Canadian schools have witnessed a parade of subcultures. The majority of youth has always had a conventional appearance, but many have embraced alternate and recognizable styles. The 1950s saw "greasers" and "beatniks," the 1960s saw "hippies," the 1970s saw "rockers" and "stoners," the 1980s saw "punks," the 1990s saw various "hip-hop" fashions, and today there is an assortment of groups, ranging from "gangstas" to "emos." And, common categories of youth such as "jocks," "nerds," "popular kids," and "brains" have been mainstays of high schools throughout those decades.

Internal Competitors: Peer Hierarchies

The 1950s and 1960s human capital rationales were emerging to support the expectation of high school graduation (e.g., Gary Becker's *Human Capital*, 1964). Simultaneously, early theories about post-industrialism and knowledge economies were emerging, as seen in Burton Clark's *Educating the Expert Society* (1962). This new normative climate inspired sociologists to study high schools and determine whether more students in this era were raising their level of engagement in their studies and were thus meeting these new expectations. Some found the new situation to be disappointing. James Coleman (1961), for instance, found that studying, learning, and achieving were hardly the top priority of students. Instead, being well-placed in peer groups seemed to be becoming increasingly important to teens. Popularity was ever-sought, and was broadly achieved by looking good and being (hetero) sexually attractive. The process of gaining peer status was gendered, of course. Masculine popularity was rooted in toughness and athleticism, while female popularity demanded physical attractiveness. These bases of peer ranking seemed to dominate school life, Coleman believed. Importantly, the hierarchy that schools officially sponsored and attempted to promote—rankings based on academic prowess— did *not* bring peer status. At best, academic ability was irrelevant to popularity with peers, and at worst, it was a liability. Top students, sometimes branded by their peers as "brains," often were found at the bottom of peer hierarchies. For Coleman, this was a problem. By actively discouraging students from excelling in their studies, the new peer cultures were subverting high school goals, and by extension, were becoming cultural impediments to the evolution of the new knowledge society. Coleman noted that school officials were attempting to co-opt this new culture and bind youth to school culture by offering extracurricular activities. Sports teams, dances, and clubs would hopefully channel students' social interests within the school community, rather than have it thrive at a distance from educational authorities.

What about contemporary peer hierarchies? More recently, award-winning sociologist Murray Milner (2004) examined the inner workings of peer cultures in several American high schools. His book *Freaks, Geeks, and Cool Kids* begins with questions posed by many exasperated parents: why are high school teens obsessed with clothing brands, popularity, and cliques? Why does high school culture so often have a "mean" edge? For Milner, these phenomena are not direct products of physical or emotional immaturity. Instead, he traced them to the intensification of social conditions that emerged after the Second World War. Most high schools continued to be age-graded institutions that did not place heavy intellectual demands on students. Family disposable income continued to rise. But he emphasized that youth wield little economic and political power. Schools, Milner reminds us, are ultimately run by adults. Except in rare schools like Summerhill (discussed in Chapter 8), students cannot hire or fire staff, create rules, or design curriculum. Milner reckons that this lack of institutional power combines with homogenous age-groupings, considerable spare time, and disposable money to encourage youth to focus on their peer lives. They enjoy only enough power to control their *social* realm, and so they make that realm ubiquitous. Their place in that social world matters a lot to them. And, that world is highly ranked and stratified.

To Milner, these conditions make youth very status-conscious. High school cliques reminded Milner of castes, of all things, as in India! A follower of Max

Weber and an expert on castes, Milner saw both high school cliques and castes as acting like "status groups." Status groups are social collectives that resemble economic classes to the extent that higher-ranked groups are almost always richer than lesser-ranked groups. But status groups are distinguished by their associations with social prestige and honour. Unlike money, status is a "zero-sum" game. One group gains prestige only when another loses some. Status groups tend to form in contexts with few avenues for upward mobility among lower-ranked people. As a result, status groups, more than economic classes, have elaborate norms, rituals, and thick social boundaries. Dominant groups tend to create elaborate social norms to signal their status. Their members face intense pressures to conform to codes for dress and social interaction, especially for intimacies such as eating and romantic relationships. If lower-ranked groups either defy or imitate those rituals, higher-ranked groups will maintain their standing by continually reinforcing or complicating those rituals.

According to Milner, castes and high school cliques are commonly obsessed with their physical appearance and social ranking. Both strive to maintain social distance from those considered their social inferiors. Both care much about intimacies such as whom they eat with and whom they hang out with. If a high school teen is seen eating with or dating someone of lower status, she or he risks being socially demoted. Both engage in small cruelties, put-downs, and harassments of their lower-status peers. To Milner, such "mean" acts are not mere forms of immaturity. They are also a strategy to maintain status boundaries.

Status consciousness also explains why some teens are so preoccupied with conforming to clothing fashions and wearing brand labels. To Milner, the isolated world of high school encourages youth to symbolize their status through consumer commodities because they are largely excluded from "producer" roles. Teens rarely have prestigious and high-paid jobs; most are relegated to menial, low-paying tasks. But our society freely grants them "consumer" roles, as long as they (or their parents) can pay for it. Teen fashions in clothes, music, TV, and movies have become billion-dollar, global industries that provide status-defining symbols for many youth. In recent years these industries have reached down to younger and younger children.

But this particular status system mostly breaks down when youth leave high school and enter new settings, such as workplaces or post-secondary institutions. Old conformity pressures mostly weaken in these new situations. Why? Milner traces these changes not to a sudden maturing among youth, but to new social conditions. In these new settings, youth have alternative sources of social recognition and new and more dispersed social networks. As a result, their reputations circulate less widely but more variably, and forms of status competition change.

In sum, youth culture and peer hierarchies have been deeply ingrained in school life over recent decades. They fuel a central dynamic in modern high schools: a continual antagonism between educational goals and social demands on youth. Peer life can distract students from learning. Recent advances in communication technologies, in many respects, are intensifying these dynamics. They represent a double-edged sword for educators. On one side, technologies are new resources used to revitalize schooling and make it appear more relevant in today's world. As discussed in Chapter 8, tools like podcasts, YouTube, and Skype are enabling new modes of distance education, self-study, and student research. But on the other side, they are often mere social gizmos that intrude into the classroom and distract students. While there is little systematic research on this topic, anecdotes and media reports suggest that students use cell phones, texting, laptops, Facebook, Twitter, and beepers mainly for social purposes. Their usage thickens the social realm of schooling, envelops teens further into peer life, and widens the autonomous "space" for youth. Much use of new technologies is mostly harmless teen fun, but sometimes it veers into something worse.

Forms of Opposition and Bullying

So far we have portrayed student subcultures as mostly mild entities that offer youth some independent cultural space and an alternative status system. They rarely pose a real physical danger to anyone. But in rarer cases, student deviance can take more severe forms. These problems are very much a post–Second World War phenomenon. Sociologists in the 1950s and 1960s were finding that student populations were less compliant and deferential than in previous decades. School officials were increasingly concerned with classroom control. Most school deviance only consisted of short outbursts of rule-breaking, irreverence, apathy, tardiness, and truancy. Only a fraction of students were overtly violent or posed serious physical threats. But these mundane acts disrupted classroom learning and hindered the schooling process. Some sociologists believed a new youth culture was competing with schools for students' attention—and that culture was winning.

These subculture theorists traced this new antagonism not only to new youth cultures, but also to the very structure of schooling. Deviance, they contended, was a symptom of schools' own selection function, namely, the stratifying role played by grading and streaming systems (e.g., Cohen, 1955; Miller, 1958; Stinchcombe, 1964). Those systems created academic hierarchies. Teachers rewarded only *some* students with As, and labelled others as academically unfit. Unlucky pupils who received poor grades were relegated to terminal streams and disqualified from post-secondary levels. These theorists emphasize an unintended consequence of school selection: it creates disincentives for unsuccessful students to cooperate in schools, and sparks a cultural backlash. Academic competitions impose a demeaned social status on their losers that inflicts an emotional injury. Their failure stokes low-achieving students' hunger for a more positive self-image. According to this theory, failing students react by creating alternate sources of peer recognition in the form of anti-school peer groups with their very own status hierarchies. These groups are noteworthy for their *inversion* of core school values. The kinds of student traits idealized by educators, such as abiding by the rules and, being courteous, obedient, and conscientious, get flipped on their head in these subcultures. Anti-school peers celebrate the very opposite: the rule-breaker, the insolent, the disobedient, and the hedonist. Males get peer approval by fighting, confronting authority figures, smoking, drinking, and being sexually active (in the next decade, theorists added street drugs to the list). Females get peer rewards for flaunting their emerging sexual maturity, embracing fashion trends, and being preoccupied with boys. Both subcultures were seen to express frustration from being on the wrong end of school selection, and to facilitate student disengagement from academics. Over the decades, other descriptions of school rebellion have redescribed these same processes in remarkably similar ways.

But recently, Randall Collins (2008, 2011) has devised a distinctly sociological understanding of peer life in schools. We outline his framework next and then use it to comprehend a particularly ugly component of school life, bullying. To begin, Collins highlights key aspects of schooling that we alluded to above. High schools, more than most other institutions, can have a "total institution" quality. They can structure relatively dense and bounded peer networks. By dense, we mean that almost everyone knows each other. By bounded, we mean that much information tends to remain within the network, and not flow to outsiders. This is the case in communities that have strong "no-snitch" norms. Bounded and dense networks facilitate the emergence of strong status hierarchies, as we described in our discussion of Milner above. Students get ranked into a pecking order of status, and those rankings shape how much of the social life of peer groups proceeds. Those at the top of those hierarchies are highly popular and socially influential; those at the bottom tend to be socially isolated, with few friends and little influence.

Collins's theory of interaction rituals, discussed in Chapter 3, further animates his thinking about peers and bullying. Recall that informal social interactions and rituals can generate collective effervescence and fill their participants with emotional energy. Successful interaction facilitates emotional entrainment, the process by which participants become synched with each other's emotional rhythms and share the same focus of attention. These ideas can be applied to the tension between education goals and peer social life. School goals can be undermined when peer hierarchies increasingly seize, dominate, and channel much of schools' emotional energy and collective effervescence. Class time can be deadening, with little dynamism and inspiration, while social times can become the main source of peer interest and attention.

One problem with energized peer hierarchies is that they become breeding grounds for bullying (see Box 12.1). Collins defines bullying as a social situation in which the target is a low-status isolate who endures repeated abuse and harassment. The offenders are usually students in the middle of a peer-status hierarchy. Offenders use bullying as a tactic to maintain and raise their status. Canadian research shows that bullying takes gendered forms in which victims and offenders are usually same-sex. Boys are more likely to partake in physical bullying, while girls are more likely to engage in social bullying or "relational aggression" in which the attempt is to ostracize a girl from a group (Currie, Kelly, and Pomerantz, 2009). But both forms of bullying are products of informal status and network hierarchies in schools.

Those groupings can also structure other forms of conflict that are often confused with bullying, but which Collins (2011) sees as having different dynamics

Box 12.1 Applying Collins's Theory of Violence to Schools

Randall Collins (2008) has developed an innovative theory of violence. He notes that violence is "Horrible and heroic, disgusting and exciting, the most condemned and glorified of human acts" (1). He takes a uniquely sociological approach. Biological and psychological approaches presume that violent tendencies are hard-wired in people and need to be repressed through socialization. But they cannot explain why actual occurrences are relatively rare, he notes. Go into the most violent neighbourhoods, or observe the most violent kinds of people—typically young males—and you will see that actual outbursts of violence are uncommon. Most confrontations end with only bluster and bluff. Sociological understandings are hampered by common myths that don't fit the facts. Movies often portray fights as long, drawn-out battles. But real fights are mostly quick, over in a matter of seconds. We glorify violence that pits evenly matched combatants, and stage such matches in sports events like boxing. But most real violence occurs when the strong prey on the weak. We idealize stone-cold warriors who do not flinch in a confrontation. But few of us are actually "good" at violence. Most get nervous and wish to flee confrontations. Data from army battles shows that most soldiers perform poorly and almost freeze at the height of combat.

Collins turns many common assumptions about violence on their head, using ideas from "interaction ritual theory." Rather than requiring constant repression, violence is actually very difficult for most people. Why? We are hard-wired for emotional entrainment. When in close contact, it is more natural for people to fall in sync with each other's emotional rhythms. The threat of violence causes most to experience confrontational fear and tension, and so most such episodes do not escalate beyond bluster and bluff. And, rather than being contagious, in which one outbreak of violence causes others to begin fighting, as depicted in quintessential barroom brawls of movie lore, most people become spectators, and fuel the original combatants with emotional energy.

For Collins, violence occurs only through a series of pathways in which the combatants are able to overcome their natural tendency to feel confrontational tension and fear. One such pathway, unfortunately, is offered by picking on the weak. Targets of bullying are often network isolates at the bottom of status hierarchies. As such, bullies have little fear of reprisal and can repeatedly harass their victims. And, the bullied often know their tormentors, creating strange relations based on emotional entrainment, akin to relations in domestic violence, in which offenders get "inside the head" of their victims. For Collins, the bullied experience a particularly damaging form of victimization because their social isolation prevents them from getting assistance and alternate sources of emotional energy. So, Collins (2011) sees some interventions as more effective than others. He doubts the power of solutions that rely on the victim, such as coaching them to stand up to their bullies, or forming "restorative justice circles" for the two parties to meet and gain mutual empathy. Victims are usually too afraid of their bullies, he notes, and bullies often *want* to hear of the damage they inflict. Collins instead recommends solutions that provide emotional supports to victims and lessen their social isolation. GSA (Gay-Straight Alliance) organizations, for instance, provide assistance and comradery, and stigmatize acts of bullying. The former can heighten threat of retaliation in the minds of bullies, and block one of their pathways to violence.

and consequences. "Honour conflicts" are battles against status equals, and rarely have the damaging effects of true bullying. "Scapegoating" is when several students gang up on a single individual and generate their own group solidarity in the process. For instance, a peer scandal can encourage bystanders to join in an attack on a target in fear than they might suffer from contagious blame if they fail to support the condemning majority. Unlike bullying, which is about seeking individual dominance, scapegoating is a mass-participation ritual. It generates self-righteous Durkheimian unity in its ugliest guise. School-based peer groups are staging grounds for scapegoating because they are relatively tightly integrated communities that generate a great mutual focus and social pressure. Homophobic attacks in schools are often in the form of individual bullying, but can escalate when many unite and gang up on the victim, beginning with mocking, jeering, and pranking and progressing to violence. This kind of scapegoating, as opposed to bullying, requires educators to change the entire culture and social dynamics of a school, rather than trying to control a smaller group of offenders. Malette (2017) has found extensive support for Collins' framework in Canada.

Bullying has received a great deal of media attention in recent years, in part prompted by a series of high profile "bullycides" around North America (Howells, 2012). Bullying appears to occur in all kinds of school situations, across all kinds of neighbourhood settings, rich or poor (Hango, 2016). It is a product of micro-situations, generated by peer processes that have much independent social space in schools, and that limit schools' socializing power. Much research is underway in efforts to curb bullying. We see promise in interventions that locate youth bullying within status hierarchies and peer cultures that form in schools. We next turn to forms of conflict with different contexts and dynamics.

The Outer Limits: Crime and Violence

An even weaker instance of school socializing power is borne out in studies of juvenile crime and delinquency. Success in school, employment, or relationships can provide youth with stability, offering what criminologists call "stakes in conformity." Young people with full-time jobs, stable marriages, or academic success are less likely to engage in types of crime that, in the eyes of most observers, make little sense. Being caught for petty crimes can jeopardize one's career or marriage. However, youth with weaker stakes in conformity are more likely to engage in crime. Criminologists have long found close correlations between school failure and criminal behaviour (Tanner, 2015). Further, much youth crime appears to be silly and senseless. Drawing graffiti, drag racing, small-time shoplifting, stealing, and fighting, offer only tiny, if any, economic rewards. And, committing these crimes poses a substantial chance of being caught, much more than sophisticated and high-yield crimes such as fraud, illegal gambling, embezzling, and so on.

Yet, "senseless" crimes appeal to some youth. Crime data suggest that youth are the predominant offenders for crimes like breaking and entering and public fighting, while older adults are more prone to lucrative crimes. Why? Criminologists argue that youth engage in "high-risk/low-yield" crimes because youth culture creates incentives for otherwise "senseless" behaviour. Males in particular reward each other for risk-taking behaviour (Hagan and McCarthy, 1987; Steffensmeir et al., 1989).

This theory also explains a key fact: most youth crime is sporadic and episodic. Youth criminality is largely short-lived; most "grow out" of crime in a few short years. For decades, sociologists have likened youth offending to a "moral holiday;" a short period in which youth temporarily suspend their values and beliefs in the name of fun and excitement. These "holidays" usually result in stupid, risky crimes that offer little monetary gain. But they impress peers and thereby offer status. Much school crime falls into this category, such as stealing, vandalism, breaking and entering, and so on. Canada's Youth Criminal Justice Act (or YCJA, formerly known as the Young Offenders Act) recognizes the short-lived nature of most youth crime and thus prescribes leniency to most non-violent offenders. Many responses attempt to minimize the stigma of criminal labelling by banning public identification of young criminals, and diverting them from adult jails. Increasingly, the YCJA is using "educational" solutions in diversion programs as an alternative for wayward youth.

Box 12.2 School "Rampage" Killings

The image of school shootings has become a major cultural meme since the late 1990s, at least in the United States. In 1997, ninth grader Michael Carneal marched into his Kentucky school with a loaded rifle and quickly killed three students and wounded five others. The next year, sixth grader Andrew Golden and eighth grader Mitchell Johnson sat in a wooded hill overlooking their Arkansas schoolyard and opened fire as their schoolmates exited the school, killing three and injuring 10 others. A string of similar incidents soon erupted across the United States. The most notable was Colorado's Columbine High School massacre in 1999, whose image of the "Trench Coat Mafia" stalking their classmates is inscribed in popular culture. One week after the Columbine shootings, 14-year-old Todd Cameron Smith killed one classmate and injured another at W.R. Myers High School in Taber, Alberta, the first such killing in a Canadian high school in over 20 years. More recently, on 14 December 2012, the Sandy Hook (Connecticut) rampage shootings took the lives of 28 people, including the shooter and his mother. Between 2013 and 2016 another 200 school shootings occurred in the US (https://everytownresearch.org/school-shootings/). By way of comparison, about a dozen shootings have occurred in Canadian schools, colleges, and universities since the 1970s.

Yet these crimes in the US went against the tide of broader trends. As sociologist Katherine Newman and her colleagues contend (Newman and Fox, 2009), most varieties of reported crime have declined across North America, including those in schools. Yet, one species rose in the late 1990s: "rampage" school shootings. These are extraordinary attacks on randomly selected parties, not acts of personal revenge,

continued

and thus represent an assault on the entire institution. In 2000, Newman assembled a team of researchers to explain how young boys could repeatedly wreak such tragic violence. They visited the Kentucky and Arkansas communities, conducting interviews with all concerned parties, and also compiled information on each American rampage shooting since 1974. Because school shootings are rare, and because millions of American teens endure all sorts of problems without resorting to violence, Newman's team needed to understand how atypical conditions converge to generate a shooting.

Their findings cast doubt on popular explanations. No shooter suddenly "snapped" in a psychotic rage; each carefully planned his assault well in advance. Rather than erupting in violent inner cities, almost all rampages occurred in small, tight-knit, family-oriented, and relatively peaceful communities that are typically praised as places where everyone knows each other. But such settings can suffocate some youth, particularly local "misfits." School-based peer groups in small towns are homogeneous. Lacking another social refuge, unpopular youth can experience an unbearable claustrophobia and feel compelled to seek revenge. As one of the few public stages in rural districts, schools are convenient targets of rage. But this rage has a gendered dimension. All shooters were males who struggled to live up to masculine ideals, and wanted to *defy* their images as ineffectual nerds or geeks. All were influenced by cultural scripts that glorify armed attack and connect manhood to the thrill of terrifying the innocent. Would-be shooters were convinced that violence could provide a "masculine exit" from their social subordination and bolster their standing. A final condition for shootings was the availability of guns, something that is unfortunately plentiful in American rural regions.

At their most extreme, schools are scenes of tragic violence. School shootings send shockwaves through their communities. When pondering such tragedies, one can ask: are schools complicit? Are school shootings "normal accidents" caused by the very design of schools, or are they problems with origins from the outside? Most data shows schools to be relatively safe places, though some are more dangerous than others. Acts of extreme violence are rare in schools, even though youth spend many of their waking hours there. Further, school violence like assaults and killings has declined in the United States and Canada over the past decade or more (Howells, 2012). Other forms of crime in schools are more prevalent in poorer neighbourhoods that are crime-ridden, as would be predicted by social disorganization theorists (Astor et al., 2009; Welsh et al., 2000). Canadian data also suggests a paradox: school crime and violence are on the decline, while public concern over school safety is on the rise (Howells, 2012). This paradox reveals the outer limits of schools' socializing power while also signalling the reliance of our schooled society on education to cure a variety of social problems. But beyond these generic limits to schools' socializing power, in what ways does that power vary across different kinds of schooling?

Varying Impacts within Schools: Core versus Extracurricular

In many respects, the socializing experience of school depends on whether one examines core or extracurricular. For instance, sports are obviously a popular

and vital component of schools' daily life. But they are not part of the core curriculum in most schools. Sports represent what organizational theorists call a
"structural add-on" in schools, something peripheral to an organization's prime
mandate. The public expects schools to offer gym classes and an assortment of
athletic teams, but governments do not continually reform and assess physical
education as they do math, science, or languages. There is no standardized testing for PE, and rarely are Canadian students ranked internationally on athletics.
Sports are more like drama presentations and other extracurricular activities:
they are important to many people and can help forge school community, but
they are not treated as essential.

Historically, schools have embraced physical education as a way to help build
character and a well-rounded person. Indeed, it was a central component in late
nineteenth- and early twentieth-century education, which emphasized "muscu-
lar Christianity" as a way to keep preternaturally unruly boys on the straight and
narrow path. But seeing sports teams as an indispensable aspect of school identity is a relatively modern invention. North American educators largely embraced
school teams and intramural sports to accommodate students who were otherwise
uninterested in academic work and to make schools a focal point in local communities (Hurn, 1993). Team sports have far more marginal roles in schools in most
other world regions. But in North America, they have assumed greater prominence.
Proficiency at a sport offers status among peers if not among teachers. Research
has shown that sports offer informal peer esteem across schools with varying class
and race compositions (Karen and Robinson, 2015). School sports are sociologically
interesting in light of questions about school socialization, highlighting how it can
be uneven and inconsistent.

Consider how sports are much more gendered (and racialized in some contexts) than are core school activities. In fact, sports are the most gender-segregated
activities in today's schools. Much more than math, science, or language, physical
education is likely to be single-sexed. School teams are rarely co-ed. Athletics have
norms of interaction that differ sharply from those in academic classrooms. The
latter are typically co-ed and encourage polite and orderly conduct. In contrast,
physical education tolerates far more masculine rough-housing, while cheerleading (mostly a unique North American phenomenon) is usually a feminine "supporting" role without parallel in the core academic curriculum. In what other
school activity do females merely cheer male combatants? There are now far more
female student athletes than before, but they are marginalized in a way unparalleled in the core curriculum. Sports, therefore, are vehicles by which informal peer
hierarchies and older notions of gender infuse student life. Sports can be bastions of
old-fashioned norms of masculinity and femininity. Many educators deem sports
teams and cheerleading to be expensive and retrograde distractions from their core
mandates, but retain them due to popular demand. Thus, these comparisons of core
and extracurricular suggest that schools are progressively gendered institutions:
their main mission subverts many traditional gender norms, while their peripheral
activities often reassert those norms.

Varying Impacts between Schools: Revisiting the Continuum of Socialization

To repeat, different kinds of schools offer a broad continuum in their socializing power. Boarding schools are most like "total institutions" in their all-enveloping influence because they house students for almost all of their waking hours. Online education is at the other end of the continuum.

Today, higher education is a dynamic arena for this continuum. As post-secondary schooling continues to expand, variations in its socializing power are widening. In the archetypal image of the university experience, young adults move out of their parental homes, attend leafy institutions with well-worn dorms, encounter new experiences, and enhance their self-images as they gain a sound liberal education. This idealized rite of passage has much lore in upper-middle-class culture, and holds symbolic power for many professors. It very much represents *the* bar for comparing academic experiences. But today's continual expansion has altered that ideal, at least for much of the public, and for many policy-makers. The new image of higher education is far more about providing skills, improving access to good jobs, and providing instruction in a cost-efficient manner (for a Canadian example, see Clark et al., 2011). But are these ideals grounded in contemporary research?

Ann Mullen, a University of Toronto sociologist, recently compared two very different kinds of universities: Yale University and Southern Connecticut State University (Mullen, 2010). These two institutions offer a strategic contrast. Though situated less than three miles apart in the US town of New Haven, their students have very different experiences. Despite close *geographical* proximity, those institutions represented very different *social* worlds.

Yale is a wealthy private institution, renowned internationally as a top university. Its alumni include several American presidents. Its financial endowment surpasses many nations. Its professors are often top experts in their research specialties. The university takes pride in its liberal arts teaching tradition. As a self-described global leader in advanced learning, Yale is a destination for elite students well beyond New Haven. Most of its fortunate enrolees had tremendous childhood advantages. "Yalies" commonly hail from affluent backgrounds (for a history, see Karabel, 2005). Mullen found that almost all of her interviewees expected to attend a prestigious university from a young age. Few ever considered attending a local public institution. Many attended private high schools, were closely guided by highly educated parents, and were groomed to enter society's upper crust. Full-time tuition fees for undergraduates in 2012–13 were $42,300, though room and board boosted the annual cost to $55,300.

In contrast, Southern Connecticut State University (known as "Southern" to locals) has a public mandate to serve the state of Connecticut. Most of its students are local commuters. Its admission procedures are not particularly selective or competitive. The university instead strives to accommodate its 12,000 students by offering courses at odd hours, part-time options, child-care services, and vocational counselling. Full-time tuition fees for undergraduates in 2012–13 were $8,450.

Mullen interviewed dozens of students at each campus. She found they had strikingly different experiences immediately after arriving. Many Southern students adopted a practical, goal-minded approach to their studies. Higher education was to prepare them for a career and get a springboard into white-collar employment. They wanted skills and credentials that would facilitate upward mobility into a chosen occupation. Education was a means to an end, an exchange of time, effort, and tuition for a decent job and the chance to purchase a home. But it was not anything more deeply personal or life-changing. And, as commuters, their university experience was simply an extension of their existing lives, and left only a small imprint on them. As one Southern commuter put it:

> I don't think I got the whole, complete experience. I was talking to my girlfriend yesterday, I was like, "I don't think I got the whole college experience, I don't know why." Maybe because I don't socialize . . . they say college life is supposed to be the best years of your life. It was regular to me. I didn't have any high points. (Mullen 2010: 196)

In contrast, Yale students thought about education very differently. They were far more ambitious, less instrumental, and more susceptible to new influences. Life on campus exposed them to new social activities, social networks, and lifestyles. Their residences provided a "college life" that prized personal and intellectual growth. While most Yale students had already lived a version of what Annette Lareau (2011) dubs the "ethos of concerted cultivation," Yale extended that ethos into young adulthood and into Ivy League culture (see Karabel, 2005).

Importantly, Yale students saw college as more than career preparation, but also as a vehicle to nurture their intellect and develop their character. They personally identified with their courses. They had lofty ambitions. They *expected* to make an impact in the world and eventually become leaders of industry, professional life, and/or government. Their "name brand" Yale degree nearly assured them of a high-ranking job.

These interviews led Mullen to a compelling conclusion: the "university experience" varies greatly. Students come with dissimilar resources and dispositions, and their institutions can amplify those differences. Yale students got the full "university experience," while Southern students did not. Studies of other American universities come to similar conclusions (e.g., Professor X, 2012; Stevens, 2007; Stuber, 2011). As horizontal inequality grows, discussed in Chapter 5, the university experience ranges more and more. Some still live the liberal-education ideal, but others are experiencing long commutes, large or online classes, more part-time, non-permanent instructors, and business-oriented course work.

Are there similar variations among Canadian campuses? As we discussed in earlier chapters, Canadian higher education institutions are arrayed on a flatter prestige hierarchy, and may be less likely to breed the kind of cohesive social elites that populate Ivy League colleges and England's Oxbridge (though consider that private elite high schools in Canada send many of their graduates to Yale and other Ivy institutions). Nonetheless, Canadian universities probably differ profoundly in their socializing impact, particularly if we compare older, more prestigious, and residence-based institutions versus newer, lesser-known and commuter-oriented institutions.

Class Dismissed? The Conflicting Experiences of Working-Class Students on Campus

Universities have long prided themselves as transformers of people's lives. They promise not only to impart new skills and boost job chances, but to also re-socialize and reinvent students, exposing them to new thinking, cultures, and styles of living. Many university graduates fondly recall their student days as life-changing, personal transformations. But as liberating as this process can be, is it class neutral? The theories of Pierre Bourdieu and Randall Collins (Chapter 3) suggest it may not be; the cultures of contemporary universities may instead be rooted in the outlooks of the global, gentrifying upper-middle class. If this is indeed the case, what happens when local working-class kids encounter this cosmopolitan culture?

Here's one quick answer: it depends. Students who commute to university from their parents' homes may change little if they are minimally exposed to that culture, encountering it only in the occasional lecture, tutorial, or social event. For those youth, home-grown orientations are likelier to remain intact. But among students more fully immersed in campus life—living in residence, joining clubs, pouring themselves into their studies—that exposure can be far more intense. What happens to them? According to sociologist Wolfgang Lehmann (2014), what occurs is a complicated and conflicting process.

Lehmann interviewed 22 undergraduates from working-class backgrounds in an Ontario university, one known to attract mostly affluent students. They had mixed experiences. On the one hand, they were absorbed by campus life, enjoying academic success, and aspiring to graduate and professional degrees. Further, they spoke of new-found personal freedoms and cultural transformations, offering comments such as "It's been an amazing experience," "It's a nice change knowing friends that have parents who are doctors or dentists," "My eyes have been opened to so much, and it makes me wonder how much more is out there. Culturally I've grown," and "It's been life altering really. I'm more open-minded, more receptive to different ideas, and more willing to recognize differences in opinion." These students warmly embraced their new lifestyles, becoming foodies; going to museums, galleries, and alternative rock concerts; sampling wines, and so on. University had exposed them to a diversity of, well, virtually everything! They encountered a far greater range of cultures, nationalities, foods, political outlooks, and sexualities than ever before. And, they were deeply impressed. They were thriving on cosmopolitanism.

Yet on the other hand, Lehmann also detected something less joyful and more unsettling. For many students, these transformations came with a cost: new conflicts in their relationships with their parents and former friends. Their working-class habits and mores now seemed like burdens. They struggled with leaving their old world behind, and felt guilty for doing so.

One student said "I feel like I can't relate to my parents. I love 'em to death, but they're both very close minded, not having an education, and just working your whole life. I can't have an intellectual conversation with my mom, it's really just surface conversations. I can't get too deep because then it's whoosh right over her heard. Where I grew up they're all factory workers, and so it is a lower class mentality down there. It's really hard coming from university, being open minded and writing about racism and sexism and feminist studies and then going back home to the same-old, same-old. I'm happy to get away from that." Another said: "I go home rarely now because my high school friends haven't changed at all, I can't communicate and relate to them. I get the feeling that they think that we, the university students, are better than them."

The young men and women in Lehmann's study were becoming upwardly mobile, joining the ranks of the professional middle class, while also adopting new outlooks, dispositions, and tastes. But they were also "breaking up" with their former communities, peers, and families, seeing them as narrow-minded and unambitious at best, and racist, sexist, and homophobic at worst. Yet, no student questioned this subtle devaluation of working-class culture, one that implicitly reduced it to a series of social and moral deficiencies. As a result, their "break-up" brought vague feelings of unease, of being caught between two worlds. For this chapter's theme, Lehmann's study has a discomforting implication. On the one hand, contemporary universities appear to be living up to some of their expressed ideals. But on the other hand, they may be encouraging working-class students to see their former communities as limiting, even pathological, while also discouraging any recognition of higher education's own biases. If so, are universities imparting a fully critical understanding of society?

Conclusion

Today's public schools are constrained in their efforts to socialize students. This chapter raises an important question: to what extent are social scripts imported into school from the outside, and to what extent do schools create, reinforce, or combat them outright? Our reading of sociological research suggests a mix of these possibilities. Entrenched social inequality can give rise to cultural expressions that distract youth from advanced schooling. Traditional working-class communities, types of social disorganization, and some forms of racial subordination can each create distance between many youth and educators. The rise of popular youth culture has similarly altered relations between students and schools over the past 60 years, providing youth with an autonomous social space that schools must sometimes accommodate. It provides a medium for a variety of subcultures, including those among low-achieving youth. Schools' selection function can provoke a generic reaction among low achievers. Otherwise, the core curriculum generally integrates students more evenly, at least by gender, than do extracurricular. More extreme forms of opposition to school are rare, and tend to reflect a lack of integration into the school community.

More than 60 years ago, Canadian sociologists argued that "the school exists both as a creation of the society and as a perpetuating institution of that same society" (Seeley et al., 1956: 245). This flat conclusion, we think, fails to account for the equalizing efforts of educators. Schools are more egalitarian than are many surrounding institutions, such as religious sites, workplaces, or families. Their organizational form tends to undermine traditional roles and integrate students, particularly by gender. But their efforts are often undermined by forces beyond schools' control. They must compete with several other socializing agents, including popular culture, peer groups, families, neighbourhoods, communication technologies, and job markets. Any further heightening of schools' socializing impact would necessitate great structural change in both schools and society. Might this happen in the foreseeable future? The next chapter concludes this book by discussing changes we believe are likely to occur in Canadian education.

Questions for Critical Thought

1. Think of your own experiences of extracurricular high school activities. Did they reinforce your gender, class, or racial identity? Comment on why or why not.

2. Revisit your grandparents once again. Did they experience anything resembling modern student subcultures, such as skinheads, punks, boarders, or hippies? What does this tell us about social change and schooling?

3. How did your school promote safety? Did those measures protect students, or did they backfire in some unintended ways?

Suggested Readings

Lehmann, Wolfgang. 2014. "Habitus Transformation and Hidden Injuries: Successful Working-Class University Students," *Sociology of Education* 87(1): 1–15. Lehmann probed the lives of some working students in his university, and found them to have mixed experiences.

Milner, Murray, Jr. 2013. "Paradoxical Inequalities: Adolescent Peer Relations in Indian Secondary Schools," *Sociology of Education* 86(3): 253–67. Milner took his conceptual framework to schools in India, and found a complex pattern of peer groups.

Mullen, Ann. 2010. *Degrees of Inequality: Culture, Class, and Gender in American Higher Education.* Baltimore: Johns Hopkins University Press. This is an intriguing comparison of student life in a renowned Ivy League college versus a local commuter university.

Tanner, Julian. 2015. *Teenage Troubles*, 4th edn. Toronto: Oxford University Press. This is a solid Canadian text on youth culture and delinquency.

Web Links

University of British Columbia: Early Learning
www.earlylearning.ubc.ca
The HELP website is dedicated to providing interdisciplinary research-based evidence that can improve the learning of younger British Columbians.

The Offord Centre
www.offordcentre.com
This centre focuses upon "improving the life quality and life opportunities of the one in five Canadian children and youth who suffer from serious social and emotional problems."

National Institute for Child Health and Human Development
www.nichd.nih.gov/about/overview
This US centre is a good resource for basic interdisciplinary research on child development issues, some with an eye to the importance of social context.

Part V
Conclusion

13 Future Directions for Canadian Education

Learning Objectives

- To review several themes presented throughout the book
- To consider how these various factors are steering a future course for Canadian education
- To determine which changes in Canadian education are likely to be short-lived and which are likely to last a long time

Introduction: The Tricky Art of Prediction

The preceding chapters have covered considerable ground. We outlined how transformations in families, economies, and politics shape schools. We sketched the main characteristics of a "schooled society," a society in which education is a central institution with increasing connections to other institutions *and* where education is sought by ever-more diverse people at more stages of their lives. Yet it is also a society where schools are increasingly scrutinized and criticized. We will return to this paradox after completing one remaining task: linking our sociological insights on schooling to emerging trends in Canadian education. This final chapter looks to the future and offers several predictions for change in major areas of Canadian education.

Prediction is tricky. Schools can be quite faddish and ever-changing, yet simultaneously staid and inert. They often stand accused of adopting and then discarding pedagogical fashions at will. Think of the fate of open schools, the revolving redesign of sex education curricula, or various physical fitness programs. But they can be portrayed as old-fashioned relics from a bygone era. Think of the continuing use of "chalk and talk" teaching methods in today's digital age.

One reason for the former charge is that schools are vulnerable to surrounding societal pressures. They are, after all, governed ultimately by a political party, subject to the whims of politicians.

Yet, schools do not respond to *every* pressure. One reason for stasis is that as bureaucratic organizations they can *buffer* their prime processes—classroom instruction and core curricula—from outside influences. While peripheral activities are subject to the wishes of politicians or professional consultants, core teaching methods have remained relatively stable for decades (Tyack and Cuban, 1995). Previous chapters showed that schools are loosely coupled organizations that delegate much discretion to teachers. This organizational form insulates classrooms from outside forces. For instance, loose coupling ensures teachers are rarely told *how* to teach. "Chalk and talk" methods of instruction remain common. Moreover, core subjects like math, science, and language are much less likely to be politicized or tampered with by non-professionals than are supplementary modules such as sex education.

Schools thus can be faddish *and* unchanging, trendy *and* inert. Being governed by politicians they must respond to some external pressures, but as loosely coupled organizations they can buffer their central processes from those forces.

Some even depict education reform as akin to a hurricane over an ocean (e.g., Tyack and Cuban, 1995). There may be incredible turmoil on the surface, with crashing waves and surges, but below the waters are far more placid. At the ocean floor, there are only faint echoes of the raging storm above. This analogy helps to reconcile connections between high-level reform proposals and their classroom impacts. Schools endure harsh criticism from politicians, who sometimes demand major overhauls. But once such demands enter the labyrinth of school bureau-cracy (e.g., boards and ministries), they can be "tamed" and transformed into more routine reforms. Teacher unions will obstruct some initiatives; parent groups will oppose others; social activists will undermine others. By the time some proposed changes hit the classroom, their impact is barely detectable. This buffering process gives teachers some discretion in their relatively solitary classrooms, and within cer-tain limits they can ensure that change proposals impact their classroom modestly.

Another buffering process comes from the tendency for reforms in one direc-tion to trigger opposing reactions. For instance, reforms aiming to enhance equal-ity of opportunity, such as de-streaming, attract opponents who worry that such measures will dilute the quality of education and then push counter-initiatives to bolster schools' sorting roles. In turn, reforms that aim to enhance quality usu-ally spark concerns over equity. This continual to-and-fro has led some analysts to regard educational change as a series of "reform cycles" in which there is a regular storm of initiatives, but in which most are transitory, constantly coming and going. As a result, true change in education is slow and gradual. Indeed, some say that schools have been merely "tinkered" with repeatedly over the past century, leaving the core process of teaching largely unchanged (Cuban, 1990).

Nonetheless, schools are changing in important ways, and we believe they will continue to do so. Acknowledging the often transient nature of school reform, we see powerful forces that are continually, if slowly, reshaping schooling. Pressures to send more youth to higher education, to accommodate all high school and ele-mentary students, to provide choice, and to be accountable to governments all are very real. How might these pressures affect schooling in lasting ways, not just in transitory, short-term fashions? The best work in the sociology of education gives us enough confidence to offer a set of "big picture" predictions for Canadian schooling. Below we offer several predictions, and end by highlighting a central paradox of our schooled society.

The Most Likely Directions for Canadian Education

Selection: More Expansion of Higher Education

Chapter 4 described how secondary schooling has become a universal experience for Canadians and how post-secondary enrolments have grown to unprecedented levels. Contemporary theorists have understood this in different ways. Marxists and functionalists have long debated whether school selection is meritorious and aimed at upgraded cognitive skills, or whether it inhibits the mobility of working-class, female, and minority students. Credentialists and institutionalists reframed this issue by emphasizing the looseness of the links between school content and workplaces and how that looseness triggers rampant credential inflation and intense competition for the most highly sought-after post-secondary programs and institutions.

Future thinking, we believe, needs to be more sensitive to structural shifts that are occurring in schooling. Chapters 4 and 5 described a change from "sponsored" to "contest" forms of competition and a migration of education's selection function upward to the post-secondary level. We also know that enrolments for university appear to be growing more than those for community college. Further, more college-level institutions are vying for university status, while no university is moving in the other direction, although universities are quickly adding more practical professional short term post-baccalaureate degrees (e.g., Applied or Professional Masters degrees; Early Learning Professionals, Intercultural Studies, Sustainability Specialists). Many former colleges have become "university colleges" and have attained the authority to grant degrees. In Ontario, Ryerson Polytechnic Institute and Nipissing Community College have gained university status, while an entire stratum of "university colleges" was created in British Columbia, some of which are now universities (e.g., Thompson Rivers University). In Alberta, Grant McEwan Community College became McEwan University. This structural upgrading has occurred in part to meet rising public demand for university education.

In addition, higher education will likely become even more differentiated, not only by field of study but also between institutions. Provincial governments want their universities to increasingly distinguish themselves from others, urging some to improve their standing on the world research stage, and others to focus on undergraduate teaching (Pizarro Milian, Davies, and Zarifa, 2016).

We believe these trends of expanding enrolments and structural upgrading will continue, with one proviso: if sizeable tuition hikes occur then enrolment growth may slow. Otherwise, if tuition is held in check and student loans do not hemorrhage, enrolments will continue to expand. Why?

On the surface, the popularity of university is surprising. The majority of Canadian high school graduates enter universities with vague career plans. Most graduate from the general arts and science fields rather than from professional programs, and most then enter mass labour markets rather than particular occupational paths. Except for professional programs, university courses are coupled loosely with labour markets. But as we have seen, employers do appear to prefer university graduates over others, despite their lack of direct job training. Social scientists debate whether this is because employers are seeking diffuse, higher-order cognitive skills, or whether it reflects credential inflation. In either case, however, holding a degree continues to enjoy a cachet in the job market.

Before the 1970s, young people with bachelor's degrees were rarities and employers could rate them as having well-above-average ability. At that time, there was no stigma attached to the *absence* of a degree. High school graduates could vie for solid middle-class jobs because the vast majority of job applicants lacked post-secondary credentials. But as more young people earned degrees over the decades, those degrees could no longer offer elite status. Even though many with BA or BSc degrees may be exceptionally able, their credentials can no longer offer entrée into any elite. Nonetheless, a degree continues to appeal to many high school graduates. As long as employers continue to link degrees with *some* measure of ability, they may increasingly associate the absence of a degree with mediocrity. Most young people want to avoid that label, and many are scrambling for a degree to dissociate themselves from the lower sector of the labour pool. Even if few are "adolescent econometricians" who closely calculate the financial costs and benefits of schooling as depicted in human capital theory, they do implicitly place wagers on the likely consequences of attaining credentials. Table 13.1 illustrates their implicit thinking.

Furthermore, a general university degree provides a ticket to *more* higher education. High school and community college diplomas have the disadvantage of being terminal credentials that cannot lead to advanced graduate or professional degrees, such as a teaching certificate, an MBA, or a PhD. The BA or BSc, though often maligned as lacking job relevance, has the virtue of being recognized by higher levels of schooling, which can offer very real occupational rewards. In a changing service-based economy, and within a culture that encourages people to switch careers and jobs, such flexibility can be valuable. In the parlance of a risk society, the credential is a subtle form of insurance.

Higher education expansion may balloon for another reason, one that lies beyond schooling. The world is changing, fast. Artificial intelligence, genomics, and robotics are all accelerating the complexity of life. New school forms have emerged in this context, from early childhood programs aimed at boosting general

Table 13.1 The Student's Dilemma

	A University Degree Offers	A College Diploma or Less Offers
Upside	Some chance of very high salary	Low cost, secure reward, quicker entry to labour force
Downside	High costs, possible low rewards, lost wages while studying	Little access to high salaries, very tough transition to professional jobs or graduate school

Source: Adapted from Wolf (2002: 183).

literacy and cognitive skills, to a series of specialized education "top-ups" emerging later over people's life courses. Accelerated change in technology may require even more frequent skill updating in adulthood. To meet this emerging era, some have called for the creation of "micro-credentials" or "badges" in higher education. But who among adults typically seeks additional schooling? Those with degrees. If this particular trend were to take root, and if micro-credentials were increasingly valuable, this could create a sharper gap between those able to keep pace with change and those who cannot.

Selection: The Upward Migration of Accommodation

Chapter 5 discussed how high schools are in some ways more competitive and in other ways more "mall-like." Vocational programs in high schools are a traditional form of accommodation, but have a troubled reputation in the sociology of education. They have been alternatively blamed for limiting the opportunities of disadvantaged youth, who usually are over-represented in applied streams, or seen to be insufficiently relevant for the job market. Educational historians have accused early twentieth-century reformers of "elitism" for assuming that many youth simply could not handle a demanding academic curriculum (Ravitch, 2000). Yet, these same programs are also seen to lack strong connections to good jobs.

Today there is an unresolved tension among policy-makers about vocational high school programs. On the one hand, those believing we are now in a "knowledge economy" assume all young workers need higher-order cognitive skills, and regard manual vocational training to be anachronistic. On the other hand, many are aware of the "forgotten half" of students who do not proceed to post-secondary levels. Many educators believe these students need more vocational programs and are ill-served by a general academic curriculum. As a consequence, many Canadian school boards are implementing new vocational programs, hoping that they will be embraced by low-achieving youth as a job-relevant form of schooling.

But recent experience suggests that youth will snub any vocational options that are seen to be incapable of delivering good jobs, regardless of their program quality. Even those youth who feel ill-suited for academic curricula will avoid vocational programs that appear to lead to dead-end jobs. Evidence from Britain (Wolf, 2011) and from Germany (Lehmann, 2000) suggests that fewer youth want these new vocational credentials if they can secure only lower-level jobs.

This lesser demand for secondary-level vocational education may be fuel for higher education. And it may be having another, unanticipated impact: pressures for institutional accommodation in *higher education*. While highly sought-after programs are increasingly selective, such as Ivy League universities in the United States and professional studies in Canada, less selective programs are increasingly expected to accommodate students. In an era of rising college and university enrolments, non-elite programs are becoming more "mall-like." Administrators want to retain greater numbers of students, sometimes in a spirit of equity, but often to generate tuition and government revenue (i.e., money that both universities and colleges get on a per-student basis). This accommodation can take a variety of forms.

To compete for students, many universities and colleges are proclaiming a new priority on student satisfaction. After decades in which undergraduates' fees bought only classes in cavernous lecture halls, housing in substandard dorms, and lengthy commutes to distant campuses, today's universities are thinking about their "customers." Some institutions are taking student course evaluations more seriously; others are pouring money into student centres, pubs, and exercise facilities. More Canadian universities and colleges are holding classes at night, on weekends, and in new suburban campuses. These options are more easily accessed by "non-traditional" students, who, juggling careers and families with their studies, want a more convenient post-secondary experience. Many colleges and universities have added online programs to supplement their regular programs, and they are successfully competing with mostly online universities such as the University of Phoenix (www.phoenix.edu). There is even evidence of some grade inflation, at least in Ontario universities (Anglin and Meng, 2000; Côté and Allahar, 2011). Just like the shopping mall high school in the 1980s, today's post-secondary institutions are more accommodating.

To emphasize these accommodations is not to deny the thousands of excellent undergraduates in Canadian universities, nor is it to necessarily claim that academic quality is plummeting, though some are saying precisely those things, penning titles like *Lowering Higher Education* (Côté and Allahar, 2011). But there is a tension between the noble goal of expanded access and older notions of academic standards. Whereas student failure rates in universities and colleges were once seen to be badges of rigour, they are now increasingly interpreted as indicating problems in particular academic *programs*, rather than indicating problems in the quality of their students. Expanded enrolments are likely to bring more students who have only a casual interest in their studies. This is not to imagine a romantic past in which all undergraduates were enraptured by their history, biology, or sociology coursework. But it is probable that those smaller and more elite student bodies had fewer individuals with strong dislikes for lectures, deep reading, and essay-writing. Some professors, at least those in non-elite programs, are claiming that universities want them to relax their standards for mandatory class attendance and reading lists, or well-crafted essay-writing. This trend of accommodating students may crash headfirst into another, namely, that professors are increasingly judged for their research. Critics are charging professors with treating teaching as a sideline, as a necessary diversion rather than a focal interest (e.g. Clark et al., 2011). Nevertheless, regardless of their impact on academic standards, near-universal rates of post-secondary attendance will probably alter the character of universities by legitimizing a range of new accommodations for students.

Box 13.1 Student Satisfaction and Ranking in Canadian Universities

The spirit of accommodation is raising the stature of student evaluations, evident in the practice of ranking Canadian universities. These rankings now sometimes include student satisfaction measures. For instance, the inaugural *Maclean's* rankings consisted mainly of "hard" measures such as the average grades of incoming students, research grants won, library holdings, and so on. However, now *Maclean's* and the *Globe and Mail* are including ratings of the satisfaction of students (see, for instance, www.macleans.ca/universities/index.jsp). And, interestingly, the rankings of universities for student satisfaction sometimes diverge rather dramatically from the rankings based on conventional measures of academic prestige. On some occasions, in fact, satisfaction rankings almost invert those for academic reputation. For undergraduate students, larger and more established research-intensive institutions may seem aloof, while small, teaching-oriented universities may seem more accommodating.

Some could argue that this new spirit of accommodation has let the "genie out of the bottle," and that established universities will have to either embrace new business models, or lose good students to those newer institutions that can offer cheaper, more flexible, and more convenient online delivery. We believe that this is doubtful, however. Mainstream universities are surely inconvenient in some respects, but they retain a key advantage: they are more *difficult to enter than their competitors*. For-profit and online universities need to attract students, and they generally have lower entry standards. That simple fact puts them at a disadvantage due to the basic dynamics of credential competition. As long as employers continue to interpret a degree as a general marker of ability and trustworthiness, they will regard graduates from more selective institutions as more able and trustworthy. As long as online degrees receive less recognition from employers, they will be sought out mainly by those students who lack other academic options. Accommodations have their limits.

Selection: Change and Stability at the Individual Level

As the structure of school selection changes, how will different groups fare within that evolving structure? Chapters 6 and 7 showed that while all youth are attaining more education, class disparities remain largely static, and gender and racial disparities in attainment have shrunk to the extent that variations *within* races and genders are more noteworthy than those between these groups.

The future of class disparities is uncertain. In Canada they may worsen if tuition increases steepen. Mounting financial barriers for poorer students can make academic contests less meritorious, especially in professional schools (Frenette, 2005). This Canadian trend might mirror international trends in which the impact of social background on school attainment appears to be strengthening with time. That is, once schooling becomes a stable and institutionalized device for rationing positions to labour markets, advantaged families learn how to "play the game" and develop strategies to boost their children's competitive advantage. Parental agency in the form of strategies to manipulate school outcomes grows in importance, whether in the form of hiring tutors, sending children to private schools, or actively intervening in schooling. These strategies are more easily adopted by already advantaged families. As contests to enter selective universities and fields of study (e.g., law or medicine) intensify, advantaged parents in turn strive to improve their children's preparation. In effect, equality and inequality occur simultaneously. University systems are widening access, but as they differentiate between mass and elite institutions and selective and unselective fields of study, they create more structural inequality. Students from advantaged families will likely continue to benefit most from these changes.

In contrast, most remaining areas of female disadvantage will likely dwindle, with women moving slowly into non-traditional fields (though relatively few men will move in the other direction). One possibility is that as traditional male-dominated paths in manual labour close, young men may be more accepting of the student role, and that could close part of the current gender attainment gap. In terms of race, we are forced to offer a more pessimistic forecast: unless societal conditions improve, Indigenous students will remain Canada's most disadvantaged group. Their existing levels of poverty and living conditions simply are not conducive to school success, although some individual Indigenous people will continue to excel.

Organization: More Privatization?

Earlier we described schools as having moved from "traditional" to "legal-rational" forms of authority. This process will continue, though perhaps in more market-styled guises. Public school systems are increasingly pressured to offer more choice in types of schools and programs. Parents and students increasingly see themselves as "customers" who deserve to choose from a menu of offerings. Schools of choice and private schools are on the rise in many Canadian urban locales. In higher education, many universities are nurturing their brand identities and emphasizing (at least in rhetoric) the customer satisfaction of their students (Kirp, 2003). Within universities, business schools in particular are presenting themselves as stand-alone entities, with their own names and individuality. Think of how MBA programs are increasingly known for their benefactors—Haskayne, Rotman, Ivey—instead of their host institution—Calgary, Toronto, Western. These and other programs want to charge tuition fees that are limited only by market demand, not government regulation. In other parts of campus, certain course offerings are valued more for their revenue-generating potential than their academic prestige.

But beyond these limited forms of choice and private governance, are we likely to see fuller forms of privatization? For instance, might provinces seek reforms such as large-scale voucher programs for private schools or home-school expenses? We doubt it, unless there are drastic political changes. Advocates will justify these initiatives for their ability to extend choice, but opponents can easily harpoon them for their lack of public accountability. Because private schools and home-schoolers usually want to retain much of their independence from government, this very fact limits their appeal to politicians. Without government subsidy, the sheer expense of these alternatives places a "natural cap" on their enrolments. However, if more conservative-leaning provincial governments are elected, and if they choose to subsidize private schools through tax breaks to families, this natural cap might soften. Without such funding changes private schooling is unlikely to grow far beyond current levels because most families cannot afford them. Instead, more provinces and school boards may look to Alberta and Quebec for inspiration and create more choice *within* the public system, bolstering their existing stock of public schools with a variety of specialty schools and programs. The form of fully private education that is most likely to grow is tutoring and supplementary education because it is affordable to more families.

As many kinds of educational businesses arise, their advertisements sometimes borrow from sociological research.

Photo by David Zarifa. Reprinted with permission.

Organization: The Loose Impact of the Knowledge Economy

Social scientists have long looked to the surrounding economy to understand schools. This reasoning is more pervasive today, with many predicting that the emerging "knowledge economy" will have a momentous impact on education. Many claim that new jobs increasingly require higher-order cognitive skills, and they are urging more young people to attend post-secondary institutions in order to keep the Canadian economy competitive. Business representatives and politicians in particular are calling for a rapid rise in the production of graduate students (i.e., master and doctoral levels) in order to raise the aggregate skill levels of the workforce.

No one can doubt that the economy has changed in recent decades. But how strong is the connection between school expansion and these economic shifts? In some ways, this is a "glass half-full/glass half-empty" issue. There are certainly more jobs in information technology. There are more professional occupations than ever. There are certainly fewer jobs in manufacturing and farming. Highly educated young people earn much higher salaries than their less educated peers. Basic literacy is required in the vast majority of jobs. But in some respects, talk of the knowledge intensiveness of many new jobs appears to be exaggerated. *Most* new jobs in Canada are in the service sector, not in the high-tech sector. Only a small proportion of these new jobs require advanced computer training. More university enrolments are in social science, humanities, and education programs than in engineering and other sciences, and there appears to be little movement from that pattern (see Figure 13.1). Many university graduates report quite loose fits between their post-secondary education and their jobs (Walters, 2004). As credentialists like Randall Collins (2002) remind us, many sectors of the economy have a limited capacity to absorb all of the skills that are being taught to undergraduates (see also Smith, 2000).

This "glass half-empty" phenomenon can be traced to a feature of loose coupling: schools have very few feedback mechanisms that directly link classroom content to job requirements. Course curricula and tests are designed by education professionals, with little input from business executives or personnel departments (whose influence continues to be resisted by many educators). Graduates face few independent inspections of their learned skills. With the exception of some professional programs, most schooling continues to nurture generic cognitive and literacy skills, rather than intricate high-tech skills, *pace* the futuristic images conjured by advocates of the knowledge economy. And, current trends in higher education may be partly undermining ongoing efforts to build student skill. Enrolment expansion has brought, on average, larger classes, fewer intimate seminars, less personal contact between students and professors, and more use of assessments like multiple-choice tests rather than lengthy essays. Without additional resources, continued enrolment expansion may make university education less enriching, and arguably less skill-intensive.

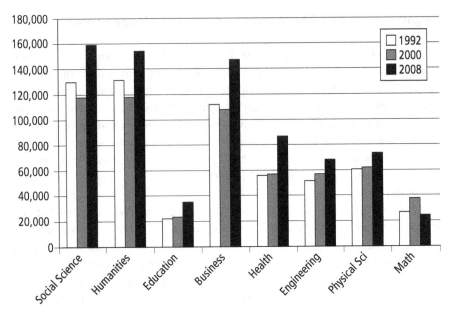

Figure 13.1 University Undergraduate Enrolment by Field of Study and Year
Source: Statistics Canada, CANSIM Table 4770013 (latest data available).

Organization: The Continual Rationalization of Curriculum

Never before has there been so much talk of school "accountability." Politicians are demanding that schools scrutinize budgets. Policy-makers are increasingly developing performance indicators, comparing schools on standardized tests. Many educators have forcefully criticized these understandings. But while this or that measure may be discarded, we doubt that the grand notion of accountability will soon vanish. Provinces spend tens of billions of dollars on education, and so politicians will continue to feel entitled to inspect schools. For all their faults, standardized test scores allow provinces to indirectly influence schooling in ways that are not overly onerous or taxing. And because educational performance indicators are being institutionalized around the world, standardized testing regimes will be difficult to dismantle. International comparisons attract the attention of government officials and media and provide readily available benchmarks for goal-setting agendas. As international testing becomes an increasingly common feature of an emergent world culture of education, few jurisdictions can avoid keeping an eye on their placement internationally or nationally.

These accountability initiatives may not actually promote efficiency, either at the K–12 level or at the post-secondary level. Critics have revealed the misleading nature of comparisons of high schools and of university rankings (e.g., Dill and Soo, 2005). But those initiatives may have an unintended outcome: to promote isomorphism. For instance, if standardized test scores are used to determine a school's funding level, that school will have a disincentive to stray from approved curricula or to use experimental teaching methods. Fewer deviations bring more isomorphism.

Curricula likely will continue to be justified in terms of their "social utility" rather than older notions of tradition, charisma, or the "sacred" qualities of knowledge (Ramirez, 2004). Educational content will be defended when it is seen to aid an individual's development. This trend will continue to erode the humanities, weakening the intellectual authority of canons of art, literature, and high culture lineages. In contrast, it will bolster business-related forms of schooling, though not necessarily in a directly vocational manner. Schooling may not *become* more directly vocational, but it will be *justified* in those terms, labelled as "applied," even if most of its skill content remains abstract. These shifts are more evident in higher education, where professional and business programs have become more numerous, at least compared to the liberal arts (Brint, 2002). Interestingly, these programs are not necessarily tightly connected to the daily realities of professional work, and some have been criticized by professional associations for such irrelevance (Grubb and Lazerson, 2005). One of the brakes on any future dominance of overly practical curricula is the continuing popularity of critical thinking and discovery-oriented forms of learning, as have been championed by progressive pedagogues for decades.

Box 13.2 "Freakonomics" of Standardized Testing

The Chicago public school system created a "high-stakes" testing program in 1996. This new policy would punish schools with low reading scores by placing them on probation and threatening to shut them down. Teachers with poor-performing students could be passed over for a raise or even fired, while those who improved their class scores could receive large bonuses. Proponents argued that this initiative would motivate teachers to work harder for their students. But as economist Steven Levitt argues (Levitt and Dubner, 2005: 26–37), it also created another incentive—for teachers to cheat! One problem was that this testing program rarely examined *how* teachers reported their students' scores. After seeing a rise in average test scores in the first few years of the program, authorities suspected some teachers of altering some of their students' wrong answers. So, the Chicago board compiled a database of all test results and created a computer program to search for unusual answer patterns within each classroom. For instance, the program would flag cases where otherwise low-achieving students might suddenly get correct answers on consecutively difficult questions. A subsequent analysis of all Chicago schools revealed evidence of teacher cheating in more than 200 classrooms each year, roughly 5 per cent of the total. Cheating teachers tended to be younger, less qualified, and in the lowest-scoring classrooms—precisely those with more incentive to raise their pay through the program. It seems that high-stakes testing initiatives are not immune from the types of unintended consequences that we find in other areas of schooling.

Organization: Exporting School to Other Institutions

As regular schooling expands, other institutions are also turning to educational procedures and structures. Chapter 4 discussed how the "school form" has been exported to corporations, the criminal justice system, and health care. Ivan Illich's worst fear is now a reality. The very social relation he found so insidious—formal teacher/student roles, prescribed and standardized curricula, accreditation, and certification procedures—is spreading fast to other institutional settings.

These examples mostly represent a spread of schooling *without* credentialism. Most school forms in corporations or in criminal justice cannot be "cashed in" for jobs or other positions, and are instead adopted for legitimacy, usefulness, or cost-effectiveness. Schooling has been institutionalized to the point where society takes it for granted, regardless of its immediate utility. As such, more social problems are being defined as educational in nature. This is analogous to the process of "medicalization," described by sociologists Conrad and Schneider (1980). New ways of thinking seep into our common culture when some institutions gain prominence over old ones, and even become enshrined in law. A century ago alcoholism was seen as a moral problem, an "evil" trait requiring the spiritual aid of a church. The rise of science eventually persuaded people to view it as a disease in need of medical treatment.

Likewise, in schooled societies, more public problems are seen to be rooted in ignorance or a lack of cognitive reasoning. Education is increasingly prescribed to solve those problems. For instance, the rationale for diversion programs for soliciting prostitution or shoplifting is that perpetuators simply haven't thought through the consequences of their acts; if given some facts and reasoning tools, we assume they are less likely to reoffend. These examples illustrate how the notion of using education to solve a variety of societal ills has spread beyond public schools.

Organization: The Continuing Impact of Consumers

Consumers, and by that we mean families and their children, have been major forces in shaping the evolution of Canadian schooling. Many educators think of schooling as a common good, an important institution to promote a range of public policies from citizenship enrichment to literacy and numeracy enhancement. Families understand schooling very differently. For most families schooling is a private good, an individualized product that has payoffs and opportunities as its most important attribute. Why have schools expanded? Because parents wanted their children to have the advantages that they perceived came with more and more advanced education. Why did some fields of study professionalize? Because parents in concert with professionals, wanted opportunities for their offspring to become lawyers, accountants, or architects. As Labaree (2010) argues, education for families is less about use-value (what you learn) and more about exchange-value (what doors it opens). Acquiring badges of ability is the greatest benefit the school system bestows on individuals.

Will this emphasis on education as a private good change? No, and indeed it might intensify even further. Certainly some families resist the factory-like nature of schooling by home-schooling their children. There are, as well, some alternative forms of schooling, such as Montessori and Waldorf. However, these are the exceptions and there is no evidence of a trend toward either of these approaches becoming widely popular. Families and students as consumers will continue to be important, but very individualized, forces for change in the system. Their quest for private returns to education will continue.

Socialization: Making Space for Youth

Among theorists, Durkheim's interest in moral education long ago gave way to the functionalist emphasis on modern values and the Marxist contention that schools largely engage in social control. What implications does more recent research have for theories of socialization? Our reading of trends suggests that future theories of school socialization should focus on its *limits*, and examine how schools must compete for influence in a world of student part-time jobs, changing youth cultures, and changing parenting approaches.

The expansion of higher education serves to prolong the school careers of young people. That prolonging will likely have crosscutting effects on the socializing power of schools. On the one hand, it will make youth culture increasingly autonomous. Stretching full-time schooling from the late teens into the mid-twenties allows for continual cultural separatism, fuelling industries that manufacture music, clothes, and youth entertainment. On the other hand, the sheer necessity of credentials ensures that most youth will be at least instrumentally attached to education. With fewer and fewer good jobs not requiring some formal schooling, almost everyone will want to attain some credential. The outcome of these two trends will be that student peer groups will increasingly make an autonomous space for themselves in schools; some may be rebellious, most will not—the latter will develop forms of cultural autonomy that rarely challenge school authority. Their transitory subcultures might create a self-absorbing social world, but they will comply with school dictates, at least in a minimal and perfunctory manner. The rebellious few will be deemed "at-risk," unlike dropouts from a generation ago, who could still be considered "normal" as they entered other, non-criminal adult roles that awaited them after high school.

These examples highlight a paradox: as schooling becomes more pervasive, its singular socializing impact weakens. As schools do more to accommodate students, influence shifts to the *opposing* direction and more socializing agents compete with schools. Consider the competition that schools face from families. Recent research suggests middle-class families are embracing child-rearing styles to cultivate educational advantages, guiding their children's schooling by hiring tutors, engaging in a wide array of after-school lessons, sending their children to educationally intensive summer camps, and expending greater amounts of effort choosing schools and colleges (Quirke, 2006; Lareau and Weininger, 2003; Stevens, 2007). Most teachers welcome these kinds of activities outside of schooling, but this "intensive parenting" can only reinforce the impact of family environment on education. Families will increasingly influence students' literacy skills, their expectations for schooling, and their work habits, even more than they do now. And, of course, families (and schools) will do so in competition with an expanding youth culture industry that sends, through entertainment, material goods, and advertising, a set of often diverging messages about the "good" life.

Arguably, schools will have less of an impact on shaping racial and gender identities. Critics of schools' gender and race biases are turning their focus to extracurricular activities. Sports, for instance, can disturb standard educational routines with by-products such as hazing rituals, physical aggression, indifference to academics, and forms of gender segregation. But school sports continue to be incredibly popular among the public and students, if not among educators. Educators will face the challenge of balancing this popularity with co-ed norms that guide the rest of the curriculum.

Finale: The Paradox of a Schooled Society

We conclude this book with a mixed message. Schools are institutional success stories. All citizens attend educational institutions for part of their youth. The vast bulk graduate from high school and well over half are proceeding to post-secondary levels. Yet, schools are also receiving the brunt of unprecedented criticism. Go to any bookstore and you will see manifestos for saving our schools, rescuing our children, all written in dramatic, crisis-language. Why has this paradox emerged? The reason is that the very act of serving unparalleled numbers of people for longer periods of their lives creates a diffused "**disenchantment.**" We use disenchantment in Max Weber's sense: education loses its "magical" quality to command traditional deference. Schooling may have become a "motherhood" item that everyone supports in the abstract, but it has lost its time-honoured association with elite rituals, aristocratic cultures, and pageantry. The caps and gowns, the great halls, and Latin-inscribed coats of arms as depicted in *Harry Potter* films have largely disappeared. They have been replaced by rationalized bureaucracies that merely promise access to labour markets for individuals and hopes of wealth creation to elites. More families are school-savvy and have high expectations for what education should be. Ask not what you can do for your school, but what your school can do for you.

Yet, this disenchantment should not cloud a sunnier accomplishment: school systems now offer extraordinary opportunities for more and more individuals. They have extended literacy to even the poorest segments of the globe. Almost all forms of corporal punishment are thankfully gone from the classroom. Unprecedented numbers of youth and adults are flooding universities to learn advanced forms of biology, business, nursing, or sociology. Few people are reminiscing for bygone eras in which schooling was a privilege for the tiny elite. Today, such an idea provokes a sense of outrage, and is rightly seen to deny basic rights. Schooling may now be demystified, yet we cannot manage without it.

Conclusion

Schools are both ever-changing organizations and rather inert institutions. Because they are ultimately regulated by government bodies, public schools must respond to many political initiatives, and reforms in one direction can trigger reactions in the opposite direction. Yet, as loosely coupled bureaucracies, they have the organizational capacity to buffer their core practices from external influences. While reform can often be transient, powerful forces are slowly transforming Canadian education. Likely directions include more expansion of higher education, some continuation of class disparities in attainment, an ongoing rationalization of curriculum, and a further weakening of schools' singular socializing impact on students. These trends pose a central paradox: as schools become more deeply institutionalized into the fabric of society, they are subject to an unprecedented barrage of criticism. People's greater familiarity with schooling generates higher expectations and erodes the ability of education to command traditional deference. Yet this "disenchantment" should not obscure the unparalleled opportunities that schools now offer to individuals.

Questions for Critical Thought

1. Go to a good local bookstore and find the section on schooling. Take note of some of the titles you find, especially those that comment on social change, quality of education, school reform, and the like. Based on these titles, reflect on the hurricane imagery with which we began this chapter.
2. Which "likely direction" for Canadian education did we leave out that would have been prominent on your own list?
3. What would it take to stop credential inflation? Is this change plausible?

Suggested Readings

Alexander, Karl, Sarah Pitcock, and Matthew Boulay, eds. 2016. *The Summer Slide: What We Know and Can Do about Summer Learning Loss*. New York: Teachers College Press. This state-of-the-art volume ties together themes about inequality, achievement, and school effects versus family influences.

Grabb, Edward, Jeffrey Reitz, and Monica Hwang, eds. 2017. *Social Inequality in Canada: Dimensions of Disadvantage*, 6th edn. Toronto: Oxford University Press. This book is for anyone wishing a comprehensive examination of trends in social inequality in this country.

Kirst, Michael, and Mitchell Stevens, eds. 2015. *Remaking College: The Changing Ecology of Higher Education*. Stanford, CA: Stanford University Press. This book is an ambitious attempt to chart the dynamism of today's higher education.

Web Links

Future of Education
www.futureofeducation.com
This website is devoted to the "future of education" and is dedicated to "charting the future of teaching and learning in a networked world."

Imaginative Education Research Group
www.ierg.net
The Imaginative Education Research Group hosts a site featuring "new theories, principles, and practical techniques for making education more effective."

Glossary

Abella image A conception of racial and ethnic inequality that is sharply dichotomized between whites and visible minorities, so-named after the report on employment equity by Canadian Judge Rosalie Abella.

charter school When a government body funds an independent school in exchange for offering a special theme or meeting various performance indicators.

class struggle A contest for power or rewards between social classes, often the capitalists/ownership class versus the working/labouring class.

collective effervescence A momentary state in which social interaction creates an intense shared experience in which people deepen their emotional attachments and mutual awareness of each other; it can provide emotional fuel for forms of collective action, identity formation, and group solidarity; see also *interaction rituals*.

correspondence principle Bowles and Gintis's term for the tendency of schools to be stratified and shaped according to needs of capitalist workplaces.

credential inflation A reciprocal process in which labour market competition continually encourages individuals to acquire educational certificates, degrees, or diplomas, and in which employers continually require higher credential levels.

Critical Pedagogy An educational style encouraging learners to critically question what they are learning, why they are learning it, and how they are learning it; a form of progressive education designed to raise consciousness of injustices and inequalities.

cultural capital Pierre Bourdieu's term for the tendency for prestigious forms of culture to be rewarded by institutions such as schools.

curricular block A formal division of learning activities into discrete and sequenced subjects and into instruction days and hours per year, schedules, timetables, and grade levels.

disenchantment Weber's term for an unintended consequence of rationalization; when societies create an intellectual environment in which virtually anything is explained by scientific analysis or calculation, they are less likely to view institutions in spiritual, magical, or aesthetic ways.

emotional entrainment A state produced by intimate social interaction in which people's moods and rhythms feed off of each other and become synched.

hidden curriculum Beyond schools' overt content, the school rules, procedures, structures, and covert norms that can shape students.

human capital theory When schooling serves as an investment that enhances productive skills and generates wealth.

individualism A belief in the importance and virtue of self-development, self-reliance, and personal independence.

in loco parentis When teachers can legitimately wield a parent-like authority over their students.

interaction rituals Patterned social interactions that create emotional energy and a sense of group membership; can range from the informal to the highly formal, as in a religious ceremony.

isomorphism From new institutional theory, the notion that organizations increasingly resemble one another over time in order to appear legitimate.

knowledge economy When economic innovation is increasingly driven by the production of knowledge, and where knowledge becomes an asset on par with land, productive capital, and manual labour power.

legal-rational authority A term from Weber's typology, in which institutions derive their legitimacy from a contractual understanding of legal rules, rights, and obligations.

legitimation When an institution or individual is granted a widely recognized authority.

linguistic codes Basil Bernstein's contention that members of social classes speak in subtly different ways, and that schools largely reward only the speech patterns of the middle class.

logic of institutionalization Institutions (e.g., schools, prisons) develop their own logics, their own vision and values, that shape member activity and also influence how others outside the institution react to it; institutions may have multiple logics (universities stress learning, research, and community engagement, as examples).

loose coupling From new institutional theory, a form of organization in which formal structures are weakly connected to technical processes. In schools, this takes the form of strongly regulating teacher and curricular certification, but then weakly monitoring classroom instruction.

magnet school Refers to public schools that have specialized programs designed to recruit students with particular interests (e.g., science or sports). The specialized programs act as a magnet to attract students.

modernization A process of societal evolution toward a more developed, more democratic, and more economically affluent society.

professionalization The process by which an occupation attempts to raise its standing.

The creation of formal educational credentials is a typical component of this process.

professional jurisdiction A term from the sociology of professions to understand battles among occupational groups to claim authority over a task area.

progressive education A pedagogical movement associated with John Dewey and often contrasted to traditional philosophies of schooling, it emphasizes student-centred learning, less structured curricula, and critical thinking.

rationalization One of Weber's core concepts, referring to a process in which elements of social life are subject to impersonal and efficiency-seeking calculation.

ruling class ideology The ideas of the ruling class that justify the power and privilege that they possess.

schooled society When formal schooling becomes a focal institution, and becomes a central force in individual lives, knowledge production, and all economic processes.

seasonal learning design A research technique that measures student characteristics near the beginning and near the end of the school year. These designs attempt to isolate the impact of summer vacation, and thereby distinguish school effects from other influences on students.

semi-monopoly Some professions, through government legislation, tightly control professional membership (e.g., physicians). They have a monopoly on the professional designation. Teachers have a semi-monopoly since within the provincial public sector tight legislation controls who can be a teacher, whereas in private or independent schools, teachers do not require the same legislated credential.

semi-professional When occupations possess some of the traits that distinguish the "classic" professionals such as doctors and lawyers, but also lack the same levels of autonomy, self-regulation, and authority.

social capital When strong norms of trust and reciprocity allow groups to achieve various goals.

social mobility The ability of individuals to move up (or down) in a society conceived as a finely gradated hierarchy.

socio-economic gradient A statistical analysis of educational attainment in which students' socio-economic backgrounds are seen to influence their school success.

status groups Ranked groups formed through cultural processes that are relatively autonomous from economic and political processes.

stratification A conception of inequality as a hierarchical ladder with finely gradated degrees, as opposed to a "class" conception of inequality as large, antagonistic clusters or groups.

streaming A highly structured form of ability grouping that directs students into distinct educational paths.

subculture When groups assume identities and values that are distinct from the mainstream.

traditional authority A term from Weber's typology, in which institutions derive their legitimacy from a belief in the sanctity of tradition.

vertical mosaic John Porter's theory of inequality as consisting of a series of ranked ethnic groups, as delineated in his 1965 book, *The Vertical Mosaic*.

voluntary and involuntary minorities John Ogbu's distinction between racial minorities whose incorporation in a society stems from forcible conquest versus those that stem from immigration.

world culture A term used by John Meyer and his colleagues to describe the formation of international bodies and their norms in the post–Second World War era. Often associated with world polity; a growing communality of cultural orientations across societies.

References

Chapter 1

Albanese, Patrizia. 2016. *Children in Canada Today*, 2nd edn. Toronto: Oxford University Press.

Baer, Douglas. 2004. "Educational Credentials and the Changing Occupational Structure," in J. Curtis, E. Grabb, and N. Guppy, eds, *Social Inequality in Canada*, 4th edn. Toronto: Pearson/Prentice-Hall, 115–30.

Bell, Daniel. 1973. *The Coming of Post-Industrial Society: A Venture in Social Forecasting.* New York: Basic Books.

Bibby, R. 2011. *Beyond the Gods & Back: Religion's Demise and Rise and Why It Matters.* Lethbridge: Project Canada Books.

Buckley, K.A.H., and M.C. Urquhart. 1965. *Historical Statistics of Canada.* Toronto: Macmillan.

Clement, Wallace, and John Myles. 1994. *Relations of Ruling: Class and Gender in Postindustrial Societies.* Montreal and Kingston: McGill-Queen's University Press.

Department of Finance. 2014. *Jobs Report: The State of the Canadian Labour Market.* Ottawa: Government of Canada, Department of Finance Cat. No.: F1-23/3-2014E

Doman, Glenn, and Janet Doman. 2005. *How to Multiply Your Baby's Intelligence Garden.* City Park: Square One Publishers.

Fortin, Nicole, David A. Green, Thomas Lemieux, Kevin Milligan, and W. Craig Riddell. 2012. "Canadian Inequality: Recent Developments and Policy Options," *Canadian Public Policy* 38, 2: 121–46.

Hall, Peter, and Michèl Lamont. 2012. *Social Resilience in the Neo-Liberal Era.* London: Cambridge University Press.

Hersch, Patricia. 1998. *A Tribe Apart: A Journey into the Heart of American Adolescence.* New York: Ballantine Books.

Holt, Emmett. 1894. *The Care and Feeding of Children: A Catechism for the Use of Mothers and Children's Nurses.* New York: D. Appleton and Company.

Inglehart, Ronald. 1995. "Changing Values, Economic Development, and Political Change," *International Social Science Journal* 145: 379–403.

McDiarmid, Garnet, and David Pratt. 1971. *Teaching Prejudice: A Content Analysis of Social Studies Textbooks Authorized for Use in Ontario.* Toronto: Ontario Institute for Studies in Education.

Royal Commission on the Status of Women. 1970. *Report.* Ottawa.

Spock, Benjamin. 1976 [1946]. *Baby and Child Care.* New York: Pocket Books.

Tomaskovic-Devey, D., and K.H. Lin. 2011. "Income Dynamics, Economic Rents, and the Financialization of the U.S. Economy," *American Sociological Review* 76, 4: 538–59.

Wall, Glenda. 2010. "Mother's Experiences with Intensive Parenting and Brain Development Discourse," *Women's Studies International Forum* 33, 3: 253–63.

Chapter 2

Drori, Gili, John Meyer, Francisco Ramirez, and Evan Schofer. 2003. *Science in the Modern World Polity: Institutionalization and Globalization.* Stanford, CA: Stanford University Press.

Durkheim, Émile. 1951 [1897]. *Suicide: A Study in Sociology.* Glencoe, IL: Free Press.

———. 1956 [1922]. *Education and Sociology.* Glencoe, IL: Free Press.

———. 1961 [1925]. *Moral Education: A Study in the Theory and Application of the Sociology of Education.* New York: Free Press.

———. 1964 [1901]. *The Rules of Sociological Method*, 2nd edn. New York: Free Press.

———. 1977 [1938]. *The Evolution of Educational Thought.* Boston: Routledge & Kegan Paul.

Gupta, Asha. 2015. "Caste, Class, and Quality at the Indian Institutes of Technology." *International Higher Education.* DOI: https://doi.org/10.6017/ihe.2008.53.8048

Marx, Karl. 1967 [1867]. *Capital: A Critique of Political Economy.* New York: International Publishers.

———, and Friedrich Engels. 1969 [1848]. "The Communist Manifesto," in *Karl Marx and Frederick Engels, Selected Works.* Moscow: Progress Publishers.

Ritzer, George. 2000. *The McDonaldization of Society.* Thousand Oaks, CA: Pine Forge Press.

Thomas, W.I., and D.S. Thomas. 1928. *The Child in America: Behavior Problems and Programs.* New York: Knopf.

Weber, Max. 1946. *From Max Weber: Essays in Sociology*, H. Gerth and C.W. Mills, eds. New York: Oxford University Press.

Chapter 3

Anyon, Jean. 1980. "Social Class and the Hidden Curriculum of Work," *Journal of Education* 162, 1.

Apple, Michael. 2004. *Ideology and Curriculum*, 3rd edn. London: Routledge.

Becker, Gary. 1975 [1964]. *Human Capital*, 2nd edn. New York: Columbia University Press.

Bennett deMarrais, Kathleen, and Margaret LeCompte. 1998. *The Way Schools Work: A Sociological Analysis of Education*, 3rd edn. White Plains, NY: Longman.

Bernstein, Basil. 1975. *Class, Codes, and Control*. London: Routledge & Kegan Paul.

Bourdieu, Pierre, and Jean Claude Passeron. 1990 [1977]. *Reproduction in Education, Society, and Culture*, 2nd edn. London: Sage.

Bowles, Samuel, and Herbert Gintis. 1976. *Schooling in Capitalist America: Educational Reform and the Contradictions of Economic Life*. New York: Basic Books.

———. 2002. "Schooling in Capitalist America Revisited," *Sociology of Education* 75, 2: 1–18.

Breuing, Mary. 2011. "Problematizing Critical Pedagogy," *International Journal of Critical Pedagogy* 3, 3: 2–23.

Brown, David K. 2001. "The Social Sources of Education Credentialism," *Sociology of Education* (Extra Issue): 19–34.

Coleman, James S. 1988. "Social Capital in the Creation of Human Capital," *American Journal of Sociology* 94, Supplement: 95–120.

Collins, Randall. 1979. *The Credential Society: An Historical Sociology of Education and Stratification*. New York: Academic Press.

———. 2004. *Interaction Ritual Chains*. Princeton NJ: Princeton University Press.

Davis, Kingsley, and Wilbert Moore. 1945. "Some Principles of Stratification," *American Sociological Review* 10, 2: 242–9.

Dreeben, Robert. 1968. *On What Is Learned in School*. Reading, MA: Addison-Wesley.

Erickson, Bonnie. 1996. "Culture, Class and Connections," *American Journal of Sociology* 102, 1: 217–51.

Garnett, Bruce, Neil Guppy, and Gerry Veenstra. 2005. "Careers Open to Talent: Educational Credentials, Cultural Knowledge, and Skilled Employment," Working Paper, Anthropology and Sociology, University of British Columbia.

Goldin, Claudia, and Lawrence F. Katz. 2008. *The Race between Education and Technology*. Cambridge MA: Harvard University Press.

Heckman, James. 2008. "Schools, Skills, and Synapses." Discussion Paper Series. Dublin: UCD Geary Institute.

Hyman, Herbert H. 1953. "The Value Systems of Different Classes: A Social Psychological Contribution to the Analysis of Stratification," in Reinhard Bendix and Seymour Martin Lipset, eds, *Class, Status and Power: A Reader in Social Stratification*. New York: Free Press, 426–43.

Kay, Fiona, and John Hagan. 1998. "Raising the Bar: The Gender Stratification of Law-Firm Capital," *American Sociological Review* 63, 5: 728–43.

Kincheloe, Joe L. 2007. "Critical Pedagogy and the Knowledge Wars of the Twenty-First Century: Evolution for Survival," in Peter McLaren and Joe Kincheloe, eds, *Critical Pedagogy: Where Are We Now?* New York: Peter Lang, 9–42.

Kiviat, Barbara. 2012. "The Big Jobs Myth: American Workers Aren't Ready for American Jobs," *Atlantic Monthly*, 25 July.

Lareau, Annette. 2011. *Unequal Childhoods: Class, Race, and Family Life*, 2nd edn. Berkeley: University of California Press.

McMahon, Tamsin. 2012. "The Myth of the 'Skills Mismatch,' " *Maclean's*, 26 July.

McMullin, Julie. 2010. *Understanding Social Inequality: Intersections of Class, Age, Gender, Ethnicity, and Race in Canada*, 2nd edn. Toronto: Oxford University Press.

Meyer, John W., John Boli, George Thomas, and Francisco Ramirez. 1997. "World Society and the Nation-State," *American Journal of Sociology* 103, 1: 144–81.

Paulle, Bowen. 2013. *Toxic Schools: High-Poverty Education in New York and Amsterdam*. Chicago, IL: University of Chicago Press.

Putnam, Robert. 2000. *Bowling Alone: The Collapse and Revival of American Community*. New York: Simon & Schuster.

Schultz, T. 1961. "Investment in Human Capital," *American Economic Review* 51 (Mar.): 1–17.

TRC. 2015. *Honouring the Truth, Reconciling for the Future*. Truth and Reconciliation Commission of Canada. Available at http://nctr.ca/assets/reports/Final%20Reports/Executive_Summary_English_Web.pdf.

Weeden, Kim A., and David B. Grusky. 2011. "Inequality and Market Failure." Unpublished manuscript, Department of Sociology, Cornell University.

Chapter 4

Ariès, Philippe. 1962 [1960]. *Centuries of Childhood: A Social History of Family Life*. New York: Vintage Books.

Barman, Jean.1995. "The Emergence of Educational Structures in

Nineteenth-Century British Columbia," in J. Barman, N. Sutherland, and J.D. Wilson, eds, *Children, Teachers, and Schools in the History of British Columbia*. Calgary: Detselig, 15–36.

Bibby, R., and Donald Posterski.1992. *Teen Trends: A Nation in Motion*. Toronto: Stoddart.

Bowles, Samuel, and Herbert Gintis. 1976. *Schooling in Capitalist America: Educational Reform and the Contradictions of Economic Life*. New York: Basic Books.

Brint, Steven. 1998. *Schools and Societies*. Thousand Oaks, CA: Pine Forge Press.

Butlin, George. 1999. "Determinants of Post-Secondary Participation," *Education Quarterly Review* 5, 3: 9–35.

Connolly, J., V. Hatchette, and L. McMaster. 1999. "Academic Achievement in Early Adolescence: Do School Attitudes Make a Difference?" *Education Quarterly Review* 6, 1: 20–9.

Curtis, Bruce D. 1988. *Building the Educational State: Canada West*. Philadelphia: Falmer Press.

Egan, Kieran. 1997. *The Educated Mind: How Cognitive Tools Shape Our Understanding*. Chicago: University of Chicago Press.

———. 2008. *The Future of Education: Reimagining Our Schools from the Ground Up*. New Haven, CT: Yale University Press.

Frank, David John, and Jay Gabler. 2006. *Reconstructing the University: Worldwide Shifts in Academia in the 20th Century*. Stanford, CA: Stanford University Press.

Freeman, Richard. 1976. *The Overeducated American*. New York: Academic Press.

Gidney, R.D., and W.P.J. Millar. 2012. *How Schools Worked: Public Education in English Canada, 1990–1940*. Montreal and Kingston: McGill-Queen's University Press.

Guppy, Neil, and Scott Davies. 1998. *Education in Canada: Recent Trends and Future Challenges*. Ottawa: Statistics Canada.

Katz, Michael B., and Paul H. Mattingly, eds. 1975. *Education and Social Change: Themes from Ontario's Past*. New York: New York University Press.

Leacy, F.H., ed. 1983. *Historical Statistics of Canada*, 2nd edn. Ottawa: Minister Responsible for Statistics Canada and the Social Science Federation of Canada. Cat. no. 11–516E. (Series W68).

Manzer, Ronald. 1994. *Public Schools and Political Ideas: Canadian Public Educational Policy in Historical Perspective*. Toronto: University of Toronto Press.

O'Day, Rosemary. 1982. *Education and Society, 1500–1800: The Social Foundations of Education in Early Modern Britain*. London: Longman.

Prentice, Alison. 1977. *The School Promoters: Education and Social Class in Mid-Nineteenth Century Upper Canada*. Toronto: McClelland & Stewart.

Ravanera, Zenaida, Fernando Rajulton, and Thomas Burch. 2004. "Patterns of Age Variability in Life Course Transitions," *Canadian Journal of Sociology* 29, 4: 527–42.

Rubenson, Kjell, Richard Desjardins, and Ee-Seul Yoon. 2007. *Adult Learning in Canada: A Comparative Perspective. Results from the Adult Literacy and Life Skills Survey*. Statistics Canada. Cat. no. 89-552-MIE–Number 17.

Schofer, Evan, and John Meyer. 2005. "The Worldwide Expansion of Higher Education in the Twentieth Century," *American Sociological Review* 70: 898–920.

Statistics Canada. 2002. *A Report on Adult Education and Training in Canada: Learning a Living*. Ottawa: Census Profile. Cat. no. 81-586-XIE.

Thomas, Eleanor M. 2009. "Canadian Nine-Year-Olds at School." Ottawa: Statistics Canada, Cat. no. 89-599-M.

Chapter 5

Anisef, Paul, Paul Axelrod, E. Baichman-Anisef, C. James, and T. Turrittin. 2000. *Opportunity and Uncertainty: Life Course Experiences of the Class of '73*. Toronto: University of Toronto Press.

Arum, Richard, and Josipa Roksa. 2011. *Academically Adrift: Limited Learning on College Campuses*. Chicago: University of Chicago Press.

Aurini, Janice, and Linda Quirke. 2011. "Does Market Competition Encourage Strategic Action in the Private Education Sector?" *Canadian Journal of Sociology* 36, 2: 173–97.

Baer, Douglas. 2004. "Educational Credentials and the Changing Occupational Structure," in J. Curtis, E. Grabb, and N. Guppy, eds, *Social Inequality in Canada*, 4th edn. Toronto: Pearson/Prentice-Hall, 115–30.

Brint, Steven. 2017. *Schools and Societies*, 3rd edn. Stanford: Stanford University Press.

———, and Jerome Karabel. 1989. *The Diverted Dream: Community Colleges and the Promise of Educational Opportunity in America, 1900–1985*. New York: Oxford University Press.

Butlin, George. 2001. "Bachelor's Graduates Who Pursue Further Post-Secondary

Education," *Education Quarterly Review* 7, 2: 22–41.

Canadian Council on Learning. 2007. "Survey of Canadian Attitudes toward Learning: Canadian Attitudes toward Tutoring." Available at www.ccl-cca.ca/ CCL/Reports/SCAL/2007Archive/ SCALStructuredTutoring.htm.

Chmielewski, Anna. 2015. "Tracking and Streaming in an International Perspective: An Interview with Dr. Anna K. Chmielewski." AJE Forum. Available at http://www.ajeforum.com/ tracking-and-streaming-in-an-international-perspective-an-interview-with-dr-anna-k-chmielewski-by-will-smith/.

Clanfield, David, and George Martell, eds. 2014. *Restacking the Deck: Streaming by Class, Race and Gender in Ontario Schools.* Toronto: Canadian Centre for Policy Alternatives.

Clifton, Rodney. 2015. "Some Other Truths about Indian Residential Schools." *C2C Journal.* Available at http://www.c2cjournal .ca/2015/05/some-other-truths-about-indian-residential-schools/.

Collins, Randall. 2002. "Credential Inflation and the Future of Universities," in Steven Brint, ed., *The Future of the City of Intellect: The Changing American University.* Stanford, CA: Stanford University Press, 23–46.

Côté, James, and Anton Allahar. 2007. *Ivory Tower Blues: A University System in Crisis.* Toronto: University of Toronto Press.

———. 2011. *Lowering Higher Education: The Rise of Corporate Universities and the Fall of Liberal Education* Toronto: University of Toronto Press.

Davies, Scott, and Janice Aurini. 2011. "Exploring School Choice in Canada: Who Chooses What and Why?" *Canadian Public Policy* 37, 4: 459–77.

———, and Neil Guppy. 1997. "Fields of Study, College Selectivity, and Student Inequalities in Higher Education," *Social Forces* 75, 4: 1417–38.

———, and David Zarifa. 2012. "The Stratification of Universities: Horizontal Inequality in Canada and the United States," *Research in Social Stratification and Mobility* 30, 2: 143–58.

Dennison, John, ed. 1995. *Challenge and Opportunity: Canada's Community Colleges at the Crossroads.* Vancouver: University of British Columbia Press.

Desjardins, Pierre-David. 2009. *Nouvelles regulations en education et strategies de postionnement des etablissements scolaires dans deux espaces urbains au Canada.* Doctoral dissertation, Université de Montreal.

Dierkes, Julian. 2013. "The Insecurity Industry: Supplementary Education in Japan," in Janice Aurini, Scott Davies, and Julian Dierkes, eds, *Out of the Shadows: The Global Intensification of Supplementary Education.* Bingley, UK: Emerald.

Duncan, Greg J., and Richard J. Murnane, eds. 2011. *Whither Opportunity? Rising Inequality, Schools, and Children's Life Chances.* New York: Russell Sage.

Dougherty, Kevin. 2002. "The Evolving Role of the Community College: Policy Issues and Research Questions," in John Smart and William Tierney, eds, *Higher Education: Handbook of Theory and Research.* Amsterdam: Kluwer.

Frenette, Marc, and Kristyn Frank. 2016. *Earnings of Postsecondary Graduates by Detailed Field of Study.* Ottawa: Statistics Canada.

Gardner, Howard. 1999. *Intelligence Reframed: Multiple Intelligences for the 21st Century.* New York: Basic Books.

Gerber, Theodore P., and Sin Yi Cheung. 2008. "Horizontal Stratification in Postsecondary Education: Forms, Explanations, and Implications," *Annual Review of Sociology* 34: 299–318.

Gidney, R.D., and W.P.J. Millar. 2012. *How Schools Worked: Public Education in English Canada, 1990–1940.* Montreal and Kingston: McGill-Queen's University Press.

Goldthorpe, John, and Michelle Jackson. 2008. "Education-Based Meritocracy: The Barriers to Its Realization," in A. Lareau and D. Conley, eds, *Social Class: How Does It Work?* New York: Russell Sage.

Guppy, Neil, Edward Grabb, and Clayton Mollica. 2013. "The Canada Foundation for Innovation, Sociology of Knowledge, and the Re-engineering of the University," *Canadian Public Policy* 39, 1: 1–19.

Hällsten, Martin. 2011. "The Structure of Educational Decision Making and Consequences for Inequality: A Swedish Test Case," *American Journal of Sociology* 116, 3: 806–54.

Hoxby, Caroline. 2009. "The Changing Selectivity of American Colleges," *Journal of Economic Perspectives* 23, 4: 95–118.

Kerckhoff, Alan. 2002. "Education and Social Stratification Process in Comparative Perspective," in Jeanne H. Ballantine and Joan Z. Spade, eds, *Schools and Society: A*

Sociological Approach to Education, 2nd edn. Toronto: Thomson Wadsworth, 432–48.

Krahn, Harvey. 2017. "Choose Your Parents Carefully: Social Class, Post-Secondary Education, and Occupational Outcomes," in E. Grabb, J Reitz, and M. Hwang, eds, *Social Inequality in Canada: Dimensions of Disadvantage*. Toronto: Oxford University Press, 90–103.

———, and Alison Taylor. 2007. "'Streaming' in the 10th Grade in Four Canadian Provinces in 2000," *Education Matters* 4, 2. Statistics Canada: Ottawa (e-journal).

Labaree, David. 2010. *Someone Has to Fail: The Zero-Sum Game of Public Schooling*. Cambridge, MA: Harvard University Press.

Lehmann, Wolfgang. 2000. "Is Germany's Dual System Still a Model for Canadian Youth Apprenticeship Initiatives?" *Canadian Public Policy* 26, 2: 225–40.

———. 2007. *Choosing to Labour? School-Work Transitions and Social Class*. Montreal and Kingston: McGill-Queen's University Press.

Lucas, Samuel. 2001. "Effectively Maintained Inequality: Education Transitions, Track Mobility, and Social Background Effects," *American Journal of Sociology* 106, 6: 1642–90.

Montt, Guillermo. 2011. "Cross-National Differences in Educational Achievement Inequality," *Sociology of Education* 84: 49–68.

Mullen, Ann, Kimberly Goyette, and Joseph Soares. 2003. "Who Goes to Graduate School? Social and Academic Correlates of Educational Continuation after College," *Sociology of Education* 76, 2: 143–69.

Pike, Robert. 1970. *Who Doesn't Get to University and Why*. Ottawa: Association of Universities and Colleges of Canada.

Porter, John, Marion Porter, and Bernard Blishen. 1982. *Stations and Callings: Making It through the School System*. Toronto: Methuen.

Powell, Arthur, Eleanor Farrar, and David Cohen. 1985. *The Shopping Mall High School: Winners and Losers in the Educational Marketplace*. Boston: Houghton Mifflin.

Raftery, Adrian E., and Michael Hout. 1993. "Maximally Maintained Inequality: Expansion, Reform, and Opportunity in Irish Education, 1921–75," *Sociology of Education* 66, 1: 41–62.

Richardson, John G. 2006. "Institutional Sequences, Pedagogical Reach, and Comparative Educational Systems," in David P. Baker and Alexander Wiseman, eds, *The Impact of Comparative Educational Research on Institutional Theory*. Oxford, UK: Elsevier, 27–48.

Ross, Alec. 2016. *The Industries of the Future*. New York: Simon and Schuster.

Shavit, Yossi, Richard Arum, and Adam Gamoran. 2007. *Stratification in Higher Education: A Comparative Study*. Stanford, CA: Stanford University Press.

Sizer, Theodore. 2004. *The Red Pencil: Convictions from Experiences in Education*. New Haven, CT: Yale University Press.

Stevens, Mitchell. 2007. *Creating a Class: College Admissions and the Education of Elites*. Cambridge, MA: Harvard University Press.

Sweet, Robert, and Anthony Roberts. 2009. "Tutoring as an Investment in Children's Education." Unpublished manuscript. Lakehead University.

Turner, Ralph. 1960. "Sponsored and Contest Mobility and the School System," *American Sociological Review* 25: 855–67.

Tyack, David. 1974. *The One Best System: A History of American Urban Education*. Cambridge, MA: Harvard University Press.

Walters, David. 2004. "Recycling: The Economic Implications of Obtaining Additional Post-secondary Credentials at Lower or Equivalent Levels." *Canadian Review of Sociology* 40(4): 463–80.

Walters, David, Jerry White, and Paul Maxim. 2004. "Does Post-Secondary Education Benefit Aboriginal Canadians? An Examination of Earnings and Employment Outcomes for Recent Aboriginal Graduates," *Canadian Public Policy* 30, 3: 283–301.

Wanner, Richard A. 1999. "Expansion and Ascription: Trends in Educational Opportunity in Canada, 1920–1994," *Canadian Review of Sociology and Anthropology* 36, 3: 409–43.

———. 2000. "A Matter of Degree(s): Trends in Occupational Status Returns to Educational Credentials in Canada," *Canadian Review of Sociology and Anthropology* 37, 3: 313–43.

Willis, Paul. 1977. *Learning to Labour: How Working Class Kids Get Working Class Jobs*. Westmead, UK: Saxon House.

Willms, J. Douglas. 2004. *Variation in Literacy Skills among Canadian Provinces: Findings from the OECD PISA*. Ottawa: Statistics Canada. Cat. no. 81–595–MIE2004012.

Wolf, Alison. 2002. *Does Education Matter? Myths about Education and Economic Growth*. New York: Penguin.

Chapter 6

Alexander, Karl L., Doris R. Entwisle, and Linda Steffel Olson. 2007. "Lasting Consequences of the Summer Learning Gap," *American Sociological Review*, 72, 2: 167–80.

Anderson, Elijah. 1999. *Code of the Street: Decency, Violence, and the Moral Life of the Inner City*. New York: Norton.

Aneshensel, Carol S. 2009. "Toward Explaining Mental Health Disparities." *Journal of Health and Social Behaviour* 50, 4: 344–77.

Baker, David, and Gerald LeTendre. 2005. *National Differences, Global Similarities: World Culture and the Future of Schooling*. Stanford, CA: Stanford University Press.

Baron, Stephen. 1989. "The Canadian West Coast Punk Subculture: A Field Study," *Canadian Journal of Sociology* 14, 1: 289–316.

Beattie, I.R. 2002. "Are All 'Adolescent Econometricians' Created Equal? Racial, Class, and Gender Differences in College Enrollment," *Sociology of Education* 75, 1: 19–43.

Borman, Geoffrey, Michael Goetz, and Maritza Dowling. 2009. "Halting the Summer Achievement Slide: A Randomized Field Trial of the KindergARTen Summer Camp." *Journal of Education for Students Placed at Risk* 14, 2: 133–47.

Bourdieu, Pierre. 1988. *Homo Academicus*. Stanford, CA: Stanford University Press.

———, and Jean Claude Passeron. 1990 [1977]. *Reproduction in Education, Society, and Culture*, 2nd edn. London: Sage.

Brint, Steven. 1998. *Schools and Societies*. Thousand Oaks, CA: Pine Forge Press.

Burkam, David, Douglas Ready, Valerie Lee, and Laura LoGerfo. 2004. "Social Class Differences in Summer Learning between Kindergarten and First Grade: Model Specification and Estimation," *Sociology of Education* 77: 1–31.

Calarco, Jessica McCrory. 2011. " 'I Need Help!' Social Class and Children's Help-Seeking in Elementary School," *American Sociological Review* 76, 6: 862–82.

Coleman, James S., E. Campbell, J. Hobson, J. McPartland, A. Mood, F. Weinfall, and R. York. 1966. *Equality of Educational Opportunity*. Washington: Government Printing Office.

Curtis, Bruce D., David Livingstone, and Harry Smaller. 1992. *Stacking the Deck: The Streaming of Working-Class Kids in Ontario Schools*. Toronto: Our Schools/Our Selves Educational Foundation.

Davies, Scott. 1994. "Class Dismissed? Student Opposition in Ontario," *Canadian Review of Sociology and Anthropology* 31, 4: 421–44.

———. 1995. "Reproduction and Resistance in Canadian High Schools: An Empirical Examination of the Willis Thesis," *British Journal of Sociology* 46, 4: 662–87.

———, and Janice Aurini. 2013. "Summer Learning Inequality in Ontario," *Canadian Public Policy* 39, 2: 287–307.

———, and Neil Guppy. 1997. "Fields of Study, College Selectivity, and Student Inequalities in Higher Education," *Social Forces* 75, 4: 1417–38.

———, and Magdalena Janus. 2009. *A Systematic: Review of Longitudinal Effects of Family SES on Child Cognition and Social-Emotional Well-Being*. Ottawa: HRSDC.

———, Vicky Maldonado, and Darren Cyr. 2017. "Changing Times, Stubborn Inequalities: Explaining Socio-economic Stratification in Canadian Schooling," in E. Grabb, J. Reitz, and M. Hwang, eds, *Social Inequality in Canada: Dimensions of Disadvantage*. Toronto: Oxford University Press, 113–25.

DiMaggio, Paul. 1982. "Cultural Capital and School Success: The Impact of Status Culture Participation on the Grades of US High School Students," *American Sociological Review* 47: 189–201.

Downey, Doug, and Shana Pribesh. 2004. "When Race Matters: Teachers' Evaluations of Students' Classroom Behavior," *Sociology of Education* 77: 267–82.

Dumais, Susan A. 2006. "Elementary School Students' Extracurricular Activities: The Effects of Participation on Achievement and Teachers' Evaluations," *Sociological Spectrum* 26, 2: 117–47.

Duncan, Greg J., and Katherine Magnuson. 2011. "The Nature and Impact of Early Achievement Skills, Attention Skills, and Behavioral Problems," in Greg J. Duncan and Richard J. Murnane, eds, *Whither Opportunity? Rising Inequality, Schools, and Children's Life Chances*. New York: Russell Sage.

Duncan, Greg J., and Richard J. Murnane (eds). 2011. *Whither Opportunity? Rising Inequality, Schools, and Children's Life Chances*. New York: Russell Sage.

Farkas, George, and Jacob Hibel. 2008. "Being Unready for School: Factors Affecting Risk and Resilience," in Alan Booth and Ann C. Crouter, eds, *Disparities in School Readiness: How Families Contribute to Transitions into School*. New York: Taylor and Francis.

Finnie, Ross, and Dejan Pavlic. 2013. "Background Characteristics and Patterns of Access to Postsecondary Education in Ontario: Evidence from Longitudinal Tax Data." Working Paper. Toronto: Higher Education Quality Council of Ontario.

Flynn, James R. 2016. "No Population Is Frozen in Time: The Sociology of Intelligence," *Psychological Inquiry* 27, 3: 205–9.

Fortin, Nicole, David A. Green, Thomas Lemieux, Kevin Milligan, and W. Craig Riddell. 2012. "Canadian Inequality: Recent Developments and Policy Options," *Canadian Public Policy* 38, 2: 121–46.

Frenette, Marc. 2005. *Is Post-Secondary Access More Equitable in Canada or the United States?* Ottawa: Statistics Canada, Analytical Studies Branch. Cat. no. 11F0019MIE No. 244.

———. 2007. "Why Are Youth from Lower-Income Families Less Likely to Attend University? Evidence from Academic Abilities, Parental Influences, and Financial Constraints." Ottawa, ON: Statistics Canada, Analytical Studies Branch Research Paper Series 11F0019MIE.

Gamoran, Adam. 2001. "American Schooling and Educational Inequality: A Forecast for the 21st Century," *Sociology of Education* (extra issue): 135–53.

Goldthorpe, John, and Michelle Jackson. 2008. "Education-Based Meritocracy: The Barriers to Its Realization," in A. Lareau and D. Donley, eds, *Social Class: How Does It Work?* New York: Russell Sage.

Guppy, Neil, and Bruce Arai. 1993. "Educational Attainment in Canada: Differences by Sex, Class, and Ethnicity," in J. Curtis et al., eds, *Social Inequality in Canada*, 2nd edn. Toronto: Prentice-Hall, 214–32.

Heckman, James. 2008. "Schools, Skills, and Synapses." Discussion Paper Series. Dublin: UCD Geary Institute.

Herrnstein, R., and C. Murray. 1994. *The Bell Curve: Intelligence and Class Structure in American Life*. New York: Free Press.

Hertzman C. 2000. "The Case for an Early Child Development Strategy for Canada," *ISUMA* Autumn: 11–18.

———, and John Frank. 2006. "Biological Pathways Linking the Social Environment, Development and Health," in J. Heymann et al., eds, *Healthier Societies: From Analysis to Action*. Oxford, UK: Oxford University Press.

———, A. Siddiqi, E. Hertzman, L. Irwin, Z. Vaghri, T.A.J Houweling, et al. 2010. "Tackling Inequality: Get Them While They're Young," *British Medical Journal* 340, 7742: 346–48.

Heyneman, S., and W. Loxley. 1983. "The Effect of Primary-School Quality on Academic Achievement across Twenty-Nine High- and Low-Income Countries," *American Journal of Sociology* 88: 1162–94.

Hou, Feng, and Aneta Bonikowska. 2016. *Educational and Labour Market Outcomes of Childhood Immigrants by Admission Class*. Analytical Studies Branch Research Paper Series 2016377e, Ottawa: Statistics Canada.

Janus, M., and E. Duku. 2007. "The School Entry Gap: Socioeconomic, Family, and Health Factors Associated with Children's School Readiness to Learn," *Early Education and Development* 18, 3: 375–403.

Johnson, David. 2005. *Signposts of Success: Interpreting Ontario's Elementary School Test Scores*. Toronto: C.D. Howe Institute.

Karen, David. 2002. "Changes in Access to Higher Education in the United States: 1980–1992," *Sociology of Education* 75, 3: 191–210.

Kingston, Paul. 2001. "The Unfulfilled Promise of Cultural Capital Theory," *Sociology of Education* (extra issue): 88–99.

Lareau, Annette. 2000. *Home Advantage: Social Class and Parental Intervention in Elementary Education*, 2nd edn. Lanham, MD: Rowman and Littlefield.

———. 2011. *Unequal Childhoods: Class, Race, and Family Life*, 2nd edn. Berkeley: University of California Press.

———, and Elliot Weininger. 2003. "Cultural Capital in Educational Research: A Critical Assessment," *Theory and Society* 32: 567–606.

Lehmann, Wolfgang. 2009a. "Class Encounters: Working-Class Students at University," in C. Levine-Rasky, ed., *Canadian Perspectives on the Sociology of Education*. Toronto: Oxford University Press, 197–212.

———. 2009b. "Becoming Middle Class: How Working-Class University Students Draw and Transgress Moral Class Boundaries," *Sociology* 43: 631–47.

———. 2014. "Habitus Transformation and Hidden Injuries: Successful Working-Class University Students," *Sociology of Education* 87, 1: 1–15.

Ma, Xin. 2001. "Stability of Socio-Economic Gaps in Mathematics and Science Achievement among Canadian Schools," *Canadian Journal of Education* 26, 1: 97–118.

Macleod, Jay. 1987. *Ain't No Makin' It: Aspirations and Attainment in a Low-Income Neighbourhood*. Boulder, CO: Westview Press.

Malette, Nicole, and Neil Guppy. 2017. "Educational Attainment among Canadians: Open and Competitive or Closed and Sponsored," in E. Grabb, J. Reitz, and M. Hwang, eds, *Social Inequality in Canada: Dimensions of Disadvantage*. Toronto: Oxford University Press, 104–12.

Milne, Emily. 2016. "I have the worst fears of teachers: moments of inclusion and exclusion in family/school relationships among Indigenous families in Southern Ontario." *Canadian Review of Sociology* 53(3): 270–89.

Morgan, Paul, Michelle Frisco, George Farkas, and Jacob Hibel. 2010. "A Propensity Score Matching Analysis of the Effects of Special Education Services," *Journal of Special Education* 43: 236–54.

Mullen, Ann, Kimberly Goyette, and Joseph Soares. 2003. "Who Goes to Graduate School? Social and Academic Correlates of Educational Continuation after College," *Sociology of Education* 76, 2: 143–69.

Nakhaie, Reza, Robert Silverman, and Teresa LaGrange. 2000. "Self-Control and Resistance to School," *Canadian Review of Sociology and Anthropology* 37, 4: 443–61.

Oreopoulos, Philip. 2005. *Canadian Compulsory School Laws and Their Impact on Educational Attainment and Future Earnings*. Ottawa: Statistics Canada, Analytical Studies Branch Research Paper Series. Cat. no. 11F0019MIE–No. 251.

———. 2007. "Do Dropouts Drop Out Too Soon? Wealth, Health, and Happiness from Compulsory Schooling," *Journal of Public Economics* 91: 2213–29.

Paulle, Bowen. 2013. *Toxic Schools: High-Poverty Education in New York and Amsterdam*. Chicago, IL: University of Chicago Press.

Quirke, Linda. 2006. "'Keeping Young Minds Sharp': Children's Cognitive Stimulation and the Rise of Parenting Magazines, 1959–2003," *Canadian Review of Sociology* 43, 4.

Reardon, Sean F. 2011. "The Widening Academic Achievement Gap between the Rich and the Poor," in Greg J. Duncan and Richard J. Murnane, eds, *Whither Opportunity? Rising Inequality, Schools, and Children's Life Chances*. New York: Russell Sage, 91–116.

Ridley, Matt. 2003. *Nature via Nurture: Genes, Experience, and What Makes Us Human*. New York: HarperCollins.

Rist, Ray. 1970. "Student Social Class and Teacher Expectations: The Self-Fulfilling Prophecy in Ghetto Education," *Harvard Educational Review* 40, 3: 411–51.

Rosenbaum, James E. 1976. *Making Inequality: The Hidden Curriculum of High School Tracking*. New York: Wiley.

Ross, David P., and Paul Roberts. 1999. *Income and Child Well-Being: A New Perspective on the Poverty Debate*. Ottawa: Canadian Council on Social Development.

Shavit, Yossi, Richard Arum, and Adam Gamoran. 2007. *Stratification in Higher Education: A Comparative Study*. Stanford, CA: Stanford University Press.

Statistics Canada. 2010. *Measuring Up: Canadian Results of the OECD PISA Study: The Performance of Canada's Youth in Reading, Mathematics and Science*, Ottawa: Statistics Canada, 81-590-x.

Tanner, Julian. 1990. "Reluctant Rebels: A Case Study of Edmonton High School Drop-outs," *Canadian Review of Anthropology and Sociology* 27, 1: 74–94.

———, Harvey Krahn, and Timothy Hartnagel. 1995. *Fractured Transitions from School to Work: Revisiting the Dropout Problem*. Toronto: Oxford University Press.

Trefler, Daniel. 2009. "Looking Backward: How Childhood Experiences Impact a Nation's Wealth," Rotman Lifelong Learning Lectures. Toronto: University of Toronto.

Turcotte, Martin. 2011. "Intergenerational Education Mobility: University Completion in Relation to Parents' Education Level," *Canadian Social Trends* 92: 37–43. Statistics Canada Catalogue no. 11-008.

Weinstein, Rhona S. 2002. *Reaching Higher: The Power of Expectations in Schooling*. Cambridge, MA: Harvard University Press.

Willis, Paul. 1977. *Learning to Labour: How Working Class Kids Get Working Class Jobs*. Westmead, UK: Saxon House.

Willms, J. Douglas. 2002. *Vulnerable Children*. Edmonton: University of Alberta Press.

———. 2004. *Variation in Literacy Skills among Canadian Provinces: Findings from the OECD PISA*. Ottawa: Statistics Canada. Cat. no. 81–595–MIE2004012.

Wineburg, Samuel. 1987. "The Self-Fulfillment of the Self-Fulfilling Prophecy," *Educational Researcher* 16: 28–44.

Wolf, Alison. 2002. *Does Education Matter? Myths about Education and Economic Growth*. New York: Penguin.

Worswick, Christopher. 2004. "Adaptation and Inequality: Children of Immigrants in Canadian Schools," *Canadian Journal of Economics* 37, 1: 53–77.

Chapter 7

Abbott, Andrew. 2001. *Chaos of Disciplines*. Chicago: University of Chicago Press.

Abella, Rosalie Silberman. 1984. *Equality in Employment: A Royal Commission Report*. Ottawa: Government of Canada.

Association of Universities and Colleges of Canada (AUCC). 2002, 2011. *Trends in Higher Education*. Ottawa.

Boyd, Monica. 2002. "Educational Attainments of Immigrant Offspring: Success or Segmented Assimilation?" *International Migration Review* 36, 4: 1037–60.

——. 2008. "Variations in Socioeconomic Outcomes of Second Generation Young Adult," *Canadian Diversity* 6, 2: 20–4.

Breen, Richard, Ruud Luijkx, Walter Müller, and Reinhard Pollak. 2009. "Long-term Trends in Educational Inequality in Europe: Class Inequalities and Gender Differences." *European Sociological Review*, 26(1): 31–48.

Brym, Robert J., with Bonnie Fox. 1989. *From Culture to Power: The Sociology of English Canada*. Toronto: Oxford University Press.

Charles, Maria. 2011. "What Gender Is Science?" *Contexts* 10(2): 22–28.

——, and David Grusky. 2004. *Occupational Ghettos: The Worldwide Segregation of Women and Men*. Stanford, CA: Stanford University Press.

——, and Karen Bradley. 2009. "Indulging Our Gendered Selves? Sex Segregation by Field of Study in 44 Countries," *American Journal of Sociology* 114, 4: 924–76.

Cook, Ramsay, and Wendy Mitchinson, eds. 1976. *The Proper Sphere: Woman's Place in Canadian Society*. Toronto: Oxford University Press, 167.

Davies, Scott, and Janice Aurini. 2011. "Exploring School Choice in Canada: Who Chooses What and Why?" *Canadian Public Policy* 37, 4: 459–77.

Davies, Scott, and Neil Guppy. 1998. "Race and Canadian Education," in Vic Satzewich, ed., *Racism and Social Inequality in Canada: Concepts, Controversies and Strategies for Resistance*. Toronto: Thompson Publishing.

Demerath, Peter. 2009. *Producing Success: The Culture of Personal Advancement in an American High School*. Chicago, IL: University Of Chicago Press

Deroche, Christina. 2012. "Re-Examining Labelling Theory within a Therapeutic Context." Unpublished manuscript, McMaster University.

DiPrete, Thomas A., and Claudia Buchmann. 2013. *The Rise of Women: The Growing Gender Gap in Education and What It Means for American Schools*. New York: Russell Sage Foundation.

Fetner, Tina, Athena Elafros, Sandra Bortolin, and Coralee Drechsler. 2012. "Safe Spaces: Gay-Straight Alliances in High Schools," *Canadian Review of Sociology* 49, 2: 188–207.

Frideres, James, and Rene Gadacz. 2011. *Aboriginal Peoples in Canada*, 9th edn. Toronto: Pearson Education Canada

Frohard-Dourlent, Hélène. 2016. " 'I Don't Care What's Under Your Clothes': The Discursive Positioning of Educators Working with Trans and Gender-Nonconforming Students," *Sex Education* 16, 1: 63–76.

Gaskell, Jane. 2009. "Feminist Approaches to the Sociology of Education in Canada," in C. Levine-Rasky, ed., *Canadian Perspectives on the Sociology of Education*. Toronto: Oxford University Press.

Guppy, Neil, and Nicole Luongo. 2015. "The Rise and Stall of the Gender Equity Revolution in Canada," *Canadian Review of Sociology* 52, 3: 241–65.

Hao, Lingxin, and Yingyi Ma. 2011. "Immigrant Youth in Postsecondary Education," in Cynthia Garía Coll and Amy Marks, eds, *The Immigrant Paradox in Children and Adolescents: Is Becoming American a Developmental Risk?* Washington, D.C.: American Psychological Association, 275–96.

Ho, Anita. 2004. "To Be Labelled, or Not to Be Labelled: That Is the Question," *British Journal of Learning Disabilities* 32: 86–92.

Hoff Somers, Christina. 2015. *The War Against Boys*. New York: Simon and Schuster.

Hou, Feng, and Aneta Bonikowska. 2016. *Educational and Labour Market Outcomes of Childhood Immigrants by Admission Class*. Analytical Studies Branch Research Paper Series 2016377e, Ottawa: Statistics Canada.

Kao, Grace, and Jennifer S. Thompson. 2003. "Racial and Ethnic Stratification in Educational Achievement and Attainment," *Annual Review of Sociology* 29: 417–42.

Labaree, David. 2010. *Someone Has to Fail: The Zero-Sum Game of Public Schooling*. Cambridge, MA: Harvard University Press.

Leicht, Kevin T. 2016. "Getting Serious about Inequality," *Sociological Quarterly* 57, 2: 211–31.

Liodakis, Nikolaos. 2002. *The Vertical Mosaic Within: Class, Gender and Nativity within Ethnicity*. Doctoral dissertation, McMaster University.

Looker, E. Dianne. 2011. "Implications of the 'Gender Gap' in Academic Achievement: A Think Piece." Ottawa: Human Resources and Skills Development Canada.

Malette, Nicole. 2017. "Forms of Fighting: A Micro-Social Analysis of Bullying and In-School Violence." *Canadian Journal of Education* 40(1): 1–29.

McAndrew, Marie. 2013. *Fragile Majorities and Education: Belgium, Catalonia, Northern Ireland, and Quebec*. Montreal and Kingston: McGill-Queens University Press.

Milligan, Kevin, and Michael Baker. 2016. "Boy-Girl Differences in Parental Time Investments: Evidence from Three Countries," *Journal of Human Capital* 10, 4: 399–441.

Milne, Emily. 2016. "I have the worst fears of teachers: moments of inclusion and exclusion in family/school relationships among Indigenous families in Southern Ontario." *Canadian Review of Sociology* 53(3): 270–89.

Ogmundson, Richard. 2002. "The Canadian Case: Cornucopia of Neglected Research Opportunities," *American Sociologist* 33, 1: 55–78.

Porter, John. 1965. *The Vertical Mosaic: An Analysis of Social Class and Power in Canada*. Toronto: University of Toronto Press.

Rothon, Catherine, Anthony Heath, and Laurence Lessard-Phillips. 2009. "The Educational Attainments of the 'Second Generation': A Comparative Study of Britain, Canada, and the United States." *Teachers College Record* 111, 6 (June): 1404–43.

Royal Commission on the Status of Women. 1970. *Report*. Ottawa.

Shavit, Yossi, Richard Arum, and Adam Gamoran. 2007. Stratification in Higher Education: *A Comparative Study*. Stanford CA: Stanford University Press.

Sirin, Selcuk R. 2005. "Socioeconomic Status and Academic Achievement: A Meta-Analytic Review of Research." *Review of Educational Research* 75, 3: 417–53.

Smagorinsky, Peter. 2011. "Confessions of a Mad Professor: An Autoethnographic Consideration of Neuroatypicality, Extranormativity, and Education." *Teacher's College Record* 113: 1701–32.

St. Germain, Gerry, and Lillian Dyck. 2011. *Reforming First Nations Education: From Crisis to Hope*. Ottawa: Report of the Standing Senate Committee on Aboriginal Peoples.

Sweet, Robert, Paul Anisef, Rob Brown, Maria Adamuti-Trache, and Gillian Parekh. 2012. "Special Needs Students and Transitions to Post-Secondary Education." Toronto: Higher Education Quality Council of Ontario.

Thiessen, Victor. 2009. "The Pursuit of Postsecondary Education: A Comparison of First Nations, African, Asian and European Canadian Youth," *Canadian Labour Market and Skills Researcher Network*. Working Paper Number 19.

Turcotte, Martin. 2011. "Intergenerational Education Mobility: University Completion in Relation to Parents' Education Level," *Canadian Social Trends* 92: 37–43. Statistics Canada Catalogue no. 11-008.

Tyack, David, and Larry Cuban. 1995. *Tinkering Toward Utopia: A Century of Public School Reform*. Cambridge, MA: Harvard University Press.

Villar, Paz, and Neil Guppy. 2016. "Gendered Science: Representational Dynamics in British Columbia Science Textbooks over the Last Half Century," *Canadian Journal of Education* 38, 3: 1–14.

Wolf, Alison. 2013. *The XX Factor: How the Rise of Working Women Has Created a Far Less Equal World*. Toronto: Allen Lane.

Chapter 8

Aurini, Janice. 2012. "Petterns of Tight and Loose Coupling in a Competitive Marketplace: The Case of Learning Center Franchises," *Sociology of Education* 85, 4: 373–87.

———, and Linda Quirke. 2011. "Does Market Competition Encourage Strategic Action in the Private Education Sector?" *Canadian Journal of Sociology* 36, 2: 173–97.

Axelrod, Paul. 1997. *The Promise of Schooling: Education in Canada, 1800–1914*. Toronto: University of Toronto Press.

Bosetti, Lynn, and Diane Gereluk. 2016. *Understanding School Choice in Canada*. Toronto: University of Toronto Press.

Chubb, John and Terry Moe. 1990. *Politics, Markets, and America's Schools*. Washington, DC: Brookings Institute.

Collins, Randall. 1979. *The Credential Society: An Historical Sociology of Education and Stratification*. New York: Academic Press.

Davies, Scott. 2002. "The Paradox of Progressive Education: A Frame Analysis," *Sociology of Education* 75, 4: 269–86.

——, and Janice Aurini. 2011. "Exploring School Choice in Canada: Who Chooses What and Why?" *Canadian Public Policy* 37, 4: 459–77.

——, and Janice Aurini. 2013. "Summer Learning Inequality in Ontario," *Canadian Public Policy* 39, 2: 287–307.

Desjardins, Pierre-David. 2009. *Nouvelles regulations en education et strategies de postionnement des etablissements scolaires dans deux espaces urbains au Canada.* Doctoral dissertation, Université de Montreal.

Edwards, Carolyn Pope. 2002. "Three Approaches from Europe: Waldorf, Montessori, and Reggio Emilia," *Early Childhood Research and Practice* 4(1). Available at http://digital-commons.unl.edu/famconfacpub/2/.

Gidney, R.D., and W.P.J. Millar. 2012. *How Schools Worked: Public Education in English Canada, 1990-1940.* Montreal and Kingston: McGill-Queen's University Press.

Guppy, Neil, Robert Crocker, Scott Davies, Claire LaPointe, and Larry Sackney. 2005. "Parent and Teacher Views on Education: A Policymaker's Guide." Kelowna: Society for the Advancement of Excellence In Education.

Hurn, Christopher. 1993. *The Limits and Possibilities of Schooling: An Introduction to the Sociology of Education.* Boston: Allyn and Bacon.

Illich, Ivan. 1970. *Deschooling Society.* New York: Harper and Row.

Johnson, David. 2009. *Ontario's Best Public Schools, 2005/6 to 2007/8: An Update to Signposts of Success.* Toronto: C.D. Howe Institute. Available at www.cdhowe.org/pdf/ebrief_85.pdf.

Lee, Valerie, and Susanna Loeb. 2000. "School Size in Chicago Elementary Schools: Effects on Teachers' Attitudes and Students' Achievement." *American Educational Research Journal* 37: 3–31.

Meyer, John W. 1977. "The Effects of Education as an Institution," *American Journal of Sociology* 83: 55–77.

——, David H. Kamens, and Aaron Benavot. 1992. *School Knowledge for the Masses.* Washington, DC: Falmer Press.

——, and Francisco Ramirez. 2000. "The World Institutionalization of Education," in Jurgen Schriewer, ed., *Discourse Formation in Comparative Education.* Frankfurt: Peter Lang.

Meyer, Heinz-Dieter, and Aaron Benavot (eds). 2013. *PISA, Power and Policy.* Oxford UK: Symposium Books.

Nuhoglu, Hasret. 2013. "Evaluation of Alternative Preschool Education Programs Regarding Their Perspectives on Teaching Science and Nature," *Mevlana International Journal of Education* 3, 4: 236–49.

Pizarro Milian, Roger, and Scott Davies. 2017. "Open Competition or Balkanized Coexistence? The Effects of Market Segments on Toronto Private Schools," *Education Policy Analysis Archives.*

Prentice, Alison. 1977. *The School Promoters: Education and Social Class in Mid-Nineteenth Century Upper Canada.* Toronto: McClelland & Stewart.

Quirke, Linda. 2013. "Rogue Resistance: Sidestepping Isomorphic Pressures in a Patchy Institutional Field," *Organization Studies* 34, 11: 1675–99.

Ruch, Richard S. 2001. *Higher Ed, Inc.: The Rise of the For-Profit University.* Baltimore: Johns Hopkins University Press.

Swidler, Ann. 1979. *Organizations without Authority: Dilemmas of Social Control in Free Schools.* Cambridge, MA: Harvard University Press.

Tyack, David, and Larry Cuban. 1995. *Tinkering Toward Utopia: A Century of Public School Reform.* Cambridge, MA: Harvard University Press.

Chapter 9

Apple, Michael. 1997. *Official Knowledge: Democratic Education in a Conservative Age.* London: Routledge.

Baker, David, and Gerald LeTendre. 2005. *National Differences, Global Similarities: World Culture and the Future of Schooling.* Stanford, CA: Stanford University Press.

Barakett, Joyce, and M. Ayaz Naseem. 2009. "Multicultural, Anti-Racist Education and Black Feminist Pedagogy," in Cynthia Levine-Rasky, ed., *Canadian Perspectives on the Sociology of Education.* Toronto: Oxford University Press.

Benavot, Aaron, Y.K. Cha, D. Kamens, J. Meyer, and S.Y. Wong. 1991. "Knowledge for the Masses: World Models and National Curricula, 1920-1986," *American Sociological Review* 56, 1: 85–100.

Bernstein, Basil. 1975. *Class, Codes, and Control.* London: Routledge & Kegan Paul.

Binder, Amy J. 2002. *Contentious Curricula: Afrocentrism and Creationism in American Public Schools.* Princeton, NJ: Princeton University Press.

Bourdieu, Pierre, and Jean Claude Passeron. 1990 [1977]. *Reproduction in Education, Society, and Culture,* 2nd edn. London: Sage.

Bowles, Samuel and Herbert Gintis. 2002. "Schooling in Capitalist America Revisited," *Sociology of Education* 75, 2: 1–18.

Brint, Steven, Mary F. Contreras, and Michael T. Matthews. 2001. "Socialization Messages in Primary Schools. An Organizational Analysis," *Sociology of Education* 74: 157–80.

———, Mark Riddle, Lori Turk-Bicakci, and Charles S. Levy. 2005. "From the Liberal to the Practical Arts in American Colleges and Universities: Organizational Analysis and Curricular Change," *Journal of Higher Education* 76: 2.

Bromley, Patricia, John W. Meyer, and Francisco O. Ramirez. 2011. "Student Centrism in Social Science Textbooks: 1970-2005," *Social Forces* 90, 2: 1–24.

Carr, David. 2003. *Making Sense of Education: An Introduction to the Philosophy and Theory of Education and Teaching*. London: Routledge Falmer.

Carter, Prudence. 2006. *Keepin' It Real: School Success Beyond Black and White*. New York: Oxford University Press.

Cuban, Larry. 2001. *Oversold and Underused: Computers in the Classroom*. Cambridge MA: Harvard University Press.

Davies, Scott. 2002. "The Paradox of Progressive Education: A Frame Analysis," *Sociology of Education* 75, 4: 269–86.

———, and Neil Guppy. 1997. "Globalization and Educational Reforms in Anglo-American Democracies," *Comparative Education Review* 41, 4: 435–59.

Dei, George Sefa. 2009. "Theorizing Anti-Racism," in Cynthia Levine-Rasky, ed. *Canadian Perspectives on the Sociology of Education*. Toronto: Oxford University Press.

DiMaggio, Paul. 1982. "Cultural Capital and School Success: The Impact of Status Culture Participation on the Grades of US High School Students," *American Sociological Review* 47: 189–201.

Downey, Douglas B., Paul T. von Hippel, and Melanie Hughes. 2008. "Are 'Failing' Schools Really Failing? Using Seasonal Comparison to Evaluate School Effectiveness." *Sociology of Education* 81(3): 242–70.

Dreeben, Robert. 1968. *On What Is Learned in School*. Reading, MA: Addison-Wesley.

Egan, Kieran. 1997. *The Educated Mind: How Cognitive Tools Shape Our Understanding*. Chicago: University of Chicago Press.

Farkas, George, Robert Grobe, Daniel Sheehan, and Y. Shuan. 1990. "Cultural Resources and School Success: Gender, Ethnicity, and Poverty Groups within an Urban School District," *American Sociological Review* 55: 127–42.

Garnett, Bruce, Neil Guppy, and Gerry Veenstra. 2005. "Careers Open to Talent: Educational Credentials, Cultural Knowledge, and Skilled Employment," Working Paper, Anthropology and Sociology, University of British Columbia.

Guppy, Neil, and K. Lyon. 2012. "Multiculturalism, Education Practices and Colonial Legacies: The Case of Canada," in C. Kassimeris and M. Vryonides, eds, *The Politics of Education: Challenging Multiculturalism*. New York: Routledge, 114–135.

Heckman, James. 2008. "Schools, Skills, and Synapses." Discussion Paper Series. Dublin: UCD Geary Institute.

Kamens, David, John Meyer, and Aaron Benavot. 1996. "Worldwide Patterns in Academic Secondary Education Curricula," *Comparative Education Review* 40 (May): 116–38.

Khan, Shamus Rahman. 2012. *Privilege: The Making of an Adolescent Elite at St. Paul's School*. Princeton NJ: Princeton University Press.

Kingston, Paul. 2001. "The Unfulfilled Promise of Cultural Capital Theory," *Sociology of Education* (extra issue): 88–99.

———, Ryan Hubbard, Brent Lapp, Paul Schroeder, and Julia Wilson. 2003. "Why Education Matters," *Sociology of Education* 76, 1: 53–70.

Kliebard, Herbert. 1995. *The Struggle for the American Curriculum, 1893-1958*, 2nd edn. New York: Routledge.

Kraatz, Matthew S., and Edward J. Zajac. 1996. "Exploring the Limits of the New Institutionalism: The Causes and Consequences of Illegitimate Organizational Change." *American Sociological Review* 61(5): 812–36.

Labaree, David. 2010. *Someone Has to Fail: The Zero-Sum Game of Public Schooling*. Cambridge, MA: Harvard University Press.

Lehmann, Wolfgang. 2000. "Is Germany's Dual System Still a Model for Canadian Youth Apprenticeship Initiatives?" *Canadian Public Policy* 26, 2: 225–40.

McAndrew, Marie. 2013. *Fragile Majorities and Education*. Montreal: McGill-Queen's University Press.

McDiarmid, Garnet, and David Pratt. 1971. *Teaching Prejudice: A Content Analysis of Social Studies Textbooks Authorized for Use in Ontario*. Toronto: Ontario Institute for Studies in Education.

McEneaney, Elizabeth H., and John Meyer. 2000. "The Content of the Curriculum: An Institutional Perspective," in Maureen T. Hallinan, ed., *Handbook of the Sociology of Education*. New York: Kluwer/Plenum.

Meyer, John W. 1977. "The Effects of Education as an Institution," *American Journal of Sociology* 83: 55–77.

Molnar, Alex. 2001. *Giving Kids the Business: The Commercialization of America's Schools*. Boulder, CO: Westview Press.

Nagy, Philip. 2000. "The Three Roles of Assessment: Gatekeeping, Accountability, and Instructional Diagnosis," *Canadian Journal of Education* 25, 4: 262–79.

Ontario Ministry of Education. 2008. *Reaching Every Student*. http://www.edu.gov.on.ca/eng/document/energize/energize.pdf

Paulle, Bowen. 2013. *Toxic Schools: High-Poverty Education in New York and Amsterdam*. Chicago, IL: University of Chicago Press.

Polster, Claire. 2009. "The Privatization of Higher Education in Canada," in C. Levine-Rasky, ed., *Canadian Perspectives on the Sociology of Education*. Toronto: Oxford University Press.

Ramirez, Francisco O. 2004. "The Rationalization of Universities." Unpublished manuscript, Stanford CA: Stanford University.

Rezai-Rashti, Goli M. 2009. "The Neo-Liberal Assault on Ontario's Secondary Schools," in C. Levine-Rasky, ed., *Canadian Perspectives on the Sociology of Education*. Toronto: Oxford University Press.

Rizk, Jessica. 2017. *The 21st Century Classroom: Technology as a Transformative Tool in Educational Routines, Rules, and Rituals*. Doctoral dissertation, McMaster University.

Snyder, Benson. 1971. *The Hidden Curriculum*. New York: Alfred A. Knopf.

Ungerleider, Charles. 2003. *Failing Our Kids: How We Are Ruining Our Public Schools*. Toronto: McClelland & Stewart.

Veenstra, Gerry. 2015. "Class Position and Musical Tastes: A Sing-off between the Cultural Omnivorism and Bourdieusian Homology Frameworks," *Canadian Review of Sociology* 52, 2: 134–59.

Villar, Paz, and Neil Guppy. 2016. "Gendered Science: Representational Dynamics in British Columbia Science Textbooks over the Last Half Century," *Canadian Journal of Education* 38, 3: 1–14.

Young, Michael F.D. 1998. *The Curriculum of the Future: From the "New Sociology of Education" to a Critical Theory of Learning*. London: Falmer Press.

Chapter 10

Abbott, Andrew. 1988. *The System of Professions: An Essay on the Division of Expert Labor*. Chicago: University of Chicago Press.

Aurini, Janice. 2012. "Patterns of Tight and Loose Coupling in a Competitive Marketplace: The Case of Learning Center Franchises," *Sociology of Education* 85, 4: 373-87.

Brint, Steven. 1994. *In an Age of Experts*. Princeton, NJ: Princeton University Press.

———. 2017. *Schools and Societies*, 3rd edn. Stanford, CA: Stanford University Press.

———, Mary F. Contreras, and Michael T. Matthews. 2001. "Socialization Messages in Primary Schools: An Organizational Analysis," *Sociology of Education* 74: 157–80.

Canadian Teachers Federation. 2001. "June 2001 Workplace Survey." Available at www.ctffce.ca/en/press/2001/Workplc.htm.

Chetty, Raj, John N. Friedman, and Jonah E. Rockoff. 2014. "Measuring the Impacts of Teachers II: Teacher Value-Added and Student Outcomes in Adulthood," *American Economic Review* 104, 9: 2633–79.

Clifton, R.A., and L.W. Roberts. 1993. *Authority in Classrooms*. Toronto: Prentice-Hall.

Crocker, R., and D. Dibbon. 2008. *Teacher Education in Canada: A Baseline Study*. Kelowna, BC: Society for the Advancement of Excellence in Education (SAEE).

Cummings, William. 2003. *The Institutions of Education: A Comparative Study of Educational Development in the Six Core Nations*. Oxford: Symposium Books, Oxford Studies in Comparative Education.

Dooner, A.M., D. Mandzuk, P. Obendoerfer, G. Babiuk, G. Cerqueira-Vassallo, V. Force, M. Vermette, and D. Roy. 2009. "Examining Student Engagement and Authority: Developing Learning Relationships in the Middle Grades," *Middle School Journal*. 41(4): 28–35.

Etzioni, Amitai, ed. 1969. *The Semi-Professions and Their Organization*. New York: Free Press.

Fullan, Michael. 2011. *Choosing the Wrong Drivers*. Available at http://edsource.org/wp-content/uploads/Fullan-Wrong-Drivers1.pdf.

Gidney, R.D., and W.P.J. Millar. 2012. *How Schools Worked: Public Education in English Canada, 1990–1940*. Montreal and Kingston: McGill-Queen's University Press.

Glazer, Joshua. 2008. "Educational Professionalism: An Inside-Out View," *American Journal of Education* 114, 2: 169–89.

Guppy, Neil, and Scott Davies. 1996. "Labour Market Dynamics in the Teaching Profession," *Education Quarterly Review* 3, 4: 33–43.

——, Robert Crocker, Scott Davies, Claire LaPointe, and Larry Sackney. 2005. "Parent and Teacher Views on Education: A Policymaker's Guide." Kelowna: Society for the Advancement of Excellence in Education.

Hart, Doug, and Arlo Kempf. 2015. *Public Attitudes towards Education in Ontario 2015: The Nineteenth OISE Survey of Educational Issues.* Available at http://www.oise.utoronto.ca/oise/UserFiles/Media/Media_Relations/Final_Report_-_19th_OISE_Survey_on_Educational_Issues_2015.pdf.

Ingersoll, Richard. 2003. *Who Controls Teachers' Work: Power and Accountability in America's Schools.* Cambridge, MA: Harvard University Press.

King, Alan J.C., and Marjorie J. Peart. 1992. *Teachers in Canada: Their Work and Quality of Life.* Ottawa: Canadian Teachers Federation.

Krahn, Harvey, Graham Lowe, and Karen Hughes. 2015. *Work, Industry, and Canadian Society,* 7th edn. Toronto: Thomson Nelson.

Leicht, Kevin, and Mary L. Fennell. 2001. *Professional Work: A Sociological Approach.* Malden, MA: Blackwell.

Lortie, Dan C. 1975. *Schoolteacher: A Sociological Study.* Chicago: University of Chicago Press.

Mehta, Jal. 2013. *The Allure of Order: High Hopes, Dashed Expectations, and the Troubled Quest to Remake American Schooling.* New York: Oxford University Press.

Meyer, John W. 1977. "The Effects of Education as an Institution," *American Journal of Sociology* 83: 55–77.

Paulle, Bowen. 2013. *Toxic Schools: High-Poverty Education in New York and Amsterdam.* Chicago, IL: University of Chicago Press.

Prentice, Alison. 1977. *The School Promoters: Education and Social Class in Mid-Nineteenth Century Upper Canada.* Toronto: McClelland & Stewart.

Quirke, Linda, and Janice Aurini. 2016. "Teachers Can't Be Made, They're Born: Teaching and Professionalism in Ontario's Private Education Sector," in Wolfgang Lehmann, ed., *Education and Society: Canadian Perspectives.* Toronto: Oxford University Press, 172–89.

Raham, Helen, Neil Guppy, Susan Phillips, and Kristen Bennett. 2008. *Beyond the Grid: A Canadian Look at the Terrain of Teacher Compensation.* Kelowna: Society for the Advancement of Excellence in Education.

Rivkin, S.G., E. Hanushek, and J.F. Kain. 2005. "Teachers, Schools, and Academic Achievement," *Econometrica* 73, 2: 417–58.

Rowan, Brian. 2002. "The New Institutionalism and the Study of Education: Changing Ideas for Changing Times." Paper presented at the conference "Advancing the Institutional Research Agenda in Education," Albany: State University of New York.

Scott, W. Richard, and John W. Meyer. 1994. "The Rise of Training Programs in Firms and Agencies," in W. Richard Scott et al., eds, *Institutional Environments and Organizations: Structural Complexity and Individualism.* Thousand Oaks, CA: Sage.

Stevens, Mitchell. 2001. *Kingdom of Children: Culture and Controversy in the Homeschooling Movement.* Princeton, NJ: Princeton University Press.

Van Nuland, Shirley. 2011. "Teacher Education in Canada," *Journal of Education for Teaching* 37, 4: 409–21.

Waller, Willard. 1965 [1932]. *The Sociology of Teaching.* New York: Wiley.

Young, J. 2004. "Systems of Educating Teachers: Case Studies in the Governance of Initial Teacher Education," *Canadian Journal of Educational Administration and Policy* 32.

Chapter 11

Alison, Derek J., Sazid Hasan, and Deani Van Pelt. 2016. *A Diverse Landscape: Independent Schools in Canada.* Vancouver: Fraser Institute. Available at www.fraserinstitute.org/sites/default/files/a-diverse-landscape-independent-schools-in-canada.pdf.

Arum, Richard, and Josipa Roksa. 2011. *Academically Adrift: Limited Learning on College Campuses.* Chicago: University of Chicago Press.

Aurini, Janice. 2008. "Understanding the Private Tutoring Revolution in Canada," *Our Schools/Our Selves* 17, 3: 93–106.

Axelrod, Paul. 1997. *The Promise of Schooling: Education in Canada, 1800–1914.* Toronto: University of Toronto Press.

Basham, Patrick, John Merrifield, and Claudia R. Hepburn. 2007. *Home Schooling: From the Extreme to the Mainstream,* 2nd edn.

Available at www.fraserinstitute.org/
commerce.web/product_files/
Homeschooling.pdf.

Bourdieu, Pierre. 1988. *Homo Academicus*.
Stanford, CA: Stanford University Press.

Brint, Steven, Mary F. Contreras, and Michael
T. Matthews. 2001. "Socialization Messages
in Primary Schools: An Organizational
Analysis," *Sociology of Education* 74: 157–80.

Calear, Alison L., and Helen Christensen.
2009. "Systematic Review of School-Based
Prevention and Early Intervention Programs
for Depression," *Journal of Adolescence* 30: 1–10.

Carter, Prudence. 2006. *Keepin' It Real: School
Success Beyond Black and White*. New York:
Oxford University Press.

Charles, Maria, and Karen Bradley. 2009.
"Indulging Our Gendered Selves? Sex
Segregation by Field of Study in 44
Countries," *American Journal of Sociology*
114, 4: 924–76.

Côté, James, and Anton Allahar. 2011. *Lowering
Higher Education: The Rise of Corporate
Universities and the Fall of Liberal Education*.
Toronto: University of Toronto Press.

Daly, Kerry. 2004. *The Changing Culture of
Parenting*. Ottawa: Vanier Institute for the
Family.

Davey, I. 1978. "The Rhythm of Work and the
Rhythm of School," in N. McDonald and
A. Chaiton, eds, *Egerton Ryerson and His
Times: Essays on the History of Education*.
Toronto: Macmillan.

Davies, Scott. 1999. "From Moral Duty to
Cultural Rights: A Case Study of Political
Framing in Education," *Sociology of
Education* 72, 1: 1–21.

———, and Janice Aurini. 2011. "Exploring School
Choice in Canada: Who Chooses What and
Why?" *Canadian Public Policy* 37, 4: 459–77.

Dei, George Sefa. 2009. "Theorizing Anti-
Racism," in Cynthia Levine-Rasky, ed.
*Canadian Perspectives on the Sociology of
Education*. Toronto: Oxford University Press.

Gidney, R.D., and W.P.J. Millar. 2012. *How
Schools Worked: Public Education in English
Canada, 1990–1940*. Montreal and Kingston:
McGill-Queen's University Press.

Government of Ontario. 1950. *Royal
Commission on Ontario Education*. Toronto.

———. 1968. *Living and Learning: The Report
of the Provincial Committee on Aims and
Objectives of Education in the Schools of
Ontario*. Toronto: Newton.

Gross, Neil, and Ethan Fosse. 2012. "Why Are
Professors Liberal?" *Theory & Society* 41:
127–68.

Guhin, Jeffrey. 2016. "Why Worry about
Evolution? Boundaries, Practices, and Moral
Salience in Sunni and Evangelical High
Schools," *Sociological Theory* 34, 2: 151–74.

Guppy, Neil, and Nicole Luongo. 2015. "The Rise
and Stall of the Gender Equity Revolution in
Canada," *Canadian Review of Sociology* 52,
3: 241–65.

———, and K. Lyon. 2012. "Multiculturalism,
Education Practices and Colonial Legacies:
The Case of Canada" in C. Kassimeris and
M. Vryonides, eds, *The Politics of Education:
Challenging Multiculturalism*. New York:
Routledge: 114–35.

Harrigan, Patrick. 1990. "The Schooling of Boys
and Girls in Canada," *Journal of Social
History* 23, 4: 803–14.

Hart, Doug, and Arlo Kempf. 2015. *Public
Attitudes towards Education in Ontario
2015: The Nineteenth OISE Survey of
Educational Issues*. Available at http://
www.oise.utoronto.ca/oise/UserFiles/Media/
Media_Relations/Final_Report_-_19th_
OISE_Survey_on_Educational_Issues_
2015.pdf.

Hout, Michael. 2012. "Social and Economic
Returns to College Education in the United
States," *Annual Review of Sociology* 38:
379–400.

Jackson, Philip W., Robert E. Boostrom, and
David T. Hansen. 1998. *The Moral Life of
Schools*. San Francisco: John Wiley and Sons.

Kingston, Paul, Ryan Hubbard, Brent Lapp, Paul
Schroeder, and Julia Wilson. 2003. "Why
Education Matters," *Sociology of Education*
76, 1: 53–70.

Labaree, David. 2010. *Someone Has to Fail:
The Zero-Sum Game of Public Schooling*.
Cambridge, MA: Harvard University Press.

Legewie, Joscha, and Thomas DiPrete. 2012.
"School Context and the Gender Gap in
Educational Achievement," *American
Sociological Review* 77, 3: 463–85.

Looker, E. Dianne. 2011. "Implications of the
'Gender Gap' in Academic Achievement: A
Think Piece." Ottawa: Human Resources
and Skills Development Canada.

Lyon, Katherine, and Neil Guppy. 2018.
"Canada: Race and Ethnic Inequalities in
Education" in P. Stevens and G. Dworkin,
eds, *The Palgrave Handbook of Race and
Ethnic Inequalities in Education*, 2nd edn.
London: Palgrave, Macmillan.

Manzer, Ronald. 1994. *Public Schools and
Political Ideas: Canadian Public Educational
Policy in Historical Perspective*. Toronto:
University of Toronto Press.

Meyer, John W. 1977. "The Effects of Education as an Institution," *American Journal of Sociology* 83: 55–77.

Pallas, Aaron. 2000. "The Effects of Schooling on Individual Lives," in Maureen T. Hallinan, ed., *Handbook of the Sociology of Education*. New York: Kluwer/Plenum.

Pizarro Milian, Roger, and Scott Davies. 2017. "Open Competition or Balkanized Coexistence? The Effects of Market Segments on Toronto Private Schools," *Education Policy Analysis Archives*.

Prentice, Alison. 1977. *The School Promoters: Education and Social Class in Mid-Nineteenth Century Upper Canada*. Toronto: McClelland & Stewart.

Quirke, Linda. 2006. "'Keeping Young Minds Sharp': Children's Cognitive Stimulation and the Rise of Parenting Magazines, 1959–2003," *Canadian Review of Sociology* 43, 4: 387–406

Raudenbush, Stephen W., and Robert D. Eschmann. 2015. "Does Schooling Increase or Reduce Social Inequality?" *Annual Review of Sociology* 41: 443–70.

Rosenbaum, D.P., and G.S. Hanson. 1998. "Assessing the Effects of School-Based Drug Education: A Six-Year Multilevel Analysis of Project D.A.R.E.," *Journal of Research in Crime and Delinquency* 35, 4: 381–412.

Sayer, Liana C., Suzanne M. Bianchi, and John P. Robinson. 2004. "Are Parents Investing Less in Children?: Trends in Mothers' and Fathers' Time with Children," *American Journal of Sociology* 110, 1: 1–43.

Steffensmeier, D., E.A. Allan, M.D. Harer, and C. Streifel. 1989. "Age and the Distribution of Crime," *American Journal of Sociology* 94: 803–31.

Tyack, David. 1974. *The One Best System: A History of American Urban Education*. Cambridge, MA: Harvard University Press.

Villar, Paz, and Neil Guppy. 2016. "Gendered Science: Representational Dynamics in British Columbia Science Textbooks over the Last Half Century," *Canadian Journal of Education* 38, 3: 1–14.

Winks, Robin. 2005. *The Blacks in Canada*, 2nd edn. Montreal and Kingston: McGill-Queen's University Press.

Chapter 12

Anderson, Elijah. 1999. *Code of the Street: Decency, Violence, and the Moral Life of the Inner City*. New York: Norton.

Astor, Ron Avi, Rami Benbenishty, and Jose Nuñez Estrada. 2009. "School Violence and Theoretically Atypical Schools: The Principal's Centrality in Orchestrating Safe Schools," *American Educational Research Journal* 46, 2: 423–61.

Becker, Gary. 1975 [1964]. *Human Capital*, 2nd edn. New York: Columbia University Press.

Boyd, Monica. 2002. "Educational Attainments of Immigrant Offspring: Success or Segmented Assimilation?" *International Migration Review* 36, 4: 1037–60.

Carter, Prudence. 2006. *Keepin' It Real: School Success Beyond Black and White*. New York: Oxford University Press.

Clark, Burton. 1962. *Educating the Expert Society*. San Francisco: Chandler.

Clark, Ian, David Trick, and Richard Van Loon. 2011. *Academic Reform: Policy Options for Improving the Quality and Cost-Effectiveness of Undergraduate Education in Ontario*. Kingston: McGill-Queen's University Press.

Cohen, Albert. 1955. *Delinquent Boys: The Culture of the Gang*. Glencoe, IL: Free Press.

Coleman, James S. 1961. *The Adolescent Society: The Social Life of the Teenager and Its Impact on Education*. New York: Free Press.

Collins, Randall. 2008. *Violence*. Princeton NJ: Princeton University Press.

———. 2011. "The Inflation of Bullying: From Fagging to Cyber-Effervescent Scapegoating." Available at http://sociological-eye.blogspot.ca/2011/07/inflation-of-bullying-from-fagging-to.html.

Currie, D., D. Kelly, and S. Pomerantz. 2009. *Girl Power: Girls Reinventing Girlhood*. New York: Peter Lang.

Downes, David. 1966. *The Delinquent Solution*. London: Routledge & Kegan Paul.

Downey, Doug. 2008. "Black/White Differences in School Performance: The Oppositional Culture Explanation," *Annual Review of Sociology* 34: 107–26.

———, and Shana Pribesh. 2004. "When Race Matters: Teachers' Evaluations of Students' Classroom Behavior," *Sociology of Education* 77: 267–82.

Farkas, George. 2003. "Racial Disparities and Discrimination in Education: What Do We Know, How Do We Know It, and What Do We Need to Know?" *Teachers College Record* 105, 6: 1119–46.

Fordham, Signithia, and John U. Ogbu. 1986. "Black Students' School Success: Coping with the Burden of 'Acting White'," *Urban Review* 18, 3: 176–206.

Goyette, Kimberly, and Yu Xie. 1999. "Educational Expectations of Asian American Youths:

Determinants and Ethnic Differences," *Sociology of Education* 71, 1: 24–38.

Hagan, John, and Bill McCarthy. 1987. "Gender, Delinquency, and the Great Depression: A Test of Power-Control Theory," *Canadian Review of Sociology and Anthropology* 24: 153–77.

Hango, Darcy. 2016. "Cyberbulling and CyberStalking among Internet Users aged 15 to 29 in Canada," *Insights on Canadian Society*, Statistics Canada, Catalogue No. 75-006-X.

Harris, Angel. 2011. *Kids Don't Want to Fail: Oppositional Culture and the Black–White Achievement Gap*. Cambridge, MA: Harvard University Press.

Howells, Stephanie. 2012. "In Search of a Culture of Fear: Understanding the Gap between the Perception and Reality of School Dangers." Doctoral dissertation, McMaster University.

Hurn, Christopher. 1993. *The Limits and Possibilities of Schooling: An Introduction to the Sociology of Education*. Boston: Allyn and Bacon.

Ingram, Nicola. 2011. "Within School and beyond the Gate: The Complexities of Being Educationally Successful and Working Class," *Sociology* 45, 2: 287–302.

Karabel, Jerome. 2005. *The Chosen: The Hidden History of Admission and Exclusion at Harvard, Yale, and Princeton*. New York: Houghton Mifflin.

Karen, David, and Robert E. Robinson, eds. 2015. *Sociological Perspectives on Sports*. New York: Routledge.

Lareau, Annette. 2011. *Unequal Childhoods: Class, Race, and Family Life*, 2nd edn. Berkeley: University of California Press.

Lehmann, Wolfgang. 2014. "Habitus Transformation and Hidden Injuries: Successful Working-Class University Students," *Sociology of Education* 87, 1: 1–15.

Lieberson, Stanley. 1961. "A Societal Theory of Race and Ethnic Relations," *American Sociological Review* 26: 92–110.

Malette, Nicole. 2017. "Forms of Fighting: Bullying and Youth Violence in Ontario," *Canadian Journal of Education*, in press.

Miller, Walter. 1958. "Lower Class Culture as a Generating Milieu of Gang Delinquency," *Journal of Social Issues* 14, 3: 5–19.

Milner, Murray, Jr. 2004. *Freaks, Geeks, and Cool Kids: American Teenagers, Schools, and the Culture of Consumption*. New York: Routledge.

Mullen, Ann. 2010. *Degrees of Inequality: Culture, Class, and Gender in American Higher Education*. Baltimore, MD: Johns Hopkins University Press.

Newman, Katherine S., and Cybelle Fox. 2009. "Repeat Tragedy: Rampage Shootings in American High Schools and College Settings, 2002–2008," *American Behavioral Scientist* 52, 9: 1286–308.

Ogbu, John U. 1992. "Understanding Cultural Diversity and Learning," *Educational Researcher* 21, 8: 5–14.

Professor X. 2012. *In the Basement of the Ivory Tower: Confessions of an Accidental Academic*. New York: Viking Books

Riley, Tasha, and Charles Ungerleider. 2012. "Self-Fulfilling Prophecy: How Teachers' Attributions, Expectations, and Stereotypes Influence the Learning Opportunities Afforded Aboriginal Students," *Canadian Journal of Education* 35, 2: 303–33.

Rothon, Catherine, Anthony Heath, and Laurence Lessard-Phillips. 2009. "The Educational Attainments of the 'Second Generation': A Comparative Study of Britain, Canada, and the United States," *Teachers College Record* 111, 6 June: 1404–43.

Seeley, John R., R. Alexander Sim, and Elizabeth Loosley. 1956. *Crestwood Heights: A Study of the Culture of Suburban Life*. Toronto: University of Toronto Press.

Steffensmeier, D., E.A. Allan, M.D. Harer, and C. Streifel. 1989. "Age and the Distribution of Crime," *American Journal of Sociology* 94: 803–31.

Stevens, Mitchell. 2007. *Creating a Class: College Admissions and the Education of Elites*. Cambridge, MA: Harvard University Press.

Stinchcombe, Arthur. 1964. *Rebellion in a High School*. Chicago: Quadrangle Books.

Stuber, Jenny M. 2011. *Inside the College Gates: How Class and Culture Matter in Higher Education*. Lanham, MD: Lexington Books.

Tanner, Julian. 2015. *Teenage Troubles: Youth and Deviance in Canada*, 4th edn. Toronto: Oxford University Press.

Thiessen, Victor. 2009. "The Pursuit of Postsecondary Education: A Comparison of First Nations, African, Asian and European Canadian Youth," *Canadian Labour Market and Skills Researcher Network*. Working Paper Number 19.

Tyson, Karolyn, William Darity Jr., and Domini Castellino. 2005. "It's Not 'a Black Thing': Understanding the Burden of Acting White and Other Dilemmas of High Achievement," *American Sociological Review* 70, 4: 582–606.

Welsh, Wayne N., Robert Stokes, and Jack R. Greene. 2000. "A Macro-Level Model of School Disorder," *Journal of Research in Crime and Delinquency* 37, 3: 243–83.

Willis, Paul. 1977. *Learning to Labour: How Working Class Kids Get Working Class Jobs.* Westmead, UK: Saxon House.

Wotherspoon, Terry. 2014 .*The Sociology of Education in Canada*, 4th edn. Toronto: Oxford University Press.

Chapter 13

Anglin, Paul M., and Ronald Meng. 2000. "Evidence on Grades and Grade Inflation at Ontario's Universities," *Canadian Public Policy* 26, 3: 361–8.

Brint, Steven, ed. 2002. *The Future of the City of Intellect: The Changing American University.* Stanford, CA: Stanford University Press.

Clark, Ian, David Trick, and Richard Van Loon. 2011. *Academic Reform: Policy Options for Improving the Quality and Cost-effectiveness of Undergraduate Education in Ontario.* Kingston: McGill-Queen's University Press.

Collins, Randall. 2002. "Credential Inflation and the Future of Universities," in Steven Brint, ed., *The Future of the City of Intellect: The Changing American University.* Stanford, CA: Stanford University Press, 23–46.

Conrad, P., and J.W. Schneider. 1980. *Deviance and Medicalization: From Badness to Sickness.* St Louis: Mosby.

Côté, James, and Anton Allahar. 2011. *Lowering Higher Education: The Rise of Corporate Universities and the Fall of Liberal Education.* Toronto: University of Toronto Press.

Cuban, Larry. 1990. "Reforming Again, Again, and Again," *Educational Researcher* 19, 1: 3–12.

Dill, David D., and Maarja Soo. 2005. "Academic Quality, League Tables, and Public Policy: A Cross-National Analysis of University Ranking Systems," *Higher Education* 49, 4: 495–534.

Frenette, Marc. 2005. *Is Post-Secondary Access More Equitable in Canada or the United States?* Ottawa: Statistics Canada, Analytical Studies Branch. Cat. no. 11F0019MIE No. 244.

Grubb, W. Norton, and Marvin Lazerson. 2005. "Vocationalism in Higher Education: The Triumph of the Education Gospel," *Journal of Higher Education* 76, 1: 1–25.

Kirp, David. 2003. *Shakespeare, Einstein, and the Bottom Line: The Marketing of Higher Education.* Cambridge, MA: Harvard University Press.

Labaree, David. 2010. *Someone Has to Fail: The Zero-Sum Game of Public Schooling.* Cambridge, MA: Harvard University Press.

Lareau, Annette, and Elliot Weininger. 2003. "Cultural Capital in Educational Research:

A Critical Assessment," *Theory and Society* 32: 567–606.

Lehmann, Wolfgang. 2000. "Is Germany's Dual System Still a Model for Canadian Youth Apprenticeship Initiatives?" *Canadian Public Policy* 26, 2: 225–40.

Levitt, Steven D., and Stephen J. Dubner. 2005. *Freakonomics: A Rogue Economist Explores the Hidden Side of Everything.* New York: William Morrow.

Pizarro Milian, Roger, Scott Davies, and David Zarifa. 2016. "Barriers to Differentiation: Applying Organizational Studies to Ontario Higher Education," *Canadian Journal of Higher Education* 46, 1: 19–37.

Quirke, Linda. 2006. "'Keeping Young Minds Sharp': Children's Cognitive Stimulation and the Rise of Parenting Magazines, 1959–2003," *Canadian Review of Sociology* 43, 4.

Ramirez, Francisco O. 2004. "The Rationalization of Universities." Unpublished manuscript, Stanford University.

Ravitch, Diane. 2000. *Left Back: A Century of Battles Over School Reforms.* New York: Simon & Schuster.

Smith, Dorothy. 2000. "Schooling for Inequality," *Signs: Journal of Women in Culture and Society* 24, 4: 1147–51.

Stevens, Mitchell. 2007. *Creating a Class: College Admissions and the Education of Elites.* Cambridge, MA: Harvard University Press.

Tyack, David, and Larry Cuban. 1995. *Tinkering Toward Utopia: A Century of Public School Reform.* Cambridge, MA: Harvard University Press.

Walters, David. 2004. "Recycling: The Economic Implications of Obtaining Additional Post-Secondary Credentials at Lower or Equivalent Levels." *Canadian Review of Sociology* 40(4): 463–80.

Walters, David, Jerry White, and Paul Maxim. 2004. "Does Post-Secondary Education Benefit Aboriginal Canadians? An Examination of Earnings and Employment Outcomes for Recent Aboriginal Graduates," *Canadian Public Policy* 30, 3: 283–301.

Wolf, Alison. 2002. *Does Education Matter? Myths about Education and Economic Growth.* New York: Penguin.

———. 2011. *Review of Vocational Education— The Wolf Report.* Available at https://www.gov.uk/government/uploads/system/uploads/attachment_data/file/180504/DFE-00031-2011.pdf.

Index